Where is the Fear of GOD?

Finding the Treasure of the Lord

by
Charles von Hammerstein

More Abundant Life
San Jose, California

Where is the Fear of GOD?
Finding the Treasure of the Lord
by Charles von Hammerstein

Published by:
More Abundant Life
Post Office Box 24526
San Jose, CA 95154 USA
www.MoreAbundantLife.com

All rights reserved. This book or parts thereof may not be reproduced in any form, stored in a retrieval system, or transmitted in any form by any means – whether electronic, mechanical, photocopy, recording, or otherwise – without prior written permission from the author, except for the inclusion of brief quotations in a review.

All scripture references are proudly and with great assurance of the truth taken from the King James Bible (KJB) – the finest and most accurate translation available anywhere, bar none. Its accuracy and fidelity to the original manuscripts is without compare among any modern version and can easily be proven to be so. "Where the word of a king *is, there is* power" (Ecc 8:4).

Copyright © 2010 by Charles von Hammerstein.
First Printing 2010

Publisher's Cataloging-in-Publication
(Provided by Quality Books, Inc.)

von Hammerstein, Charles.
Where is the Fear of God?. Finding the Treasure of the Lord /
by Charles von Hammerstein.
p. cm.
Includes bibliographical references and index.
Library of Congress Control Number: 2009912059
Soft Cover ISBN: 0-9760302-1-7 / 978-0-9760302-1-8
Hard Cover ISBN: 0-9760302-2-5 / 978-0-9760302-2-5
1. God (Christianity)—Worship and love. 2. Fear of God—Christianity. 3. Fear of God—Biblical teaching.
I. Title.

BV4817.V66 2010   248.4   QBI09-600220

Printed in the United States of America

Selah

And <u>fear not</u> them which kill the body,
but are not able to kill the soul:

but rather <u>fear him</u> which is able to destroy both soul and body in hell.
<u>fear him</u> which is able to destroy both soul and body in hell. Mt 10:28

And his mercy is on them that <u>fear him</u>
from generation to generation. Lk 1:50

O that there were such an heart in them,
that they would fear me,

and keep all my commandments always,
that it might be well with them,
and with their children for ever! Dt 5:29

Table of Contents

Introduction:	The Choice Set Before Us	10
Chapter 1.	Why We Should Fear the LORD	22
Chapter 2.	God's Judgment, A Cause for Fear	36
Chapter 3.	The Spirit of the Fear of the LORD	58
Chapter 4.	Fearing God, Far More Than Reverence	72
Chapter 5.	Trembling in the Presence of the Almighty	92
Chapter 6.	Understanding the New Covenant of Grace & Fear	112
Chapter 7.	The Door of Mercy to All Those who Fear the LORD	126
Chapter 8.	Replacing Our Many Fears with God's Singular Fear	138
Chapter 9.	Trust and True Faith Through Our Fear of the LORD	154
Chapter 10.	True Fellowship Flows from the Fear of the LORD	164
Chapter 11.	Recapturing the Purity of the Fear of the LORD	182
Chapter 12.	Having a Heart to Learn the Fear of the LORD	196
Chapter 13.	The Inestimable Treasure of God's Fear	214
Chapter 14.	Experiencing the Genuine Fear of God	242
Appendix I.	Definition of Some Biblical Terms	268
Appendix II.	The Scriptures on Fearing God	284
Appendix III.	Words Used with Fearing God	292
Content Index:	Finding A Specific Topic	296
Thanksgiving:	The Fruit of Our Labors	306
An Epilogue:	Enduring Fear of God	308
Resources:	Table for the Hungry	318

Figures

Figure 3-1	The Candlestick of the Spirit	61
Figure 6-1	The Pillars of Grace and Fear	119
Figure 13-1	Finding the Fountain of Life	221

Tables

Table 6-1	Comparing the Two Pillars of Grace & Fear	118
Table 12-1	Recapturing the Fear of God – David's Outline	200
Table 13-1	The Blessings of the LORD on those who Fear Him	225

Format notes:

1. In quotations where clarifying notes or pronoun changes have been needed these are always enclosed in square brackets to signal the reader. Underlining and **bolding** of certain words have been added for emphasis to help the reader know what is being drawn from the scripture. Where the KJB uses *italics* or small caps (e.g. LORD) these have been preserved.

2. The definitions for certain Hebrew and Greek words have been included for clarity or amplification. These are always taken from the Strong's definition of Hebrew and Greek words,[1] except where noted for English definitions. When the Strong's definition is for a phrase or a longer definition they are enclosed in single quotes ('this is an example'). Where Strong's uses italics in the definition these have usually been preserved. When the Strong's number is supplied it is either Hnnnn or Gnnnn, where H is for Hebrew words & G is for Greek.

3. Outside of quotes, italics are sometimes used to emphasize certain words.

---

[1] Strong, James, <u>Strong's Exhaustive Concordance</u>, Compact Edition, Grand Rapids, Michigan, Baker Book House, 1984.

Abundant Blessings

This book uncovers the hidden balance of grace, the strength to overcome besetting sins, and the source of intimacy that we so often long for from our heavenly Father. This book is the first of a two-part set on discovering "Where is the Fear of GOD?" We cannot look at the fear of God without touching so many other areas of our heart and life in Christ. As a result there are found an abundant supply of blessings on many different subjects that many would not even consider when thinking about the fear of God. Hence, let me enumerate a few of them so that you may refer to this book when needed. In these pages we will discuss:

- Should we fear God as our Father?
- How to be intimate with the Lord GOD
- Why Satan hates the fear of God so much
- Learn the hidden wisdom that defeats the enemy
- Renewing ourselves with the washing of repentance
- Revealing the Salt of the Covenant: the Fear of the LORD
- The Fear of God is the doorway to mercy and the way of peace
- Understanding the work of the Spirit of God through the Candlestick

The next book, Where is the Fear of GOD? Losing the Treasure of the Lord,[2] uncovers why we lose the precious gift of the fear of God, which the Spirit plants in every one of our hearts as soon as we are born again. It covers the following areas.

- Unveiling the religion of the Samarians that exists in Christianity today
- The foundation of being correctable in our relationship with the Lord
- How to prevent the Pharisee spirit from taking root in our heart
- Warnings on losing God's fear from Good Kings Gone Bad
- Heart surgeries the fear of God needs to perform on us
- Why we needn't be ashamed of the name of Jesus
- How the fear of God changes how we worship
- A detailed list of beguiling counterfeits
- The heart of integrity & friendship
- The banner of brokenness

---

[2] Where a relevant subject is covered in the other book it will be referred to in short as Losing the Treasure of the Lord.

Introduction: The Choice Set Before Us

*"And I saw another angel fly in the midst of heaven, having
the everlasting gospel to preach unto them that dwell on the earth, and to
every nation, and kindred, and tongue, and people, Saying with a loud voice,
<u>Fear God, and give glory to him; for the hour of his judgment is come</u>" Rev 14:6-7*

Reasons for Writing: The Master Plan

*"A man's heart deviseth his way: but the LORD directeth his steps.
The preparations of the heart in man, and the answer of the tongue,
is from the LORD." Pr 16:1,9*

Jude so wanted to write to the saints to share with them the common salvation that we all have and to encourage them, but because of the severity of the times he was living in and how many were falling from the faith he was moved to change what he was going to write to them about. Hear his words,

> Beloved, when I gave all diligence to write unto you of the common salvation, <u>it was needful for me</u> to write unto you, and exhort *you* that ye should earnestly contend for the faith which was once delivered unto the saints. For there are certain men crept in unawares, who were before of old ordained to this condemnation, ungodly men,

Introduction: The Choice Set Before Us

turning the grace of our God into lasciviousness, and denying the only Lord God, and our Lord Jesus Christ. Jude 1:3-4

So it is with me. When this book started it was concerning a different subject altogether. The Lord had put on my heart to write concerning overcoming defeat in the life of the believer. That book may still be written by the grace and timing of God, for I so want to see each follower of the Lord Jesus become an overcomer – for the pangs of defeat have left deep ruts in the pathways of my own heart. Hope is the starting point of faith upon which our life in the Lord is built, but hope without any means of obtaining what is hoped for leads to utter despair. Many fellow soldiers of the Lord have struggled with such despair. The danger of living in repeated defeat, or worse yet, the ignorance even that one is being continually defeated, will bring great devastation. You cannot long remain in a state of repeated defeat without coming into bondage of one form or another. Your resolve to hold on will eventually wear away through discouragement to where you will one day give up.

As I was writing that book, the section on the Fear of the LORD was initially only one chapter. But the more I wrote, the more I found only this one chapter was being written. It became so central and vital that I soon saw there can be no repeated victory in our life, no escaping the snares of the enemy that are set for us, if we do not possess a deep and abiding fear of the LORD. The life of the follower of Jesus must be fortified with the nutrients and the foundations that only the fear of the LORD can provide, or it will become deformed and sickly. Thus, it was more needful for me to write unto you concerning the fear of the LORD by which we may earnestly contend for the faith.

God has an amazing way of taking the things we are learning and putting us to the test in those very things. Repeatedly, Jesus taught his own disciples and immediately put them to the test to see if they truly understood. "And this he said to prove him: for he himself knew what he would do." Jn 6:6 Through certain circumstances in my own life, both in the struggles of my own heart and in failures spiritually, as well as seeing the fulfillment of the end times of people's hearts growing hard and cold and departing from the living God (Mt 24:12-13, Heb 3:12-13), I was awakened to the absolute necessity of having the fear of God rooted, grounded, and planted in my heart.

Thus, began a hunt to discover how I had lost the fear of God as well as how to recapture it. I had always been moved by those in the scriptures who truly knew God. I always wanted to know God the way they did, yet every one of them had the fear of God in their life. The more I studied, the more the fear of God began to be the master key that opened door after door of our walk with our Master. The fear of God touches our worship, our service, our obedience, our giving, our relationship to man, our relationship to God, and it will even be the key to understanding ourselves. It is its own reward.

For me this book has been life-changing, not because it is the first book I have written (for there are others), nor because it was the longest book I have written (even though it is), nor because it was the easiest to write (for the hand of the LORD has been with me in this as I have never experienced before), but because it has been the most important book for my own life. I believe this will be one of the most important books (after the scripture) that you will ever read. This book uncovers the hidden balance of grace, the strength to overcome besetting sins, and the source of intimacy that we so often long for from our heavenly Father. Every fall in scripture has been because the fear of God was lost, and I can certainly attest to this in my own life. Yet, what I had missed until now was that every restoration of God's people was always the result of restoring his fear in their hearts and finding that true balance of trust and fear.

> Every restoration of God's people was always the result of
> restoring his fear in their hearts
> and finding that true balance of trust and fear.

The Testimony of the Word of God

"But I receive not testimony from man:
but these things I say, that ye might be saved." Jn 5:34

Let me add one postscript concerning how this book was purposefully written. In Christianity today, God's people are often more interested in testimony than they are in the Word of Life, the Bible. Yet the Lord in these last days is wondering when he returns will anyone have true faith? Now we know where true faith comes from and that is from the word of God. "So then faith *cometh* by hearing, and hearing by the word of God." Rom 10:17 So what Jesus is really wondering today is is anyone listening to the word of God? Is anyone hearing what he spoke? Is anyone hearing the testimony of the Lord.

> **WARNING**: Be assured the 'testimony' here is *not* the testimony of men, nor the testimony of the working of God in men's lives, but rather the testimony of the Word of God itself. "And he said unto them, Set your hearts unto all the words which I testify among you this day, which ye shall command your children to observe to do, **all the words of this law.**" Dt 32:46 The testimony *is* the Word of God.

What we so need in this land of religious activity is a resurrection of hearing the word of the Lord, not the word of self-appointed prophets, but the word of the Lord found in the holy writ of the Bible! We are in the greatest famine of hearing the word of the Lord of all time. Where are the people humbling themselves before the word of God to be obedient to what saith the scriptures? This

Introduction: The Choice Set Before Us

is why it was revealed to Isaiah, "Bind up the <u>testimony</u>, seal the law among my disciples. To the law and to the <u>testimony</u>: if they speak not according to this word, *it is* because *there is* no light in them." Isa 8:16,20

Because of the irreverence of these times, the great apostasy from truth that is taking place throughout the church, and so many who are lovers of pleasures more than lovers of God, it is not a time for men's testimonies of their experiences. Who can speak in the light of God's awe-inspiring glory and the fearfulness of his judgments? No one could stand to minister because of God's cloud that came down (1K 8:11, 2Ch 5:14). You will never learn the fear of the LORD from hearing a man's testimony.[3] The fear of the LORD is not about hearing someone's experiences and being awed.

Rather, it is about hearing the testimony of the Word of God, hearing the words of The Man, Jesus Christ, and being awed in God. I could share my testimonies and experiences concerning the fear of the LORD, and the lack of it, both from my own life as well as from those I have ministered to. But what we truly need to have awakened in us is the fear of God – the burning truth of God's word that cuts away the hypocrisy of our hearts. May you be molded, shaped, and conformed to the image of his Son as you recapture the fear of God in your life. The LORD God has always desired his fear to be in the hearts of his children. May it be thriving in yours.

The Snare of our Soul

"And blessed is he, whosoever shall not be offended in me." Mt 11:6

Jesus encouraged the disciples of John, and John the Baptist himself, not to be offended by the truth and the power by which he spoke. Jesus did not fit people's molds or their expectations, then, even as it is today. He is, Peter declares, "a stone of stumbling, and a rock of offence" (1Pe 2:8). If any man of God truly following Jesus is to bring forth the truth as it is in Jesus, then some of our religious tables <u>must</u> be overturned. Many things in this book confront compromise and false doctrine, many of which will be in you, some of which will be in those you personally admire and maybe even trust. To be a faithful witness of the kingdom of God and of our Lord Jesus Christ, I must be willing to speak the truth, and not to spare your soul – even where it hurts. This is the impact of the kingdom of God. It always comes with a two-edged sword to turn cities and peoples' thinking upside down. I am convicted by much that is written herein; I pray you will be also.

---

[3] As evidence of the surety of this fact, note that the only extended teaching that we have on the fear of the LORD in the Bible (i.e. in Psalm 34) is given by David after his own experience of forsaking the fear of the LORD, and yet it is not filled with any of those experiences, but rather with exhortations to hold fast to the truth.

Know it is not my intention to shame any man or woman, but many things being done in Christianity in God's eyes are indeed shameful. We cannot apologize for the truth, no matter whom it offends. I am a man like anyone else. I am no better than the least of God's servants, but I am a servant of God, and he has given me a message for the Church of these last days. My prayer is that whoever hears these words will have the fear of God to depart from their compromise by acknowledging truth through repentance. Do not let your soul, through the offense that may come to it, stop you from hearing the truth, for only in the truth may we find deliverance. May the fear of God be stoked into a blazing flame in your heart to consume the chaff of compromise and to bring you into the treasure of the Lord.

The Need to Receive Correction

"I said, Surely thou wilt fear me, <u>thou wilt receive instruction</u>; so their dwelling should not be cut off, howsoever I punished them: but they rose early, and corrupted all their doings." Zep 3:7

If we are to recapture the fear of God, we must know how it is learned. Now there is both a true fear of God (Ps 34:11) as well as a false fear of God (Isa 29:13), both of which can be taught to us. Interestingly, the word for 'teach/taught' in both Psalm 34:11 and Isaiah 29:13 is the same. It is *lamad* (H3925), which means 'to *goad*, i.e. (by implication) to *teach* (the rod being an Oriental *incentive*)'. The fear of God cannot be taught as one teaches a university course, just the communication of information. The fear of God is far more than knowledge. It must be taught with the rod of correction. This is why men who teach the true fear of God must be broken men, men who have already been willing to be much corrected by the LORD and by other men. Men may teach the false fear of God as the command of men with mere knowledge, but the true fear of God must be taught with correction and reformation as its goal.

If any of us is to learn the true fear of God, we must receive correction. This is God's expectation, "I said, Surely thou wilt fear me, <u>thou wilt receive instruction</u>" (Zep 3:7). This word 'instruction' means 'properly *chastisement*; figurative *reproof, warning* or *instruction*'. To fear God is to receive instruction, warning, reproof, and chastisement. To reject any of these, and not to have an ear to hear, is to reject the fear of God.

> To fear God is to receive instruction, warning, reproof, and chastisement. To reject any of these, and not to have an ear to hear, is to reject the fear of God.

Why is the receiving of correction so important? Because the "reproofs of instruction *are* the way of life" (Pr 6:23). The primary way the fear of the LORD

Introduction: The Choice Set Before Us

is learned is as a parent teaches a child. So David invites us to come as children to learn it, "Come, <u>ye children</u>, hearken unto me: I will teach you the fear of the LORD." Ps 34:11 It is because of this that we will have to deal with many issues of correction not only to the individual, but also to the body of Christ. If we would learn the true fear of God and not the false, we must prepare ourselves to return to the narrow way of the kingdom, which brings back the rule of God.

The Weightier Matters

Jesus condemned the scribes and Pharisees for omitting the weightier matters of the law. What are these weightier matters of the law? The first and foremost of them is judgment (Mt 23:23). Jesus said they should not have left judgment <u>undone</u> or put it away. We have done in Christianity exactly what the Pharisees of old did by putting away judgment. Is this not why there is so little true fear of God in Christianity today? For the very fact that we do NOT recognize that God, "without respect of persons", judges every man according to his works and NOT according to his profession only.

In the early church we see open correction, yet today correction of any sort is being scorned. It is being left undone (Mt 23:23). This then becomes the expected norm. Because the church so often follows the world instead of the Lord, and there is no correction in the schools or workplaces, therefore there is now no correction in the church. The one who tries to bring correction according to the word of God is thus seen to be the one in error, the one with a judgmental spirit, and the one who is erring and who *needs* the correction!

Many Christians have been lulled into a faith of compromise, rather than a faith to <u>become</u> the righteousness of God in Christ Jesus.[4] And they have been lulled into a permissive grace allowing them to do as they please, rather than a grace that enables them to stand in the will of God. Peter testified, "I have written briefly, exhorting, and testifying that this is the true grace of God wherein ye stand <u>so that we sin not</u>." 1Pe 5:12 Is this not why Paul many times had to warn and protect his spiritual son in the faith, Timothy, to fight the good fight, to lay hold on eternal life, to keep sound doctrine, and to be warned of those who err and depart from the faith?[5]

Consider the case of Peter and Paul. Peter was the great leader, the rock and supposed pillar of the Jerusalem church (Gal 2:9), an extensive traveling apostle, a worker of many unusual miracles (Ac 5:15), *and* one of the closest apostles to

---

[4] God's purpose is "that we might be made the righteousness of God in him." 2Co 5:21 The faith to become is seen in Abraham, "Who against hope believed in hope, that he might <u>become</u> the father of many nations; according to that which was spoken, So shall thy seed be." Rom 4:18

[5] Paul warns and charges Timothy repeatedly: 1Tim 1:4,18-20, 3:2-6, 4:1-2,7,16, 6:3-5,11-14,20-21, 2Tim 1:14-15, 2:1-4,14-18,22-24, 3:1-9, 4:1-5,14-15.

Jesus. Yet Paul, though he was younger in the faith and had not been one of the original twelve who walked with Jesus, when he saw Peter caught up in hypocrisy, which was contrary to the truth, Paul did not remain silent, nor did he deal with it in private later. Rather, he rebuked Peter, the Bible says, "before *them* all" (Gal 2:14). He brought a sobering warning that if Peter continued in his hypocrisy that he was making Christ die in vain (Gal 2:21)!

Paul spent much time in his letters to the Corinthians on how to deal with those who were living in sin. He had to secure the principles of correction of Matthew 18:15-17, which were being violated. If they would not hear the witnesses, then the erring parties were to be brought before the church and to be openly reproved. If they would not hear this, then they were to become "as an heathen and a publican." They were to be disfellowshipped, removed from participation in the local body. Why does God demand this? Because we hate or despise them? No, because we love them enough to know that they need the fear of God restored in their life. So Paul tells Timothy, "Them that sin rebuke before all, <u>that others also may fear.</u>" 1Tim 5:20 Yes, at times it must be "before all", so that others also may fear. The preservation of the fear of God through God's judgment is of vital consequence and must be preserved. It must be relearned if the Church is to be Christ's undefiled, spotless bride.

Will We Hear His Voice?

> But this thing commanded I them, saying, Obey my voice, and I will be your God, and ye shall be my people: and walk ye in all the ways that I have commanded you, that it may be well unto you.
>
> But they hearkened not, nor inclined their ear, but walked in the counsels *and* in the imagination of their evil heart, and went backward, and not forward.
>
> Since the day that your fathers came forth out of the land of Egypt unto this day I have even sent unto you all my servants the prophets, daily rising up early and sending *them*:
>
> Yet they hearkened not unto me, nor inclined their ear, but hardened their neck: they did worse than their fathers.
>
> Therefore thou shalt speak all these words unto them; but they will not hearken to thee: thou shalt also call unto them; but they will not answer thee. Jer 7:23-27

Today is little different than Jeremiah's day or Jesus' day when there were so many different ways of believing, so many different sects and denominations and independent non-denominations, and so little ability to hear the word of correction from our heavenly Father. Jesus continually had to confront those who claimed God was their father and who were the children of the covenant. There were the Pharisees, the Sadducees, the Herodians, the scribes, the doctors of the law, and so many others that we know not of, such as the Essenes, yet all

Introduction: The Choice Set Before Us

of these are very much alive in kind in the church today.[6] But who of all these people was willing to come under the rule of God into the kingdom of God by hearkening to the word of God? Only a remnant of disciples! Even still, who is willing to hear the reproof, correction, rebuke, and admonishment of the scriptures? Look today at the largest churches worldwide and especially in America and you will see a complete lack of proper reverence and godly fear toward the great and dreadful King of kings and the laws of his kingdom.

I have never seen in all my years of ministry those who are Christians less able to hear correction by the word of God. People today are flocking after the smooth things. They do not want the hard sayings of Jesus. Sadly, much of the church is still basking in its selfish self-centered worship. Much of the church comes to God primarily for what they can get. The judgment of the Lord truly draws near, not only for the wickedness of the evil generation that we live in, but even more so because God's own people have become like the people in the days of Noah – they are NOT moved by fear to prepare for the judgment which is most certainly to come. As in Noah's day, when a man of God becomes a preacher of righteousness and warns of the coming judgment of God, people dismiss and mock rather than hear and take to heart. Out of all the times Jesus could have picked, Jesus picked the very days of Noah to warn us of.

> But as the days of Noe *were*, so shall also the coming of the Son of man be. For as in the days that were before the flood they were eating and drinking, marrying and giving in marriage, until the day that Noe entered into the ark, And knew not until the flood came, and took them all away; so shall also the coming of the Son of man be. Mt 24:37-39

They didn't know what was coming! Not because they hadn't heard, for in 120 years of preaching everyone had heard of Noah and his ark and his call to repentance.[7] "But I say, Did not Israel know? … But to Israel he saith, All day long I have stretched forth my hands unto a disobedient and gainsaying people." Rom 10:19,21 The problem is not that people have not heard, but in hearing they do not open their ears or their hearts. The same was true in the early church, for so Stephen says to the religious of his day. "Ye stiffnecked and uncircumcised in heart and ears, ye do always resist the Holy Ghost: as your fathers *did*, so *do* ye." Ac 7:51 The problem is no one believed the word that was

---

[6] Just because they do not carry the same name, does not mean they are not of the very same spirit. There are indeed many groups who walk today as Pharisees, Sadducees, Herodians, scribes, doctors of the law, and Essenes. The names have all been changed to hide the guilty (as Satan always does), but the spirit is the same.

[7] Though we have no record of such, the news of Noah and his message would easily have spread around the world in this length of time, for there have always been travelers roaming the world telling of distant news, and Noah would have been a spectacle, a laughingstock to all the earth.

preached, neither by Noah, nor by Stephen, because it was not a smooth word. It brought rebuke and reproof. Have we forgotten that Noah condemned the world as a preacher of righteousness (Heb 11:6, 2Pe 2:5)? Jesus said when he returns, "Nevertheless when the Son of man cometh, shall he find faith on the earth?" Lk 18:8 And we know where true faith comes from. It comes from hearing and hearing by the word of God.

> But they have not all obeyed the gospel. For Esaias saith, Lord, who hath believed our report? So then faith *cometh* by hearing, and hearing by the word of `God. But I say, Have they not heard? Yes verily, their sound went into all the earth, and their words unto the ends of the world. Rom 10:16-18

Jesus then seriously wonders if when he comes he will find anyone hearing by the word of God. Will anyone truly hear what the word of God says – not what men say, not the doctrines and teachings of your church or denomination, not the views and opinions of your favorite teacher, but "what saith the scriptures" (Rom 4:3, Gal 4:30)! Men take great liberty with the word of God to pick and choose the parts they like and to discard the parts they do not like. They do not give the whole counsel of the word of God (Ac 20:27), but only their pet doctrines. So many use the sweet parts of the word of God to draw disciples after themselves but cast away anything that might cause one to walk away on account of truth. But not so Jesus! He was willing to lose all for the sake of truth and the will of his Father. To his own devoted twelve he gives this challenge, "Will ye also go away?" Jn 6:67

So many in charge of congregations whom God has called to be servants are doing exactly what God warned in condemnation not to do. They are eating and drinking with the drunken (Lk 12:45-46). They are sitting down and having fellowship with the ungodly and the worldly. Large churches around the country invite unsaved celebrities and politicians (religious but not born again) into their church to have the holy pulpit to speak. God has reserved the altar of God to be a holy place where only those who know him are allowed and only the word of God is to be spoken.

For the Sake of His Kingdom
"But rather seek ye the kingdom of God." Lk 12:31

This book is dedicated first and foremost to the expanding of the kingdom of God, God's rule and reign in the earth,[8] that a people would be set apart and

---

[8] The kingdom is the 'king's domain', where the king rules and reigns and his voice or word is law. Thus, the kingdom of God is where Jesus alone is exalted. It is where he, as the Word of God, has final authority. His kingdom is manifest on earth whenever his will is done. So it is written, "Thy kingdom come. Thy will be done, as in heaven, so in earth." Lk 11:2 Where his will is done on earth (as it is in heaven), then *there* is where

Introduction: The Choice Set Before Us

prepared as a holy people for the coming of the Lord – not the wonderful day of rejoicing that men say it will be, but the great and terrible day of the Lord that the word of God says it will be (Joel 2:31)! My hope is this book may be used to awaken God's people back unto righteousness and bring back the holy fear that causes his people to stop willfully sinning so that they may truly know the one they say they believe in. "Awake to righteousness, and sin not; for some have not the knowledge of God: I speak *this* to your shame." 1Co 15:34

So many who claim to be sons and daughters of God today are truly asleep and the gathering gloom and darkness of wickedness in high places is overtaking many. This is both in subtleness as well as in open rebellion through compromise. That this book would be used by God to bring back the fear of God and to remind his people that they are called to a disciplined life of self-denial and of putting the Lord's concerns above their own. This is true discipleship, to willingly submit to his will by putting aside our will and our ways. "Wherefore he saith, Awake thou that sleepest, and arise from the dead, and Christ shall give thee light. See then that ye walk circumspectly, not as fools, but as wise, Redeeming the time, because the days are evil." Eph 5:14-16

We are living in the days of Noah, yet no one is watching! "Watch therefore: for ye know not what hour your Lord doth come. Therefore be ye also ready: for in such an hour as ye think not the Son of man cometh." Mt 24:42,44 In light of the Lord's coming and that that day should not overtake us as a thief, we are warned as children of light and children of the day to not be of the night, nor of darkness. "Therefore let us not sleep, as *do* others; but let us watch and be sober." 1Th 5:4-6 The slumber the Church has fallen into is the result of the loss of the fear of God. It will be impossible to first awaken the Church and then to keep her awake and alert without the restoration of the fear of God. We are fast approaching the judgment of the Last Days which no one can appropriately be prepared for if they do not truly fear God. This is the crying need of the Church: to recapture the inestimable treasure of the fear of God.

---

his kingdom is. That is why Jesus said, "Behold, the kingdom of God is within you." Lk 17:21

Introduction: The Choice Set Before Us

*Dedicated to the recapturing
of the inestimable treasure
of the fear of the LORD and
to those who want to maintain
a pure conscience before the Lord
that they might not lose their first love.
May this poor vessel and you my chosen reader
live in the fullness that is in the fear of the LORD.*

Chapter 1. Why We Should Fear the LORD
Our Discarded Inheritance

"thou hast given me the heritage of those that fear thy name." Ps 61:5
"Surely thou wilt fear me, thou wilt receive instruction;
so their dwelling should not be cut off" Zep 3:7

Why is the fear of the LORD needed today? Why do we even need to consider it when we have faith, grace, love, and mercy through Jesus Christ our Lord? Why the fear of the LORD at all? *Firstly*, we need it because the fear of the LORD is the very life that Jesus lived here on this earth. The Bible declares Jesus was the stumbling block to all who reject the word. "And he shall be for a sanctuary; but for a stone of stumbling and for a rock of offence to both the houses of Israel, for a gin and for a snare to the inhabitants of Jerusalem." Isa 8:14 To them that receive him he is a sanctuary. To them that reject him he will be for a stone of stumbling and for a rock of offense.

Therefore, we will see the extent or lack of our fear of God by the reflection we see in our response to the Word. As it is with our response to the Word, which was made flesh, so it is with our response to the fear of God. For those who despise the fear of God it is truly a stumbling block – which is exactly what God said it would be! Isn't it amazing, how <u>immediately</u> after making

1 – Why We Should Fear the LORD

the LORD of hosts our fear and our dread that <u>then</u> he becomes a sanctuary unto us, but a stone of stumbling and a rock of offense to others!

> Sanctify the LORD of hosts himself; and <u>*let* him *be* your fear,</u> and <u>*let* him *be* your dread</u>. And he shall be for a sanctuary; but for a stone of stumbling and for a rock of offence Isa 8:13-14

Secondly, we need it because the fear of God is part of our spiritual inheritance which we were born with by the Spirit of God. The fear of God and the grace of God seem to be opposites in the minds of most present day Christians, yet the same Spirit of grace is the same Spirit of the fear of the LORD (Isa 11:2). Most see the fear of God as something opposed to the grace of God, when in fact, it is its fraternal twin. Some think of God's fear as nothing more than a vestigial holdover from the old covenant that has outlived its present day usefulness, yet still remains – something akin to tonsils, which if it causes any problems we can safely remove it and be done with it. For many, the fear of God is something despised, something evil. They feel it takes away from the gentle understanding that God is love and mercy. Yet the Psalmist declares, "*Oh* how great *is* thy <u>goodness</u>, which thou hast laid up for them that fear thee; *which* thou hast wrought for them that trust in thee before the sons of men!" Ps 31:19

God does not look at the fear of God as something we can do with or without. To God, losing the fear of God is a manifest form of backsliding and forsaking him.

Thirdly, we need to see the fear of God not as unimportant, but as **the** most important part, the very capstone that holds up the magnificent ramparts and archways of grace. There are more promises, rewards, and blessings associated with the fear of the LORD than with any other grace in all scripture. This seems beyond even our imagination. Can the fear of the LORD compare to the supreme and sublime majesty in any way with our new covenant inheritance or graces which we have received by faith in Jesus Christ? This may seem an astounding idea, yet we shall see it more than compare. It will be shown that the fear of God is at the heart of New Testament grace more than any of us realize.

God does not look at the fear of God as something we can do with or without. To God, losing the fear of God is a manifest form of backsliding and forsaking him: "know therefore and see that *it is* an evil *thing* and bitter, that thou hast forsaken the LORD thy God, that my fear *is* not in thee, saith the Lord GOD of hosts." Jer 2:19 That the fear of the LORD should be the capstone of grace takes many aback, but we shall find that the fear of the LORD is an inestimable treasure. Without the fear of God, the grace of God becomes something God never intended, for it is turned by ungodly men (i.e. men who do not fear God) into lasciviousness (i.e. *incontinence* and *licentiousness*, Jude 1:4). Only the fear of the LORD can keep the grace of God balanced and pure.

Fourthly, we need it because the fear of God is designed by God to be an integrated part of our trust in God and our love for God. This is so contrary to what most of us have been taught. We have thought of the fear of God as the enemy of or at least a stranger to trust, love, peace, mercy, and grace. In fact, it is the life-giving force behind all these. The Bible says we are exhorted to "Serve the LORD with fear, and rejoice with trembling." Ps 2:11 Thus, serving, rejoicing, and trembling with fear all coexist perfectly in God's miraculous balance. Similarly, in one New Testament verse God says we are to love *and* to fear (1Pe 2:17)! Daniel lived under and understood God's covenant of mercy and was greatly loved of God and loved God greatly, yet in that love he still trembled in fear before the Word of the LORD (Dan 10:11).

Do we know what the LORD required first and foremost of his people that came out of Egypt? "And now, Israel, what doth the LORD thy God require of thee, but to fear the LORD thy God, to walk in all his ways, and to love him, and to serve the LORD thy God <u>with all thy heart and with all thy soul</u>" (Dt 10:12). Fearing God, loving God, and serving God are not strangers at all in the pages of scripture, but in fact, are covenant companions.

> The fear of the LORD acts as the root upholding the tree of life within our heart, producing abundant fruit unto God's glory, praise, and honor.

The fear of God is in fact, the strength of our walk with God and determines the depth of our relationship with him. The fear of the LORD is like the roots of the great oak of scripture. Our strength is to come from the power of the Word of God working within us. Though the Word itself is full of strength and power it cannot stand in our life unless it is planted, rooted, grounded, and settled in our heart through the fear of God. So the fear of the LORD acts as the root upholding the tree of life within our heart, producing abundant fruit unto God's glory, praise, and honor.

Fifthly, that the fear of God needs to be recaptured, as if it were once ours, then lost, and now needs to be regained, sounds as unnecessary as relearning how to ride a bicycle. Many who do believe in the fear of God think that because they believe in God, surely they by default fear him – but nothing could be farther from the truth! The fear of the LORD affects every part of our walk with God and even our relationship to one another.

Sixthly, the fear of God is our primary protection from hypocrisy and from departing from the Lord. If we would keep the fear of the LORD working in our hearts, it would be a watchman that never sleeps, nor slumbers, keeping us from compromise and from denying the Lord who bought us. The knowledge of scripture by itself is often seen to puff up the mind and to produce an arrogant pride that is void of life and brings forth religious death (1Co 8:1). The greatest scholars of the Bible reside in seminaries today, and they are worse than the scribes and Pharisees of old that crucified the Lord! As Jesus said, concerning their supposed knowledge and teachings, "But woe unto you, scribes and Pharisees, hypocrites! for ye shut up the kingdom of heaven against men: for ye neither go in *yourselves*, neither suffer ye them that are entering to go in." Mt 23:13

This is the quintessential problem: people know *of* the Lord Jesus, are familiar with the Bible, attend religious functions, and even teach others, but they have never taken to heart that which they see in the scriptures. Through the lack of the fear of God they are not daily converted from their thoughts and their ways to those of God. Without the fear of God there is **no** knowledge of the holy (Pr 9:10). The scribes and Pharisees of Jesus' day could not hear what Jesus, the living Word of God, was saying to them. They rejected what he spoke and despised it as something worthless.

The scribes and Pharisees of today do the same, be assured. They cannot hear the word of the kingdom. They will not endure it, nor will they enter into it, but they will keep others (by their false authority) from hearing it. Some will condemn this book because it exposes, through the power of the word of God, the darkness of men's hearts. Those who love darkness cannot endure the teaching of the kingdom, for the teaching of the kingdom exposes the hearts of men. "For the time will come when they will not endure sound doctrine; but after their own lusts shall they heap to themselves teachers, having itching ears" (2Tim 4:3). The modern scribes and Pharisees will despise such things as the fear of God as worthless and kick against the pricks of God's word. As it is written, even as their fathers did before them, so do they (Ac 7:51). We so need the fear of God that alone can strip us of the hypocrisy that tries as leeches to suck the life out of all of our hearts.

Seventhly, the fear of the LORD is itself a grace of God, and no service is acceptable to God without it (Heb 12:28). It is a treasure, enriching our lives, and provides us with an inheritance better than any earthly king could give. With it we will abide satisfied, without it we are adrift on our own strength, will, and desires. It gives us the ability to depart from the snares of death and from evil. It will deliver us from a host of selfishness including covetousness, dishonesty, and envy. It is the beginning of wisdom and knowledge. It alone is able to slay the Goliath of pride that continues to threaten us and to mock our God. The fear of the LORD is a fountain of life, and from it flows faith, hope, humility, singleness of heart, self-denial, enlargement of heart, and compassion for others. Most of all, God takes pleasure in them that fear him. You are invited and wooed by the Spirit of the LORD to come and learn the fear of the LORD which is clean and enduring. But let that which you glean from these pages not be a passing doctrine as so many things are in the church today. Let it be a foundational grace in your walk that you never let go of.

For Whom is the Fear of the LORD?

"Who would not fear thee, O King of nations? for to thee doth it appertain: forasmuch as among all the wise men of the nations, and in all their kingdoms, there is none like unto thee." Jer 10:7

The word of God contains the simplicity that is in Christ (2Co 11:3) as well as the deep things that be of God (1Co 2:9-10, Job 12:22). That is why we can enjoy its treasures as soon as we are a new creation, and yet be challenged by its depth of truth and majesty when we are seasoned and mature in the things of God. But to understand the meat of the word we must "Study to shew thyself approved unto God, a workman that needeth not to be ashamed, rightly dividing the word of truth." 2Tim 2:15 In the same way, to understand the fear of the LORD properly we will have to dig into the word of God and look at many areas of our walk with the Lord. The subject of the fear of God contains much milk which the babe in Christ will rejoice in and be well satisfied. These, all can enjoy, but some will involve issues of meat and are not appropriate for young or unlearned believers.

> **WARNING**: The fear of the LORD will cut to the core of every man's heart – for so it is designed of God to do. Some of the issues that will require cutting open will be matters of strong meat. These a babe in Christ or one who is unlearned is not ready to understand or to <u>keep in a proper balance</u>. Therefore, certain subjects covered in this book will be hard to understand. Even Peter stated that Paul at times in his epistles wrote "some things hard to be understood" for those who were unlearned[9] as well as for those who were unstable.[10,11] When that is encountered feel free to skip those sections and continue on.

---

[9] The unlearned are those who have not been taught the principles of discipleship of what a person must do to follow the Lord. They are in fact believers and not disciples. Interestingly, the root word of 'unlearned' is '*a*' (which means 'not') and *manthano* (Greek 3129), another form of which is *matheo*, which is the root word for 'disciple'! The unlearned are literally 'not discipled'.

[10] The unstable are those who are *vacillating*. The word for 'unstable' is '*a*' (which means 'not') and *sterizo* (Greek 4741), which means 'to *set fast*, i.e. (literal) to *turn resolutely* in a certain direction, or (figurative) to *confirm*'. Thus, we are not surprised to find this word used repeatedly of those who are disciples. "<u>Confirming</u> the souls of the disciples, *and* exhorting them to continue in the faith, and that we must through much tribulation enter into the kingdom of God." Ac 14:22 The word 'confirming' is *episterizo*, which means 'to *support further*'.

[11] The unlearned and unstable, therefore, are the undiscipled who need a foundation in the doctrine of Christ laid in their life by expert builders so that they will "be no more

1 – Why We Should Fear the L ORD

The fear of God is for everyone who will (i.e. to everyone who will choose it). The fear of the LORD is NOT given to only the mature. A child by their simple trust may understand and possess God's fear in simplicity many times better than an adult. The child needs merely to hold onto that good thing which they have and not allow it to be stolen through false doctrine or by neglect. Thus, the fear of God is NOT for those who are specially gifted or endowed, or of a certain maturity level any more than salvation is for a special group. Know that the fear of the LORD is NOT given to favorites or to them that God specially 'chooses', anymore than wisdom or any other grace of the Spirit – for God has chosen all of his children. O how men twist the true character of the merciful and just God by their false concepts concerning predestination and election. Here is what Jesus said,

> For <u>every one that asketh receiveth</u>; and he that seeketh findeth; and to him that knocketh it shall be opened. Or what man is there of you, whom if his son ask bread, will he give him a stone? Or if he ask a fish, will he give him a serpent? If ye then, being evil, know how to give good gifts unto your children, <u>how much more shall your Father which is in heaven give good things to them that ask him</u>? Mt 7:8-11

God is grieved with those who turn him by their false doctrines into a respecter of persons who picks some and rejects others for salvation.[12] These are those who put a stumblingblock in the way of God's people,[13] who have no fear of God (Lev 19:14), and who make others to doubt what God says he will freely give! Wisdom is given to all those who ask in faith believing, when it is for the purpose of bringing glory to God. He will not withhold what he has promised to freely give as long as we believe in his word. Let us ask in faith, nothing doubting for the fear of God, for it is the very beginning of wisdom. "The fear of the LORD *is* the beginning of wisdom" (Ps 111:10).

> If <u>any of you</u> lack wisdom, let him ask of God, that giveth to <u>all *men*</u> liberally, & upbraideth not; and it <u>shall be given him</u>. But let him ask in faith, nothing wavering. For he that wavereth is like a wave of the sea driven with the wind & tossed. Ye ask, and receive not, because ye ask amiss, that ye may consume *it* upon your lusts. Jam 1:5-6, 4:3

So it is with the fear of God, it is given to those who desire it for the purpose of bringing glory to God by being more willing and obedient to him. The scriptures are clear to those who know the Lord in truth, God desires for **all** to

---

children tossed to and fro, and carried about with every wind of doctrine, by the sleight of men, *and* cunning craftiness, whereby they lie in wait to deceive" (Eph 4:14).

[12] If we would know anything of God, then know this first, "For there is <u>no</u> respect of persons with God." Rom 2:11 (also see Eph 6:9, Col 3:25, 1Pe 1:17) And as Peter had to painfully learn, "Of a truth I perceive that God is <u>no</u> respecter of persons" (Ac 10:34, also see 2Ch 19:7).

[13] Stumblingblock: Rev 2:14, Rom 14:13, Isa 57:14.

be saved and for **all** to come to the knowledge of the truth (1Tim 2:4), and so he freely gives to **all** who ask. He has left the choice of salvation into our hands per our choice. So it is with possessing the wisdom of God and the foundation of that heavenly wisdom, the fear of the LORD. It is our choice to choose. He desires for all to have the fear of God abiding deeply and growing in them. "O worship the LORD in the beauty of holiness: fear before him, all the earth." Ps 96:9 Did you hear that? God would have <u>all the earth</u> to worship him and to fear before him. And so he commands it, "Fear before him, <u>all the earth</u>" (1Ch 16:30). But alas, so few choose the fear of the LORD. But be assured dear reader it is for you, if you would have it! Let us then choose while we may, while the word of exhortation is near.

The Fear of God and Unbelievers

There is far, far too much to consider concerning the fear of the LORD, if we did not restrict our view to the most important parts. The fear of the LORD affects unbelievers as well as believers. The focus in this work has been restricted to that which concerns the believer in order not to weary, nor distract the reader from that most important work that God wants to do in perfecting those who call upon the name of the LORD. God desires those who follow him to be devoted to his fear (Ps 119:38). The greatest emphasis on the fear of God in scripture is in bringing God's people to a place where they truly are prepared to meet their God. Yet there are also many scriptures where God uses the fear of God in unbelievers' lives to draw them unto himself. Some of these are discussed in the appendix.[14]

God's Amazement, Why We Don't Fear God!
"Fear ye not me? saith the LORD" Jer 5:22

Many in their thinking ask, "Why should we fear God?" So many in their religious thinking wonder why anyone should fear God if they really knew him. Rather, if we knew God better, we ought to ask, "Why shouldn't we fear God?" The LORD himself incredulously asks us, "Fear ye not me? saith the LORD: will ye not tremble at my presence" (Jer 5:22). We have every reason to fear God, if we would see ourselves properly in the light of his glory and power. We ought first and foremost to fear God because of who he is! Do we really know "him that <u>ought</u> to be feared" (Ps 76:11)? This word 'feared' means 'a fearful thing' and is translated 'dread, terribleness, terror'. We are commanded to "Sanctify the LORD of hosts himself; and *let* him *be* your fear, and *let* him *be* your dread." Isa 8:13 The repentant thief on the cross has words that we all need to hear: "But the other answering rebuked him, saying, Dost not thou fear God, seeing

---

[14] See the appendix entitled "The Fear of God and Unbelievers" in the book <u>Losing the Treasure of the Lord</u> for more information on this.

1 – Why We Should Fear the LORD

thou art in the same condemnation?" Lk 23:40 God truly wonders why we all do not fear him! "I said, <u>Surely thou wilt fear me</u>, thou wilt receive instruction; so their dwelling should not be cut off, howsoever I punished them: but they rose early, *and* corrupted all their doings." Zep 3:7 God is in fact looking for us to fear him, for it is part of his lordship (i.e. his sovereign right to be Lord and Master).

> A son honoureth *his* father, and a servant his master: if then I *be* a father, where *is* mine honour? and if I *be* a master, <u>where *is* my fear</u>? saith the LORD of hosts unto you, O priests, that despise my name. And ye say, Wherein have we despised thy name? Mal 1:6

The LORD is sure that we would indeed fear him, if we *truly* knew him. So many today claim to know him, but scoff at the idea of fearing him. This is a contradiction in God's eyes. God says it cannot be. Men may weave their webs of deceit, which slowly put God's people asleep and deaden them to the conviction of truth, but truly God is asking today why we despise his name, and do not give him the honor AND fear that are due him.

Of all things that God required of his people it was this thing first, the very thing that men would leave off today: the fear of God. "And now, Israel, **what doth the LORD thy God require of thee**, <u>but to fear the LORD thy God</u>, to walk in all his ways, and to love him, and to serve the LORD thy God with all thy heart and with all thy soul" (Dt 10:12). Now maybe we see why the Almighty God is truly amazed that we do not fear him when we ought to. Certainly those who have had a Biblical encounter with the living God, wonder why others do not fear him. Listen to the hearts of Jeremiah the prophet and John the apostle:

> Forasmuch as *there is* none like unto thee, O LORD; thou *art* great, and thy name is great in might. <u>Who would not fear thee</u>, O King of nations? for to thee doth it appertain: forasmuch as among all the wise *men* of the nations, and in all their kingdoms, <u>*there is* none like unto thee</u>. Jer 10:6-7

> <u>Who shall not fear thee</u>, O Lord, and glorify thy name? <u>for *thou* only *art* holy</u>: for all nations shall come and worship before thee; for thy judgments are made manifest. Rev 15:4

This is why we do not fear him as we ought to: because we fail to see that the fear of God appertains (i.e. it belongs by divine right) to God. We do not comprehend how different he is than all of us. Truly, there is none like him, not in power, might, wisdom, strength, or glory. We, as mere men created by God, continually try to reduce the Alpha and Omega, the Dreadful and Infinite God to man's standard and man's ways. Why does Revelation, that reveals to us not only Jesus Christ but also him who sits on the throne, declare we must fear the Lord? Because **only** God is holy! We ought *not* to fear man, because he is not holy, not by nature, by essence, or by his works. But God Almighty on the other hand is holy in all ways, and therefore it is written, "**Who** shall not fear thee"? We have all the reasons to fear him and no reason not to fear him.

- Should not the outshining brilliance of his **glory** (Heb 1:3) cause us to fear before him? Yes.
- Because he is beyond finding out and is **excellent** in power, judgment, and justice, should we not therefore fear him (Job 37:23-24)? Yes.
- Because he <u>only</u> is **holy**, should we not fear him (Rev 15:4)? Yes.
- Since he is our **Master**, should we not therefore fear him (Mal 1:6)? Yes.
- The inescapable witness that surrounds us, that by his Word he spoke all of creation into existence, should we not fear the **Creator** (Jer 5:22)? Yes.
- For his **mercy** at giving rain in its season and bringing forth the increase of our harvest for which we are so totally unworthy and undeserving, should we not continually fear him (Jer 5:24)? Yes.

Grace that Teaches us to Fear God

"But there is forgiveness with thee, that thou mayest be feared." Ps 130:4

Most of all, should we *not* fear him because of his forgiveness? Yes, we should fear God, and maybe for this reason more than all the rest combined. As Elihu revealed concerning the Almighty, "he will not afflict. Men do therefore fear him" (Job 37:23-24). Though he is excellent in justice and in judgment, and has every right to condemn us, yet the scripture records that "he will not afflict". The word 'afflict' in Hebrew means '*looking* down or *browbeating*' and comes from a word which means to shout. Though God is *mighty* and excels in power, judgment, and justice, he does not despise us or beat us down with his judgments, yelling at us when we fall short.

> If we have received more abundant grace and the overflowing of forgiveness in the new covenant, ought we not to fear God *more* than any Old Testament saint?

This is cause for great rejoicing *and* humility, which should lead us to fearing God. The psalmist in one of the songs of degrees sings, "If thou, LORD, shouldest mark iniquities, O Lord, who shall stand? But *there is* forgiveness with thee, <u>that thou mayest be feared</u>." Ps 130:3-4 Because the Lord has redeemed us, forgiven us, and delivered us, we ought to fear him. Men today think we should not fear God because he is forgiving, gracious, and merciful, but the saints of old knew contrariwise. It is because he forgives us that we should fear him. So it was with the Israelites whom God had delivered out of the land of bondage. "But the LORD, who brought you up out of the land of Egypt with great power and a stretched out arm, <u>him shall ye fear</u>, and him shall ye worship, and to him shall ye do sacrifice." 2K 17:36 His forgiveness is the greatest motivation we should have today to fear the LORD. If we have received more abundant grace and the overflowing of forgiveness in the new covenant, ought we not to fear God *more* than any Old Testament saint?

Forgiveness is at the Root of the Fear of God

The wonder of God's forgiveness is designed to create in us the fear of God. The mercy of forgiveness and answered prayer should move us to fear the one true God. Only the Lord GOD can bring the reality of forgiveness to us. No other false God can do this. After experiencing God's forgiveness, of a truth "we know that an idol *is* nothing" and that there is only one true God (1Co 8:4). This was the test of Elijah the prophet: the God who *answers* "let him be God." 1K 18:24 God answering our prayers and forgiving our sin should move others to fear him. Hear why Solomon sought for God's blessing in dedicating the temple.

> What prayer and supplication soever be *made* by any man, *or* by all thy people Israel, which shall know every man the plague of his own heart, and spread forth his hands toward this house: Then <u>hear thou in heaven</u> thy dwelling place, <u>and forgive</u>, and do, and give to every man according to his ways, whose heart thou knowest; (for thou, *even* thou only, knowest the hearts of all the children of men;) <u>That they may fear thee</u> all the days that they live in the land which thou gavest unto our fathers. 1K 8:38-40

God has always intended for his handiwork in our life, his hand of deliverance from sin and death, and his cleansing us from all unrighteousness, to be on display for a witness to all who see us. We, now, are the light of the world (Mt 5:14, Jn 9:5) to give light by our life. Salvation and sanctification are the double-fruitedness of his wisdom that the LORD desires to display to all the world (Eph 3:8-10). And what does God expect the result to be when others observe these blessings? That they would fear him. As it is written, "God shall bless us; and all the ends of the earth shall fear him." Ps 67:7

Gaining a Desire for What has been Lost
"where is my fear? saith the LORD of hosts unto you" Mal 1:6

The scripture implores us to fear God and not to fear the fear of God. Rather, we ought to delight in it and to desire it. When Nehemiah in his intercession to God mentions those whose prayer the LORD ought to hear and answer, he specifically mentions those "who <u>desire</u> to fear thy name" (Neh 1:11). The word 'desire' here is in Hebrew means '*pleased* with'. It is translated 'delight in, desire, favour, please, have pleasure, whosoever would, willing, wish'. This ought to be our attitude toward the fear of God. We ought to take great pleasure in fearing him and to desire it with all our heart. O that God's people would again be pleased with the fear of God and would diligently seek after it.

Where is the Fear of GOD? Finding the Treasure of the Lord

Before God can ever bring us into what he has for us, we must first stop looking back and longing for what we've had and start desiring and looking forward for the promise. Faith enables us to reach forward for what he has, but the fear of God enables us to leave the old behind. The fear of God is what enables us to depart from the iniquity we still desire and to exchange our selfish, sinful desires into a longing for his perfect, selfless will.

> Be not wise in thine own eyes: fear the LORD, and <u>depart from evil</u>. By mercy and truth iniquity is purged: and by the fear of the LORD *men* <u>depart from evil</u>. Pr 3:7, 16:6

This is why the promise of God and the fear of God go hand in hand, both need each other. Without the promise of God, the fear of God becomes oppressive and defeating. Without the fear of God, the promise of God is either unattainable or unenjoyable. Even if the promise is received, it cannot be kept or enjoyed without the fear of God.

> Religious men wonder why men fear God when "God is loving and merciful", but God himself wonders why we do NOT fear him for those very same reasons!

The hall of faith was filled with those that "having seen [*the promises*] afar off, and were persuaded of *them*, and embraced *them*, and confessed that they were strangers and pilgrims on the earth." By this they openly declared that they were seeking a country which was not the one they had come from, but a better country, a heavenly one (Heb 11:13-16). Because they desired what God had for them, he was able not only to show it to them, but also to bring them into it. So will he do for us when we desire the fear of God. We must become as those in Nehemiah's day, servants of God who saw the ruins of Jerusalem [i.e. the church today] and to see her rebuilt, they desired to fear God (Neh 1:11).

Religious men wonder why men fear God when "God is loving and merciful", but God himself wonders why we do NOT fear him for those very same reasons! O how different are the ways and thoughts of men from the LORD!

> <u>Fear ye not me</u>? saith the LORD: <u>will ye not tremble</u> at my presence, which have placed the sand *for* the bound of the sea by a perpetual decree, that it cannot pass it: and though the waves thereof toss themselves, yet can they not prevail; though they roar, yet can they not pass over it?
>
> But this people hath a revolting & a rebellious heart; they are revolted & gone. <u>Neither say they in their heart, Let us now fear the LORD our God</u>, that giveth rain, both the former & the latter, in his season: he reserveth unto us the appointed weeks of the harvest. Jer 5:22-24

1 – Why We Should Fear the LORD

Men do not fear God today because they think they do not need to. They think they are enlightened and more mature in their love toward God to *not* fear him. God states contrariwise. Until we seek after the fear of God as for silver and gold, then we truly understand nothing concerning the fear of God, nor even of God himself! "If thou seekest her as silver, and searchest for her as *for* hid treasures; Then shalt thou understand the fear of the LORD, and find the knowledge of God." Pr 2:4-5 God says we do *not* fear him because we have a revolting and rebellious heart – a heart that is literally *turning* away from him and *bitter*. To him, not having the fear of God within us is a manifest form of backsliding and forsaking him: "know therefore and see that *it is* an evil *thing* and bitter, that thou hast forsaken the LORD thy God, that my fear is not in thee, saith the Lord GOD of hosts." Jer 2:19

> This is the wickedness of our generation:
> that there is no fear of God before our eyes.

Understanding the Fear of God and Perfect Love

"what doth the LORD thy God require of thee, but to fear the LORD thy God, to walk in all his ways, and to love him, and to serve the LORD thy God with all thy heart and with all thy soul" Dt 10:12

Enlightened Christianity has no true fear of God. They teach it away, believing it is not truly fear at all. They think it away, believing it is only an old covenant artifact having no place in our relationship through Jesus Christ as sons and daughters of God. They say, "How can a loving God and Father desire us to have any fear toward him?" So many, in fact today, despise the fear of God when we ought to cherish it and be devoted to it.[15]

Those who truly encountered God fell on their faces as if struck dead by their fear, and we in our new covenant smugness would put all that aside and, along with cults like Unity, believe that we should have no fear at all. They hold fast to one verse, but they do not take the whole counsel of God to understand the context of how John the apostle's words fit in. He says, "There is no fear in love; but perfect love casteth out fear: because fear hath torment. He that feareth is not made perfect in love." 1Jn 4:18 The fear being spoken of here in 1John 4:18 *cannot* be the fear of God or else the scripture is made to contradict itself. "God forbid: yea, let God be true, but every man a liar" (Rom 3:4).

No, the perfect love of God casts out all earthly and natural fear, but NOT the fear which is from above, that the scripture says is clean and enduring (Ps

---

[15] David, who most assuredly was the writer of Psalm 119 (by Proverbs 4:4), says he was *devoted* to the fear of God (Ps 119:38)! This is because David knew how much he had been delivered from, through God's fear, as he testifies for us in Psalm 34.

19:9). Jesus himself, who was surely perfected in love, had the fear of God and taught the fear of God (e.g.: Lk 18:2). This is the incredible deception of religion, that men can actually believe they are loving God by *not* fearing him, when on the contrary it shows that they are falling out of love with God and their heart is becoming more estranged toward him daily. This is the wickedness of our generation: that there is no fear of God before our eyes. "The transgression of the wicked saith within my heart, *that there is* no fear of God before his eyes." Ps 36:1 Is it any wonder the Proverbs exhort us to be "in the fear of the LORD all the day long" (Pr 23:17)?! So Peter instructs us to live the rest of our life in the fear of God. "And if ye call on the Father, who without respect of persons judgeth according to every man's work, pass the time of your sojourning *here* in fear" (1Pe 1:17). So where is the fear of God today?

Chapter 2. God's Judgment, A Cause for Fear
Putting God Back on His Throne of Judgment

"thou hast given me the heritage of those that fear thy name." Ps 61:5

We Shall All Be Judged – Let Us Fear

"For the time is come that judgment must begin at the house of God: and if it first begin at us, what shall the end be of them that obey not the gospel of God?" 1Pe 4:17

We must worship the LORD for ALL that he is – both for his mercies AND for his judgments! "Behold therefore the goodness and severity of God: on them which fell, severity; but toward thee, goodness, <u>if thou continue</u> in *his* goodness: otherwise thou also shalt be cut off." Rom 11:22 The fear of God's judgment must be a part of our relationship with the Lord for it is the proper response to his authority. As he himself asks, "and if I *be* a master [*sovereign*, i.e. *controller*: lord], where *is* my fear? saith the LORD of hosts unto you" (Mal 1:6).

Elihu instructs us that we must fear God not only for his forgiveness, but also for his judgment. Let us now examine how God is excellent in judgment and in justice so that we may know further why we ought to fear him (Job 37:23-24). Be assured that God *does* express his anger at times even against his

2 – God's Judgment, A Cause for Fear

own children. If we are to worship the true and living God, we must worship him as he is and not a one-dimensional Santa Claus or the great candy machine in the sky – neither of which we can have a personal relationship with. God is a living person who has every emotion we do – for we are created in his image. Many today would emasculate God[16] and make him only a kindly old grandmother who never disciplines and is never angry with her children – but <u>judgment</u> lies in the hands of God as well as mercy.

God has repeatedly revealed that he *does* get angry with his disobedient children. We see the anger of the LORD flare up even against his most devoted servants when their ways confront his divine, perfect will.[17] In all the Old Testament, there is no greater servant than Moses. He is called the servant of the LORD or "My servant" more than any other person. Yet, God's anger arises against him on more than one occasion.

> And the anger of the LORD was kindled against Moses Ex 4:14
>
> Also the LORD was angry with me for your sakes Dt 1:37
>
> Furthermore the LORD was angry with me for your sakes Dt 4:21

From modern Christianity we get the mistaken message that the judgments of God are only for the lost. But hear the warning of scripture: "Therefore is the anger of the LORD kindled against **his people**" (Isa 5:25). Solomon came to the wisdom that "God shall judge <u>the righteous</u> and the wicked: for *there is* a time there for every purpose and for every work." Ecc 3:17 Job in his wisdom understood that if we cannot receive evil from God, even though we be the righteous, then we are fools. Or worse yet, if we think that God cannot or will not send evil our way, then we think and speak as fools. Often we speak as foolishly as Job's wife when we think that God will not judge the righteous.

> But he said unto her, Thou speakest as one of the foolish women speaketh. What? shall we receive good at the hand of God, and <u>shall we not receive evil</u>? In all this did not Job sin with his lips. Job 2:10

The Beginning of Wisdom: Knowing the Fearfulness of God's Judgments

Many speak as fools today and sin with their lips, declaring that God only wants to bless his children, when his primary purpose has always been to *perfect us* by conforming us to the image of his Son. God has many tools by which he

---

[16] Thus, even some translations of the holy scriptures have had the sheer folly and the lack of any fear of God to change the very words of God in order to neuter him! God forbid that we should modify the word of God with our views and for our purposes, rather than allowing the word of God to determine our views and set our purposes.

[17] Here is a short list of servants with whom God was angry: Moses (Ex 4:14), Aaron (Nu 12:1,9, Dt 9:20), David (2Sam 24:1+), and Solomon (1K 11:9). We could also mention the disciples of Jesus whom he was at times angered with.

does this, blessing is one of them, but there are others he must use – causing us to suffer lack at times (Dt 8:2-3). He will never use only one. He will conform us to his Son through both grace, mercies, and blessings as well as through afflictions, chastenings, and judgments. We have his repeated promise on this.

> Before I was afflicted I went astray: but now have I kept thy word. Ps 119:67

> As many as I love, I rebuke and chasten: be zealous therefore, and repent. Rev 3:19

> And ye have forgotten the exhortation which speaketh unto you as unto children, My son, despise not thou the chastening of the Lord, nor faint when thou art rebuked of him: For whom the Lord loveth he chasteneth, and scourgeth every son whom he receiveth. If ye endure chastening, God dealeth with you as with sons; for what son is he whom the father chasteneth not? Heb 12:5-7

WARNING: The false prophets so often heard today continually cry 'bless-me', 'bless-me' prophecies for this is what the itching ears of people want to hear (2Tim 4:3). We are full of man-trained 'prophets' who deliver "personal prophecies" of blessing. But *where* are the true men of God who fulfill the true prophetic office which is to warn God's people? See Ezekiel's call as a watchman which was to warn the people (Eze 33:2-9). Notice it says seven times to warn them![18]

All of the Old Testament judgments are written for our admonition, not our dismissal! The word admonition in 1Corinthians 10:11 is *nouthesia* (G3559) and means 'calling *attention* to, i.e. (by implication) mild *rebuke* or *warning*'. Consider this, Paul in writing the Greek, non-Jewish believers in Corinth used the Old Testament destructions in order to warn them of what would happen if they continued in the way they were headed. Paul says by the Holy Ghost,

> Now all these things happened unto them for ensamples: and they are written <u>for our admonition</u>, upon whom the ends of the world are come. Wherefore let him that thinketh he standeth <u>take heed</u> lest he fall. 1Co 10:11-12

We are called to take heed in our spiritual life, lest we fall after the same example of disobedience of those who were destroyed (Heb 4:11). Remember, it

---

[18] Remember, Micaiah of whom it was said, "*There is* yet one man, by whom we may enquire of the LORD: but I hate him; for <u>he never prophesied good unto me</u>, but always evil: the same is Micaiah the son of Imla. And Jehoshaphat said, Let not the king say so." 2Ch 18:7 Few are the men who respond as Jehoshaphat, desiring to hear the voice of the one who will bring forth God's true judgments. Sadly, though Jehoshaphat desired to hear God's voice through a true prophet, yet he did not hearken to his warning! How much like today. So many claim to want to hear the word of the Lord, but when they hear it they are not so keen on doing it.

was in the New Testament church that believers were judged on the spot by God for lying to the apostle of God (Ac 5:1-2), not once, but twice to let us know that the thing is "established by God" (Gen 41:32). This was one of the ways that God kept the fear of God alive in the midst of the New Testament believers in Jerusalem (Ac 5:5,11).

Jesus was certain about his heavenly Father's power to judge unto destruction. So we should be certain of this also. "But I will forewarn you whom ye shall fear: Fear him, which after he hath killed <u>hath power to cast into hell</u>; yea, I say unto you, Fear him." Lk 12:5 These words are very significant, because they were not primarily spoken to the multitudes. Verse 1 says these words were *specifically* spoken to his own disciples! Jesus wanted to forewarn his own closest followers so that they would not be smug in their walk with God. Jesus wants us all to know these things beforehand – before it is too late to make a difference.

Why Does God Judge His Own?

We are moved to fear God and to worship him BECAUSE judgment is with him. If we turn from our iniquities, he is gracious and just to forgive us. But what makes us appreciate and remember his grace and his mercy is that he is the judge who holds all judgment in his hands. God has judged his own people repeatedly over the centuries for their willful disobedience and unwillingness to fear his rod. His rod of judgment is intended by God to stir up in his people fear and godly caution and the service of our worship unto him. In our fear, we are able to more deeply worship him, not in song only, but now with a heart that is circumcised and exposed to his inspection. Today, we have forgotten that God is the judge not only of the lost, but also of his own people.

> But **ye are come** unto … God <u>the Judge of all</u> Heb 12:22-23
>
> brethren, lest **ye be condemned**: behold, <u>the judge</u> standeth before the door. Jam 5:9

We must allow God to be all that he says he is. Fear must be rendered unto every judge as a result of their office, not only by man's appointment, but by God's own ordinance. "Render therefore to <u>all</u> their dues: … fear to whom fear; honour to whom honour." Rom 13:7 The faith of God and the fear of God must work hand in hand in this. Faith, not despair or resignation, must arise in the midst of judgment.[19] Remember, it was in the very face of total destruction that Moses secured deliverance for all Israel, and Abraham secured safety for Lot. The true fear of God will birth an assurance in the surety of God's word – our true security.

---

[19] For more on the need of faith, see 'A Trusting Spirit: the Instruction of His Deliverances' in the chapter entitled "The Testings of the Fear of the LORD" in the book <u>Losing the Treasure of the Lord</u>.

The Purpose of God's Judgments

The fear of God is designed not to have us flee from God, but rather to have us flee from what causes God to be angry with us, from that which displeases him. This is why David says, "Deliver me, O LORD, from mine enemies: I flee <u>unto thee</u> to hide me." Ps 143:9 We must flee from the enticements of the world's system (which is represented by Babylon). We must flee from her abominations, her pleasures, and from trusting in the world's wisdom. As God warned his people in Jeremiah's day, "Flee out of the midst of Babylon, and deliver every man his soul: be not cut off in her iniquity; for this *is* the time of the LORD's vengeance; he will render unto her a recompence." Jer 51:6 So the word instructs us everywhere to flee from iniquity:

- Flee fornication. 1Co 6:18
- Flee from idolatry 1Co 10:14
- Flee also youthful lusts 2Tim 2:22
- Flee these things [i.e. covetousness & false doctrine] 1Tim 6:11

God uses judgment in our life to cause us to flee, not from him, but to flee to him. As he ministers judgment, it is written that "The LORD also will be a refuge for the oppressed, <u>a refuge in times of trouble</u>." Ps 9:8-9 The fear of the LORD which causes us to fear his judgments is actually our refuge from his judgment (Pr 14:26)! "But I will sing of thy power; yea, I will sing aloud of thy mercy in the morning: for thou hast been my defence and <u>refuge in the day of my trouble</u>." Ps 59:16 Our fear of God's judgments keeps us from coming *under* his judgments. This is why the true grace of God must teach our heart to fear. If we do not fear God's judgments, as so many in Christianity do not, then we will come under many of his judgments. Why? Because God's judgments are designed by him to restore his fear so that we may turn from our way.

The Mercy of His Judgments

If we only knew, God's judgments are actually a part of his mercy! The expression of God's anger, if we could see the whole of eternity, is *also* an expression of his mercy. You may be astounded at this, but listen. God *must* remind us of his mercy by sending his judgments! You say, "How can this be?" Because if God only showed mercy, we would forget who he is, what he is capable of, and the greatness of his anger, the pure and holy hatred he has against sin and rebellion. The world at large already despises God for his mercy, but sadly even God's own children are beginning to do so. God in his mercy will be despised. For what cause would God, the merciful one, be despised? For the sake of his intense love, his great mercy, and his longsuffering graciousness to spare mankind and as long as possible not to send his judgment.

2 – God's Judgment, A Cause for Fear

This is why the judgments that shall hit the earth in these last days shall be like no other. God shall rain down his hail of judgment to sweep away the refuge of lies that 'God will not judge us' – when he has promised to do exactly that, to judge us for our iniquities. Even in his judgment, though, he is merciful, for he never executes the full measure of his wrath – not at least until the final judgment, when the *fierceness* of the wrath of God shall for the first time be meted out. Remember who Jesus is, "he shall rule them with a rod of iron: and he treadeth the winepress of the fierceness and wrath of Almighty God." Rev 19:15

As men have had their hard (i.e. '*harsh, severe*: fierce') speeches against the Lord (Jude 1:15), so shall he bring forth his harsh and severe and fierce judgments. Let this get deep in our spirit. The fact of the Father's capability *and* purpose to judge is to move us to fear, not to complacency. The judgments of God are meant to be an anchor point for his fear to stay fixed in our heart. "For if we would judge ourselves, we should not be judged. But when we are judged, we are chastened of the Lord, that we should not be condemned with the world." 1Co 11:31-32 The mere fact that Paul had to bring this to the remembrance of the Corinthians shows that they had not been judging themselves.

> The judgments of God are meant to be an anchor point for his fear to stay fixed in our heart. God's judgments are designed by him to restore his fear so that we may turn from our way.

Why did the Corinthians not judge themselves? Because they did not believe that God would judge them – just like this generation. It also shows they had already been judged of the Lord! Both first and second Corinthians are written because God had already judged their deeds and actions – they just didn't know it. Instead of refusing and rejecting his judgment of us when we are walking in disobedience, let us rather humble ourselves under his mighty hand and fear him. "My flesh trembleth for fear of thee; and I am afraid of thy judgments." Ps 119:120 He is right and just to judge his disobedient servants and his own children.

We cannot dismiss his judgments coming upon us as his children and still worship the true God, for this is who he has revealed himself to be. God has looked forward to the last days when his people will truly consider his judgments and destructions. May all of us fulfill this prophetic promise which God spoke twice to Jeremiah, and may we consider perfectly why God brings forth his fierce anger. In these last days we will see the judgments of God again poured out, for they are prophesied in detail by Jesus, both in the gospels and in Revelation, and they are yet to be fulfilled.

The fierce anger of the LORD shall not return, until he have done *it*, and until he have performed the intents {the thoughts} of his heart: <u>in the latter days ye shall consider it {perfectly}</u>. Jer 30:24 {23:20}

Hear and Fear: The Wisdom of His Judgments

Let us more perfectly consider the anger of the LORD and his judgments further. We have seen God brings his judgments so that those who come afterward would consider it and fear him (Jer 30:24, 23:20). So the psalmist says, "And all men shall fear, and shall declare the work of God; for they shall wisely consider of his doing." Ps 64:9 All of God's fiercesome acts and deeds are done so that *"men* should fear before him." Ecc 3:14 As soon as God brought his people out of Egypt, he instituted judgments which were to be executed upon those who were rebellious. These judgments were so that his people upon hearing of it would then fear the LORD. This was how he showed them and us the seriousness of his word. Through the judgments of the LORD each of us ought to learn to obey his voice, not just when we feel like doing it, but upon the hearing of it. God ensured at all times with his people that proper respect for authority was maintained. God records for us three specific groups which were punished in order to produce fear in the hearts of his people.

1. <u>Those that enticed others to serve other gods</u>: death by stoning.

   And thou shalt stone him with stones, that he die; because he hath sought to thrust thee away from the LORD thy God, which brought thee out of the land of Egypt, from the house of bondage. And all Israel <u>shall hear, and fear</u>, and shall do no more any such wickedness as this is among you. Dt 13:10-11

2. <u>Those who would not hearken to the voice of authority</u>:

   a. Those who would not listen to the counsel of the priests on disputes: death by stoning.

      And the man that will do presumptuously, and will not hearken unto the priest that standeth to minister there before the LORD thy God, or unto the judge, even that man shall die: and thou shalt put away the evil from Israel. And all the people <u>shall hear, and fear</u>, and do no more presumptuously. Dt 17:12-13

   b. a stubborn, rebellious son who won't obey the voice of his father or mother: death by stoning.

      And all the men of his city shall stone him with stones, that he die: so shalt thou put evil away from among you; and all Israel <u>shall hear, and fear</u>. Dt 21:21

3. <u>Anyone who bore false witness</u>: same punishment as the one being tried.

2 – God's Judgment, A Cause for Fear

> Then shall ye do unto him, as he had thought to have done unto his brother: so shalt thou put the evil away from among you. And those which remain <u>shall hear, and fear</u>, and shall henceforth commit no more any such evil among you. And thine eye shall not pity; *but* life *shall go* for life, eye for eye, tooth for tooth, hand for hand, foot for foot. Dt 19:19-21

We see the importance of God's judgments not only in the scriptures above, but also in the representation of the millennial rule of Christ foreshadowed in Solomon. Two women came forth unto him each saying the child was theirs. When his wisdom was put to the full test, his judgment came forth to show forth the wisdom of God. God's wisdom is to use the godly fear of judgment to bring forth truth and honesty. "And all Israel heard <u>of the judgment</u> which the king had <u>judged</u>; and <u>they feared the king</u>: for they saw that the wisdom of God *was* in him, <u>to do judgment</u>." 1K 3:28 All the people by his wisdom which he had from God to bring forth judgment saw both the severity and the goodness of God (Rom 11:22).

Today, the characteristics of respect for authority, honesty, and integrity are so easily cast aside because there is no fear of God. Yet the first judgment of God that hit the New Testament church involved these very issues: lack of respect for God's authorities in the earth (i.e. the apostles) and a lack of honesty and integrity in business matters. God took it into his own hands to put to death first Ananias and then Sapphira because of this. And what did the wisdom of God's judgments produce? The same as what God has desired throughout time that his people would hear and fear (Ac 5:5,11). If the wisdom of God was in Solomon "to do judgment", do we think this same wisdom is not in God himself? If the people feared the king for the judgment he judged, let us more so fear the God of heaven for the judgment that lies in his lap.

God's judgments are for both the righteous as well as the wicked to take notice. Concerning the destruction of the proud, Psalm 52:6-7 lets us know that "The righteous also shall see, and fear". Though men may foolishly find wrongdoing with God for his judgments, yet his wisdom is beyond fathoming. As it is written, "The meek will he guide <u>in judgment</u>: and the meek will he teach his way." Ps 25:9 God does not dispense his judgments only on the unjust. He sends them also upon the righteous to produce godly character through testing and suffering. "God judgeth the righteous" (Ps 7:11). Again it is written, "thou executest judgment and righteousness in Jacob." Ps 99:4

The Preservation of God's Judgments

We need to wisely consider and meditate on his judgments. There is a great depth of wisdom, understanding, counsel, and knowledge to glean from his judgments. As the scripture says, "Thy judgments *are* a great deep: O LORD, thou preservest man and beast." Ps 36:6 It is hard, at first, to perceive how

God can use judgments to *preserve* man, but he does indeed preserve us by his judgments. As David said, "Before I was afflicted I went astray: but now have I kept thy word." Ps 119:67 In the book of Job we see that God brings forth his chastenings (Job 33:19) so "that he may withdraw man *from his* purpose, and hide pride from man. He keepeth back his soul from the pit, and his life from perishing by the sword." Job 33:17-18 God's chastenings keep us from our purpose and turn away the pride of our rashness to continue in our way, while ignoring his way. The chastenings of the LORD keep us from perishing. This is why we cannot put away judgment in the church.

The judgments of the LORD are to produce the fear of God in us. Once we have the fruit of God's fear working in our heart, then we will understand the value and the righteousness of God's judgments. Without the fear of God we will never understand how totally true and righteous the judgments of the LORD are, or why we really need them. Notice how the fear of God immediately precedes the understanding of God's judgments. "The fear of the LORD *is* clean, enduring for ever: the <u>judgments</u> of the LORD *are* <u>true *and* righteous</u> altogether." Ps 19:9 This is confirmed by Proverbs where the result of understanding the fear of the LORD (Pr 2:5) is that "**then** shalt thou understand righteousness, and <u>judgment</u>, and equity" (Pr 2:9).

We must learn how to receive the judgments of God in our life. Remember, even Jesus suffered in his obedience as a son and learned from it (Heb 5:8). Revelation declares that those who have lost their lives for the Lord will *know* the righteousness of God's judgments, for they say, "Even so, Lord God Almighty, true and righteous *are* thy judgments." Rev 16:7 One day all those in heaven will join in this same refrain, "For <u>true and righteous</u> *are* his <u>judgments</u>" (Rev 19:2). His judgments are indeed a great deep, and if we continue with the LORD, we will indeed see how God uses them to preserve us (Ps 36:6).

So why do we find fault with God for the sovereignty of his judgments, when scripture says they are good (Ps 119:39)? Because we so lack the fear of God that we cannot see the judgments of the LORD as true *and* righteous altogether. "The fear of the LORD *is* clean, enduring for ever: the judgments of the LORD *are* true *and* righteous altogether." Ps 19:9 As it was in Jeremiah's day, so it is today,

> no man repented him of his wickedness, saying, What have I done? every one turned <u>to his course</u>, as the horse rusheth into the battle. Yea, the stork in the heaven knoweth her appointed times; and the turtle & the crane & the swallow observe the time of their coming; but **my people know not the judgment of the LORD**. Jer 8:6-7

The Need for God's Judgments

This is the modern church's problem. As those of Jeremiah's day, we do not observe the time of his coming, nor do we know the judgment of the

2 – God's Judgment, A Cause for Fear

LORD, for we have left it undone; we have put it aside. Without an understanding of his judgments, we can never regain the true fear of the LORD for the judgment of the LORD is the foundation of the fear of God.[20] If God's judgments are not real to us, then neither will his fear be real to us, for his judgments are to bring us to his fear.

> He that chastiseth the heathen, <u>shall not he correct</u> [*us*]? he that teacheth man knowledge, *shall not he know?* The LORD knoweth the thoughts of man, that they *are* vanity. <u>Blessed *is* the man whom thou chastenest</u>, O LORD, and teachest him out of thy law Ps 94:10-12

This is the sound doctrine of Biblical truth which must be recaptured. If God cannot judge his own people, his own family, then he will never have true respect. Remember, judgment is the *habitation* of his throne.[21] God rules and reigns through judgment (as every king does). It is by sitting in his throne of judgment that God scatters away all evil (Pr 20:8). This is an integral part of his being our father: the ability to correct and to admonish (Eph 6:4, 1Th 2:11). The rod of correction is essential to drive foolishness out of all of our hearts as God's children, for "foolishness *is* bound in the heart of a child; *but* the rod of correction shall drive it far from him." Pr 22:15 Because of the need for correction and chastisement, we are encouraged throughout the scripture not to be wearied by it, not to reject it, but to understand that it is for our good.

> Behold, <u>happy</u> *is* the man whom God correcteth: therefore <u>despise not</u> thou the chastening of the Almighty: For he maketh sore, and bindeth up: he woundeth, and his hands make whole. He shall deliver thee in six troubles: yea, in seven there shall no evil touch thee. Job 5:17-19

> My son, <u>despise not</u> the chastening of the LORD; <u>neither be weary</u> of his correction: For whom the LORD loveth he correcteth; <u>even as a father</u> the son *in whom* he delighteth. Pr 3:11-12

> And <u>ye have forgotten</u> the exhortation which speaketh unto you as unto children, My son, <u>despise not</u> thou the chastening of the Lord, <u>nor faint</u> when thou art rebuked of him: For whom the Lord loveth he chasteneth, and scourgeth every son whom he receiveth. Furthermore we have had fathers of our flesh which corrected *us,* and we gave *them* reverence: shall we not much rather be in subjection unto the Father of spirits, and live? Heb 12:5-6,9

It was as a father that Paul was being forced to come to the Corinthians with a rod, because they were unwilling to hearken to his authority (1Co 4:21). So even our heavenly Father, as a father, corrects us with the chastening rod.

---

[20] To see more how foundational the judgment of God is to God's fear see the figure entitled 'The Pillars of Grace and Fear'.

[21] The habitation of his throne: Ps 89:14, 97:2, Isa 9:7, Mt 19:28.

God's correction is for the purpose of delivering our soul from hell (Pr 23:13-14), so that we will give God rest and bring delight unto his soul (Pr 29:17).

We Must Fear Our Father: The Impartial Judge

"And if ye call on the Father, who without respect of persons judgeth according to every man's work, pass the time of your sojourning here in fear" 1Pe 1:17

Lastly, Elihu gives us the reason to fear God that "he respecteth not any *that are* wise of heart." Job 37:24 So Peter in the new covenant confirms this for us. "And if ye call on the Father, who without respect of persons judgeth according to every man's work, pass the time of your sojourning *here* in fear" (1Pe 1:17). Even though God is our father, he is an impartial judge, so we must walk in godly fear before him. We have seen how God uses both mercy and judgment individually to bring us to his fear. Let us look at them together for a moment to see how God would remove from us the pride, the being "wise of heart", that he disrespects.

Will We Humbly Receive His Warnings and Judgments When They Come?

So how did God attempt to restore the fear of God which had been so lost in Jeremiah's day? The answer will give us great insight into what he is doing today. To restore the fear of God, God must restore the fear of his judgments. But before he brings his judgments he will always warn his people and give them time and space to repent.[22] As God spoke to Isaiah,

> And therefore will the LORD wait, that he may be gracious unto you, and therefore will he be exalted, that he may have mercy upon you: for the LORD *is* a God of judgment: blessed *are* all they that wait for him. Isa 30:18

God warned his people and brought in rebuke and correction through his messengers. Eleven times in Jeremiah alone,[23] God says he arose early and sent his prophets to speak, even to protest, to turn his people from their evil ways back to the LORD. But his own people did not hear. When his warnings go unheeded, God *must* then chasten and correct through afflictions, judgments, and yes, punishments. Will God leave his children unpunished? The scripture says, "No." In the following scriptures it is *because* God has *not* abandoned us and is with us that he promises to punish us for our waywardness as his children.

> **For I *am* with thee**, saith the LORD, to save thee: ... but I will correct thee in measure, and will not leave thee <u>altogether unpunished</u>. Jer 30:11

---

[22] See in particular Isa 42:9 and Am 3:7.

[23] God arose early: Jer 7:13,25, 11:7, 25:3-4, 26:5, 29:19, 32:33, 35:14-15, 44:4.

2 – God's Judgment, A Cause for Fear

> Fear thou not, O Jacob my servant, saith the LORD: **for I *am* with thee**; ... but I will not make a full end of thee, but correct thee in measure; yet will I not leave thee <u>wholly unpunished</u>. Jer 46:28

Let us repent and receive God's correction and believe in his chastisements and judgments, so that we may be humbled and instructed in the good paths of the LORD and have the fear of the LORD restored. May we not end up as those of Jeremiah's day of whom God had smitten (Jer 2:29-30), yet they still refused to receive the correction which he had dealt out to them.

> O LORD, *are* not thine eyes upon the truth? thou hast stricken them, but they have not grieved; thou hast consumed them, *but* they have <u>refused to receive correction</u>: they have made their faces harder than a rock; they have refused to return [i.e. to repent]. Jer 5:3

> But thou shalt say unto them, This *is* a nation that obeyeth not the voice of the LORD their God, <u>nor receiveth correction</u>: truth is perished, and is cut off from their mouth. Jer 7:28

God told Jeremiah "my people know not the judgment of the LORD." Jer 8:7 This word 'know' means 'to know (by *seeing*)'. We must ask ourselves do we know by having seen (i.e. do we know firsthand) the judgment of the LORD? Does it produce godly fear in us as it ought to? Many will not know, nor will they understand that the devastations and tragedies that are coming are the very judgments of God! They will either attribute them to the devil and continue in the pride of their own way, or they will blame and condemn God for his actions. Though it overturns many a present day Bible teacher's theology, the scripture says God creates darkness and evil (Isa 45:7). That people *will* blame and condemn God for his judgments is prophesied throughout the scripture. When the judgments of God hit this earth, scripture records men (because of the hardness of their own hearts and the wickedness of their deeds) will blaspheme his holy name, blaming God, but they will not repent.

> [men] blasphemed the name of God, <u>which hath power over these plagues</u>: and they repented not to give him glory. And blasphemed the God of heaven because of their pains and their sores, and repented not of their deeds. Rev 16:9,11 (also v21)

> every morning doth [the just LORD] bring his judgment to light, he faileth not; but the unjust knoweth no shame. I said, Surely thou wilt fear me, thou wilt receive instruction; so their dwelling should not be cut off, howsoever I punished them: but they rose early, *and* corrupted all their doings. Zep 3:5,7

This is the way of those who refuse the fear of God. They refuse to be held accountable to 'their own deeds'. Thus, God's purpose is lost of bringing about meekness and his God through the demonstration of his authority and power. They lose the fear of God that could be theirs. By afflicting us he would chase us back to himself. Through his judgments he desires to open our deaf ears.

> Thou, *even* thou, *art* to be feared: and who may stand in thy sight when once thou art angry? Thou didst cause judgment to be heard from heaven; the earth feared, and was still, When God arose to judgment, **to save all the meek** of the earth. Selah [i.e. *stop and think about it!*]. Ps 76:7-9

When God's judgments are seen or heard, they cause the earth to stand still. This is the LORD trying to capture our attention through the demonstration of his power. "Who shall not fear thee, O Lord, and glorify thy name? for *thou* only *art* holy: for all nations shall come and worship before thee; for thy judgments are made manifest." Rev 15:4 The manifestation of God's judgments is to remind us of his holiness and to humble us so that we truly come and worship before him. God would arrest all our attention so that we might fear him.

Consider again what the psalmist said. God uses his judgments to "save all the meek of the earth." Thus, who are the meek of the earth, but those who will hear his judgments and humble themselves to fear him? Through hearing and through humbling ourselves, God is able to save us from our own destructive ways. This is why God must use judgment at times to bring about brokenness and meekness, so that we might have ears to hear and fear.[24]

Through his awesome judgments the LORD saves the meek of the earth. The meek will behold his mighty acts and fear unto repentance. Thus, the scripture says, "Surely his salvation *is* nigh them that fear him" (Ps 85:9). Often God has allowed and ordained disaster and loss, along with intense suffering and pain. He uses tragedies and suffering to bring the stubborn, hardened unbelieving soul and the erring believer who is walking in pride or willful disobedience and even his faithful servants to all come to the priceless place of brokenness. Here the preciousness of his gift of grace and restoration can be received and the fellowship of his sufferings can be treasured (Php 3:10).

So often we are tempted to think of God's judgments as evil, when the scripture declares that his judgments are good (Ps 119:39). May we now see better why, for they are for our salvation and humbling. May we see that his judgments may lead to destruction in those who harden their hearts, but to everlasting life in those who soften their hearts and fear before him.

Judging without Respect of Persons: The Call to Obedience

We would do well to regularly consider the judgments of God in order to keep our heart from becoming puffed up and losing our fear of God. As the Judge, God judges in perfect righteousness. He will judge without respect for

---

[24] Hear and fear: Dt 13:11, 17:13, 19:20, 21:21. Hear and learn to fear: Dt 4:10, 31:12-13, 2Ch 20:29, Ps 34:11, 66:16, 76:8, Ecc 12:13, Jer 33:9, Ac 5:5,11.

persons (this we must be assured of, for it is throughout the Word).²⁵ This alone ought to cause us to live our short and pilgrim's life here on this earth in fear. Though he is our father, yet he is our judge. "And if ye call on the Father, who <u>without respect of persons judgeth</u> according to every man's work, pass the time of your sojourning *here* in fear" (1Pet 1:17). The fact that God our Father judges every man's works, regardless of who they are, should cause us to fear. What we have repented of and is under the blood has been erased, but what we still walk willfully and obstinately against God's commandments in will be judged. Let us learn to pass the time of our residence here on earth as strangers and pilgrims in the fear of God.

If for all these, we still are slow in coming to a ready acceptance of the fear of God, then we ought to fear God simply because he himself repeatedly and continually commands it in both testaments.

- "fear him" – Dt 8:6, 13:4, Mt 10:28, Lk 12:5
- "Fear God." – 1Pe 2:17, Rev 14:7
- "fear thou God." – Ecc 5:7
- "Thou shalt fear thy God" – Lev 19:14,32, 25:17,36,43
- "fear the LORD" – numerous²⁶

Our whole obligation as his people is to fear God and to obey him. So Solomon says, "Let us hear the conclusion of the whole matter: Fear God, and keep his commandments: <u>for this is the whole duty of man</u>." Ecc 12:13 Over and over again the scripture puts forth for us to fear him and to obey him.²⁷ "O that there were such an heart in them, that they would fear me, and keep all my commandments <u>always</u>, <u>that it might be well with them</u>, and with their children for ever!" Dt 5:29 It is given specifically to us as saints of God and as servants that we are to fear him. "O fear the LORD, ye his saints" (Ps 34:9). Servants are to "obey in all things" in the fear of God (Col 3:22).

Truly, the LORD knows what is best for us. He knows that the fear of the LORD and the obedience that comes from it is for our good, as he says, so "that it might be well with [us], and with [our] children for ever!" The fear of the LORD is meant by God to be a great blessing in our life, but men have turned it into a cursing. This is why God must correct our thinking.

> O LORD, I know that the way of man *is not in himself*: *it is* not in man that walketh to direct his steps. <u>O LORD, correct me</u>, but with judgment; not in thine anger, lest thou bring me to nothing. Jer 10:23-24

---

[25] There is **no** respect of persons with God: Ac 10:34; Rom 2:11; Eph 6:9; Col 3:25; Jam 2:1,9; 1Pe 1:17; 2Sam 14:14; 2Ch 19:7; Pr 28:21.

[26] Dt 6:13, 10:20, Jos 24:14, 1Sam 12:14,24, Ps 33:8, 34:9, Pr 3:7, Jer 5:24

[27] Fear and obey: Dt 6:2, 8:6, 13:4, 17:19, 1Sam 12:14.

The LORD must correct us at times in order to direct our steps, for he must teach us the way that we should go. So often we think that we know the way we ought to go, but the scripture warns us it is not in us. "What man *is* he that feareth the LORD? him shall he teach in the way *that* he shall choose." Ps 25:12 The fear of the LORD opens up our heart to hear correction. The LORD has a way that he has chosen for us. He knows which way we ought to go. It is not a way that originates in us, but in his mighty plan and counsel. We must come to know the way he has chosen for us, and through the fear of God he will. He can then teach us which way that is. And even when we do not see or understand the value of what he asks us to do, we may still please him by the obedience of faith.[28]

For the Sake of His Glory
"that glory may dwell in our land." Ps 85:9

We have yet one more reason why we need the fear of God in our home, in our church, in our city, and in our country. It is so that, in the dark and evil days we live in, glory may dwell in our land! "Surely his salvation *is* nigh them that fear him; that glory may dwell in our land." Ps 85:9 The glory of God can be seen by others through our lives. That glory will never be seen unless we are glorifying God by how we live in accordance with his character and his commandments. It is the fear of God which produces both of these: his character in us and obedience to him (by departing from iniquity). Thus, the fear of the LORD in us is the key to others beholding the glory of God. O how we need his glory to be seen.

America once had such a glory, for America once had salvation *and* the fear of God. In the New England Primer[29] of 1777 which taught American children in public school how to read, it contained the alphabet with a phrase for each letter that was to be memorized. The phrase for each letter was a scripture from the Bible. Notice the first two letters and the significance of what was being taught as the foundation of knowledge to school children:

- A – "A wise son maketh a glad father:
  but a foolish man despiseth his mother." Pr 15:20
- B – "Better *is* little with the fear of the LORD
  than great treasure and trouble therewith." Pr 15:16

What is truly astonishing about this, is that this was not the elementary primer for private Christian schools. No, this was in use for nearly 200 years in

---

[28] The obedience of faith: Rom 1:5, 16:26-27.

[29] *The New England Primer* was the first textbook ever printed in America and was used to teach reading and Bible lessons in its **public** schools until the twentieth century. [Please see the WallBuilders website (www.wallbuilders.com) for more information.]

2 – God's Judgment, A Cause for Fear

<u>public</u> schools! The foundation of what was once taught in public schools is astounding when we compare it with the antagonism toward anything Christian today. While learning the alphabet all school children in America once learned the scriptures. In doing so, they would immediately learn first to honor their father and mother; they would thus learn respect for God-ordained authority. Second, they would learn to fear God, to depart from covetousness, *and* to have godly contentment! O how America has fallen from its godly heritage. Where once the commandments of God were in its textbooks going into the hearts of its children to keep them from evil, now they are taken from before their eyes so that they cannot be publicly displayed – lest they be "influenced" or feel compelled to obey them! She has lost so much. She has lost her fear of God. Today in the church we have salvation being taught, but we have no fear of God, and because we do not have it, therefore we have no glory in our land.

Consider, from God's perspective, the importance of people coming to know his fear. In the days of the dispersion God removed his people from the promised land because they did not fear him and sent them into captivity into lands amongst people that feared not the LORD. He then brought some of these foreign people back to settle the land. Of these resettled people it is written, "And *so* it was at the beginning of their dwelling there, *that* they <u>feared not the LORD</u>: therefore the LORD sent lions among them, which slew *some* of them." 2K 17:25 Isn't it amazing again, how God chose to reveal himself to these deportees? He chose to reveal himself not by mercy and comforts, not by longsuffering and loving-kindness, but rather by fearful judgments, which were to produce in them the fear of God.

> Today in the church we have salvation being taught, but we have no fear of God, and because we do not have it, therefore we have no glory in our land.

If the fear of God can be incorporated into the hearts and the gatherings of God's people, as once was in early America, then glory will again dwell in that land. What few people realize is that the glory that attended America for so many years was not due to America's inventiveness, her educational system, hard work, or technical industrialization – as her history books would say. No, it was the result of godly men and women who worshipped God in spirit and in truth and who held fast to the authority of the Bible as the ultimate truth. This was the glory of America, a people unashamed to worship, to pray to, and to speak of their God and of his word in every facet of their life, both private and public, both domestic and civil.

Where is the Fear of GOD? Finding the Treasure of the Lord

The Source of America's Past Greatness

Once, the Bible was used as the standard of law. The scriptures were regularly quoted in the legal system of America as the authority of truth. Now they are cast aside for man's wisdom. Many of the original universities and colleges in America were either overtly Christian and started to advance the Christian faith, or they were at least founded on the word of God. America once used the scriptures as a guide to teaching her children how to read, but now such things are inadmissible; they are in fact outlawed – to America's shame. She once heard God's cries,

> <u>Receive my instruction</u>, and not silver; and knowledge rather than choice gold. For wisdom *is* better than rubies; and all the things that may be desired are not to be compared to it. I wisdom dwell with prudence, and <u>find out knowledge of witty inventions</u>. **The fear of the LORD** *is* to hate evil: pride, and arrogancy, and the evil way, and the froward mouth, do I hate. Pr 8:10-13

Wisdom from God, we are instructed, finds out the knowledge of witty inventions. This is why historically many of the greatest scientists of past generations were believers in God. God gave America's founding fathers wisdom because they feared him, for the beginning of wisdom is the fear of the LORD. It was the fear of the LORD that enabled America to excel and to invent witty inventions.

Notice how in Proverbs 8:12-13, Solomon immediately goes from the discovery of inventions to the fear of the LORD. America was once a nation, through its trust in the Lord GOD and its holding fast to the Bible as the very word of God, that hated evil, pride, arrogancy, the evil way, and lying. With the loss of the fear of God that has all changed. America now loves evil – buying and selling it for pleasure! America is number one in the world in exporting pornography. Its movies are filled with filthy language, illicit sex, crudity of every form, and graphic violence unbounded. Soap operas captivate the minds of housewives and young women with adultery, fornication, lying, deceiving, even murders, where once the scriptures and the fear of God was a woman's glory.

America at one time despised pride and haughtiness and was part of the reason she declared independence from Britain, but now she has become worse than the ones she rebelled against. America is a high-minded nation, full of itself. Where once it was full of the fear of God, and in truth it could be said, "In God we trust", now it is a blatant lie, a hypocrisy of the highest order. America trusts in its weapons, its armies, its technology, its economic power, and its own intelligence, but she does not trust in God. The true God is far, far from her ways and her thoughts. There is little doubt to any non-American that America is the proudest nation on earth.

2 – God's Judgment, A Cause for Fear

In the beginning, America stood on truth, for the sake of truth. Now it stands on lies and speaks lies, as evidenced, among other things, by her politicians and the open, unashamed lies they have been caught in – yet, sadly, no one cares anymore. It is almost expected. Yet, it was the fear of God that brought forth the glory of America politically, industrially, technically, and economically, but in her prosperity and her advancement she has become proud in her own eyes. She thought that *she* had produced all these things and that these things were all for *her* pleasure and enjoyment. Rather, these things were the result of the blessings of Almighty God for her faithfulness to him, not so that she could spend them upon herself, but so that America might bless the nations with truth, righteousness, and mercy for the poor and downtrodden. But she has been deceived by her riches and prosperity.

Judgment after judgment has begun to hit America, and God must wonder why we still do not fear him. "I said, <u>Surely thou wilt fear me</u>, thou wilt receive instruction; so their dwelling should not be cut off, howsoever I punished [i.e. *visited*] them: but they rose early, *and* corrupted all their doings." Zep 3:7 She has been visited with God's judgments, yet as soon as the judgment is over, she rises early and corrupts all her doings. Terrific weather phenomena have ravaged America's food supply. The worst flooding, hurricanes, tornadoes, earthquakes, droughts, and fires of America's history are all taking place now. They are increasing in frequency and destructiveness. Pestilence and every kind of sickness and cancer are afflicting America. Waves of disease hit America every year, attacking the old and the young.[30] Hardly a prophecy that God spoke to ancient Israel, concerning what would come upon them if they forsook the commandments of God, has not come to pass against America, in her forsaking of him. God said, "Thou shalt betroth a wife, and another man shall lie with her" (Dt 28:30); how true this is with the escalation of adultery. God has warned America, but she has no ear to hear.

> If thou wilt not observe to do all the words of this law that are written in this book, that thou mayest <u>fear this glorious and fearful name,</u> THE LORD THY GOD; Then the LORD will make thy **plagues wonderful**, and the plagues of thy seed, *even* **great plagues**, and **of long continuance**, and **sore sicknesses**, and **of long continuance**. Moreover he will bring upon thee all the diseases of Egypt, which thou wast afraid of; and they shall cleave unto thee. Also every sickness, and every plague, which *is* not written in the book of this law, them will the LORD bring upon thee, until thou be destroyed. Dt 28:58-61

How can anyone doubt what has happened to America and not see the fearful judgments he has brought against her for her sins? Only the deception of

---

[30] We have been smitten with the botch (i.e. *burning ulcers*) of Egypt and with emerods (i.e. *tumors*) as scripture itself warns will fall upon those who once followed the LORD, but now have forsaken him (Dt 28:27,35).

a prideful, covetous, and hardened heart can so blind one. How can anyone not see that the LORD is trying to bring her back to the fear of God she once possessed? Through fearful judgments he is trying to bring America to her knees and to repent before a holy God, so that she will put away all other false gods – but that is the *one* thing she will not do, for she has become the land of every god under heaven. She considers this 'liberty and freedom for all', when it is in fact the greatest bondage of all. She is as ancient Israel. She honors foreign gods and their worship more than the true God, though it was the true God that established them both in such miraculous ways. As God warned them of turning away from him, so it could be equally as true for America today,

> Or hath God assayed to go *and* take him a nation from the midst of another *nation,* by temptations, by signs, and by wonders, and by war, and by a mighty hand, and by a stretched out arm, and by great terrors, according to all that the LORD your God did for you? Dt 4:34

We are called by God to "neither make mention of the names of their gods, nor cause to swear *by them,* neither serve them, nor bow yourselves unto them" (Jos 23:7), yet America has spiritual and natural leaders who not only take up their names and who swear by them, but who even bow down to them, and go into their places of worship, and allow their followers to come into the LORD's place of worship and speak of their gods upon altars that were once dedicated to the LORD God. God's commandments cannot be displayed in her places of justice. Her children cannot publicly pray to him in her schools. Yet the total hypocrisy that "In God we trust" is on her money, and every session of the congress opens with prayer. But America knows not to which god she is even praying! People are made to swear to the truth upon the Bible, even though its truth is no longer admissible by judges for jurors to make decisions based on truth, when once her laws were made from the very pages of the same Bible!

The plagues and sicknesses, the famines and droughts, the judgments and cursings of God will only increase, and the day will come as God himself promised, when we will be "smitten before thine enemies: thou shalt go out one way against them, and flee seven ways before them" (Dt 28:25). Like Egypt of long ago, God will be glorified whether by her destruction, to prove the word of God true, or whether by her repentance and turning to him. God desires to deliver her, as well as every nation, from themselves and from the enemy, so that he may again show mercy and bring his glory into that land. This is all of our choice. Will we choose the fear of the LORD or not? "<u>Now</u> therefore fear the LORD, and serve him in sincerity and in truth: and put away the gods which your fathers served on the other side of the flood, and in Egypt; and serve ye the LORD." Jos 24:14

The fear of God that was upon the early founding fathers of America spread a blessing that God Almighty freely gave, according to his promise to the generations that followed. Here is God's promise to the generations who follow those who fear him: "But the mercy of the LORD *is* from everlasting to everlast-

2 – God's Judgment, A Cause for Fear

ing upon them that fear him, and his righteousness <u>unto children's children</u>" (Ps 103:17). The blessing of the fear of God is not given only to those who have it, but to their children's children as well. The grandchildren of those who were possessed with the fear of the LORD are blessed with mercy from God. God shows or demonstrates mercy and justice or fairness to the offspring of those who feared him – even though they begin to depart from him. Solomon was blessed because of his father David's heart toward God. So the prodigal son was blessed with a great inheritance (even though he squandered it), not because of his own goodness, but because of the goodness and provision of his father.

> **WARNING**: The time of America's blessing from having godly forefathers has run out. She truly is living on borrowed time. Her godly inheritance has been squandered. Now is the last chance for America to repent and return to the LORD, for his judgments and his wrath are stored up and are brimming over. Only the recapturing of the fear of the LORD can save her, divert the disasters that are looming over, and return to her his abundant mercies.

Complete destruction has always come to every great and proud civilization which forsakes the fear of God. The glory of Egypt fell and is no more. The glory of Babylon fell and is no more. The same with Assyria, Persia, Medo-Persia, Greece, and even all the glory of Rome – they have all fallen and are no more. There are no exceptions. Only repentance and a return to the fear of God can stay God's hand of judgment.

Consider the case of Nineveh. Nineveh was spared God's judgment but for a season[31] because they heard the word of judgment which God proclaimed by Jonah and with prayer, fasting, and breaking off of their sins of wickedness they repented. America is very little different than Nineveh today, in terms of her sins and being under God's judgment. But America has not repented as Nineveh did. O that teachers faithful to the truth would arise before it is altogether too late! That they might come and dwell in the house of God ('Bethel') and teach us <u>how</u> we should fear the LORD (2K 17:28). Let us do as those of Nineveh did to repent, before God's anger is unleashed.

> But let man and beast be covered with sackcloth, and cry mightily unto God: yea, let them turn every one from his evil way, and from the violence that *is* in their hands. Who can tell *if* God will turn and repent, and turn away from his fierce anger, that we perish not?
>
> And God saw their works, that they turned from their evil way; and God repented of the evil, that he had said that he would do unto them; and he did *it* not. Jnh 3:8-9

---

[31] Later, the Ninevites returned to these same sins and they were destroyed, approximately 150 years after Jonah's preaching.

The Witness of our Heart
"that glory may dwell in our land." Ps 85:9

Our own heart, whether believers or unbelievers, witnesses to us that there is a judgment that we must all face. So Solomon in his search for truth and meaning comes to the clear witness of his own heart, "I said in mine heart, God shall judge the righteous and the wicked: for *there is* a time there for every purpose and for every work." Ecc 3:17 Solomon reminds youth that they ought to be sure of God's judgments of the choices they make: "know thou, that for all these *things* God will bring thee into judgment." Ecc 11:9 It is because God will judge "every work … with every secret thing" that Solomon is brought to the conclusion that we *must* fear God (Ecc 12:13-14).

This is why when believers are taught or falsely believe that they will not face any judgment for their works, because they are in Christ, a great contradiction is set up in their heart. Instead of this bringing peace it actually robs us of peace. Our heart continually through the knowledge of truth warns us that there is a price to pay for sin, disobedience, and compromise. It is only by acknowledging God's judgment and allowing him to search our heart daily to show us what displeases and angers him that the cause for his judgment can be removed. Then through repentance the evil desires of our heart can be cleansed, and through the renewing by the Word our minds are no longer enemies unto God by wicked thoughts (Jam 4:4).[32] Only then can our heart be made to be at peace with the Lord. Remember, it was to born again believers that Paul wrote and warned them that they were storing up wrath from God, if they were not continually coming before God in repentance and a softening of their heart. "But after thy hardness and impenitent heart treasurest up unto thyself wrath against the day of wrath and revelation of the righteous judgment of God." Rom 2:5

Thus, judgment is the key to having peace. If we disallow God's judgments on his children we deny the witness of our own heart as children of God, we deny all the Old Testament scriptures, and we even deny the Spirit of God who is witnessing to us of judgment (Jn 16:8-11).[33] So Isaiah warned of a disobedient

---

[32] So Paul warns the Ephesians not to walk anymore as the lost do, "in the vanity of their mind" for this produces alienation from God (Eph 4:17-23).

[33] When Jesus says the Comforter "will reprove the world of sin, and of righteousness, and of judgment" we may get the wrong impression and believe that the Comforter will only do these things for the lost (i.e. the world). But "the world" here is not in the specific sense of those who are of the world, but in the general sense of being all people. The Spirit of God clearly convicts not only the lost but also the believer of sin, for without his work of conviction the saved would truly be in bondage to the elements of the world. The Spirit of God will also convict the saved of righteousness (i.e. what he/she ought to do) and of judgment (i.e. the Judgment seat of Christ).

2 – God's Judgment, A Cause for Fear

and gainsaying people (Rom 10:20-21) who would not know the way of peace because they did not know God's judgments:

> The way of peace they know not; and *there is* no judgment in their goings: they have made them crooked paths: whosoever goeth therein shall not know peace. Isa 59:8

If we would know the way of peace, let us have "judgment in [our] goings". For if we come to know the judgment of God and its redemptive purpose, then we will see its good fruit: the fear of God.

Chapter 3. The Spirit of the Fear of the LORD
Recognizing Our Spiritual Birthright
"*the spirit ... of the fear of the LORD*" Isa 11:2

The Revelation of the Spirit
"*that which is born of the Spirit is spirit.*" Jn 3:6

When anyone confesses Christ Jesus as Lord of their life unto eternal salvation, the fear of the LORD is planted in their heart as a part of the process of being born again, though many do not know it. Like me, you were most likely never taught that. At the moment of salvation we are translated out of the kingdom of darkness and brought into the kingdom of his dear Son (Col 1:13). As adopted sons and daughters, the heavenly Father gives us a down payment of our eternal inheritance. He grants that greatest gift of the sealing of the Holy Spirit which is called the indwelling, the earnest or down-payment of our inheritance (Eph 1:13). This is the same Spirit which indwelt our Lord, yet, we forget that that Spirit which is given to us is "the spirit ... of the fear of the LORD" (Isa 11:2)! Let us go back to the beginning of the work of the Spirit in us when we were born again and learn more about the Spirit and his work.

3 – The Spirit of the Fear of the LORD

The Spirit of God is called "the seven Spirits of God",[34] or as we would better understand today, the seven-fold Spirit of God. The foreshadowing of the characteristics of the Spirit are seen in the candlestick, which was in the holy place of Moses' tabernacle. It had a central main shaft and three pairs of shafts extending out to the right and to the left, making seven total shafts. At the top of each was a bowl and a lamp, making seven total lamps (Ex 25:31-37). This is pictured in Figure 3-1, The Candlestick of the Spirit. Nowhere in scripture are these seven attributes or characteristics of the Spirit described for us except in one place (and even there not completely).

Let us take a moment to understand a little more about the Spirit of God, for he has much to do with growing the grace of the fear of the LORD in our hearts, for he is its planter. In Isaiah 11:2 we have what appears to be, and what all wrongly claim to be, all 7 attributes of the Holy Spirit. In reality we have only 6 of his 7 attributes here. Many try to force it to be seven by ridiculously claiming that the first is "the spirit of the LORD", but this is who he is, not an attribute. Look at this verse closely. "And the spirit of the LORD shall rest upon him, the spirit of [1] wisdom and [2] understanding, the spirit of [3] counsel and [4] might, the spirit of [5] knowledge and of [6] the fear of the LORD" (Isa 11:2). It is clear from this verse that those attributes listed are paired up into three sets, making a total of six,[35] so that again "the spirit of the LORD" is clearly seen not to be one of the attributes listed, but rather his identification.

The Spirit of Love

The seventh attribute of the Spirit is never specifically or openly mentioned in the entire Old Testament or either in the gospels (though it is there, but concealed). It is not until the New Testament epistle to a young, growing and faithful disciple, named Timothy, that the seventh or fullness of the Spirit is openly revealed – for only the heart of a disciple can learn the perfection of the Spirit of God. There, Paul reveals the seventh attribute or perfection of the Spirit. He summarizes the characteristics of the Spirit, saying we have received the spirit "of power, and of love, and of a sound mind." 2Tim 1:7

The Spirit 'of power' is none other than the second half of the three pairs of the attributes of the Spirit. These are the spirit of understanding, might [i.e. power], and the fear of the LORD. The Spirit 'of a sound mind' is none other than the first half of these three pairs, which are the spirit of wisdom, counsel, and knowledge. That only leaves us with the core characteristic of the spirit 'of love'. This would be the candlestick's main shaft, the seventh or core attribute of the Spirit, and would explain why it alone is not paired with any other attrib-

---

[34] The seven spirits of God: Rev 3:1, 4:5, 5:6.

[35] Namely, we see the pairings as: wisdom and understanding, counsel and might, knowledge and the fear of the LORD.

ute. This should explain to us why the fullness of the Spirit of love could not be fully revealed and demonstrated until the coming of his dear and beloved Son through whom "God so loved the world, that he gave his only begotten Son" (Jn 3:16). This is why the Spirit of the LORD is indeed the Spirit of Christ.[36]

> Without the fear of God we can only be an unstable footstool for the LORD, not having that third leg of the Spirit's working: his power.

The Spirit of love is made known to us in the new covenant in several precious ways, unforeseen under the old covenant. The Spirit of God is both the source of love for God and the bringer of God's love to us. As it is written, "the love of God is shed abroad in our hearts by the Holy Ghost which is given unto us." Rom 5:5 Paul speaks of our "love in the Spirit" (Col 1:8, see also Rom 15:30). The first fruit of the Spirit is none other than love (Gal 5:22). Thus, immediately following "the Holy Ghost" in 2Corinthians 6:6 we see "love unfeigned", and immediately following "the Spirit" in 1Peter 1:22 we again see an "unfeigned love of the brethren". So because we are "born of God"[37] and because "God is love" (1Jn 4:8), therefore we can see that through the Spirit of love which first came to indwell us and to give us spiritual birth that we are truly born of love.

Returning again to the characteristics of the spirit, we see that the spirit of the fear of the LORD is the foundational beginning of the spirit of power. Remember, the second half of the characteristics of the spirit are summarized by Paul as the spirit of power (2Tim 1:7). They are the spirit of the fear of the LORD, might, and understanding. Thus, the fear of the LORD is the foundational root of the spirit of might or power. If we are lacking power in our walk with God, it can often be traced back to a loss of the fear of the LORD!

We need to recapture the fear of the LORD with all our heart. Without the fear of God we can only be an unstable footstool for the LORD, not having that third leg of the Spirit's working: his power. We must have all three workings of the Spirit in our life to be stable: power, love, and a sound mind. We may have the spirit of love (through the new birth) and the spirit of a sound mind (through the word of God), but be completely lacking the fear of the LORD and therefore have no spirit of power working in us. Without the fear of God we will have no power in prayer, no might to overcome sin, and no depth of spiritual understanding of what is going on in our life.

---

[36] The Spirit of Christ is identified as the Spirit of God and the Holy Ghost: Rom 8:9, 1Pe 1:11-12, Php 1:19.

[37] Born or begotten of God: Jn 1:13, 1Jn 2:9, 4:7, 5:1,4,18.

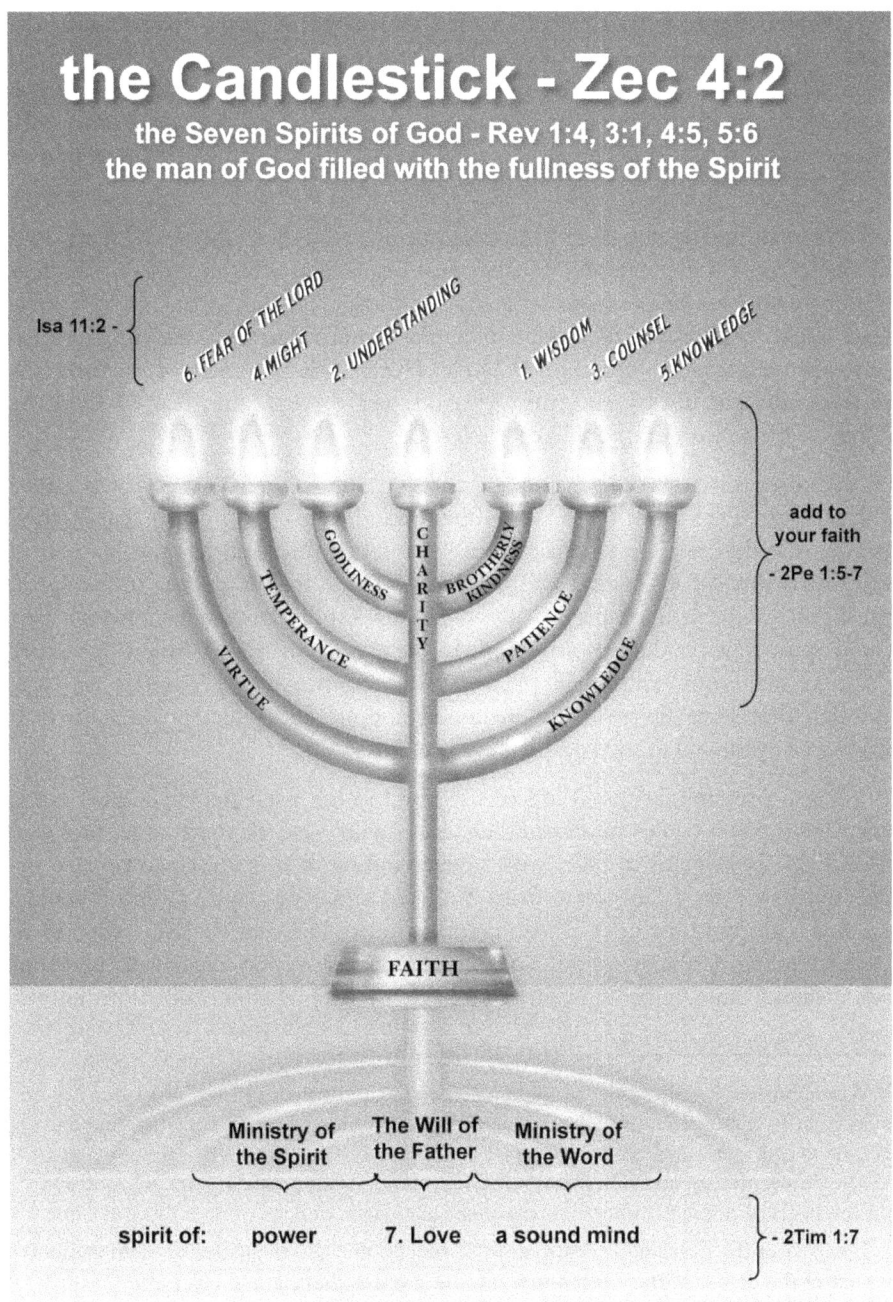

Where is the Fear of GOD? Finding the Treasure of the Lord

From Fear to Wisdom: Growth in the Spirit

By studying how these attributes are developed in us as we mature in the Lord it becomes evident that this is a listing of the characteristics of the Spirit of the LORD in *reverse* order. The fullness of what he works is mentioned first and it works backwards to the root from which it came. Thus, they are from God's perspective (i.e. in God coming to man), rather than from our perspective of the way in which we grow into these graces of the Spirit.

No man having just been born again begins to walk in the spirit of wisdom or the spirit of understanding. Rather, they begin first with the spirit of the fear of the LORD, and they begin to learn knowledge by the Spirit of God as he leads them to the word of God. This is the pattern that God has designed for our spiritual maturity in being led of the Holy Spirit. The fear of the LORD is birthed into our life by the Spirit of God, and through that fear of God the Spirit is able to produce godly knowledge.

God promised, "And I will make an everlasting covenant with them, that I will not turn away from them, to do them good; but I will put my fear in their hearts, that they shall not depart from me." Jer 32:40 God has put his fear in our hearts through the new covenant. He has done this by putting in his Spirit, the Spirit of the fear of the LORD, within us. Godly knowledge through that same Spirit now produces spiritual might (*force, valor,* or *victory*). Might or victory through that same Spirit will produce wise counsel. Wise counsel, in turn, through that same Spirit results in understanding, and understanding through that same Spirit will in the end produce great wisdom.

It is a principle in the Word of God and in life itself that first must come knowledge, then comes understanding, and finally wisdom may come, that is, *if* knowledge is properly applied with understanding. We never go in reverse order, unless we are falling away from the Lord and losing spiritual intuitiveness. Each is built upon the next. Wisdom comes in our life after we have come to an understanding. Understanding can only come after we have received his counsel. Counsel must be brought after we have might.[38] Might comes from knowl-

---

[38] Wise counsel *must* always be brought after we have might or victory. This may not be evident at first, but when we are strong and have might is when we truly become dangerous to our own selves and to others. Suffice it to say that after we have won a great victory, more than at any other time, we often stand at our greatest peril. Note, it was on the heels of overwhelming victories that the greatest defeats of men of God came.

It was after the miraculous destruction of Jericho that the tragic defeat of Ai came. It was after the defeat of the Ammonites and the Syrians that Bath-sheba came (2Sam 10-11). It was but a short time after Peter's declaration of Jesus as "the Christ, the Son of the living God" that he was rebuked by Jesus for speaking the words of Satan (Mt 16:16-23). Need we continue? The need for counsel is needed most when we are gaining our greatest victories in the LORD and are at our strongest. It is all too easy to feel over-edge, and true spiritual knowledge comes, yes, from the Spirit of God, but in particular from 'the spirit of the fear of the LORD', for it is through the fear of the LORD that we gain the knowledge of the holy (Pr 9:10).

Let us look at one more evidence to secure our heart that indeed these attributes of the Spirit are listed in reverse order. It is not written that wisdom or knowledge is the beginning of the fear of the LORD. Rather, it is written "The fear of the LORD *is* the beginning of wisdom" (Pr 9:10, also Ps 111:10). So there can be no godly wisdom in the absence of the fear of God. The fear of God always precedes godly wisdom. So also it is with true knowledge. "The fear of the LORD *is* the beginning of knowledge" (Pr 1:7). The fear of the LORD opens the door to spiritual knowledge, then understanding, and in time wisdom. Thus, the very *first* attribute the Spirit of the LORD desires to manifest in us is his fear.

We may speak rightly then when we say that we were born again by the Spirit of the fear of the LORD. Now this is yet another of the great paradoxes of salvation. "For God hath not given us the spirit of fear; but of power, and of love, and of a sound mind." 2Tim 1:7 Consider this, though we have *not* been given "the spirit of fear", God has in fact given us 'the spirit of the fear of the LORD'! The spirit we have received is *not* the spirit of the fear of man, nor the spirit of the fear of circumstances, nor of the future, but it **IS** the spirit of the fear of the LORD. The Spirit of God from our new birth moves us, guides us, and inspires each of us to fear nothing but the Almighty God. It is upon this foundation of the fear of the LORD that the Spirit will build all the rest of his characteristics.

Born in Fear and Reborn in Fear

"I will praise thee; for I am fearfully and wonderfully made" Ps 139:14

Creation itself has been so molded, shaped, and formed that everything around us from his innate glory, to his Word, to his forgiveness, to his Wonders, to the natural creation – both its beauties and its catastrophes – even to our own lives, should lead us to the fear of the LORD. It should not seem strange then that our very being has been fashioned in fear. The Bible shows us the very core of our being has been created "fearfully" (Ps 139:14) or literally 'in fear'. This is the very same Hebrew word (H3372) used many times for the fear of God. We are fearfully made. We are literally 'made in fear'. Thus, not only our spiritual birth was in the fear of God, but even our natural birth was in the fear of God! So from beginning to new beginning, God has orchestrated his fear to be in us.

---

ly confident when we have done something for the Lord that has made a difference. Let us remember, "we have this treasure in earthen vessels, that the excellency of the power may be of God, and not of us." 2Co 4:7 The pride of our heart will always deceive us (Ob 1:3) and remove the fear of God from our heart, if we are not continually watchful.

Where is the Fear of GOD? Finding the Treasure of the Lord

We were created to fear God. We dare not put that away. Our fulfillment in life and our purpose cannot be established without the fear of God being unleashed and developed. God has promised to "fulfil the desire of them that fear him" (Ps 145:19). How then can we ever find our true fulfillment without the fear of God? Everyone in scripture that grew with God in intimacy grew simultaneously in the fear of God. Is it any wonder, as we shall see, that there are so, so many blessings associated with the fear of God? When we give place to the fear of God and, like the early church, learn to walk in it, then we will fulfill our created destiny. The fear of the LORD is at the very root of both our created being and of our re-created being through the new birth. Thus, the fear of the LORD should be the life-giving root out of which our knowledge, strength, counsel, understanding, wisdom, and love are all based.

Those who Must be Saved with Fear

Jude tells us that some may **only** be saved through fear, because of the depth of sin that they are involved in (and presumably how much they still love it). So he warns, "And others save with fear, pulling *them* out of the fire; hating even the garment spotted by the flesh." Jude 1:23 Often we think this is *our* fear, meaning we need to approach them *in* fear and save them. But remember, we don't save anyone. God does the saving. We plant and water, but he gives the increase. This scripture says "save with fear". This fear is specifically the fear of God that we must awaken in their hearts to flee the depth of depravity that they have entered into and that is drawing them to the very edge of the pit.

Make no mistake, all sin kills, by bringing separation from the life that only is found in God, but all sin does not kill at the same rate or in the same way. Many diseases lead to death; some kill slowly, others exceedingly swiftly. The picture here that Jude sees is when one has covered themselves in a flammable substance and their body is being engulfed by flames. These are close to utter destruction, having only moments left to hear.[39] In this case only the fear of God can save them. They must be saved with fear.

Jude implies that most are saved without fear. For those who are saved without the fear of God, they are often missing the first characteristic or "character" of the Spirit, in terms of their understanding of the gospel. Yet, this is exactly how most people come to the Lord. The Spirit of the LORD expects they will be taught the fear of God by the governors and tutors that are to be over them. But in so many churches this is not being done, because the fear of the Lord has been deliberately set aside. As a result, the fear of the LORD must be engrafted in later in order to grow up beyond childhood – for if we would go on to maturity, we shall see, we *must* have the fear of God.

---

[39] When the Lord opens a door to speak to such, we often are the only ones who will have the opportunity.

3 – The Spirit of the Fear of the LORD

Fear for Growth

The fear of God is essential for growing up in our salvation, for Paul says, "Wherefore, my beloved, as ye have always obeyed, not as in my presence only, but now much more in my absence, <u>work out your own salvation with fear and trembling</u>." Php 2:12 As we *work out* our salvation with fear and trembling, the Lord is able to *work in* us "both to will and to do of his good pleasure". This is because his salvation is being worked out by us, or exercised by us, and it will grow stronger in us. Salvation will begin to affect or take possession of more and more parts of our life. If we would see our salvation worked out in our lives, then we must have the fear of God working in us. So we need *faith* for salvation and *fear* for growth and obedience. It is because of the lack of the fear of God in us that we are often so weak in the strength or might of our salvation and its dominion in our life.

> **QUESTION**: How can we work out our salvation with fear and trembling, if we have no fear of God in us and no reason to tremble? Answer: We cannot! Thus, if we are to see God working in us "both to will and to do of his good pleasure" (Php 2:13), then we must get the fear of God working in us. Let our salvation be exercised by the fear of God through the keeping of a good conscience.

Let us look at an analogy, so that we can understand the difficulty of receiving the fear of God later in our spiritual life. Circumcision as an infant is far wiser and easier than as an adult. The infant to be circumcised has no choice in the matter. It is strictly the will of their father. But as a youth or even an adult we now have a will and a choice that can refuse to be circumcised. It is the same with engrafting in the fear of God *after* a person has been saved for a number of years. Often, when we are older we do not see the benefits, we only see the discomfort and pain it will bring, and it is easy to say no or even to abort the process in midstream. This is the great difficulty of the apostolic mantle bringing in the fear of God to a believer's life who has never known it. It is very easy to reject and, after the pain begins to come, even to despise. The analogy of the circumcision of our heart and the engrafting of the fear of the LORD are so close that it can be said that the fear of the LORD *is* the circumcision of our heart – for they are part of the same work done by apostles.

A Fear that will Never Pass Away
"The fear of the LORD is clean, enduring forever." Ps 19:9

Let us be assured that the fear of God is not an Old Testament artifact to be done away with in the new covenant or the dispensation of grace. The fear of the LORD cannot be locked up under the old covenant dispensation, for if we study the scriptures we see it is *not* part of the old covenant only. Consider these promises of the fear of God being in God's people for all time:

> The fear of the LORD *is* clean, <u>enduring for ever</u> Ps 19:9
>
> They shall fear thee as long as the sun & moon endure, <u>throughout all generations</u>. Ps 72:5
>
> Afterward shall the children of Israel return, and seek the LORD their God, and David their king; and shall fear the LORD and his goodness <u>in the latter days</u>. Hos 3:5
>
> And they shall be my people, and I will be their God: And I will give them one heart, and one way, <u>that they may fear me for ever</u>, for the good of them, and of their children after them: And I will make an everlasting covenant with them, that I will not turn away from them, to do them good; but <u>I will put my fear in their hearts</u>, that they shall not depart from me. Jer 32:38-40

The promise to the prophets of the covenant that was to come was that God's people would have the fear of God in the latter days.[40] In fact, God promised to put his fear into our hearts. God has planted his fear in us so that we will not depart from him and so that he may do us good. O the cunning craftiness of so many teachers who would by their teachings extract the fear of God from our hearts. It is the Father's heart that ALL people would have the fear of God. He is grieved when we do not fear him, and he does not change in his judgment (Mal 3:5-6). He would have us always fear him. It is not for a select few, but for all. "Let <u>all the earth</u> fear the LORD: let <u>all the inhabitants of the world</u> stand in awe of him."[41] Ps 33:8 "God shall bless us; and <u>all the ends of the earth</u> shall fear him." Ps 67:7 It is both: for all people and for all time! God even worked his mighty wonders to deliver his people so that they might always fear him. "That all the people of the earth might know the hand of the LORD, that it *is* mighty: that ye might fear the LORD your God <u>for ever</u>." Jos 4:24 It has by no means passed away – except, sadly, before the eyes of men.[42]

The continual record of scripture of those who truly knew God shows a people that when in the presence of the LORD and when receiving his commandments had great fear – so great, they even quaked and trembled in fear! Think on that, dear reader. Men of God in the past <u>trembled</u> when they thought

---

[40] With so many despising or ignoring the fear of God today, one may wonder where are these last days covenant people who are walking in the promised new covenant, for they are certainly not in the masses of Christianity! This is why we must understand, that the prophets always only spoke of a last days <u>remnant</u> which would be truly saved and would enter into God's promises. Such people are not in the mega-churches of today, or if there, they cannot long remain without putting away the precious fear of God.

[41] The phrase 'stand in awe' in the Hebrew may also mean here 'to *shrink* in *fear*'.

[42] "And the way of peace have they not known: There is no fear of God <u>before their eyes</u>." Rom 3:17-18

3 – The Spirit of the Fear of the LORD

on God's name. They trembled when they heard God's word. Daniel records his own reaction, "And when he had spoken this word unto me, I stood trembling." Dan 10:11 Daniel stood '*shuddering* (more or less violently)' when he heard the words of God! In Ezra's day it was "those that tremble at the commandment of our God" that made a covenant with God (Ezr 10:3, 9:4). God declares that "to this *man* will I look, *even* to *him that is* poor and of a contrite spirit, and <u>trembleth at my word</u>." Isa 66:2 How we have lost this kind of heart today! The record of scripture is crammed full of those who feared God in every generation:

- Noah feared God (Heb 11:7).
- Job feared God (Job 1:1,8, 2:3).
- Abraham feared God (Gen 22:12).
- Isaac feared God (Gen 31:42,53).
- Jacob feared God (Gen 31:53, Ps 22:23).
- Levi the priest feared the LORD (Mal 2:4-5).
- The Jewish midwives feared God (Ex 1:17,21).
- Moses feared God (Ex 3:6, Ac 7:32, Heb 12:21).
- The Exodus people at times feared God (Ex 20:20).
- Joshua taught the people to fear the LORD (Jos 24:14).
- David particularly feared the LORD (Ps 5:7, 119:38,120).[43]
- Obadiah the governor greatly feared the LORD (1K 18:3-4).
- Hezekiah king of Judah feared and sought the LORD (Jer 26:19).
- Many of God's prophets also feared the LORD (e.g.: Jonah, Jnh 1:9).
- Those who heard the prophets sometimes feared the LORD (Hag 1:12).
- Those of the restoration feared God (e.g.: Neh. & Hanani, Neh 5:15 & 7:2).

The Banner of the Fear of the LORD

*"Thou hast given a banner to them that fear thee,
that it may be displayed because of the truth. Selah." Ps 60:4*

The LORD has given us evidence of the fear of God throughout the scriptures. After this, we will look at the New Testament witness concerning it, but before we leave the Old Testament, let us look at the place that is given to the fear of God. The Bible declares that God has "given a banner" to those who fear him "that it may be displayed because of the truth. Selah." Ps 60:4 The banner of truth that is displayed is the testimony of the lives of those who fear him. This testimony is reflected in their thoughts, words, actions, and choices. There are so many that we could consider, but let us look at the banner that is more conspicuously displayed in the lives of a few of the saints in scripture who feared God.

---

[43] Many also feared the LORD during the times of the kings.

Where is the Fear of GOD? Finding the Treasure of the Lord

1. <u>Job: the patient servant, tested by fire, rewarded double for his trouble</u>[44]

    And the LORD said unto Satan, Hast thou considered my servant Job, that *there is* none like him in the earth, a perfect and an upright man, **one that feareth God**, and escheweth evil? and still he holdeth fast his integrity, although thou movedst me against him, to destroy him without cause. Job 2:3

2. <u>Noah: the heir of righteousness which is by faith</u>

    By faith Noah, being warned of God of things not seen as yet, **moved with fear**, prepared an ark to the saving of his house; by the which he condemned the world, and became heir of the righteousness which is by faith. Heb 11:7

    But Noah <u>found grace</u> in the eyes of the LORD. … Noah was a <u>just</u> man *and* <u>perfect</u> in his generations, *and* Noah walked with God. And the LORD said unto Noah, Come thou and all thy house into the ark; for thee have I seen <u>righteous</u> before me in this generation. Gen 6:8-9, 7:1

3. <u>Abraham: the friend of God & father of faith, imputed righteousness</u>

    for now I know that **thou fearest God**, seeing thou hast not withheld thy son, thine only *son* from me. … And said, By myself have I sworn, saith the LORD, for because thou hast done this thing, and hast not withheld thy son, thine only *son*: That in blessing I will bless thee, and in multiplying I will multiply thy seed as the stars of the heaven, and as the sand which *is* upon the sea shore; and thy seed shall possess the gate of his enemies; And in thy seed shall all the nations of the earth be blessed; because thou hast obeyed my voice. Gen 22:12,16-18

4. <u>Levi: the priest of God received the covenant of life and peace</u>

    ye shall know that I have sent this commandment unto you, that my covenant might be with Levi, saith the LORD of hosts. My covenant was with him of life and peace; and I gave them to him **for the fear wherewith he feared me, and was afraid before my name**. Mal 2:4-5

5. <u>Moses: the servant of God talked in intimacy face to face with God</u>

    he was **afraid** to look upon God. Ex 3:6

    Saying, I *am* the God of thy fathers, the God of Abraham, and the God of Isaac, and the God of Jacob. Then Moses <u>trembled</u>, and durst not behold. Ac 7:32

    And so terrible was the sight, *that* Moses said, I <u>exceedingly fear and quake</u> Heb 12:21

---

[44] When God wanted to boast of his servant to the enemy he displays the banner of the fear of God that was in Job (Job 1:1,8, 2:3).

3 – The Spirit of the Fear of the LORD

6. <u>Nehemiah: the faithful servant</u>

    Also I said, It *is* not good that ye do: **ought ye not to walk in the fear of our God** because of the reproach of the heathen our enemies? Neh 5:9

    But the former governors that *had been* before me were chargeable unto the people, and had taken of them bread and wine, beside forty shekels of silver; yea, even their servants bare rule over the people: but **so did not I, because of the fear of God.** Neh 5:15

7. <u>Hezekiah: the king who received correction</u>

    Micah the Morasthite prophesied in the days of Hezekiah king of Judah, and spake to all the people of Judah, saying, Thus saith the LORD of hosts; Zion shall be plowed *like* a field, and Jerusalem shall become heaps, and the mountain of the house as the high places of a forest. Did Hezekiah king of Judah and all Judah put him at all to death? **did he not fear the LORD**, and besought the LORD, and the LORD repented him of the evil which he had pronounced against them? Jer 26:18-19

We could go on and speak of so many others to whom the fear of God was given as a banner. We could speak of Isaac and Jacob, the spiritual offspring of Abraham, and children of the covenant which is by faith. The LORD that they knew was called the "fear of Isaac" (Gen 31:42,53). How many times the only or primary thing we know of an individual in scripture was that they feared God, and the works that sprung from that fear? Such were the midwives that feared God (Ex 1:17,21), Obadiah who greatly feared the LORD (1K 18:3-4), Hanani who "was a faithful man, and feared God above many" (Neh 7:2). But let this brief record suffice. In truth, we would not know these people for the examples they were, if it were not for the fear of the LORD that worked in them. They were used by God to change the destiny of many others, all because they feared God. God holds them up and all those in the hall of faith (Heb 11), because of the fear of God that worked in them and through them.

There is something unmistakable about someone who has the fear of God. The presence or the lack thereof can immediately be seen or discerned. Thus, when Abraham went down to Egypt he immediately perceived that there was no fear of God in that place (Gen 20:11). On the contrary, "a certain woman of the wives of the sons of the prophets" cried unto Elisha saying, "thou <u>knowest</u> that thy servant did fear the LORD" (2K 4:1). We truly need in these last days to be those who will "return [i.e. *repent*], and discern between the righteous and the wicked, between him that serveth God and him that serveth him not." Mal 3:18 How may we know who serves God and who serves him not (even though they appear to be)? We will know if they serve God in truth by the absence or presence of the fear of God in their life. This is the context of Malachi 3:18 (see vv16-17). There they are clearly identified as those who both fear the LORD and are in fellowship with others who fear him. Let us long for that banner of the fear of the LORD so that the truth may be displayed through our lives.[45]

Everywhere We Look We See the Fear of God

But hasn't the fear of God passed away under the new covenant? No, the New Testament is replete with examples of those who likewise feared God and found favor with him. Paul himself gives instructions for servants [which is equally as applicable to employees today] to serve their masters in the fear of God (Col 3:22). But let us start with the beginning of the new covenant. There we see Mary's praise unto the Lord while Jesus is yet in her womb. "And his mercy *is* on them that fear him <u>from generation to generation</u>." Lk 1:50 So the fear of God is the door for God's mercy for *every* generation.

Throughout the New Testament we see so many who feared God. Jesus, our example, feared God (Heb 5:7). Jesus' own disciples feared the Lord (Mk 4:40-41, Lk 9:34), as well as the women at the sepulchre (Mt 28:8). In fact, it was the way of the early church. We see "fear came upon every soul" repeatedly (Ac 2:43, 5:5,11), and it was part of their walk with the Lord (Ac 9:31). Even unsaved people, some of whom found salvation, feared the Lord, such as the thief on the cross (Lk 23:40), the Roman soldiers at the foot of the cross (Mt 27:54), and Cornelius (Ac 10:2,22). Often it was to them that feared God that Paul spoke the kingdom of God to during his apostolic journeys (Ac 13:16,26).

The fear of God was not only practiced, but also clearly taught as a New Testament doctrine. Jesus taught it (Mt 10:28, Lk 12:5) and it often issued from his ministry. "And they were all amazed, and they glorified God, and were <u>filled with fear</u>, saying, We have seen strange things to day." Lk 5:26 "And there <u>came a fear on all</u>: and they glorified God, saying, That a great prophet is risen up among us; and, That God hath visited his people." Lk 7:16 The fear of God was the constant apostolic exhortation to the saints. We see it to the Romans (Rom 11:20, 13:7, 3:18), to the Corinthians (2Co 7:1,11,15), to the Ephesians (Eph 5:21, 6:5), to the Philippians (Php 2:12), to the Colossians (Col 3:22), to the Hebrews (Heb 4:1, 10:31, 12:28), and to those "scattered throughout Pontus, Galatia, Cappadocia, Asia, and Bithynia" (1Pe 1:1 → 1:17, 2:17).

Every New Testament writer speaks of the fear of God: Matthew, Mark, Luke,[46] John,[47] Paul, James, Peter, and Jude.[48] And so Peter boldly states to

---

[45] To find out more about the banner of the fear of the LORD see the section 'The Banner of Brokenness' in the chapter entitled "The Way of Brokenness and God's Fear" in the book <u>Losing the Treasure of the Lord</u>.

[46] Matthew, Mark, and Luke each respectively in their gospels.

[47] John in Rev 11:18, 14:7, 15:4, 19:5.

[48] Jude in his epistle: 1:12,23.

3 – The Spirit of the Fear of the LORD

Cornelius and to all those gathered in his home, "But in every nation he that feareth him, and worketh righteousness, is accepted with him." Ac 10:35 Even unto the end of days we see in the book of Revelation, God still forcefully commanding the fear of God. "Saying with a loud voice, <u>Fear God</u>, and give glory to him; for the hour of his judgment is come" (Rev 14:7). What has passed away are true servants of God who know, understand, believe in, and treasure the fear of God.

Until we see how truly 'new covenant' the fear of God is and how necessary it is to our walk with God, then we will never be able to apprehend its great value and why we must recapture it. We must perceive the preciousness and inestimable value of the fear of God by faith, whether we understand it or not. Peter gives us the simple but provoking commandment "Fear God." 1Pe 2:17 As we shall see, the fear of the Lord is a grace of God. "Therefore, as ye abound in every *thing*, *in* faith, and utterance, and knowledge, and *in* all diligence, and *in* your love to us, *see* that ye abound in this grace also." 2Co 8:7

Chapter 4. Fearing God, Far More Than Reverence
Understanding the Fear of God

"God is greatly to be feared in the assembly of the saints, and to be had in reverence of all them that are about him." Psalm 89:7

The fear of God goes so much deeper than many of us think. The fear of God is not a small fear, nor a twinge of conviction, nor a gentle check received in our spirit, rather the scripture shows us it is an exceeding great fear.[49] It has no match in earthly fears. It is not merely a reverence of God or a quiet respect of him, but rather it is a literal trembling and quaking before the manifestation of his authority, whether it is his presence or his word. The greatest stumblingblock to understanding the true fear of God is confusing it with reverence.

The Substitute Fear of God: Reverence

Many say the fear of God is the reverence and deep respect of God and that it is not to tremble before God in fear. We shall see this is most assuredly

---

[49] The exceeding fear of God: Heb 12:21, Jonah 1:16, Mk 4:41.

4 – Fearing God, Far More Than Reverence

not the case. The true fear of God is to tremble before him and his word. So many replace that which God has given us to turn us from evil, with something evil in itself – a religious spirit called 'reverence for God'. But is our fear of him just a reverence, a respect, and an awe of him who is so great that we cannot understand him?

This is the spirit of religion itself, designed by well-meaning men to bring us closer to God, but which in fact pushes us further and further away. Do not misunderstand, we are to have a reverence of God, and the reverence of God in and of itself is not evil, but appropriate and commanded. Yet reverence for God does not replace the fear of God, for it is clearly distinguished from the fear of God in the scriptures, and the emphasis is overwhelmingly on the fear of God, not the reverence of God. Let us look at what the scripture says about reverence toward God. There is truly not much to look at, for only two verses in the entire Bible directly speak of reverence toward God.[50]

> God is greatly to be <u>feared</u> in the assembly of the saints, and to be had in **reverence** of all *them that are* about him. Ps 89:7

> Wherefore we receiving a kingdom which cannot be moved, let us have grace, whereby we may serve God acceptably with **reverence** and <u>godly fear</u> Heb 12:28

The fear of God and the reverence due him, as seen in both verses, are two separate things. It cannot be coincidental that the only two times 'reverence' is spoken of in relationship to God, both times the fear of God is *also* mentioned and clearly distinguished from it. If ever God was trying to show us and warn us not to substitute the true fear of God with reverence it would be this fact. Yes, as a father he deserves reverence, but he deserves so much more than that also. Think on this, Almighty God inspires fear. In both these verses the fear of God has an emphasizing qualifier: *greatly* to be feared and *godly* fear. We learn two things from this about the fear of God. First, the fear of God is not a small fear, but a great fear. Second, the fear of God is not a human or natural fear, but it is a godly fear. It's source and inspiration is God, not man. The fear of God is a trembling before the authority of God, and the dread of his power and glory.

This godly fear is birthed out of the fact that God is a consuming fire (Heb 12:29). And lest there be any doubt, this phrase in the Old Testament was first coined concerning the wrath of God that fell on his own people for their com-

---

[50] There is an indirect reference in the parable of the workers in the vineyard where the one, well-beloved son of the lord of the vineyard is sent and of whom it is said "They will reverence my son." (Mt 21:37, Mk 12:6, Lk 20:13) There is also what some would consider another indirect reference in Heb 12:9 where it says we give the fathers of our flesh reverence. And so should we not do the same to the Father of spirits? Yet the main focus in Hebrews 12:9 is not so much giving reverence as it is being in subjection unto him. An additional 2x reverence refers to God's sanctuary (Lev 19:30, 26:2).

plaining and rebellion.⁵¹ God is the judge, and he ever retains the right to judge and to condemn hypocrisy and rebellion. These, **no covenant has ever been able to set aside**, for it is a part of who he is, the Judge.⁵²

With reverence and godly fear we are to serve God acceptably. How sad that we have so removed God's authority from him and his power that we no longer fear him for these reasons. Think of this. When have you ever been taught to come before the LORD with trembling and to rejoice in such experiences? Yet the scripture commands us to do so. "Serve the LORD with fear, and rejoice with trembling." Ps 2:11 We cannot approach God with reverence and think that it can be acceptable without the fear of God. No, the fear of God enables us to approach the LORD and then he will "be had in reverence of all *them that are* about him." Ps 89:7

Other than these, the scriptures are remarkably silent about reverence for God, whereas it waxes eloquent about the fear of God. Thus, it is a general rule that fear is rendered toward God, while reverence is toward man.⁵³ Interestingly, we have no promises associated with reverence, yet all the promises are attached to the fear of God. Reverence and the fear of God are distinct and separate in the scriptures, and God's emphasis is heavily, heavily on the side of fearing God. Thus, when reverence becomes a substitute and replacement for the fear of God, then it becomes something evil.

With only two direct references of reverence to God, it should not be surprising that reverence more often is in relationship to man than it is to God. In fact, nine times it refers to men.⁵⁴ This emphasis on reverence being toward man and on fear being toward God is most clearly seen in the New Testament. In Hebrews 12:9 where it says we had fathers of our flesh, and we gave them reverence, it uses the Greek word *entrepo*. This same word is used in Luke 18:4 'regard' as follows, "And he would not for a while: but afterward he said within himself, Though I fear not God, nor regard man". There we see the unjust judge had no fear of God, nor any reverence of man.⁵⁵

Clearly, reverence or respect is less than the fear of God. We ought to be convinced of this, not only by the emphasis of reverence being primarily toward

---

⁵¹ See Dt 4:24, concerning Nu 11:1 and 16:35.

⁵² God is still our Judge even in the new covenant: 2Tim 4:8, Heb 10:30, 12:23, Jam 5:9.

⁵³ Reverence is used of God only twice and both times in connection with also fearing him (Ps 89:7, Heb 12:28). Yet, reverence is used much more often of men. Thus, a wife is called to reverence her husband (Eph 5:33), children their father (Heb 12:9), servants their master (Mt 21:37/Mk 12:6/Lk 20:13), and subjects their king (2Sam 9:6, 1K 1:31).

⁵⁴ Reverence toward man: 2x of David, 2x of Haman, 3x of the vineyard owner's son (Mt 21:37; Mk 12:6; Lk 20:13), & 1x each of husbands (Eph 5:23) & fathers (Heb 12:9).

⁵⁵ This is true hypocrisy, for every judge demands reverence and in fact his office can only be upheld with it.

4 – Fearing God, Far More Than Reverence

man, rather than God, but also by the overwhelming emphasis in scripture on the fear of God quantitatively. We have 13 total references to 'reverence' in all of scripture, but we have over 350 references to the fear of God! Reverence is a very minor emphasis in the scripture, whereas the fear of the LORD is everywhere. Remember, "A false balance *is* abomination to the LORD: but a just weight *is* his delight." Pr 11:1 Let us ensure that we are putting the proper emphasis and just and fair weight that scripture does for each thing that we do. If the scriptures speak much on the fear of the LORD (in fact, 175 times more!) and little on reverencing the LORD, then let us also emphasize and focus much of our attention on the fear of the LORD and little on reverencing him, for this is a just and fair balance in his sight.

> **WARNING**: Why then do Christian teachers ALWAYS overemphasize reverence toward God and downplay or altogether eliminate fear toward God? Why, when a minister does speak about the fear of God, is the very *first* thing they say about it, is that it is NOT fear and that it is just an awe or reverence for God? We can only conclude, after seeing the scriptures we have already seen, that they are trusting in their own ideas and thoughts about who God is and what other men say about him, rather than studying the scriptures to show themselves approved unto God and not men. We must also conclude they themselves have never experienced the true fear of God, as detailed in the Bible – otherwise they would indeed know, that it is far more than reverence, it is a literal fear, which at times includes trembling and quaking.

Is Not the Fear of God but Awe?

Let us take a moment also to discuss, what really is the 'awe' of God, for the scripture does show that we are to be in awe of him. David says, "Stand in awe, and sin not: commune with your own heart upon your bed, and be still. Selah." Ps 4:4 Let us put away our own concept of what we may think 'awe' is and not apply the awe that we may have of certain men inappropriately to the living God. The word 'awe' in Psalm 4:4 means 'to *quiver*' and is translated 'be afraid, disquieted, fret, quake, shake, tremble, troubled'. It is hardly what we think of when we speak of being in awe. Yes this is the awe that the true fear of God is to be. It is far more reverence.

This is confirmed for us a second time when the word 'awe' is used. David in his praise of the word of God declares that while some may be afraid of princes who persecute the righteous, his fear is toward God's word. Thus, he says, "but my heart standeth in awe of thy word." Ps 119:161 This word 'awe' is a different word in Hebrew and means 'to *be startled* (by a sudden alarm); hence to *fear* in general'. It is translated 'be afraid, (be in) fear, make to shake'. Thus, yes, the fear of God is awe, but not the awe that men know!

The awe of God occurs one last time (for awe is only mentioned a total of three times in all of scripture and all of these are in the the OT in psalms). We are commanded to have the fear of the LORD and to stand in awe of him. "Let all the earth fear the LORD: let all the inhabitants of the world stand in awe of him." Ps 33:8 Thus, the outworking of our fear of God will be to stand in awe of him. This word 'awe' is yet again another Hebrew word. But like both of the others it also focuses on fear and trembling. This word, according to the context, means 'to *shrink, fear* (as in a *strange* place)'. It also means 'to *turn* aside from the road (for a lodging or any other purpose)'.

Again, this is a far cry from what men think of when they say 'awe' today. The awe we are to have biblically should make us be afraid of God and his judgments, afraid to defy his commandments, and fearful to keep going our own way. The true awe of God should turn us off of our way and away from our purpose and cause us to stand before him, to listen to what he has to say. That is the awe and fear of God that we are to have today, not some nice sentimental idea of mere respect or even wonder.[56]

Who He is and What He Does Teaches us to Fear Him

"Israel saw that great work which the LORD did upon the Egyptians: and the people feared the LORD, and believed the LORD, and his servant Moses." Ex 14:31

We must fear him because of who he is and what he does. His all-surpassing greatness should put us into an all-consuming *necessity* to fear him. Many times people do not truly know who or what that they are worshipping. If we know God as he is in his awesomeness, we will surely fear him. "Shall not his excellency make you afraid? and his dread fall upon you?" Job 13:11 The fact that the LORD is *elevated* far above man's mortal state and limited ability, that he is *'exalted* in rank and character' above all of creation, ought to make us afraid. The scripture shows us time and again that the one who is *not* afraid of God is the one who does *not* know God.[57] "And *that* their children, which have not known anything, may hear, and learn to fear the LORD your God" (Dt 31:13). It was by knowing the LORD that people were to fear him.

> The scripture shows us time and again that the one who is not afraid of God is the one who does not know God.

---

[56] The Bible's use of the word 'awe' is closer to what men understand by the old English word 'awful', as inspiring dread or even terror.

[57] The scripture shows those who do not fear God, do know not God in any depth of intimacy: 1K 8:43/2Ch 6:33, Jos 4:24.

4 – Fearing God, Far More Than Reverence

What a complete turning upside down of the purpose of the knowledge of God! Today people are taught that the knowledge of God will remove their fear of him, when in fact, the knowledge of God should inspire us to fear him. Hence, we cannot talk about knowing God without talking about fearing him. And because it is his essence, his very being, that moves us to fear him, we cannot talk about worship in earnest without talking about the nature of the true God – who he is, as opposed to who we *think* he is. Yet the overwhelming majority of born again Christians today do NOT fear the living God. They may reverence him, but they do not fear him in true fear as the Bible says we must. Elihu,[58] on the other hand, being full of the Spirit and with great wisdom stated,

> *Touching* the Almighty, we cannot find him out:
> *he is* excellent in power, and in judgment, and in plenty of justice: he will not afflict. <u>Men do therefore fear him</u>:
> he respecteth not any *that are* wise of heart. Job 37:23-24

Elihu states men should fear God, why? We fear God because we cannot find him out, that is, no one knows the depth or the fullness of the characteristics of the infinite God.

1. We fear God because he *is* excellent/*mighty* in power.
2. We fear God because he *is* excellent/*mighty* in judgment & in justice.
3. We fear God because of his great mercies & forgiveness.
4. We fear God because he respects not any that are wise of heart. "And if ye call on the Father, who without respect of persons judgeth according to every man's work, pass the time of your sojourning *here* <u>in fear</u>" (1Pe 1:17).

---

[58] Elihu is sometimes misunderstood and thought to be one of Job's miserable counselors, but nothing could be farther from the truth. Some have misinterpreted God's words, when he says, "Who *is* this that darkeneth counsel by words without knowledge?" Job 38:2 These words were not directed to Elihu, but to Job, as verse 1 of that chapter makes clear. This is why God brought rebuke to Eliphaz and his *two* friends (i.e. Bildad and Zophar – Job 42:7-8), but we read no such thing about Elihu.

Elihu is a pre-incarnate visitation of the Lord Jesus – for no man could make the claims he did without being rebuked (e.g.: Job 33:4). He claimed to speak on God's behalf and to be perfect in knowledge (Job 36:2,4)! He is the only person in the book of Job who is not rebuked, and he is also the one who speaks right before God Almighty.

Job had asked God for an intermediary, one to stand between him and God (Job 9:33), and Elihu was God's answer, as Elihu himself states, "Behold, I *am* according to thy wish in God's stead: I also am formed out of the clay." Job 33:6 Thus, it is not coincidence that Elihu's name means '*God of him*' or '*He is God*', and he comes as one formed out of the dust of the earth, even as Jesus in his incarnation!

Fearing His Excellent Power

The fact that we cannot find him out is why we should fear him. We cannot plumb the depths of the power, judgment, justice, and mercy that resides in him, nor comes from him. No man can know the depth of God, nor the greatness of any of his character or characteristics. For these things do men fear him, and for that alone we are debt-bound to fear him. Even today, by the awesome deliverance of salvation through Jesus Christ, our heavenly Father intends for us to come to know his mighty power so that we might fear him. The gospel of our salvation is where the fullness of his power, judgment, justice, and mercy all come together and meet. This is why God desires:

> The eyes of your understanding being enlightened; <u>that ye may know</u> what is the hope of his calling, and what the riches of the glory of his inheritance in the saints, And <u>what *is* the exceeding greatness of his power</u> to us-ward who believe, according to the working of his mighty power Eph 1:18-19

First, let us behold the excellence of his power, and see how this produces the fear of God in us. Think about the apostles. As they came to know the Lord and walk with him, did they grow in fear of the Lord, or did they lose their fear of him? Let us see. When Jesus arose and rebuked the wind and it ceased, so that there was a great calm (Mk 4:39), what was the response of his disciples? Were they comforted? No, this caused the disciples to <u>exceedingly</u> fear, so that they said one to another, "What manner of man is this, that even the wind and the sea obey him?" Mk 4:41

Many times Jesus' disciples, because of the power with which he spoke, were afraid of him. They were at times *so* afraid of him they were afraid to ask him what he meant, even though they clearly did not understand (Mk 9:32, Lk 9:45). As Jesus headed to Jerusalem for his final Passover feast, the disciples followed behind him being afraid of him. "Jesus went before them: and they were amazed; and as they followed, <u>they were afraid</u>." Mk 10:32 This was the fear of God that the disciples walked in, as they came to know "meek and gentle" Jesus! The more they got to know Jesus and to see the Father working through him, the more (not the less) they feared him! Ought it not to be the same with us also, if we are getting to know the true Jesus? So let it be with us. As we get to know the Lord more, may we come to know his fear even more. Let us come to know what the scripture calls his <u>exceeding</u> fear.[59]

The intervention of God's direct acts in our lives are intended by his Spirit to break our pride and innate stubbornness and bring us to a place of broken-

---

[59] The exceeding fear of the Lord is mentioned three times in scripture, all of them are in relationship to those who truly knew the Lord *and* his voice: (1) Jonah (Jonah 1:16), (2) the apostles (Mk 4:41), and (3) Moses (Heb 12:21). We see men greatly feared the LORD on repeated occasions: 1Sam 12:18, 1K 18:3, Ps 89:7, 96:4, Mt 27:54.

ness. As he is, so are his works. He is majestic, sovereign, mighty, glorious, perfect, omnipotent, holy, and ultimately just. Ought we not to expect the same of his works? His works divinely and specially reveal his transcendent holiness. "The LORD *is* righteous in all his ways, and <u>holy in all his works</u>." Ps 145:17 And his holiness, that is the power or excellence of his person, produces in us the fear of God. "Who shall not fear thee, O Lord, and glorify thy name? for *thou only art* <u>holy</u>: for all nations shall come and worship before thee; <u>for thy judgments</u> are made manifest." Rev 15:4 The greatness and power of God is revealed in his work of creation, in the power, might, and devastation of storms, floods, fires, earthquakes, and volcanoes. God also displays his majesty and might through his miracles.

Great kings will build great works of architecture from houses, to palaces, to coliseums, to statues, to bridges and roads, to gardens, to pools, to works of art. So Solomon, as a great king, showed forth the glory of his kingdom (Ecc 2:4-6). Great kings will then display their works, their kingdoms, their riches, their dominion, and their armies for all to see and respect their power (Est 1:3-4). Rulers of governments will put forth such displays specially to produce awe in their subjects, fear in their slaves, and dread and terror in their enemies. So the LORD, as the King of Kings, shows forth his dominion and his works so that all people might know his might and fear him forever. "That all the people of the earth might know the hand of the LORD, that it *is* mighty: <u>that ye might fear the LORD your God for ever</u>." Jos 4:24 The specific mighty works of God toward his people referenced here in Joshua 4:24 are:

1. the parting of the Red Sea so that God's people could leave the land of bondage and escape their enemies,
2. the parting of the waters of the Jordan so that God's people could enter into the land of promise.

Though two specific events are named, it is clear God's purpose whenever he delivers his children miraculously is meant to reveal his mighty power that we might always fear him. The King of kings shows forth all his works with the specific purpose that men would consider his doings and fear him. "And all men shall fear, and shall declare <u>the work of God</u>; for they shall wisely consider of his doing." Ps 64:9 God says if we wisely consider the work of God, then it will birth his fear in us. Maybe the reason the fear of God is so much less in our generation, more than any other, is because we take so little time to consider what he has done.

The Power of His Creation Inspires us to Fear Him

The LORD's hope is that we will wisely consider his doings. When we consider the miracle of life, the wonder of creation, even the majesty of the heavens in motion, they continually speak to us that only by his hand are these things so. The LORD himself desires that we know his work, and that in wisely considering it we would know that he alone has done it; no one can take from his work, nor add anything to it. And everything God does, he does for this singular purpose: so that we would fear before him. "I know that, whatsoever God doeth, it shall be for ever: nothing can be put to it, nor any thing taken from it: and <u>God doeth *it*, that *men* should fear before him</u>." Ecc 3:14 Consider this, the fear of the LORD is so important to God that *everything* he does is to awaken in us his fear. This is the power of his doings that ought to cause us to fear him.

> And everything God does, he does for this singular purpose: so that we would fear before him.

The fear of the LORD should grow in us as we observe his wonders and consider the power of his word, both in creation at large and in our own personal lives. The creation itself witnesses to us of his eternal power and his godhead, so that we are without excuse to not glorify him as God (Rom 1:20-21). If we would only consider the heavens and the earth and all that the LORD has made, if we truly believed that he spoke and all that is invisible and visible stood fast, the fear of God would be birthed in us.[60] Because he is our Creator, therefore we fear him. So the psalmist echoes, "Let all the earth fear the LORD: let all the inhabitants of the world stand in awe of him. <u>For he spake, and it was *done*; he commanded, and it stood fast</u>." Ps 33:8-9

The works of God are to move us to fear him – from the original creation that he spoke into existence by his word, to setting the bounds of the sea, to his supply of rain for the harvest. God wonders why we don't fear him because of his great power.

> Fear ye not me? saith the LORD: will ye not tremble at my presence, which have <u>placed the sand *for* the bound of the sea by a perpetual decree</u>, that it cannot pass it: and though the waves thereof toss themselves, yet can they not prevail; though they roar, yet can they not pass over it?
>
> Neither say they in their heart, Let us now fear the LORD our God, <u>that giveth rain</u>, both the former and the latter, <u>in his season</u>: he reserveth unto us the appointed weeks of the harvest. Jer 5:22,24

The very creation itself witnesses that we ought to fear God. Is it not truly amazing that God has made all creatures to fear and dread man, so that every

---

[60] This is the integral importance of believing in the miracle of creation. It is an essential doctrine of scripture. It is key to the depth of the fear of God we would possess. The gospel is based on there being a real Adam (Lk 3:38, Jude 1:14, 1Tim 2:13-14) of whom Jesus is the second man and the last Adam (1Co 15:45,47). If we give in to "oppositions of science falsely so called" (1Tim 6:20), then our faith is weakened, the authority and truth of the word of God is destroyed, and we lose our foundation for the fear of God.

brute beast offers up to man by *nature* what is rightly deserved by God (Gen 9:2), yet man as also one of God's creation so often refuses to pay the same worship of fear and dread to his Creator who so rightly deserves it?

> He is thy Creator? Is it not seemly for creatures to fear and reverence their Creator? But what a shame is this to man, that God should subject all his creatures to him, and he should refuse to stoop his heart to God! ... art thou not ashamed that a silly cow, a sheep, yea, swine, should better observe the law of creation than thou dost the law of thy God?[61]

The Witness of the New Creation:
His Forgiveness & Deliverances Births His Fear
"But there is forgiveness with thee, that thou mayest be feared." Ps 130:4

The testimony of creation that sparks the fear of God in another's life is not limited to natural creation. Spiritual creation and spiritual growth that occur through salvation and sanctification are the greatest testimony of all to the truth and power of the gospel. Are not we God's crowning act of creation? Therefore, what rejoicing it brings when God can take us from the disobedient, lost, and carnal state that natural, unregenerate man is in and transform us into the sons of God who ...

> Do all things without murmurings and disputings: That ye may be blameless and harmless, the sons of God, without rebuke, in the midst of a crooked and perverse nation, among whom ye shine as lights in the world; Holding forth the word of life Php 2:14-16

What testimony of creation can be any greater today than the testimony of making a new creation in Christ Jesus through salvation? The continual deliverances that come as a result of walking in faith with the Lord are not only to produce and renew the fear of the LORD in ourselves, but also in others through the rejoicing of our testimony. It is both the testimony of our salvation and the witness of his deliverances that inspires others to fear the LORD and trust in him.

> He brought me up also out of an horrible pit, out of the miry clay, and set my feet upon a rock, *and* established my goings. And he hath put a new song in my mouth, *even* praise unto our God: <u>many shall see *it*, and fear</u>, and shall trust in the LORD. Ps 40:2-3

When the world sees that we are brought up out of a horrible pit (i.e. out of what we were stuck in and could not free ourself), that our feet are now set upon a rock and our goings are established, then there will be those who are

---

[61] "The Fear of God" by John Bunyan, The Religious Tract Society, London, UK, 1679 (reprinted 1839), p. 138 (first two questions), 132.

convicted and will fear the LORD and trust in him. This was the fruit when Jehoshaphat brought the people back to the word of God. Those in the neighboring kingdoms saw and feared God.

> And they taught in Judah, and *had* the book of the law of the LORD with them, and went about throughout all the cities of Judah, and taught the people. And the fear of the LORD fell upon all the kingdoms of the lands that *were* round about Judah, so that they made no war against Jehoshaphat. 2Ch 17:9-10

Once We Know the Lord,
Should We *Ever* Be Afraid of Him?
"My flesh trembleth for fear of thee; and I am afraid of thy judgments." Ps 119:120

Few believe in the fear of God today for what it is. Of those who say they believe in the fear of God, they will always as a matter of fact clarify that the fear of God is *not* fear. In an amazing twist of plain truth, they will deny that something is exactly what it claims to be! Remember, the fear of God is *not* called the respect of God, the awe of God, or the reverence of God. It is called the *fear* of God. Fear and reverence, as well as fear and respect, are always distinguished from each other in the scripture. Throughout the volume of scripture, the fear of God is never called the reverence of God, nor is it called the respect of God. Yet men will, without any scriptural foundation, state that the fear of God is not fear, but merely reverence, respect, and awe.[62] But the Bible calls the fear of God the FEAR of God. This is because it is indeed fear. Let us now convince ourselves from the scriptures that the true fear of God does involve being afraid and trembling before our God and King.

> **WARNING**: Please, friend, hear the word of God. "Hear the word of the LORD, ye that tremble at his word" (Isa 66:5). It does not say have an awe, a deep respect, a reverence for his word; it says tremble at his word! Remember, this is not even God's presence or his person, this is his word we are to shudder before,[63] and the presence of a person is always greater than their word. So even Paul says that some thought his letters were "weighty and powerful; but *his* bodily presence *is* weak, and *his* speech contemptible. Let such an one think this, that, such as we are in word by letters when we are absent, such *will we be* also in deed when we are present." 2Co 10:10-11

---

[62] The overwhelming emphasis in scripture is always laid on fearing God, not on reverencing him, nor respecting him, as we have already seen.

[63] The Hebrew word for 'tremble' in this verse means *fearful*, and it comes from the root which means 'to *shudder* with terror; hence to *fear*; also to *hasten* (with anxiety)'. This root word is translated 'quake, tremble, be afraid'.

4 – Fearing God, Far More Than Reverence

The fact that men who read the Bible and teach it will believe in the fear of God, but will claim it is NOT fear is the most obvious evidence that Satan hates the fear of God and at all costs would keep us from the true fear of God.[64] How does Satan do this? Either by causing us to deny it overtly (by saying the fear of God is not for today) or covertly (by saying it is not what it is). In another chapter we will look at imitations of the fear of God and substitutes to it,[65] but here let us look at this issue of being afraid of God. Is this actually a part of the fear of God as recorded in the scriptures, or is it as man says, something God does not want in us? The statement is made over and over again by well-meaning Bible teachers that God does not want us to be afraid of him. Yet, because of who the LORD of glory is, we will always be afraid of him. As we shall see, even his closest servants were afraid of him. God may not *desire* us to be afraid of him, but we most certainly will be – once we come to meet him face to face.

Consider an analogy. God does not *want* to chasten us. God takes no joy in chastening us. But does God chasten us? Most certainly he does. The psalmist records, "The LORD hath chastened me sore: but he hath not given me over unto death." Ps 118:18 In the same way, we may say that God does not want us to be afraid of him. God takes no pleasure in making us afraid or even in terrifying us. But does God make us afraid of himself, does he terrify his children? Most certainly he does, as the scriptures show us. When God brought forth his warnings, God expected his people to fear him. When God through Jeremiah gave a scroll to the king with the word of God's judgments on it, God expected his people in fear to turn from their ways and to hearken to his words. "Yet they were not afraid, nor rent their garments, *neither* the king, nor any of his servants that heard all these words." Jer 36:24 God was as angered by this then, as he is today when his word is despised.

Let us look at those who knew God and loved him deeply, yet were still afraid of him. Many times in the scripture when God visited his people, whether directly or through men of God or even through angelic visitations, those receiving the visitation were instantly afraid. When God had a message of exhortation for them, he always told them immediately to fear not or not to be afraid.[66] Why did God need to do this? Because the message of comfort or good news that was being brought did not require fear. But note above all, that the response to a visitation of God will *always* be one of fear. This is the rule we see in scripture. Let us touch on several saints who knew God and their experi-

---

[64] Refer to "An Epilogue: Enduring Fear of God" to see why Satan so hates the true fear of God.

[65] See the chapter entitled "Cheap Imitations and Artificial Substitutes" in the book Losing the Treasure of the Lord.

[66] Examples of this comforting to "fear not" include: Daniel (Dan 10:11-12,19), Zacharias (Lk 1:12-13), Mary (Lk 1:29-30), the shepherds in the field (Lk 2:9-10), John (Rev 1:17).

ences. For each of these saints, there were moments and events when they were manifestly afraid of God, for which God made no apology, nor does he tell them not to be afraid.

David, a Man after God's own Heart, is Afraid of God

David on several occasions is afraid of God. The most significant of these was when he first tried to bring in the ark of the covenant into Jerusalem, but he did not seek God after the due order of how it should be done (1Ch 15:13). As a result, he used worldly methods to try to bring in the presence of God, and God was angered. Why did this anger God? David employed the same method used by the Philistines to return the ark, namely an ox cart. This was not God's prescribed method. It may have been acceptable for the lost, who do not know God's commands, but only because God's primary purpose for them is to instill his fear – which he did. But this was not acceptable for God's people, who in copying those of the flesh (i.e. the uncircumcised Philistines) and ignoring God's holy commands on how it should be done, revealed that there was no fear of God in his own people. Hence, through judgment, God restores his fear amongst his people, and in particular to their leader, David.

> And <u>the anger of the LORD was kindled against Uzzah</u>; and God smote him there for *his* error; and there he died by the ark of God. And David was displeased, because the LORD had made a breach upon Uzzah: and he called the name of the place Perez-uzzah to this day. And David was <u>afraid of the LORD</u> that day, and said, How shall the ark of the LORD come to me? 2Sam 6:7-9

WARNING: Like many charismatic leaders today, David attempted to use worldly methods to try to bring in the presence of God into the congregation of the people. This is the sin of presumption that modern Christianity is so guilty of, because they have lost the fear of God and the knowledge of the holy. We must see how severely this was judged of God, and how much it angered him. If God does not change, as it is written of him (Mal 3:6), then several well-meaning but deceived servants of God just like Uzzah have also touched the holy things of God in an unsanctified manner. Similarly, they are already spiritually dead for being involved with using worldly ways of coming to God. If any of us have done such a thing, may God bring us, through repentance, into a newness of life, a spiritual resurrection, so that we may come out from such things and no longer touch them.

Can any man say after God brings forth the judgment of death – when such a thing should never have even been possible, if only the due order of God's commands had been followed – that David *should not* have been afraid of God that day?! Can any man say that God was wrong for making David afraid of him that day? Can any man say that God would not do such a thing today under the same circumstances? In fact, under the new covenant, God has done EXACTLY the same thing in slaying Ananias and Sapphira (Ac 5) when just like Uzzah they touched what was dedicated to God!

Notice how David was displeased with God, yet David was the one in error. Our first response to God's personal judgment, just like David, is often to be displeased with God. This word 'displeased' means 'to *glow* or grow warm; figurative (usually) to *blaze* up, of anger, zeal, jealousy'. Isn't that just like us, as impudent children – God shows forth his anger in his discipline of *our* disobedience, and we get angry at him. This is utterly the pride of man – and why David had to repent of it! Men would not let God get angry at his children, for they say it is not in his character, but the moment they come under God's rightful anger and displeasure, they in turn are displeased with God and get hot with anger against God!! Let us instead walk on holy ground, as David through repentance learned to do, and give fear to him that *ought* to be feared. "For we know him that hath said, Vengeance *belongeth* unto me, I will recompense, saith the Lord. And again, The Lord shall judge his people. *It is* a fearful thing to fall into the hands of the living God." Heb 10:30-31

But this was not the only time David was afraid of God, nor the only time that God was angry with David and his people. It is written, "And again the anger of the LORD was kindled against Israel, and he moved David against them to say, Go, number Israel and Judah." 2Sam 24:1 This was the sin of pride when David counted the people, and there were several acts of disobedience in it. First, there was the purpose of boasting in the strength of one's might by counting how great one's armies are. Second, there was the actual act of calling for a census, when it was God's prerogative to do so, not the king's. David would later learn and declare, "My times *are* in thy hand" (Ps 31:15). Third, there was the ignoring of wise counsel when Joab told David not to sin against the LORD in this way.

> And Joab answered, The LORD make his people an hundred times so many more as they *be:* but, my lord the king, *are* they not all my lord's servants? why then doth my lord require this thing? why will he be a cause of trespass to Israel? 1Ch 21:3

Notice how Joab, David's general, clearly sees this as an act of pride, for he immediately confronts it with a prayer to the LORD that they may continue to increase in number. Yet despite Joab's plea for wisdom, David did not listen. The fourth disobedience that was committed is that God commanded when a census was taken, that an offering be given for every man: "then shall they give every man a ransom for his soul unto the LORD, when thou numberest them; that there be no plague among them, when *thou* numberest them." Ex 30:12 This ransom for the soul, which was to be given unto the LORD, is how God would keep his people from becoming proud. This was not done for David, when confronted for his sin, his own conscience convicts him afterwards.

> And David's heart smote him after that he had numbered the people. And David said unto the LORD, I have sinned greatly in that I have done: and now, I beseech thee, O LORD, take away the iniquity of thy servant; for I have done very foolishly. 2Sam 24:10

The scripture specifically lets us know why David was afraid of God this time. "But David could not go before it to enquire of God: for he was afraid because of the sword of the angel of the LORD." 1Ch 21:30 David was afraid of God's rightful anger, his sword of judgment. We all ought to fear God for this reason. Do we fear God for *nothing* (Job 1:9)? Or do we have a reason to be afraid of him? David had reason to be afraid of God and so do we. We must fear his judgments. As David declares, "My flesh trembleth for fear of thee; and I am afraid of thy judgments." Ps 119:120 Who should not fear God? Is there anyone?

Christian teachers say, as God's children, we should not be afraid of God, yet this is, in fact, one of the signs of the Laodicean church of the last days! They will encounter the judgments of the Lord (i.e. his rebukes and his chastenings) and like the world around them they will not repent of their doings and learn to fear God. Why? Because they do not recognize the justness of God's judgments and his divine right to judge. It is said by so many men of God today, "God does not judge his people. God does not get angry with his people." But you have seen it with your own eyes, the Bible says the complete opposite – even in the New Testament. God *does* get angry with his people and *does* judge them. In fact, it is promised he will.

> For the LORD will judge his people, and he will repent himself concerning his servants. Ps 135:14
>
> For we know him that hath said, Vengeance *belongeth* unto me, I will recompense, saith the Lord. And again, The Lord shall judge his people. Heb 10:30

Let us take a moment to deal with this further. Men say, "God does not get angry with his children because he loves them." Have we lost the entire revelation of the Old Testament and even of Revelation itself?! For God shows over and over again that he indeed gets angry at his children when they are willfully disobedient and when they continually ignore and cast aside his counsel. Men say, "The Father was never angry with Jesus, and we are in his Son. We are his body. Therefore God will never be angry with us." This sounds so good to our ears, but it is not true. God *was* angry with Jesus when the sin of the world was put upon him on the cross – this was why God, the Almighty Judge, *had* to turn away. God's wrath had to fall upon his own Son because of our sin. This was why Jesus said "My God, my God, why hast thou forsaken me?" Mt 27:46

Though we *are* of his body, yet Jesus did not sin, but we do sin. Remember, sin separates us from our God (Isa 59:2). Jesus did not have to ask for forgiveness, we must ask for forgiveness. Jesus did not have to flee the wrath to come,

4 – Fearing God, Far More Than Reverence

but the scriptures say we must flee it. Whenever one of God's children holds the truth in unrighteousness, then "the wrath of God is revealed from heaven against all ungodliness and unrighteousness" (Rom 1:18)! Paul was warning the born again Christians of Rome not to have an impenitent or hardened heart, lest the wrath of God be stored up for them at the "revelation of the righteous judgment of God" (Rom 2:5, also see v8). Where is the fear of God today?

Yes, God has not appointed his children to wrath (1Th 5:19), neither is it his will that any should perish, but that all should be saved (1Tim 2:4). Yet, not all will be saved, nor will all be spared his wrath – even among his children![67] Paul was speaking of those who were saved, but who were walking in open sin when he said, "Let no man deceive you with vain words: for because of these things [i.e. *the sin they were walking in*] cometh the wrath of God upon the children of disobedience." Eph 5:6

> **WARNING**: This is the seriousness of why we cannot sit down with and even eat with willfully disobedient brethren – so that they will have the fear of God restored, and they will know they will NOT inherit eternal life if they continue in their way. Esau could not inherit the blessing, because he did not treasure it. He sold his birthright and was rejected (Heb 12:16-17). So we, if we do not treasure salvation, cannot inherit it. Those who sell their birthright, just like Esau by walking after the flesh, will receive condemnation and will not inherit the eternal kingdom.[68]

How can we *expect* the Lord not to be angry with us at times, when Jesus was angry with his very own disciples? Especially when we have the written record of what he expects, which they did not have? We may easily see God's pleasure and displeasure, his joy and his anger that he has toward the churches in the early chapters of Revelation. If God can be happy with us because of our heart toward him, then we must, even as Job did, allow the LORD also to be angry with us, especially when our hearts are contrary to him. If we worship a *living* God and not a dead god, then he will respond to our heart and actions with pleasure and displeasure. Remember, it is through faith *and* patience that the promises were obtained (Heb 6:12). Esau had no patience for God's blessings so he could not obtain them. The glory of the churches was when they had both faith and patience (2Th 1:4-5, 2Tim 3:10, Rev 2:19, 13:10, 14:12). Thus, as disciples we are exhorted to follow after both faith and patience.[69]

---

[67] We will look in more detail at the Father's wrath and the appropriate fear we should have in response, as servants of God *because* he holds the rod, in the section 'What to Fear' in the chapter entitled "Replacing Our Many Fears with God's Singular Fear".

[68] Those who will not inherit the kingdom: Gal 5:21, 1Co 5:11-13, 6:9-10.

[69] We are exhorted to have both faith and patience: 1Tim 6:11-14, Tit 2:2, Jam 1:3-4.

Job, the Perfect and Upright Man who Eschewed Evil, is Afraid of God

Job was afraid of God, yet we see Job's fear of God was not because he had done something wrong, but because of God's great power. Twice the scripture tells us that in all Job did he "sinned not, nor charged God foolishly." Job 1:22 (also Job 2:10) Let us get this in our heart, Job was not afraid of God because of anything he had done wrong. That was what his three friends tried to convince him of, but were rebuked by God for. Several times in the midst of his own struggle, it is Job who must teach his friends to fear God and be afraid of the Almighty. How much like today this is. The book of Job is literally the fear of God on trial. Thus, it should not be surprising that it reveals why we should all justly be afraid of God. Job was afraid of God for three particular characteristics of God:

1. **The Excellency of God:** Job was afraid of God because of his glory and holiness (i.e. how much greater he is than us). He says, "Shall not his excellency make you <u>afraid</u>? and his dread fall upon you?" Job 13:11 The excellency of God is his '*elevation* and *exaltation* in rank or character'. God is so much higher, so much greater, so much more powerful than we are, that we ought to be afraid of him. Job, as God himself, was shocked that his three friends were not afraid of God for this very reason. It is because we do not see how high and how holy God is compared to our small selves that we do not fear him as he ought to be feared (Ps 76:11)! Asaph says,

   "Thou *art* <u>more glorious *and* excellent</u> than the mountains of prey. At thy rebuke, O God of Jacob, both the chariot and horse are cast into a dead sleep. Thou, *even* thou, <u>*art* to be feared</u>: and who may stand in thy sight when once <u>thou art angry</u>? Thou didst cause judgment to be heard from heaven; the earth <u>feared</u>, and was still" (Ps 76:4,6-8).

   Note that this fear can only <u>increase</u> in us, not decrease, as we grow in our knowledge of the LORD. "And Israel saw that great work which the LORD did upon the Egyptians: and the people [i.e. *his people Israel*] <u>feared</u> the LORD, and believed the LORD" (Ex 14:31). "Only <u>fear</u> the LORD, and serve him in truth with all your heart: for <u>consider how great *things* he hath done for you</u>." 1Sam 12:24 The more we know of how truly great he is, the more we will be afraid of him.[70] It is a law of difference. The more different we see that he is from us, the more we will fear him, worship him, and serve him.

2. **His Sovereign Hand:** Job states that God's sovereign purposes, to do things we completely cannot understand at the time, caused him to be afraid of the LORD. "Withdraw thine hand far from me: and let not thy

---

[70] Here are a few more scriptures showing that as we learn of his greatness we should fear him more: 2K 17:36, 1Ch 16:25, Ps 96:4. Also see Job 31:23 where the word 'highness' is this same word 'excellency' in Job 13:11.

dread make me <u>afraid</u>." Job 13:21 Ought we not to fear God for this reason, the fact that he does *whatever* pleases him? Job gains a deep insight into God's sovereignty that we would do well to come to appreciate in our own life. It is because we do not consider God's free will and his sovereign right to do as he pleases that we do not fear him more!

But he *is* in one *mind,* and who can turn him? and *what* his soul desireth, even *that* he doeth. For he performeth *the thing that is* appointed for me: and many such *things are* with him. Therefore am I troubled at his presence: <u>when I consider, I am afraid of him</u>. Job 23:13-15

> **WARNING**: The sword of the word of God[71] is not only for judgment, but also for warning. Thus, his word is likened to a trumpet that warns us of approaching danger.[72] God's word was written for admonition and warning. It is the sound of a trumpet, an announcement of his plan to judge all things.[73] But God wants to know, is anyone hearkening to the trumpet call of his word, which brings warning? "Shall a trumpet be blown in the city, and the people <u>not be afraid</u>? shall there be evil in a city, and the LORD hath not done *it?* The lion hath roared, <u>who will not fear</u>?" Am 3:6,8

3. ***The Sword of God***: Because judgment and chastenings belong to the LORD we must fear him. "Be ye <u>afraid</u> of the sword: for wrath *bringeth* the punishments of the sword, that ye may know *there is* a judgment." Job 19:29 Every child is to fear the rod of correction, otherwise it is not a rod. Paul makes clear that the rod does not come in meekness or in love, it comes in power (1Co 4:20-21). Paul says, "Wilt thou then <u>not be afraid of the power</u>?" Rom 13:3 Because God has the power to bring forth judgment, we must fear him, and in that fear, Paul says, it will turn us to "do that which is good" (Rom 13:3). Our fear of the power extends even to delegated authorities among men. Thus, we are called not to be presumptuous or self-willed but to be "afraid to speak evil of dignities" (2Pe 2:10).[74]

---

[71] The word of God is the sword of the Spirit (Eph 6:17) and is sharper than any two-edged sword (Heb 4:12).

[72] We are so far from understanding God's sovereignty and his judgment that we cannot understand such prayers as Habakkuk's: "O LORD, <u>I have heard thy speech, *and* was afraid</u>: O LORD, revive thy work in the midst of the years, in the midst of the years make known; in wrath remember mercy." Hab 3:2 Who of us, by what we are being taught, would pray this way today? Yet God has not changed!

[73] The word for 'speech' in Hab 3:2 means '*a sound, rumor, announcement*'.

[74] The Greek word for 'afraid' in 2Pe 2:10 is literally used to form our English words "terrified" and "tremble"! Let us be terrified and tremble when we think of speaking evil of an authority.

Focusing on the Fear of the LORD

In the next chapter we will explore further the depth of the fear of God – how much farther it goes in true fear than mere reverence. In our liberal age, men say we should never be afraid of God, "For God is love, and what fear is there in love?" But we have seen and will see more, the great lovers of God who were men of great faith and in covenant with God, were at times afraid of the LORD because of his power, his glory, and his judgments. We will look more in the next chapter at what the Bible calls the dread and terror of the LORD. Let us first recap what we have found so that we may build strongly in our hearts a foundation for understanding what truly is the fear of God.

We have seen that God is to be *greatly* feared and that the fear of God is distinctly different and more than reverence for God. It is an exceeding fear, which is greater than all earthly fears. We have seen the fear of God is a literal fear, and it is a *godly* fear – meaning it is truly of God! Reverence is mainly toward men in properly responding to the position of authority which they have. But fear is to be rendered primarily to God. The scripture shows us the more we know God, as he really is, the more we will fear him. This is the pattern in scripture of those who grew in true intimacy with Almighty God. His fear is rooted in the greatness of his power (both in creation and in salvation), his mercies, his deliverances, his judgments, and the fact that he is not a respecter of persons. In short, it is his holiness, that he *only* is holy. That is the reason we ought all to fear him.

Because the focus of so many is on pleasing men or using men rather than on pleasing God and submitting to him, reverence is more in people's thoughts than is the fear of God. But if we truly will consider his greatness and his awesome works we will know and speak much of his fear. Let us be assured of the importance of fearing God – not just reverencing him – for everything the LORD does, he does so that we might fear him (Ecc 3:14).

4 – Fearing God, Far More Than Reverence

Chapter 5. Trembling in the Presence of the Almighty
The Depth of our Fear Toward God

"so terrible was the sight, that Moses said, I exceedingly fear and quake:" Heb 12:21

The Source of the Fear of the LORD
"Dominion and fear are with him, he maketh peace in his high places." Job 25:2

Though his mighty works, from creation to destruction, from mercy to judgment, from salvation to eternal punishment, all inspire the fear of the LORD, yet the single greatest source is still God himself. So we see that fear is with him (Job 25:2). The fear of God is a godly fear – a fear that comes from God (Heb 12:28). We must choose the fear of the LORD and let it be in us, but we must not make the mistake and think that the fear of the LORD has its source in us. We do not create it or initiate it or in any way produce it. Rather, it re-creates in us a prepared heart to meet the Lord. It makes us into what God desires. The source of the fear of the LORD is God himself. Repeatedly the scripture proclaims that it is **his** fear.

> even according to thy fear, *so is* thy wrath. Ps 90:11
> in thy fear will I worship toward thy holy temple. Ps 5:7

5 – Trembling in the Presence of the Almighty

> Stablish thy word unto thy servant,
> who *is devoted* to <u>thy fear</u>. Ps 119:38
>
> O LORD, why hast thou made us to err from thy ways,
> *and* hardened our heart from <u>thy fear</u>? Isa 63:17

> Dominion and fear are with the LORD. If we would approach him, we must submit to his rule *and* to his fear. To come any other way is to come disrespectfully ...

Choosing the fear of the LORD is about being willing to receive God for who he is – the great and awesome God that inspires fear, especially among his people who truly know him. If we come before the true God and dominion and fear are with him, then how can we not be covered by these? How can we receive and honor God as God, yet reject his dominion (i.e. his right to rule over us)? We cannot. Nor can we think that we can come before him, in any way that honors him, if we reject his fear. Dominion and fear are with the LORD. If we would approach him, we must submit to his rule *and* to his fear. To come any other way is to come disrespectfully and dishonorably.

His Dominion and Our Salvation

The need for understanding the kingdom of God is so important. Most Christians understand the kingdom of God as a place we will one day go, somewhere in heaven. Some believe the kingdom of God will come when Jesus returns. But when questioned by the Pharisees when the kingdom of God should come, Jesus answered, "The kingdom of God cometh not with observation: Neither shall they say, Lo here! or, lo there!" Lk 17:20-21 The kingdom of God is literally the king's domain, where the king rules and reigns in power and authority. Where God has dominion and his word is given undisputed authority there is the kingdom. Thus, is the kingdom of God in the heaven of heavens? Yes, but is the kingdom of God also on earth? Yes, wherever a people allow him to truly rule and reign over them. So Jesus taught his disciples to pray, "Thy kingdom come. Thy will be done <u>in earth</u>, as *it is* in heaven." Mt 6:10 The kingdom comes to earth when his will is done. It comes within our heart. So Jesus said, "for behold, the kingdom of God is within you." Lk 17:21

Can you hear what he said? His kingdom is in heaven because God's will is perfectly done there, and when we submit to his will on earth *exactly* as it is in heaven (i.e. with wholehearted obedience and with the fear of God),[75] then his

---

[75] His angels must certainly fear him for they are even more acutely aware of and are in the very presence of his glory and holiness, so that they proclaim it continually (holy, holy, holy), and it is God's holiness which inspires us to fear him (Rev 15:4). To see the link between God's holiness and our godly fear toward him, see the chapter entitled

kingdom is here as well. We can accurately say his will being done here on earth *is* his kingdom come into our midst. Now we know why the kingdom of God does not come with observation, because religious people are always looking for external manifestations and experiences but are unwilling to submit to God's word. Since they are unwilling to do what God has commanded, they are blinded from being able to see the true manifestation of his kingdom which is submission to his word. The kingdom of God can only be within us through the Lordship of Jesus Christ. If we would have his presence, we must allow his dominion to reign over us.

True salvation is not merely believing on Jesus, for the demons believe in Jesus, but it does not save them (Jam 2:19). Many believe on Jesus today, but he is the wrong Jesus. They believe with all their heart in Jesus, but the Jesus they believe in is but a teacher or a prophet or a good man, and not God come in the flesh to which we must submit our very lives in unquestioning fealty. Salvation and deliverance in our life comes when we confess him as Lord. "That if thou shalt confess with thy mouth the Lord Jesus, and shalt believe in thine heart that God hath raised him from the dead, thou shalt be saved." Rom 10:9 It is all about making him lord of our lives and not just saviour. He is saviour to the world, but he must become our lord, by us choosing to lay down our life and to pick up his.

If Jesus is the door (Jn 10:7,9) and we are to enter into that door for eternal life, then we must come under the lintel.[76] We often think of the doors of kings or cities which are wide and tall. The picture of a gate that is 10, 12, 16 feet high and higher comes to mind, but the door of the Lord is low, not high, and narrow, not wide, so Jesus said.

> Enter ye in at the strait [i.e. *narrow*] gate: for wide *is* the gate, and broad *is* the way, that leadeth to destruction, and many there be which go in thereat: Because strait [i.e. *narrow*] *is* the gate, and narrow [i.e. *crowded*, full of tribulation and suffering] *is* the way, which leadeth unto life, and few there be that find it. Mt 7:13-14

The gates of the world, based on their importance, are wide and tall and easy to enter in, but not so the gate of the Lord. It is narrow and low and one must fight and labor to enter into the rest of God. It is so low that all must bow and humble themselves to enter in. "For the LORD taketh pleasure in his people: he will beautify the meek with salvation." Ps 149:4 Only those who humble themselves (i.e. the meek) will enter into the kingdom of God. "Except ye be converted, and become as little children, ye shall not enter into the kingdom of heaven." Mt 18:3

"Holiness, Righteousness, & Faithfulness to God" in the book <u>Losing the Treasure of the Lord</u>.

[76] The lintel is that part of the door which is the horizontal beam on top.

5 – Trembling in the Presence of the Almighty

His Dominion Prepares the Way for His Fear

His dominion prepares the way for his fear. No dominion, no rule, no lordship, then no fear of God. Find a person with no fear of God and you will find a person who is not under Christ's lordship, one who at the root serves the Lord as they see fit, and not per his authoritative command. This is why God says to us, "if I *be* a <u>master</u>, where *is* my fear? saith the LORD of hosts unto you" (Mal 1:6). When the LORD is the sovereign controller who rules over us, we will fear him. When we begin to be our own master and ruler, the self-determiner of our decisions and choices, then we will have no fear of God, because we give no thought to what he thinks of our way.

We cannot be friends of God when we go our own way. Our own way always causes us to become estranged from him. So Paul warns, "Because the carnal mind *is* enmity against God: for it is not subject to the law of God, neither indeed can be." Rom 8:7 Without his continued lordship in our life, the way to the Father becomes "my way to God", the truth about the Father becomes "what I believe is true", and the life of the Father becomes merely "my life". If we would learn anything of the true fear of God we must acknowledge and submit to his authority.

> Find a person with no fear of God and you will find a person who is not under Christ's lordship, one who at the root serves the Lord as they see fit …. If we would learn anything of the true fear of God we must acknowledge and submit to his authority.

Paul in Ephesians 5 explains how a marriage between a man and a wife is the mystery of Christ and the church (Eph 5:32), Christ being the man or the head and the church being his wife. Yet even in the intimacy of marriage and the closeness of fellowship that is unsurpassed on earth, we see authority and subjection still have their place. These are not cast aside in God's order. So it comes as no surprise that

> Wives, <u>submit yourselves unto</u> your own husbands, as unto the Lord. For the husband is the head of the wife, even as Christ is the head of the church: and he is the saviour of the body. Therefore as the church is <u>subject unto Christ,</u> so *let* the wives *be* to their own husbands in every thing. Eph 5:22-24

> Likewise, ye wives, *be* in <u>subjection to</u> your own husbands; … For after this manner in the old time the holy women also, who trusted in God, adorned themselves, being in <u>subjection unto</u> their own husbands: Even as Sarah obeyed Abraham, calling him <u>lord</u>: whose

daughters ye are, as long as ye do well, and are not afraid with any amazement. 1Pe 3:1,5-6

We, as the bride of Christ, are to submit ourselves unto our husband Jesus, for this very reason, because he is the Lord and is God's ordained head of the church. The adornment, the beautifying addition of our walk with the Lord *is* our subjection to him as our husband. Our conversation (i.e. our 'behavior') is to be one of complete subjection, being subject in all things. But it is this subjection to Jesus' lordship that opens the door to godly fear. "Likewise, ye wives, *be* in subjection to your own husbands; … While they behold your chaste conversation *coupled* with fear." 1Pe 3:1-2 Godly subjection will produce godly fear.

Trembling before God
"Fear ye not me? saith the LORD: will ye not tremble at my presence" Jer 5:22

So many of us are still bound by a religious mentality that the fear of God is merely an awe or a reverence and not truly the fear that it is. So often this is an almost unconscious mindset because of all the teaching (or lack thereof) that we have concerning reverence and the fear of the Lord. Probably the best way to break through this stronghold is to consider the literal trembling people underwent throughout the scripture as a result of the true fear of God. It is far too easy for any one of us to judge from our own perspective, by our own experiences (or that of another that we greatly respect), and by where we 'stand'.

Which of us has stood in the very presence of Almighty God? Few, few indeed ever have in this life, whereas in the life to come every man, woman, and child will come before his great and dreadful presence. In the scripture we have the record of a few individuals who literally stood before God himself while still on this side of eternal judgment. We ought to glean what we can from their first hand experience and hold fast to that rather than anything else, for what God has revealed in his holy Word is more real than what we see with our own eyes or handle with our own hands. The testimony of scripture is clear. Every man of God who truly met the LORD face to face quaked and trembled.

1. *Moses*, the friend of God: The Bible says "And the LORD spake unto Moses face to face, as a man speaketh unto his friend." Ex 33:11 We have two unique times in Moses' life where God appeared unto him, and in both of them Moses trembled in fear at God's presence.
    - *Saying,* I *am* the God of thy fathers, the God of Abraham, and the God of Isaac, and the God of Jacob. Then Moses <u>trembled</u>, and durst not behold. Ac 7:32
    - And so terrible was the sight, *that* Moses said, I <u>exceedingly fear and quake</u> Heb 12:21

5 – Trembling in the Presence of the Almighty

The first reference in Acts 7:32 refers to when God appeared to Moses at the burning bush before he started leading the exodus, and the second in Hebrews 12:21 refers to when God appeared to him at Mount Horeb when he gave him the 10 commandments. Notice how both times it was what Moses **saw** that caused him to tremble:

a. "Moses trembled, and <u>durst not behold</u>"

b. "**so terrible** [so *frightful*, i.e. *formidable*] <u>was the sight</u>" that he did exceedingly fear and quake.

We cannot fully apprehend what Moses saw that was so frightful and formidable that the Bible calls it terrible, but we must know it is something beyond any of us knows. Notice that Moses, though he was the friend of God, was not just a little afraid of God, but was <u>exceedingly</u> fearful. The words 'exceeding fearful' are one Greek word *ekphobos* (1630) which means '*frightened out* of one's wits'.[77]

2. *Daniel*, the lover of God: he encountered the LORD's messenger, and received him as if God himself were speaking to him. Scripture says Daniel was a man 'greatly beloved' of God. So here too we have a man who was very intimate with the LORD, yet when God spoke to him through even a messenger Daniel trembled at God's words. "And he said unto me, O Daniel, a man <u>greatly beloved</u>, understand the words that I speak unto thee, and stand upright: for unto thee am I now sent. And when he had spoken this word unto me, I stood <u>trembling</u>." Dan 10:11 Here we see a man who loved God and yet at the same time feared God.

3. *Peter*, *James*, and *John*, Jesus' closest disciples: Jesus took these three men separately from the twelve and showed them, and them alone his transfiguration, his power to raise the dead, and the pouring out of his soul in Gethsemane in order to be obedient to the Father's will. They had an intimacy with Jesus that none of the others had. Yet when Jesus takes them to the mount of Transfiguration and the heavenly Father overshadows them in a cloud, they did not rejoice and shout and dance. The Bible says rather that "they were <u>sore afraid</u>." Mk 9:6 This phrase 'sore afraid' is the exact same Greek word used of Moses in Hebrews 12:21 that we have seen *ekphobos*, to 'exceedingly fear' or to be frightened out of one's wits. Again, it was what they *saw* that caused them to be exceedingly fearful. Thus, even the New Testament apostolic heart still has great fear in the presence of the Almighty.[78]

---

[77] Compare this with the testimony of modern faith preachers who have supposedly seen God and sat down and talked with him.

[78] Again, note how people's modern testimonies of how God spoke to them does not match up with the Biblical record of God's appearances.

4. *Paul*, the great servant of God: Paul was also very intimate with the Lord, as he himself stated, "have I not seen Jesus Christ our Lord?" 1Co 9:1 Paul the apostle spoke more about the love, mercy, and grace of God than any other Old or New Testament writer. He was used of God to pen the greatest chapter on love in all the world, 1Corinthians chapter 13. If any mere man knew and could communicate the love of God, it was he. So what of his testimony? Did perfect love cast out all fear, or did he have the fear of God in God's presence? Yes, he also trembled as a result of God appearing unto him. "And he trembling and astonished said, Lord, what wilt thou have me to do?" Ac 9:6

It was not just at his salvation that Paul trembled before God. He kept this throughout his growth in the Lord. When Paul sent messengers unto the churches and they received them as messengers of God with trembling, Paul did not correct or chastise those sent or those who received them in this way. He in fact commended them for their fear and trembling!

- And his inward affection is more abundant toward you, whilst he remembereth the obedience of you all, how with fear and trembling ye received him. 2Co 7:15
- Wherefore, my beloved, as ye have always obeyed, not as in my presence only, but now much more in my absence, work out your own salvation with fear and trembling. Php 2:12

So we see Moses, Daniel, Peter, James, John, and Paul all had intimate encounters with the Lord or with his messengers and all trembled before God's presence or his words. Can we argue or refute their testimony? No. We can only ask that the Lord would divinely change our perspective on what the real love of God is and that we also would experience the fear and trembling before him. God earnestly wonders why we do not fear him, knowing that we will most certainly tremble at his presence. "Fear ye not me? saith the LORD: will ye not tremble at my presence?" Jer 5:22 Because we **will** tremble when we are truly in his presence – without question – we ought to fear God now! The scripture calls out three specific reasons why we should tremble.

1. *God's Presence* : We should tremble because of the power and glory of God's presence. [Remember, it was what Moses, Peter, James, John, and Paul *saw* that caused them all to tremble.[79]]

    - My flesh trembleth for fear of thee; and I am afraid of thy judgments. Ps 119:120
    - Fear ye not me? saith the LORD: will ye not tremble at my presence? Jer 5:22

---

[79] What they saw made them sore afraid: Heb 12:21, Ac 7:32, Mk 9:6, Ac 9:6.

5 – Trembling in the Presence of the Almighty

2. *God's Position* : We should tremble because of the power and glory of God's position. He is the King of kings whose kingdom shall never have an end.[80]

    – The LORD reigneth; let the people tremble: he sitteth *between* the cherubims; Ps 99:1

    – men tremble and fear before the God of Daniel: for he is the living God, and stedfast for ever, and his kingdom *that* which shall not be destroyed, and his dominion *shall be even* unto the end. Dan 6:26

3. *God's Precepts* : We should tremble because of the power and glory of God's precepts.[81]

    – Then were assembled unto me every one that trembled at the words of the God of Israel Ezra 9:4

    – Now therefore let us make a covenant with our God … those that tremble at the commandment of our God Ezra 10:3

    – but to this *man* will I look, *even* to *him that is* poor and of a contrite spirit, and trembleth at my word. Hear the word of the LORD, ye that tremble at his word; Isa 66:2,5

Trembling at the Word of the King

Let us look at a example of how all of these – the fear of his presence, the fear of his position, and the fear of his precepts – function together in his role as king of kings to inspire us to rightfully tremble. Fear belongs to kings; it is their rightful due. Solomon, through the judgment he showed, was feared as king (1K 3:28). Because of Nebuchadnezzar's great power and judgment he also was feared.

> And for the majesty that [God] gave [Nebuchadnezzar], all people, nations, and languages, trembled and feared before him: whom he would he slew; and whom he would he kept alive; and whom he would he set up; and whom he would he put down. Dan 5:19

Consider the far greater judgment and majesty that the King we serve has. If men fear natural kings, should not we more so fear the King of kings? Should we not tremble at his Word who spoke all of creation into existence? Those of Ezra's day during the restoration trembled at the words of God (Ezra 9:4, 10:3). David himself the lover of God trembled at the words of God (Ps 119:120). And Solomon his son also warned us to fear God's commandments. "Whoso

---

[80] If we are exhorted to serve our "earthly masters according to the flesh, with fear and trembling, in singleness of [our] heart, as unto Christ" (Eph 6:5), how much more, how much, much more, ought we to "with **fear** and **trembling**" serve our heavenly Master who died for us while we were yet sinners?

[81] We are to literally fear the commandment of God, and we will be rewarded if we do (Pr 13:13).

despiseth the word shall be destroyed: but <u>he that feareth the commandment</u> shall be rewarded." Pr 13:13 Even the Corinthians, once repentance was brought to their hearts, received men of God with fear and trembling. "And his inward affection is more abundant toward you, whilst he remembereth the obedience of you all, how <u>with fear and trembling ye received him</u>." 2Co 7:15 It is these kind of men and women that God is looking to find and to speak to.

> For all those *things* hath mine hand made, and all those *things* have been, saith the LORD: but to this *man* will I look, *even* to *him that is* poor and of a contrite spirit, and <u>trembleth at my word</u>. Hear the word of the LORD, <u>ye that tremble at his word</u>; your brethren that hated you, that cast you out for my name's sake, said, Let the LORD be glorified: but he shall appear to your joy, and they shall be ashamed. Isa 66:2,5

Is it no wonder, without any fear of God's word that the fear of God is perishing in America?! We are called to fear the Word of our King. May you be set free from the doctrines of men and their lack of the fear of God as you study to show yourself approved unto God and not unto men, being "ready always to *give* an answer to every man that asketh you a reason of the hope that is in you with meekness and <u>fear</u>" (1Pe 3:15).

The Dread and Terror of God
"Shall not his excellency make you afraid? and his dread fall upon you?" Job 13:11

Today, no one thinks of dreading God. Who among us is invited to work on 'cultivating a profound fear of his power and being, so that we anticipate with alarm his actions'? Christians by and large consider anyone who would dread God as one who truly does not know God firsthand and certainly does not have a healthy relationship with the loving heavenly Father. They would say, "Now that we're the saved and know him, we should no longer dread him. That is only for the heathen." Indeed, the heathen ought to dread even the name of God, "for I *am* a great King, saith the LORD of hosts, and my name *is* dreadful among the heathen." Mal 1:14

But have we made God in our image in this? Does his excellency, his '*exaltation* in rank or character', not make us afraid? Job makes an amazing statement to his self-righteous friends who have judged and condemned him without showing him his fault. To them he says, "Shall not his <u>excellency</u> make you afraid? and his dread fall upon you?" Job 13:11 This is a question we ought to all ask of ourselves. Does his excellency make us afraid? Does his dread fall upon us? Or is "our God" different than Job's God?

We so often fall back on the fact that we are under God's covenant of mercy, but if we only knew the scriptures well, we would know the saints in the Old Testament were also under a covenant of mercy. Listen to Daniel's prayer

5 – Trembling in the Presence of the Almighty

and on what grounds he approaches the living God. "And I prayed unto the LORD my God, and made my confession, and said, O Lord, **the great and dreadful God**, <u>keeping the covenant and mercy to them that love him</u>, and to them that keep his commandments" (Dan 9:4). Daniel understood the covenant of mercy that God watched over them with, and yet it moved him to declare how great and how dreadful God is!

So many today are filled with natural fears that overwhelm their life, but the one thing that we ought to fear and dread we don't. The true prophetic cry is to let God be our fear and our dread: "Sanctify the LORD of hosts himself; and *let* him *be* your fear, and <u>*let* him *be* your dread</u>." Isa 8:13 The LORD of hosts will never be our dread or our fear in our gatherings until we *let him be* our fear and dread. But first we must sanctify him. We must set him apart from all other things. Men rejoice and dance, sing and shout, boast and praise before God as they should. But do they also weep and cry out, fast and pray? Do they fear and dread before the Almighty as they also should? Or do we only receive the sweet and gentle but reject the sour and strong. Is our menu with God restricted only to fast food snacks and dainty desserts? Or do we also have the hearty vegetables, strong meat, and bitter herbs that we need to grow?

Concerning the return of the Lord, so many today are looking for a feast and party mentality, when God says it will be a fearful, a dreadful day. "Behold, I will send you Elijah the prophet before the coming of the great and <u>dreadful day of the LORD</u>" (Mal 4:5). The Bible declares it will be a day of judgment – even for God's own people! He will judge the living and the dead. So many today are deceived and think that because they are in Christ all judgment has passed. They believe they no longer will be judged. Yet the Bible says on the contrary that we will be judged FIRST! "For the time *is come* that judgment must begin at the house of God: and if *it* first *begin* at us, what shall the end *be* of them that obey not the gospel of God?" 1Pe 4:17 God is a great and dreadful God (Dan 9:4) and his coming will be on a great and dreadful day (Mal 4:5). I pray that we know him who is great and dreadful and that we are truly prepared for that great and dreadful day. May we learn the dread of God and the reality of trembling before him in fear *before* that dreadful day.

"Knowing therefore the terror of the Lord" 2Co 5:11

To the typical Christian mindset, terror is something that should characterize the wicked's interaction with the LORD and not the righteous' relationship with their God. The wicked will experience terror at the coming of the Lord, for he comes to judge, and they are without Christ, without hope, and without God in the world (Eph 2:12). They are children of disobedience, and by nature children of wrath upon whom the wrath of God will come (Eph 2:2-3, 5:6, Col 3:6).

> Behold, the Lord cometh with ten thousands of his saints, To execute judgment upon all, and to convince all that are ungodly among

them of all their ungodly deeds which they have ungodly committed, and of all their hard *speeches* which ungodly sinners have spoken against him. Jude 1:14-15

Speaking of the wicked and the ungodly (Ps 73:3,12), David comes to the revelation how they shall be consumed with terrors. "Surely thou didst set them in slippery places: thou castedst them down into destruction. How are they *brought* into desolation, as in a moment! they are utterly consumed with terrors." Ps 73:18-19 Similarly, Job speaks of the terror of the rich man who was not rich toward God that lies down in peace but is taken away in terror. "Terrors take hold on him as waters, a tempest stealeth him away in the night." Job 27:20

But the terror of God was experienced also by the righteous. Let us look at righteous men and servants of God, patriarchs and prophets, all who experienced God's terror. We think only of the great signs and wonders that God worked in order to bring forth his people from Egypt, but the Bible says he also worked great terrors before the eyes of his people (Dt 4:34). We think that these were only a terror to the lost (i.e. to the Egyptians), but it was a terror even to the Israelites, God's covenant people. "And in all that mighty hand, and in all the great terror which Moses shewed in the sight of all Israel." Dt 34:12 These terrors were to be seen specifically by the Israelites that they might come to know the LORD. Do you still think that God did not have his servants experience the terrors of God? Job experienced them. David experienced them. Jeremiah experienced them. Paul experienced them. And even Paul's fellow laborers experienced them. Let us behold the terror of the LORD.

1. *Heman, the Ezrahite* : a worshipper of God
   I *am* afflicted and ready to die from *my* youth up: *while* I suffer thy terrors I am distracted. Thy fierce wrath goeth over me; thy terrors have cut me off. Ps 88:15-16

2. *Job* : a righteous man who feared God and eschewed evil
   the terrors of God do set themselves in array against me. Job 6:4
   Terrors are turned upon me: they pursue my soul as the wind   Job 30:15   For destruction *from God was* a terror to me, and by reason of his highness I could not endure. Job 31:23

3. *Jeremiah* : a prophet who would not compromise
   Behold, O LORD, and consider to whom thou hast done this. ... Thou hast called as in a solemn day my terrors round about, so that in the day of the LORD'S anger none escaped nor remained   Lam 2:20,22

5 – Trembling in the Presence of the Almighty

4. *Paul and his fellow laborers*: an apostle who forsook all[82]
   Knowing therefore <u>the terror of the Lord</u>, we persuade men; but we are made manifest unto God; and I trust also are made manifest in your consciences. 2Co 5:11

Four men have recorded the terror from God they experienced. All experienced God's terror. God was once known by his own worshippers as the terrible God who did terrible deeds, that is, he was the God who is full of terrors and who causes us to *fear* and at times to be *frightened*. "For <u>the LORD most high is terrible</u>; *he is* a great King over all the earth." Ps 47:2 His name was great and terrible, which all people were to praise (Ps 99:3). He was terrible in his works and the psalmist exhorts us to confess this very thing to God (Ps 66:3)! Even David confesses that God is terrible in coming out of his holy places (Ps 68:35). God's people expected him to answer them by terrible deeds. "By terrible things in righteousness wilt thou answer us, O God of our salvation" (Ps 65:5).

Please know the supreme greatness of your God. He frightens us merely because of who he is. He cannot but frighten us, both his presence, his workings, and even his name for they are exceeding great and his holiness beyond understanding. In this regard, we cannot compare God as our heavenly Father to us as his spiritual children the same way we do an earthly father to his own child. We are adopted children and are not of the same essence or the same glory, and though we have a special intimacy with him through his Son, Jesus Christ, yet he is God and we are not. We need to recapture so much that has been lost in our understanding and knowledge of the true God. If we will understand the depth of his holiness, then the fear of God will rightfully spring up in our heart and possess it as God has always desired. This is why every time God revealed himself to man, the terror of God, the judgment of God, and the holiness of God were always manifested.

Prepared for His Presence through the Fear of the LORD

Even Jesus, though he came as the bruised reed and with meekness and gentleness to show us the love and mercy of God, yet he also had to show forth God's holy wrath when twice he cleansed the temple and drove out all that his Father hated. Jesus terrified even his own disciples. If we are to come to know God in his fullness and not just the parts we would choose of him, then we must come to know the terror of the LORD, for it is part of who he is.

We are not to despise the chastening of the LORD (Pr 3:11), neither let us despise the fear of the LORD as so many do. It is for our deepest protection and

---

[82] Note that it was not just Paul, but also those who labored with him (the Timothy's, the Titus', and the messengers of the churches), for Paul says **"we** persuade men" and **"we** are made manifest". All of these men were in covenant relationship with God by faith even as we are today. They all experienced the terror of the Lord.

ultimately the doorway to our deepest intimacy with the God who dwells in unapproachable light (1Tim 6:16). Godly fear is for protection that we may take warning (Gen 42:28,35, 43:18). Remember, we cannot stroll in "come as you are" into the Father's throne room without being properly prepared and clothed. God has left us the story of Esther, to remind us of his holiness. Though she was a loving wife and a holy woman of God, with no cause for mistrust or unfaithfulness, yet she still had to come before her husband as the king when he sat on his throne with the greatest of fear.

> All the king's servants, and the people of the king's provinces, do know, that whosoever, whether man or woman, shall come unto the king into the inner court, who is not called, *there is* one law of his to put *him* to death, except such to whom the king shall hold out the golden sceptre, that he may live: but I have not been called to come in unto the king these thirty days. Est 4:11

Even Esther would not come arrogantly or presumptuously into the throne room of her king, though he was her own husband. Only with desperation, and the preparation of prayer and fasting, did she dare approach. Remember, we also are being prepared as a bride for our King and Lord, Jesus. So Paul exhorts us not to be deceived in how we approach God in his holiness. Let the fear of God prepare us to have the right heart in approaching his awesome presence.

> For I am jealous over you with godly jealousy: for I have espoused you to one husband, that I may present *you as* a chaste virgin to Christ. But I fear, lest by any means, as the serpent beguiled Eve through his subtilty, so your minds should be corrupted from the simplicity [i.e. the *singleness*] that is in Christ. 2Co 11:2-3

Are you willing to grow up into maturity and know the terror of the LORD? It will change your life if you do. You will now be willing to live openly in accordance with a good conscience and to be fully manifest to others, but more than that, you will now persuade men to be reconciled with God before it is too late. As Paul declares, "Knowing therefore the terror of the Lord, we persuade men" (2Co 5:11). If the true fear of God is restored to the church, a sincere spiritual fervor will awaken God's people to be the ambassadors of reconciliation they are called to be.

The Beginning of the Fear of God

"And he said, I heard thy voice in the garden, and I was afraid, because I was naked; and I hid myself." Gen 3:10

The first fear we see recorded in scripture is not any of the multitude of phobias that people are afflicted with today. This was the singular fear of God's judgment. Out of all fears that men ought to have today, this is the one most lacking, and that, if they would only acknowledge truth, would lead them back to the knowledge of God and his divine plan of restoration, fellowship, and life.

5 – Trembling in the Presence of the Almighty

Should we be afraid of the judgments of God if we are children of God? Yes! When God's anger broke forth upon Uzzah and he died, David was rightly afraid of God. "David was afraid of God that day" (1Ch 13:12). Sadly, many would do away with this fear altogether and say that the fear of God's judgment has no place in the life of a believer, yet the scripture shows otherwise.

We ought <u>always</u> to fear God's judgment, even as a child fears the rod and appropriately so of their father who bears the rod. Paul explains in Romans 13:3 that if we are afraid of the authority who bears the sword (i.e. 'the judicial *punishment*'), then we shall have praise from the authority. God is the ultimate bearer of the sword, and hence if we fear when he bears the sword, we will have praise from God himself. If we on the other hand, do not fear him who bears the sword, we will receive God's disapproval and condemnation. It is the fear of the rod that keeps all of us at times from being willingly, openly, or casually disobedient. Rather than putting this away, the true disciple of the Lord should rejoice that this aspect of the fear of the Lord is working in them. The fear of judgment, the fear of offending a holy God is a justified and righteous fear – one that Jesus himself had and exhorted us to have also.

Christians often have no righteous fear of God's judgment because the church at large has put away judgment. Why is this? Because Christians are not taught the foundational stone of *eternal judgment* (Heb 6:2). The Christian does not have clearly set before his face the judgment seat of Christ, which we must *all* stand before. And when God's people *are* taught of the judgment seat of Christ, they are taught falsely about it that it is NOT a judgment seat at all, but rather a blessing box, a place of receiving rewards for what we have done that is good and suffering loss (i.e. the loss of rewards, they say), if we have been bad.

Yet the two times the judgment seat of Christ is mentioned, this is clearly not the case. There is a soberness and a refraining from being willful that God wants to impart unto us when we think of standing before the Lord Jesus. "But why dost thou judge thy brother? or why dost thou set at nought thy brother? for we shall all stand before the judgment seat of Christ." Rom 14:10 There is an accountability to the judgment seat of Christ that we must acknowledge: we *will* be judged. Listen carefully to what Paul says in the other reference:

> For we must all appear before the judgment seat of Christ; that every one may receive the things *done* in *his* body, according to that he hath done, whether *it be* good or bad. Knowing therefore the terror of the Lord, we persuade men; but we are made manifest unto God; and I trust also are made manifest in your consciences. 2Co 5:10-11

Do we really think, if we have done bad and have not made our conscience right before God by acknowledging our sin and making it right in his eyes, that we will merely receive nothing? We deceive ourselves, if this is what we think. Why else does Paul immediately go from there into "**knowing** therefore the terror of the Lord"? Why does he *immediately* speak of having a conscience that is manifest unto all? Why then the urgent need to persuade men, if God will not deal with disobedience among his own children?

> The fear of judgment, the fear of offending a holy God
> is a justified and righteous fear –
> one that Jesus himself had and exhorted us to have also.

If we would know the judgment seat of Christ as it really is, and not as men say it is, it will not produce complacency, but fervency and terror. Remember, the terror that Paul is referring to here has NOTHING to do with the judgment of unbelievers. This has to do specifically with the judgment of disobedient believers! Let us truly understand the terror of the Lord, and fear God. Jesus said that stripes are appointed the servant of God who does not prepare for the coming of the Lord by having a right and proper fear of the Master. We must prepare ourselves for the coming of the Lord by the fear of God.

> And that servant, which knew his lord's will, and <u>prepared not *himself*</u>, neither did according to his will, shall be beaten with many *stripes*. But he that knew not, and did commit things worthy of stripes, shall be beaten with few *stripes*. For unto whomsoever much is given, of him shall be much required: and to whom men have committed much, of him they will ask the more. Lk 12:47-48

Why We are to be Afraid of God: His Exceeding Holiness

Being afraid of God began in the garden after Eve and Adam transgressed against God's commandment to not partake of the tree of the knowledge of good and evil. When Adam was questioned by God as to where was he, Adam's response is, "I heard thy voice in the garden, and I was afraid, because I *was* naked; and I hid myself." Gen 3:10 It is our nakedness (i.e. our shame) because of sin, that when we hear the voice of God, we naturally withdraw.

Only the repentant heart which is ready to turn aside from its wickedness and which lays hold of the faith that is in God will run to him. The unrepentant heart must hide from the terrible presence of God because it is under judgment and the unseared conscience knows it! Remember, Adam was the son of God (Lk 3:38). He had an intimate relationship with the LORD that many of us cannot imagine. This shows us that even a child of God can experience the driving away of the fear of the LORD, if they are unwilling to change and repent. Similarly, we find Sarah, a daughter of God (1Pe 3:6), being afraid of God because her heart was caught in denying the truth. "Then Sarah denied, saying, I laughed not; for she was <u>afraid</u>. And he said, Nay; but thou didst laugh." Gen 18:15

When Adam and Eve had sinned and were afraid (Gen 3:10), did God tell them not to be afraid? NO! Even though they were his children, albeit his dis-

5 – Trembling in the Presence of the Almighty

obedient children, they had reason to be afraid! This is what so many who say we should not be afraid of God do not perceive. We have reason to be afraid of God, because of his utter awesomeness. "The sinners in Zion are afraid; fearfulness hath surprised the hypocrites. Who among us shall dwell with the devouring fire? who among us shall dwell with everlasting burnings?" Isa 33:14 It is his *holiness* that makes us afraid. It is God's holiness that the angels and the four beasts before the throne of God continually testify to (Isa 6:3, Rev 4:8).

Many who go to church or to Bible studies or to Christian gatherings are truly not expecting to meet God there. They are going to learn or to be entertained, but not to encounter the holiness of God. This is the great problem of all our hearts in truly not expecting to meet God; therefore we have so little fear of God in the church. Whenever we find the presence of God unlooked for, when we are surprised by his holiness, we cannot but respond in fear. Thus, every recorded encounter with God or with his holy messenger is marked by fear. God is holy in his very essence. Therefore when we encounter him, we *must* fear him. Let us look at a few examples.

1. As Job suffered under the anguish of his afflictions and the awesomeness of the holy eye of God, he says, "Therefore am I troubled at his presence: when I consider, I am afraid of him." Job 23:15 'Troubled' here means 'to *tremble* inwardly (or *palpitate*), i.e. (figurative) *be* (causative *make*) (suddenly) *alarmed* or *agitated*'.
2. Jacob's response after he arose from the dream at Bethel: "And he was afraid, and said, How dreadful *is* this place! this is none other but the house of God, and this *is* the gate of heaven." Gen 28:17
3. When God revealed himself to Moses at the burning bush, Moses was afraid. "I *am* the God of thy father, the God of Abraham, the God of Isaac, and the God of Jacob. And Moses hid his face; for he was afraid to look upon God." Ex 3:6 Moses went to go "see this great sight" (v2). He was not expecting to meet God.

The Fear of Our Father

His chastening is not for our destruction, nor to drive us away from him, but for our reformation and to bring us back to him. So it is the same with his fear. His fear is not for our destruction, nor to drive us away from him,[83] but for our reformation and to bring us back to him. Until God can restore a healthy appreciation of his supreme holiness, and this can only be done through the fear of God, he cannot become intimate with us. Remember, no king of authority, of which the King of kings is supreme, can allow even his own children to dis-

---

[83] Though as we have seen, his fear, even his chastening, can drive us far from him – dependent on **our** heart. See the section 'The Response of Departing from God: Rebelling Fear' in the appendix entitled "The Fear of God and Unbelievers" in the book Losing the Treasure of the Lord.

respect and take lightly his dread, fear, power, and might. He must be in the eyes of all, the supreme authority.

This is why we are not initially in the hands of the Father. That is reserved for later, as we mature and grow. But the child, though be the heir, "is under tutors and governors <u>until the time appointed of the father</u>." Gal 4:2 Initially, we are in the hands of the Spirit and the servants of God he puts us under. The Holy Spirit as a mother nurtures and suckles us (1Th 2:7) preparing us to be presented in holiness to our holy Father (Jn 17:11). Along side comes our elder brother, Jesus, who leads us in discipleship and whose word reveals the Father and showing us what God Almighty expects of us. This is why the scripture says, "*It is* a fearful thing to fall into the hands of the living God." Heb 10:31

You may object, "But God is our Father. No father wants his children to be afraid of him." This is partially true, but not altogether. A father does not want his child to approach him in fear when there is no reason to fear, but there *are* reasons to fear at certain times. When the father speaks in authority, especially in warning to stop the child from doing something that may bring immediate harm if not hearkened to, then a father *does* want his child to fear his voice and his authority. Without this, a father cannot properly protect his child from danger by his voice alone. It is for the safety of the child. So it is with the fear of God, it is for our safety, and if God's authority is to be properly established in our heart, then the fear of God *must* be present.

Many think we ought not to fear God *because* he is our father. They often say, "As a father, I don't want my child to fear me." But the opposite is true with God! He, as our Father, **does** want us to fear him. Let us hear the testimony of scripture. He asks us, as our father, "if then I *be* a father, where *is* mine honour? and if I *be* a master, <u>where *is* my fear</u>? saith the LORD of hosts unto you" (Mal 1:6). "And if ye call on the Father, who without respect of persons judgeth according to every man's work, <u>pass the time of your sojourning *here* in fear</u>" (1Pe 1:17). We are not only to have the fear of God, we are to have it continually! "*Be thou* in the fear of the LORD all the day long." Pr 23:17 *Because* he is our Father, therefore we ought to daily fear him.

Do not forget this, God is <u>more than</u> our Father. His fatherhood cannot contain the fullness of his character or explain all of his actions. He is also the eternal judge. He is the mighty king. We dare not forget, there is a divine difference between God being our Father and an earthly father and child. The earthly father and child are of the same substance, the same nature, and the same preponderance to sin. They are both mankind. This is not altogether true of our heavenly Father and we as his children. Though he has given us *of* his nature, so that we "might be partakers of the divine nature" (2Pe 1:4), yet we are not little gods, who will one day grow up to be gods, as believed by the cults. No, we are and always will be his creation. We are not divine. Jesus, the only begotten Son

5 – Trembling in the Presence of the Almighty

of God is "true God from true God, begotten not made"[84] – we are not. Thus, his awesome presence will *always* make us afraid, while we are in this "earthly house of *this* tabernacle" (2Co 5:1).

> **WARNING**: This is the infinite difference between an earthly father and child, and between the heavenly Father and his child. Today we see God too much in our own image, so we do not fear him, nor are we afraid of him. This only betrays, as Job shows us, the lack of the depth of the true knowledge of God in these last days! What people know of God today is one dimensional. It is only grace, grace, grace. They know nothing of his severity and his judgment. The early church did not know God as grace, grace, grace. They knew both his goodness *and* his severity (Rom 11:22). Thus, they walked in a power and a holiness that is far from the modern church.

We Fear Him Because We Know Him as He is

Many say today we should *never* be afraid of God, yet the scripture shows example after example of those who truly knew God, loved him and served him, yet they at justifiable times were afraid of him. Think of God's introduction to Moses. "I *am* the God of thy father, the God of Abraham, the God of Isaac, and the God of Jacob. And Moses hid his face; for he was afraid to look upon God." Ex 3:6 As long as judgment belongs to God, we must be afraid of him, regardless of the depth of our love for him and his love for us. People are not afraid of God because they in truth have taken judgment away from God. They do not believe what the scripture says, that he **will** judge his people. Do we truly know him as he is? Hear Paul in Hebrews, "For we know him that hath said, Vengeance *belongeth* unto me, I will recompense, saith the Lord. And again, The Lord shall judge his people." Heb 10:30 Even Moses, who is the type and shadow of the new covenant believer, was afraid of God's anger. "For I was afraid of the anger and hot displeasure, wherewith the LORD was wroth against you to destroy you." Dt 9:19

If we are truly children of our heavenly Father, then should we not fear the rod of his correction? This indeed terrified Job: the rod of God. "Neither is there any daysman betwixt us, *that* might lay his hand upon us both. Let him take his rod away from me, and let not his fear terrify me" (Job 9:33-34). Consider this, it is because of the fear of God's rod that Job cried out for a daysman, an intermediary, an advocate. Therefore, it is the fear of judgment, the fear of being chastened that awakens in us the holy desire for the Saviour. Is God sorry for this? Or is this not exactly as God plans it? Should we *not* be afraid of his anger and hot displeasure, when within his reach is the rod of correction? Can we think that being adopted as sons and daughters by faith in Christ Jesus

---

[84] Taken from the Nicene Creed.

that he will not treat us as true children and be angry with us when we deliberately disobey him? Or have we once again de-masculinized the Judge of the living and the dead[85] and made him into our own image?

This is the problem with the doctrines of men, they put God in a box which limits him to the dictates of what man thinks is right and just for a particular state. But God is not bound by men's theories and thoughts, rather he acts in accordance with his word and who he is. His word proves he is angry with his own people at times, and his judgments did indeed fall on them when they refused to repent. God is both a father and a judge. He has not stopped being these once we become adopted.

We will *all* stand before the judgment seat of Christ. Paul, that great apostle of grace, said, "Knowing therefore the terror of the Lord" (2Co 5:11). Do you know the terror of God, or do the doctrines of men prevent you from seeing him as he is? Let the fire of God burn away the chaff of falsehood and your own concept of who you think God is. Let God be God, but every man a liar (Rom 3:4). Remember, the people were <u>afraid</u> of the fire on the mount. So should we be afraid of God, for our God is a consuming fire – and that is New Testament theology, not Old!

Peace & Trembling in the Fear of the LORD
"Dominion and fear are with him, he maketh peace in his high places." Job 25:2

Where we once trembled in the fear of man, now we must learn to tremble in the fear of God. Another paradox of the fear of the LORD is how trembling in the fear of God actually forms the foundation of true peace and joy. To the natural way of thinking this is an utter impossibility, but no more so than salvation through the Lord Jesus Christ. "With men *it is* impossible, but not with God: for with God all things are possible." Mk 10:27 With men there can be no peace in fear. Earthly fears rob the mind of any ability to find peace and rest. This is often the greatest cry of those who are bound up by their fears: the total lack of peace and rest. But the heavenly fear, the fear that comes from God, actually establishes our heart in peace by inviting us to trust in him and him alone. This is why "Dominion and fear *are* with him, he <u>maketh peace</u> in his high places." Job 25:2

As his dominion and fear are established in our lives and hearts, he is able to make peace in <u>his</u> high places. But what, you ask, are his high places? These are the places of our heart that are truly dedicated unto his dominion and which are given over to his fear. In the Old Testament the high places were always

---

[85] Judge of the quick and the dead: Ac 10:42, 2Tim. 4:1, 1Pe 4:5.

5 – Trembling in the Presence of the Almighty

places of worship – whether true or false! They were always places of sacrifice,[86] where God often met with his people.[87] God is able to establish the tabernacle of his peace there in the high places of our heart where he is able to freely have rule. Notice how the scriptures declare that God "treadeth upon the high places of the earth" (Am 4:13, Mic 1:3). God is able to walk with us in our heart, just like he did before the fall with Adam and Eve in the garden. As it was in the beginning before the fall, so it is again wherever God's dominion and fear are allowed to reign. In the garden of Eden before the fall, God's dominion and fear were unchallenged.[88] Adam and Eve must have walked even as the early church did having rest and being edified "walking in the fear of God, and in the comfort of the Holy Ghost" (Ac 9:31).

We must fear the LORD in order to enter into his rest. Hear what the scripture says, "Let us therefore <u>fear</u>, lest, a promise being left *us* of <u>entering into his rest</u>, any of you should seem to come short of it." Heb 4:1 This is why we cannot afford to put away the clean and enduring fear of the LORD. If we do not fear God, a promise *will* be left us of entering into his rest. Without the fear of God, we will not experience the full promise of his peace and rest. This is why some believers in Jesus never find deliverance from their fears, nor do they find the true peace of God – all because they never learn the fear of God. The fear of God is what enables us to enter into the promise of his rest. If we would enter into his rest, then let us therefore fear him! If we will only allow his dominion and fear to be with us, he will create peace in every area of our heart that is fully given over to him.

---

[86] A place of sacrifice: 1Sam 9:12, 1K 3:2-4, 1Ch 16:39-40, 21:29, 2Ch 33:17; 1K 12:31-32.

[87] A place of God's presence: Nu 23:3-4, Isa 57:15, 58:14.

[88] See the section entitled 'Back to the Beginning: Grace *and* Fear' in the chapter "Understanding the New Covenant of Grace & Fear".

Chapter 6. Understanding the New Covenant of Grace & Fear
Finding the Missing Pillar of Truth

*"And I will make an everlasting covenant with them,
that I will not turn away from them, to do them good;
but I will put my fear in their hearts,
that they shall not depart from me." Jer 32:40*

Hope is the anchor of our soul. The hope, which is set before us in the gospel to which every born again believer has fled for refuge, is both sure and steadfast (Heb 6:18-19, Col 1:5). The hope of the gospel is what steadies us and secures us in all of our weariness. This is why Paul's prayer for the saints is always that they would fully understand the mystery of the gospel (Eph 3:4, 6:19, Col 1:9-10). We need to have "the eyes of [our] understanding [be] enlightened; that [we] may know what is the hope of his calling, and what the riches of the glory of his inheritance in the saints" (Eph 1:18). How well do we understand the riches of the inheritance of the saints, which is found in the gospel? If we look to the promise of the gospel, which is the new covenant, we will better understand what are the riches of our inheritance as saints. Let us explore the foundation of the gospel, for the foundation will reveal the true treasure of our spiritual inheritance.

6 – Understanding the New Covenant of Grace & Fear

The Everlasting Gospel: Fear God

*"And I saw another angel fly in the midst of heaven,
having <u>the everlasting gospel</u> to preach unto them that dwell
on the earth, and to every nation, and kindred, and tongue, and people,
Saying with a loud voice, <u>Fear God, and give glory to him</u>;
for the hour of his judgment is come: and worship him" Rev 14:6-7*

What many think the gospel is today, is NOT the gospel. Born again Christians everywhere are taught that the gospel is "Believe on Christ and you will be saved." Remember, anyone can believe anything they want for whatever self-motivated reason they want. This is not salvation. True salvation is designed by God to come as a result of the deep conviction of sin and the fear that arises from knowing we are under the wrath of God because of our sins. The essential ingredients of salvation that are missing in modern evangelistic efforts are the preparation of repentance and the requirement for lordship. If we search the scriptures we see before such invitations to believe were given, repentance and lordship were always either preached or were manifestly already present.

Repentance[89] and the acknowledging of the Lordship of Jesus Christ are both required for true salvation. Without them we have only a mental assent, an agreement or a willful choice to serve him, but we have not been converted through salvation yet. Look at what comes before the invitation is given to the Philippian jailor to "Believe on the <u>Lord</u> Jesus Christ, and thou shalt be saved, and thy house." Ac 16:31 The jailor came trembling before them (showing the fear of God and the knowledge of his own guilt) and he spoke these words, "Sirs, what must I do to be saved?" Ac 16:30 The fear of the Lord was present, repentance was present, and the desire to come under the Lord's authority was present. Therefore all that was needed was to believe on the Lord Jesus.

Have we truly so misunderstood the gospel? Let us look at God's heavenly definition of the eternal gospel – the true gospel, uncorrupted by man's doctrines, and that has never changed – the eternal gospel. The eternal or everlasting gospel is the gospel that was "used of past time, or past and future as well." In Revelation 14:7 we see the angel from heaven that comes to earth to preach the everlasting gospel to all nations, kindreds, tongues, and people. What is the everlasting gospel that has always been preached? The everlasting gospel as we see in Revelation 14:6-7 is [1] "Fear God, and [2] give glory to him; for the hour of his judgment is come: and [3] worship him". All men of all time have been called to fear God and in that fear to give him glory and to worship him. Why? Because his judgment is coming! So many Christians look forward to Christ's return with joy and expectancy, yet we are called first to fear him for the hour of his judgment is coming. Then we are to give him glory.

---

[89] Remember, repentance biblically is turning away from our way back unto the Lord and changing our way of thinking to be in agreement with God's thinking.

The New Covenant: Grace *and* Fear

"Behold, the days come, saith the LORD, that I will make a <u>new covenant</u>" Jer 31:31

What is this new covenant that God promised? It is the covenant of grace *and* fear. What does God say about this new covenant? Three times it is used in the New Testament, all three of which are in the book of Hebrews.[90] Only one time in the Old Testament is the phrase "new covenant" used and that is in Jeremiah when he prophesies that he will make a new covenant with the house of Israel and the house of Judah (Jer 31:31). Let us look at the new covenant as it was prophesied by Jeremiah side-by-side with its fulfillment in the New Testament. When you read them side-by-side it is clear that what Jeremiah prophesied is the very new covenant that the apostles taught.

God's promise is that the new covenant would be founded on the word of God being written on our heart and that our iniquities would be remembered no more. He also promised that he would be our God through this new covenant and we would be his people, that each of us would personally know him (who are a part of this covenant). One vital part of the new covenant that is so often missed is not explained until the next chapter of Jeremiah.

> **WARNING**: At first, these scriptures may sound like they apply specially and only to the Jews, since they mention the house of Israel *and* the house of Judah, but this is not the case.[91] Some have erroneously taught that this new covenant is only for the Jews. Yet this is contradicted by the New Testament scriptures themselves, which prove that this prophecy of Jeremiah *is* the very new covenant that we have received in Jesus. This is also why the days of Jeremiah are the very days prophesied that we live in. These are the last days before the great and terrible day of the Lord's judgment.

---

[90] The 'new covenant': Hebrews 8:8,13, 12:24.

[91] Though 'the house of Israel' is specifically called out in Jeremiah 31:33, the New Testament writers directly quote this verse and apply it to the church (Heb 8:10, 10:16). The fact that this is written to the Hebrews makes no difference for us, for it equally applies. "<u>All scripture</u> *is* given by inspiration of God, and *is* profitable for doctrine, for reproof, for correction, for instruction in righteousness" (2Tim 3:16).

Remember, once we are born again we are no longer Jew, nor Greek (Gal 3:28, Col. 3:11). These things have passed away now that we are in Christ, for Christ is all in all. We become 'the church' which is separate and distinct from Jews *and* Gentiles (1Co 10:32). By applying this to the church, God clearly shows that those who are born again, by faith in the Lord Jesus (whether previously Jew or Gentile), are now partakers of this promise and this covenant! They in fact become spiritual Israel and of the Jerusalem which is from above (Gal 4:26). Though we were once strangers from the covenants of promise, we are such no longer (Eph 2:12,19)!

6 – Understanding the New Covenant of Grace & Fear

> Behold, the days come, saith the LORD, that I will make a new covenant with the house of Israel, and with the house of Judah: Not according to the covenant that I made with their fathers in the day *that* I took them by the hand to bring them out of the land of Egypt; which my covenant they brake, although I was an husband unto them, saith the LORD: But this *shall be* the covenant that I will make with the house of Israel; After those days, saith the LORD, I will put my law in their inward parts, and write it in their hearts; and will be their God, and they shall be my people. And they shall teach no more every man his neighbour, and every man his brother, saying, Know the LORD: for they shall all know me, from the least of them unto the greatest of them, saith the LORD; for I will forgive their iniquity, and I will remember their sin no more. Jer 31:31-34

> Behold, the days come, saith the Lord, when I will make a new covenant with the house of Israel and with the house of Judah: Not according to the covenant that I made with their fathers in the day when I took them by the hand to lead them out of the land of Egypt; because they continued not in my covenant, and I regarded them not, saith the Lord. For this *is* the covenant that I will make with the house of Israel after those days, saith the Lord; I will put my laws into their mind, and write them in their hearts: and I will be to them a God, and they shall be to me a people: And they shall not teach every man his neighbour, and every man his brother, saying, Know the Lord: for all shall know me, from the least to the greatest. For I will be merciful to their unrighteousness, and their sins and their iniquities will I remember no more. Heb 8:8-12

Now in Jeremiah 32, he speaks of the *everlasting* covenant. This is clearly the new covenant, not only from the context of Jeremiah itself, but also because the everlasting covenant *is* the covenant of the forgiveness of our sins. This everlasting covenant came through the sacrificial death and outpouring of Jesus' blood for us as the spotless lamb of God. This, the writer of Hebrews confirms for us by concluding his epistle with: "Now the God of peace, that brought again from the dead our Lord Jesus, that great shepherd of the sheep, through the blood of the <u>everlasting covenant</u>" (Heb 13:20). Let us look at this everlasting covenant, the new covenant, which Jeremiah speaks of in chapter 32.

> And they shall be my people, and I will be their God: And I will give them one heart, and one way, that they may fear me for ever, for the good of them, and of their children after them: And I will make an <u>everlasting covenant</u> with them, that I will not turn away from them, to do them good; but I will put my fear in their hearts, that they shall not depart from me. Jer 32:38-40

Again we see, through the everlasting, new covenant, he will be our God and we will be his people. But this time God also mentions he will give us one heart and one way and that he will put his fear in our hearts. Through salvation, God has indeed given us one way: Jesus Christ. "Jesus saith unto him, I am the way, the truth, and the life: no man cometh unto the Father, but by me." Jn 14:6 Through the new birth, God has indeed given us one heart, a new heart (Eze 36:26), the heart of Jesus. Through prayer and the baptism of the Holy Ghost, this one heart was manifested in the new covenant church.

> And when they had prayed, the place was shaken where they were assembled together; and they were all filled with the Holy Ghost, and they spake the word of God with boldness. And the multitude of them that believed were of <u>one heart and of one soul</u>: neither said any *of them* that ought of the things which he possessed was his own; but they had all things common. Ac 4:31-32

This one way and this one heart have been given for two purposes: (1) for the good of us and our children (2) and so that we may fear God forever! This is the everlasting new covenant! This is why we should not say we are under the covenant of grace alone, but under the covenant of grace *and* fear. God promised to do two works on our heart which would form the new covenant. First, he would give us a new heart through grace. Grace is 'the divine influence upon the heart, and its reflection in the life'.[92] God's grace brings about the forgiveness of sins and the deliverance from the wrath of God. This completely changes our position: from the kingdom of darkness to the kingdom of his dear Son, the kingdom of light (Col 1:13, Ac 26:18).

But what of our direction? What of the strength of salvation to *stay* saved, to remain in the grace of God? How did God promise he would do this? This he does by putting the fear of God in our heart. As he said, "but I will put my fear in their hearts, <u>that they shall not depart from me</u>." Jer 32:40 With his fear in our heart, he promises we will not depart from him. If we lose our fear of God, then we will eventually depart from him, as the example of the lives of so many who have departed from the faith so evidently testifies.

> What is this new covenant that God promised?
> It is the covenant of grace *and* fear.

Notice God's everlasting covenant has two parts to it. *First*, he will unite our heart to fear him (Jer 32:38-40).[93] Our heart must be united if we are to fear him (Ps 86:11). Through the new covenant, he puts his fear in our heart so that we will not depart from him. *Second*, the fear of the LORD then causes his word to be written on our hearts (Jer 31:31,33). This is because we so respect his word that we do not reject it or flee from it.

---

[92] Per Strong's definition of the word for grace: *charis* (Greek 5485).

[93] This is why we cannot have a divided heart and walk in the fear of God.

6 – Understanding the New Covenant of Grace & Fear

The Foundational Pillars of the New Covenant

These two foundational pillars of our salvation, grace and fear, are constantly under attack by the enemy. So many have defended the pillar of grace, but who is defending the pillar of the fear of God that we have lost? Pillars in the scripture represent the foundation of truth, that which is established, steadfast, and sure. So God promises in Revelation, if we overcome, we will be as pillars in the temple of God (Rev 3:12), speaking of a stability and permanence. So Paul speaks of the church of the living God as "the pillar [i.e. the *support*] and ground [i.e. *immovableness* or steadfastness] of the truth." 1Tim 3:15 These two pillars of the new covenant can be seen in the building of Solomon's Temple. Let us examine their significance and special representation.

God had two pillars set up in front of Solomon's Temple. Before one could enter the temple of God's presence they had to approach and pass between these two mighty pillars. Solomon's Temple represents the heavenly temple. Whoever would enter therein must come by the way of these two pillars.

> And he reared up the pillars before the temple, one on the right hand, and the other on the left; and called the name of that on the right hand Jachin, and the name of that on the left Boaz. 2Ch 3:17

The importance of these pillars is that God named them! God did not name *any* of the other parts of the temple – only these two pillars. He gave them a personal name, showing all who would come that they represented something special, something about how they were to come before him in their worship. They were called Jachin and Boaz. The meanings of their names are given to us by the King James translators in their marginal notes. According to them, **Jachin** means "he shall establish" and **Boaz** means "in it is strength".

Let us continue examining the representation of these two pillars. These two pillars, the pillars of grace and fear are what form the new covenant (as we have seen from Jer 31:31-34, 32:38-40). Grace, mercy, faith,[94] *and* the fear of God are all required for salvation to be properly established in our life. We must learn how to pass through grace and fear, mercy and faith, to get to our desired destination, the LORD in his heavenly temple. We know we are saved by <u>grace</u> through <u>faith</u> (Eph 2:8, Rom 4:16), and that we are saved by <u>mercy</u>.[95] "Not by works of righteousness which we have done, but <u>according to his mercy he saved us</u>, by the washing of regeneration, and renewing of the Holy Ghost" (Tit

---

[94] Faith is put with the fear of God because the true faith of God grows out of a fear of him, to trust in what he says over anything else. We will see how the fear of God is the door to intimacy with the LORD, which is why "we have access by faith [i.e. that which is born out of the fear of God] into this grace wherein we stand, and rejoice in hope of the glory of God." Rom 5:2

[95] Salvation by mercy is seen in these verses: Ps 109:26, 119:41, 6:4, 31:16, 85:7, 86:16, 13:5, Hos 1:7.

3:5). But it is the fear of God that brings us to salvation. "Surely his salvation *is* nigh them that fear him" (Ps 85:9). In addition, we have seen that when we are born again, we are birthed in the fear of God.

Each pillar had a capital on top and a pedestal on the bottom. The foundational pedestal would be mercy for grace and the fear of God for faith. This is because God's grace toward us springs from his mercy, and our faith is to spring from the fear of the LORD. The capital that stood on top of each pillar represented the fruit that was produced by each pillar (i.e. the end result). Thus, the fruit of grace is seen in the scriptures to be peace, and the fruit of faith is righteousness. Multiple characteristics of a single column or pillar are often seen together in the scripture. The pillar of how God *establishes* us is grace, mercy, and peace. These three parts are all found together in the New Testament repeatedly. "Unto Timothy, *my* own son in the faith: Grace, mercy, *and* peace, from God our Father and Jesus Christ our Lord."[96] 1Tim 1:2 Peace and grace are repeatedly paired together[97] and so are peace and mercy.[98] Similarly, we find the same pairings on the pillar of Boaz.

Table 6-1   Comparing the Two Pillars of Grace & Fear

the Pillar of Boaz:	the Pillar of Jachin:
• the strength of **Faith/Faithfulness**[99]: "He staggered not at the promise of God through unbelief; but was <u>strong</u> in faith, giving glory to God" Rom 4:20	• established in **Grace**[100]: "*it is* a good thing that the heart be <u>established</u> with grace" Heb 13:9 "But the God of all grace … stablish *you*." 1Pe 5:10
• the foundation of the **Fear of God**[101] based on the strength of God's **judgment** & **truth**: "In the fear of the LORD *is* <u>strong</u> confidence" Pr 14:26	• the foundation of **Mercy** based on the surety of God's **justice** & **love**: "And in mercy shall the throne be <u>established</u>" Isa 16:5
⇒ the fruit of **Righteousness**[102] (Heb 12:11, Jam 3:17)	⇒ the fruit of **Peace** (Isa 57:19)

---

[96] See this same phrase in 2Tim 1:2, Tit 1:4, 2Jn 1:3.

[97] Peace and grace: Rom 1:7, 16:20, 1Co 1:3, 2Co 1:2, Gal 1:3, Eph 1:2, Php 1:2, Col. 1:2, 1Th 1:1, 2Th 1:2, Phm 1:3, 1Pe 1:2, 2Pe 1:2, Rev 1:4.

[98] Peace and mercy: Isa 54:10, Jer 16:5, Gal 6:16, Jam 3:17, Jude 1:2.

[99] For faith/faithfulness also see Ac 3:16, Heb 11:11, Lk 22:32, 1Co 16:13. And for trust see: Ps 18:2, Isa 12:2, 26:4, Nah 1:7.

[100] For establishing in grace, also see Rom 16:24-25.

[101] Of whom shall we be afraid? The LORD only, "who *is* the strength of my life" Ps 27:1 (see also Lk 12:5, Ps 34:9, Dt 13:4). For the fear of God and the strength that is in it, see also Isa 33:6, 25:3.

[102] Fruits of righteousness: 2Co 9:10, Php 1:11, Heb 12:11, Jam 3:17, Pr 11:30, 12:12.

6 – Understanding the New Covenant of Grace & Fear

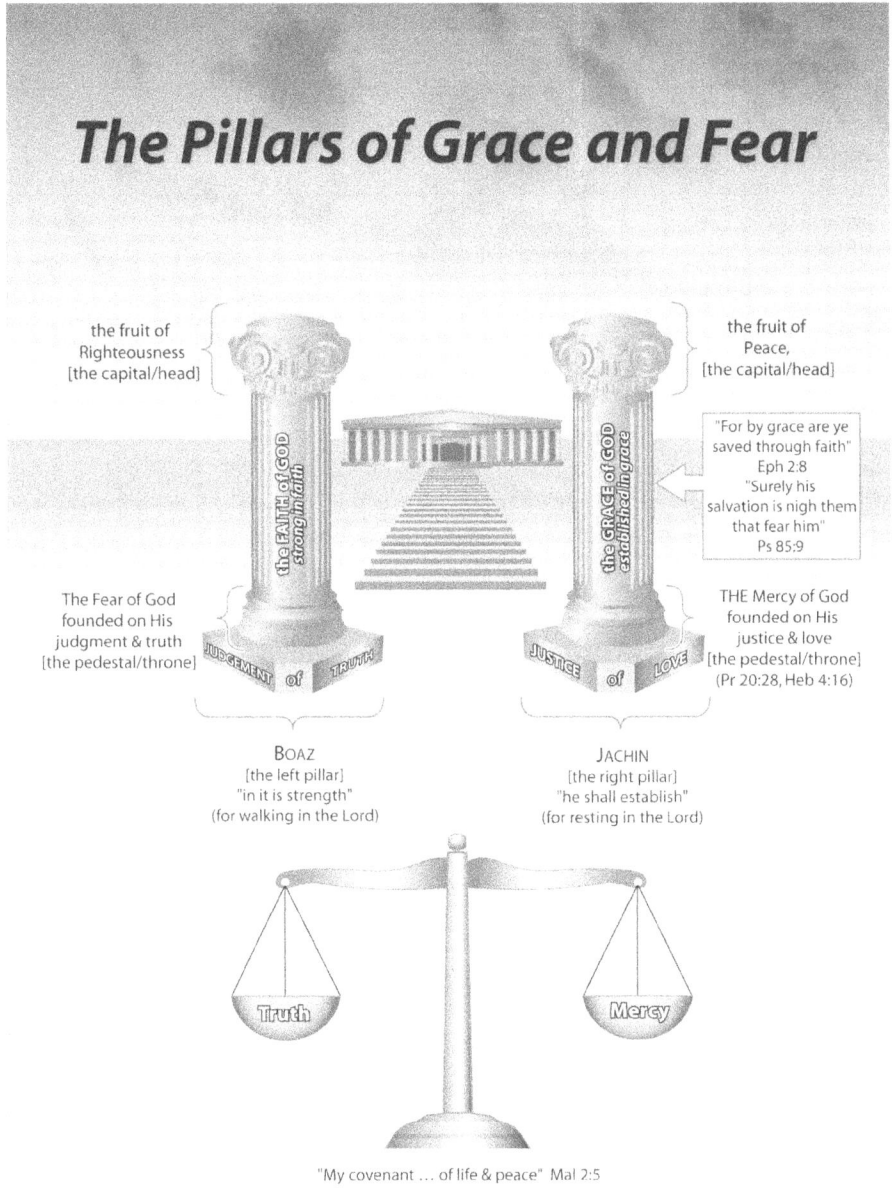

Our pillar of *strength* is found is the fear of God, faith, and righteousness. Jesus' girdle or belt was none other than righteousness and faithfulness (Isa 11:5). The righteousness of God is revealed by faith (Rom 1:17, 3:22,25), and our faith is counted for righteousness, so that the scripture speaks repeatedly of the righteousness of faith.[103] Additionally, the pedestal or throne that upholds the pillar of strength is the truth of God's word itself. Thus, we often see truth (which is the pedestal of strength) and righteousness (which is the capital or fruit of spiritual growth) together. We are to walk before God in truth and righteousness (1K 3:6, Ps 15:2, Isa 48:1), "and they shall be my people, and I will be their God, in truth and in righteousness." Zec 8:8 Truth and righteousness are often mentioned together.[104]

Even more interesting is when these two foundational pillars, the pillar of *establishing* and the pillar of *strength*, are found together in the scripture. Many of these references have to do with salvation or the forgiveness of sins. For instance, "By **mercy** and **truth** iniquity is purged" (Pr 16:6). "But the **mercy** of the LORD *is* from everlasting to everlasting upon them that **fear** him, and his **righteousness** unto children's children" (Ps 103:17). We also see grace and fear in Hebrews 12:28, and many other examples of mercy and truth,[105] as well as mercy and the fear of God.[106]

Back to the Beginning: Grace *and* Fear

"But the mercy of the LORD is from everlasting to everlasting upon them that fear him, and his righteousness unto children's children" Ps 103:17

Salvation has been preached from the very beginning, the first being right in the very garden of Eden after the fall.[107] Thus, these two foundational pillars of salvation must be from the very beginning also. As it is written, "the mercy of the LORD *is* from everlasting to everlasting upon them that fear him, and his righteousness unto children's children" (Ps 103:17). As "the mercy of the LORD *is* from everlasting to everlasting" so also the fear of the LORD endures forever (Ps 19:9). These two have always been. They will be in the end of time, and they were there in the beginning of time, even before Adam and Eve.

---

[103] Faith and righteousness: Ps 40:10, 119:138, 143:1, Isa 1:21,26, 11:5, Rom 1:17, 3:22, 3:25, 4:5-13, 9:30, 10:6, Gal 5:5, Php 3:9, Heb 11:7,33, 2Pe 1:1, Rev 19:11, 1Sam 26:23.

[104] Truth and righteousness: Ps 96:13, 119:142, Isa 26:2, Jer 4:2, 2Co 6:7, Eph 5:9, 6:14.

[105] Mercy and truth: Pr 16:6, 20:28, Ps 57:3, 57:10, 61:7, 98:3, 100:5, 117:2, 108:4, 69:13, 40:11, Pr 3:3 (us).

[106] Mercy and fear: Lk 1:50, Ps 147:11, 118:4, 103:11, 33:18, 5:7.

[107] This is seen in the seed of the woman crushing the head of the serpent (Gen 3:15), and the lamb slain from the foundation of the world (Gen 3:21, Rev 13:8).

6 – Understanding the New Covenant of Grace & Fear

Let's see how this pillar of strength has been destroyed. In the beginning, Adam and Eve lived in perfect grace and in perfect fear of God. We know this must have been the case, first, because there was no law (Rom 4:15). Therefore they lived in a covenant relationship of grace – as did all the patriarchs. This is why Abraham was the father of faith, of them under the law as well as those without the law (Rom 4:16). Second, Adam and Eve must have been walking in the fear of God because God was their master from the beginning,[108] and the scripture declares that fear is due him as a master (Mal 1:6). Third, any covenant which brings forth "life and peace" must be established through grace by the fear of God. As God says of his covenant with Levi the priest, "My covenant was with him of life and peace; and I gave them to him *for* the <u>fear wherewith he feared me</u>" (Mal 2:5).

When Adam and Eve fell because of disobedience, it was primarily the pillar of strength that was demolished. Yes, they also lost the fruit of the pillar of establishing, which is peace. Until reconciliation can take place, sin always prevents peace, but this was immediately restored as God brought reconciliation by slaying the innocent lamb and clothing them with his mercy, kindness, and grace. This enabled them to be reestablished in forgiveness and in covenant relationship to him so that, before they left the garden, the pillar of establishing (grace, mercy, peace, and love) was set upright in their lives again. But now they had no strength. It was the pillar of strength (the fear of God, faith, righteousness, and truth) that was lost in their life from the very beginning.

> All sin and disobedience to God is the direct result of the loss of his fear. This is why God's solution to our wayward ways and to departing from sin and iniquity is to recapture the fear of God.

Notice the direct result of the fall and how it completely destroyed Boaz – leaving nothing left. We will see how our intimacy with the Lord is directly dependent on how much of the fear of God we possess. Their disobedience was the direct result of their loss of God's fear. Hence, the intimacy of their relationship with God was severed (for it is through his fear that we have our deepest intimacy with him).[109] But many other things were also lost at the same time.

---

[108] The proof of Adam's complete submission to God as master, even before the fall, is that God determines in complete authority where Adam will live, what his occupation and calling will be, and what Adam is to partake of and not partake of. Yet we see absolutely no disagreement, questioning, or even discussion from Adam. Adam completely accepts God's right as supreme Lord and Master to dictate whatever he chooses for Adam's life.

[109] The relationship of intimacy with God and the fear of God will be seen in the chapter entitled "True Fellowship Flows from the Fear of the LORD".

Truth was lost, and deception entered into their hearts. Sound judgment was lost, as they thought they could hide from God! Their righteousness, of course, was lost as they were covered with the stain of sin. Their spiritual eyes were instantly closed, and their natural, carnal eyes were instantly opened. Thus, they now walked by sight, not by faith – so even their faith was corrupted.

Why did all this happen to this one pillar? Because what they lost by disobeying God and partaking of the tree of the knowledge of good and evil was they forsook the fear of God! If we only understood the importance of his fear more, we would know that all sin and disobedience to God is the direct result of the loss of his fear. This is why God's solution to our wayward ways and to departing from sin and iniquity is to recapture the fear of God.[110] Nearly all the blessings that we seek for and desire in life are dependent on the fear of God.[111] When this pedestal or throne of the fear of God was removed nearly all the blessings of God were lost. Even the clean and pure fear of God that they had was lost. It was replaced with the false fear of God which is a guilty conscience.

How Grace can be Frustrated

This is the great importance of the fear of the LORD both to him and to us – for without it, grace will ultimately be frustrated and abused. Why do I say that grace will be frustrated without the fear of God? Because grace was designed by God to work hand-in-hand with fear. This we have seen in the two pillars of the new covenant. God put his fear into our heart to keep us from departing from him (Jer 32:40). Remember, the grace of God teaches us to deny "ungodliness and worldly lusts, [*so that*] we should live soberly, righteously, and godly, in this present world" (Tit 2:11-12). It is clear, that many a saint receives the grace of God in both salvation and in forgiveness, and yet they do not learn *how* to deny ungodliness and worldly lusts so that they live soberly, righteously, and godly, in this present world. So how does grace teach us these things?

God designed the grace of God to teach our heart to fear him. The fear of God will keep our heart from departing from the LORD. God's fear keeps worldly lusts from gaining access into our heart, or if already present to become despised in our heart. The goodness of God reflected in his great mercy to forgive us is his divine highway prepared to lead us to the fear of God. If we would truly understand the depth of God's grace through forgiveness, we would indeed fear him as David the man of God did before us (Ps 130:3-4). When anyone prays to God knowing the plague of their own heart, God will forgive, and that forgiveness is designed by God to lead them to fear him.

---

[110] Through the fear of the LORD we depart from iniquity: Pr 3:7, 14:16,27, 16:6, Job 28:28. Remember, the fear of the LORD, that is wisdom.

[111] These are covered later in the chapter entitled "The Inestimable Treasure of God's Fear", when we are ready to see all that the LORD has for those who fear him.

6 – Understanding the New Covenant of Grace & Fear

> Then hear thou in heaven thy dwelling place, and **forgive**, and do, and give to every man according to his ways, whose heart thou knowest; (for thou, *even* thou only, knowest the hearts of all the children of men;) That they may fear thee all the days that they live in the land which thou gavest unto our fathers. 1K 8:39-40

God expects that his mercies will produce in us the fear of God. If his mercy is received and does not produce the expected fruit of the fear of God, he is angered. "Neither say they in their heart, Let us now fear the LORD our God, that giveth rain, both the former and the latter, in his season: he reserveth unto us the appointed weeks of the harvest." Jer 5:24 How far our understanding of God's forgiveness has drifted from the biblical purpose! In the scriptures when godly men were forgiven by God, they feared him all the more. Now, forgiveness many times does not produce the fear of God or grateful humility, but often impudence and pride instead, just like the man forgiven the great debt of 10,000 talents (Mt 18:23-35). The goodness of God's mercies are always intended by him to be a witness to others. God expects by the goodness he has shown in forgiving us, not only that we will fear him, but that others also may believe and fear him.

> And I will cleanse them from all their iniquity, whereby they have sinned against me; and I will pardon all their iniquities, whereby they have sinned, and whereby they have transgressed against me. And it shall be to me a name of joy, a praise and an honour before all the nations of the earth, which shall hear all the good that I do unto them: and they shall fear and tremble for all the goodness and for all the prosperity that I procure unto it. Jer 33:8-9

Treasures New and Old

"and at our gates are all manner of pleasant fruits,
new and old, which I have laid up for thee, O my beloved." SS 7:13

The recovery of the pillar of the fear of God, the pillar of strength, will bring such strength to our life, for so many blessings are attached to the fear of God. There is truly a heritage that God gives to those who fear him (Ps 61:5). This word 'heritage' in Hebrew means 'something *occupied*; a *conquest*'. All godly wisdom, understanding, and knowledge have their root in the fear of God. The heritage of the fear of the LORD is that of a householder whose house is filled with great treasures. Hence, it is written, "Through wisdom is an house builded; and by understanding it is established: And by knowledge shall the chambers be filled with all precious and pleasant riches." Pr 24:3-4 Our spiritual house is therefore built through the wisdom that springs from the fear of God. Through the understanding that issues from the fear of the LORD, our house is established. By the fear of the Most High (which brings the knowledge of the holy), so the chambers of our house are filled with great treasures.

Grace and fear together add a fullness to our life spiritually that cannot be compared. It is as Jesus said, "Therefore every scribe *which is* instructed unto the kingdom of heaven is like unto a man *that is* an householder, which bringeth forth out of his treasure *things* new and old." Mt 13:52 The fear of God is a great treasure (Isa 33:6), and it brings forth great treasures. The fear of God will open up the treasures of the word of God in a way that you have never seen before. For this he has promised, "He hath given **meat** unto them that fear him: he will ever be mindful of his covenant." Ps 111:5 The meat of the word of God is reserved for those who fear him. And he says again, "The secret of the LORD *is* with them that fear him; and he will shew them his covenant." Ps 25:14 The covenants of God in their true balance of both grace and fear can only be understood when we are walking in both the grace and the fear of God. This is the secret that the LORD of glory is able to add unto us. A depth of insight into the covenants of God will be added when we fear him. This is why treasures new and old are brought forth from the word of God out of our heart. Let us press on to lay hold of this forgotten pillar of truth in which is our strength.

Chapter 7. The Door of Mercy to All Those who Fear the LORD
How His Fear Opens the Door of Mercy

"By faith Noah, being warned of God of things not seen as yet, moved with fear, prepared an ark to the <u>saving</u> of his house; by the which he condemned the world, and became heir of the righteousness which is by faith." Heb 11:7

The Type & Shadow of Salvation: Noah & the Ark

We have seen that we need the fear of God to properly understand God and his plan of salvation. The very gospel of the ages is to fear God. Thus, we see an intertwining of faith and the fear of God that form the foundation for a strong salvation. Remember, the second pillar of the new covenant was named Boaz, "in it is strength". The fear of God prepares the heart for salvation and faith obtains that salvation. We grow in our salvation and maintain our salvation through both faith and the fear of God. We must learn to walk by faith (2Co 5:7) and in the fear of God.[112] We see this perfect joining of faith and fear in

---

[112] Walking in the fear of God: Ac 9:31, 2Ch 6:31, Neh 5:9.

7 – The Door of Mercy to All Those who Fear the LORD

Noah's life. Noah and the ark are an example to us of true salvation. Only Noah and the small remnant that was in the ark with him were delivered from the wrath to come (1Pe 3:20). So Jesus warned us of these last days that only a remnant would be saved (Lk 13:23-27). Those in the ark were lifted up from the floods of destruction that swept away the ungodly. The ark itself represented the fullness of salvation and our walk with God.

- It was **300 cubits long**, for 300 was the number of deliverance by faith.[113]
- It was **50 cubits wide** speaking of liberty, for it was in the fiftieth year, the year of jubilee that the slaves were set free. It was also the freedom of the Spirit witnessed at the outpouring of the Spirit at Pentecost, which is 50 days after Passover.
- It was **30 cubits high**, even as Jesus was 30 years old when he started his ministry.
- There were **three stories** representing both the trinity (the Father, Son, and Holy Ghost) and the three heavens of creation: our heaven (the natural heaven or the sky), the second heaven (where the fallen angels are warring against the angels with Michael the archangel), and the third heavens (the heaven of heavens, where the throne of God is – 2Co 12:2).
- There was **one window** in the roof, only one source of light from above, which was one cubit by one cubit representing the one and only one God.
- There was **one door** representing the Lord Jesus Christ who stated, "I am the door: by me if any man enter in, he shall be saved" (Jn 10:9).[114]

Is it any wonder then that one of the first examples of salvation by faith in the great chapter of faith (Heb 11) was Noah? "By faith Noah, being warned of God of things not seen as yet, moved with fear, prepared an ark to the **saving** of his house; by the which he condemned the world, and became heir of the righteousness which is by faith." Heb 11:7 Salvation was worked out in Noah's life (as well as his whole house) as he was moved with fear by the faith he had in

---

[113] It was by 300 men that God worked deliverance by faith through Gideon. Remember the sword of the LORD and Gideon? Gideon was a type of Christ, and the 300 were the type and shadow of true disciples who brought the water of the word to their mouth with diligence and watchfulness and who followed Gideon's example to do as he did. Similarly, Enoch was delivered by faith from this evil world as he walked with God for 300 years before he was taken up into heaven (Gen 5:22-24). To Benjamin, 'the son of the right hand', was given 300 pieces of silver speaking of the redemption given to the sons of God by faith in Christ Jesus.

[114] That one door was in the side of the ark, and it was in Jesus' side where he was pierced, opening the door of salvation unto us through his death.

what God had spoken. Though the order in this verse is 'by faith', 'warned', and then 'moved with fear', in fact, the actual order was that Noah was first 'warned', then he was 'moved with fear', and finally 'by faith' he prepared.

This is exactly what we have seen in Boaz, the pillar of strength: that the warning of God's judgments are to produce a godly fear in us which in turn is to produce a godly faith, and the end or fruit is righteousness. Noah's faith arose from his fear in the truthfulness and certainty of the warning of the judgment that was to come. Should not our faith in God move us to fear the coming judgment he has promised, and so as wise virgins to prepare? Should we not also be *moved with fear* to establish our salvation and the salvation of those around us by obedience to God's will? So Paul instructs Timothy to have this same godly fear that Noah had,

> Meditate upon these things; give thyself wholly to them; that thy profiting may appear to all. Take heed unto thyself, and unto the doctrine; continue in them: for in doing this thou shalt both save thyself, and them that hear thee. 1Tim 4:15-16

The Floodgates of Mercy to those who Fear Him

"For as the heaven is high above the earth, so great is his mercy toward them that fear him. But the mercy of the LORD is from everlasting to everlasting upon them that fear him" Ps 103:11,17

When one first begins to search out in the scriptures the fear of the LORD, it is an amazing thing to see how many times mercy is connected with it. Nehemiah's prayer for mercy in order to approach the heathen king he was serving was not based on his own righteousness, nor what he had done to serve this earthly king, but on the basis that he was a servant of God who feared God.

> O Lord, I beseech thee, let now thine ear be attentive to the prayer of thy servant, and to the prayer of thy servants, who desire to fear thy name: and prosper, I pray thee, thy servant this day, and grant him mercy in the sight of this man. Neh 1:11

The fear of God is the door to finding and obtaining the mercies of God. To see this in its fullness we need to take a moment to understand Hebrew parallelism. Much of the Psalms and Proverbs are written in a parallelism of one type or another. The primary one that concerns us is the 'synonymous' parallelism, where the joining of two descriptions represent the same thing.[115] In 'posi-

---

[115] Types of Hebrew parallelism include (1) *synonymous*, where the same thought is repeated using different words in order to amplify the point and to focus the reader's attention on it; (2) *synthetic*, in which the second thought adds to the first thought and builds upon it; and (3) *antithetic*, in which two contradictory or opposing thoughts are joined side by side [Note: this is more often used in Proverbs]. Since the first two types

7 – The Door of Mercy to All Those who Fear the LORD

tive' parallelisms, like 'synonymous' parallelism, the first thought usually represents the overall characteristic (i.e. a *summary*), whereas the second usually represents a specific detail (i.e. an *example*). Twice in the scripture the fear of God is directly equated with those that hope in the LORD's mercy using synonymous parallelism.

> Behold, the eye of the LORD *is* upon them that fear him, Ps 33:18
> upon them that hope in his mercy

> The LORD taketh pleasure in them that fear him,
> in those that hope in his mercy. Ps 147:11

> **The fear of God is the door to finding and obtaining the mercies of God.**

Those "that fear him" are clearly one and the same as those "that hope in his mercy." By Hebrew parallelism we see that those who fear the LORD are the overall category and those that hope in his mercy are the specific outworking of that fear of God. Thus, those who truly hope in God's mercy will always be those who fear him. The fear of the LORD and the receiving of mercy are put together in the scriptures many times.

> Let them now that fear the LORD say, that his **mercy** *endureth* for ever. Ps 118:4

> For as the heaven is high above the earth, *so* great is his **mercy** toward them that fear him.

> But the **mercy** of the LORD *is* from everlasting to everlasting upon them that fear him, and his righteousness unto children's children; Ps 103:11,17

God's forgiveness (among other reasons) is given for the very purpose that we would fear him. "If thou, LORD, shouldest mark iniquities, O Lord, who shall stand? But *there is* forgiveness with thee, that thou mayest be feared." Ps 130:3-4 The goodness of God reflected in his great mercy to forgive us is his divine highway prepared to lead us to the fear of God. Thus, the goal of God's mercy toward us in forgiving us our trespasses and sins is to revive in us the fear of God so that we will depart from sin.

The Ultimate Mercy: Salvation

"Surely his salvation is nigh them that fear him" Ps 85:9

---

of parallelism agree in meaning, they can jointly be referred to as *positive* parallelism, while the third is *negative* parallelism.

Is it any wonder, then, that the greatest mercy of all, salvation, is intimately involved with the fear of God? The fear of God is what he uses repeatedly in scripture to open the door of salvation. God has intended every saved person to be saved in fear, to walk in the fear of God, and to have the spirit of the fear of the LORD in them (Isa 11:2).

The gospel of Luke declares the new covenant is in fact the outpouring of God's eternal covenant of mercy upon them that fear him. "And his mercy *is* on them that fear him from generation to generation." Lk 1:50 Knowing that "according to his mercy he saved us" (Tit 3:5), we see that the fear of the LORD is truly the door to the greatest mercy of all, the mercy of salvation, for his mercy is upon them that fear him. Thus, it is by our fear of him that he saves us! God's promise is when those that fear him cry unto him, "he also will hear their cry, and will save them." Ps 145:19 Is it no wonder that the scripture says, "Surely his salvation *is* nigh them that fear him" (Ps 85:9). The fear of the LORD properly prepares our heart for salvation by bringing in the conviction of the holiness of God, so that the scripture says of it, "The fear of the LORD *is* a fountain of life, to depart from the snares of death."[116] Pr 14:27

The Fear of God: the Pathway that Leads to Salvation

Make no mistake, the fear of God does not ensure that a person is saved. Nor will the fear of God by itself save us. We are saved through the act of being born again by making Jesus Lord of our life. Not all who fear God are saved, but we will still see the fear of God is a powerful tool *unto* salvation, for it prepares the heart to receive the truth and will lead it toward salvation.

The scripture is clear that many unsaved people may fear God, and yet know nothing of salvation through Jesus Christ. Cornelius was just such a man. Cornelius was "A devout *man,* and one that feared God with all his house, which gave much alms to the people, and prayed to God alway." Ac 10:2 Cornelius' external righteousness and holiness was greater than that of most Christians today, yet he was still uncleansed, in his sin, and by nature still a child of wrath. Had he perished, Cornelius would have gone directly to hell. Yet, the fear of God was the door that the Lord was able to open so that Cornelius may hear the gospel and might receive it. Similarly, Paul preached to the Gentile proselytes known as the "God fearers", and they were the ones who oftentimes particularly believed and received the preaching of the gospel:

> **whosoever among you feareth God**, to you is the word of this salvation sent. ... And when the Gentiles heard this, they were glad, and glorified the word of the Lord: and as many as were ordained to eternal life believed. Ac 13:26,48

---

[116] Especially from the snares of eternal death.

7 – The Door of Mercy to All Those who Fear the LORD

> **WARNING**: Some may misinterpret Peter's statement, "But in every nation he that feareth him, and worketh righteousness, is accepted with him." Ac 10:35 Peter is clearly NOT saying that salvation is granted on the basis of fearing God and working righteousness, for that would deny so many other scriptures which clearly show us that salvation is "by grace … through faith; and that not of ourselves … Not of works, lest any many should boast" (Eph 2:8-9).
>
> We have no second witness that we are saved by fear and works. Jude 1:23, in fact, shows that many are saved without the fear of God. God clearly accepts no man's works for salvation – for all men's works (except his Son's) fall short being mixed with our own sin and impurity. So why does Peter say this? Because the true fear of God, which is without hypocrisy and which works righteousness, will always lead a man to salvation! Thus, God does not reject any man who fears him and works righteousness as far as his approaching him and offering that man salvation, but it is still a choice that that man must make to receive the salvation which is freely offered him.

Those Without the Fear of God

Neither are all who are saved still in possession of the fear of God that was given to them by the Spirit of God at salvation – otherwise, God would not have to question his own people why they do not fear him! People may even be saved without the fear of God. Such people who come to the Lord without it or those who have lost the fear of God often have a weak foundation to their salvation. You say, "How can that be, for the foundation which no other man can lay and which is laid is Jesus Christ? How can it be weak or strong when it is all the same foundation?" First, the strength of any foundation is not only dependent upon what it is laid upon (i.e. the strength of the rock or sand below), but also *how* it is laid upon that foundation (i.e. is it firmly attached, rooted, grounded, planted, and established, or is it merely resting atop of it). Second, we may be saved with the fear of God or without, dependent on the message that was preached unto us – that is plain both from the scripture (Jude 1:23) and from practical experience. This is why God has always expected his ordained servants[117] to teach his people the fear of God so that they might mature in obedience and in holiness.

The Salt of the Covenant: the Fear of the LORD

"All the heave offerings of the holy things, which the children of Israel offer unto the LORD, have I given thee, and thy sons and thy daughters with thee, by a statute for ever: it is a <u>covenant of salt</u> for ever before the LORD unto thee and to thy seed with thee." Nu 18:19

---

[117] Like Moses, David, Isaiah, Jeremiah, Jesus, Peter, Paul, and so many others, as ordained servants of God, they all taught the fear of God.

Where is the Fear of GOD? Finding the Treasure of the Lord

The fear of the LORD is what has been missing in our walk with the Lord. This singular issue of our heart, which has been put aside and mocked and scoffed at, is the very salt that will preserve our life, our heart, our thoughts, and our walk. We must recapture the salt of the covenant: the fear of God. This is the salt of the covenant that will enable us not to depart from God, as long as we keep it in our heart. The grace of God changes our position and our person. We are no longer children of wrath. We are a new creation. This is our establishing, but we have no strength to endure and to remain faithful without the pillar of the fear of God that produces a sound faith, based on God's judgment and his truth (and not on our desires or wants).

The Necessity of Salt in Offerings

There was a special offering that God taught the people of the Exodus about. It was the *heave offering*. It was a free will offering, an offering which came from the heart of thanksgiving toward God. It was particularly 'a *present* to the LORD'. 'Heave' is the Hebrew word *t'ruwmah*. The root words mean 'something raised up on high'. When God prescribed the law of the heave offering of the holy things (those things which were dedicated unto God as something specially set apart for him), it was called a covenant of salt.

> All the heave offerings of the holy things, which the children of Israel offer unto the LORD, have I given thee, and thy sons and thy daughters with thee, by a statute for ever: <u>it is a covenant of salt for ever</u> before the LORD unto thee and to thy seed with thee. Nu 18:19

The Israelites were called not to "suffer <u>the salt of the covenant</u> of thy God to be lacking from thy meat offering: with all thine offerings thou shalt offer <u>salt</u>." Lev 2:13 Whatever they offered unto God had to be offered with salt. So everything in our life must be done with the salt of the fear of God. "Wherefore we receiving a kingdom which cannot be moved, let us have grace, whereby we may serve God <u>acceptably with</u> reverence and <u>godly fear</u>" (Heb 12:28). Though we have the grace of God, yet still we cannot serve acceptably without reverence and godly fear. It is the salt of the covenant of our God that must not be lacking in all that we do for him.

In fact, without the fear of God it is **impossible** to serve God acceptably or agreeably to him. Why do I make such a bold statement? Because the word of God mandates it. "Wherefore we receiving a kingdom which cannot be moved, let us have grace, whereby we may serve God <u>acceptably with reverence and godly fear</u>" (Heb 12:28). Prior to these 'enlightened' days, if we lived under the times of the kings we would not *think* of coming before the king or an emperor without great fear. So, if we serve God without the fear of the LORD we

7 – The Door of Mercy to All Those who Fear the LORD

can only receive rebuke and warning for not serving the greatest of all kings as he who is rightfully the King of kings and who is worthy of all fear.[118]

When God wanted something to be sure and everlasting, he made it a covenant of salt. Notice how the kingdom that was given to David and to his sons (that foreshadowed the kingdom of God) was a covenant of salt. "Ought ye not to know that the LORD God of Israel gave the kingdom over Israel to David for ever, *even* to him and to his sons by a covenant of salt?" 2Ch 13:5

Our Speech: Seasoned with Salt

"Let your speech be alway with grace, seasoned with salt,
that ye may know how ye ought to answer every man." Col 4:6

Even our speech is to be seasoned with salt. Notice how our speech is always to be with grace, and yet that by itself is insufficient! "Let your speech <u>be alway</u> with grace, <u>seasoned with salt</u>, that ye may know how ye ought to answer every man." Col 4:6 How can we know how to answer every man? With grace alone? No. We must also have salt. Grace teaches us how to answer with mercy and patience. Grace reminds us of where we came from, and what we are without the Lord so that we may answer humbly.[119] Grace teaches us how to answer so that we point men to salvation and explain the saving work of Jesus Christ. Grace enables us to have compassion, knowing that we are compassed with the same infirmities and undergo the same trials. Grace enables us to reach out to them in their poverty, destitution, sickness, and hurt and to have a love for them that comes from the living God. As we have been loved by Christ through grace, so we are able to love others with the same love that he loved us with.

But how to answer every man according to their particular need comes *not* from grace, but from the fear of the LORD. The grace of God enables us to take their side, but the fear of God enables us to take God's side. It is the fear of God that keeps us from giving a false comfort. The fear of God keeps us speaking the truth, even when it hurts. The fear of God keeps us from giving a false peace. It enables us to show others how to be truly reconciled to God, even though it may initially bring turmoil, opposition, and a great lack of peace to

---

[118] Let us be assured, God is worthy of all fear: 1Tim 6:15, Rev 17:14, 19:16.

[119] It is grace that keeps us from the prideful spirit of the Pharisees. The Galatians had been taken captive by such a self-righteous spirit. Thus, when they had to confront someone who had been overtaken in a fault, Paul warns them to consider themselves, lest they also be tempted (Gal 6:1). And what was this temptation? But being tempted to be lifted up with pride, by thinking that they were better than the one who was overtaken. This is why the previous verse speaks of seeking after vain glory and provoking (i.e. *challenging*) one another (Gal 5:26). And the next two verses immediately bring the warning to be humble. "For if a man think himself to be something, when he is nothing, he deceiveth himself." Gal 6:3

their soul.[120] Through the fear of God we warn people of the condemnation that is the end of walking in disobedience. "Knowing therefore the terror of the Lord, we persuade men" (2Co 5:11) to be reconciled to God (v18-20).

> **WARNING**: The false prophets in Jeremiah's day, as well as our day today, heal the hurt of God's people only slightly, saying "Peace, peace", when there is no peace (Jer 6:14, 8:11). Similarly, Ezekiel exposed the false prophets who seduced God's people saying, "Peace" when *there was* no peace (Eze 13:10). So when does true peace come? Not when wickedness abides. *"There is* **no** *peace,* saith the LORD, unto the wicked." Isa 48:22 Peace can only come after righteousness is re-established through repentance, reconciliation, and truth.

Remember, it is the fear of the LORD that teaches us how to answer. As Peter, "But sanctify the Lord God in your hearts: and *be* ready always to *give* an answer to every man that asketh you a reason of the hope that is in you with meekness and fear" (1Pe 3:15). We have an answer (i.e. 'a clearing of oneself, a defense') for the reason of the hope that is in us. This defense is given to us when we answer in meekness and in the fear of God (1Pe 3:15). The answer of hope, we have, is rooted in humility and in the fear of God. Why in humility and in godly fear? First, in meekness, because we know that it is nothing that we have done that saves us, but what he has done to forgive us and to adopt us as his own. We know the great debt of sin and the depth of depravity from which we have been delivered, and we cannot help but walk humbly before our God.

Second, in fear, because we know we "call on the Father, who without respect of persons judgeth according to every man's work" so that we "pass the time of [our] sojourning *here* in fear" (1Pe 1:17). We have such a hope within us because we "sanctify the Lord God in [our] hearts" through the fear of God. When we fear the Lord, we will set him apart as holy in our heart. God says when we sanctify him we *are* fearing him (Isa 29:23). "Sanctify the LORD of hosts himself; and *let* him *be* your fear, and *let* him *be* your dread." Isa 8:13 Meekness and fear allow us to give an answer to every man that is in agreement with his particular state, but does not compromise the truth of God's word. The meekness comes from the grace of God, which we have received, but to it must be added God's fear. Jesus NEVER whitewashed or ignored sin, yet he was still able to minister compassionately without compromising the word and will of his Father. Jesus had an answer for the state of every man or woman:

- For those who are rich in the things of this life, like the rich young ruler, Jesus gave the answer that he must forsake all.

---

[120] The peace we are promised to be led by is not a soulish peace. It is a spiritual peace that passes all understanding (Php 4:7). Thus, the natural or soulish man cannot comprehend it.

7 – The Door of Mercy to All Those who Fear the LORD

- For those whose sin was hidden, like the women at the well, Jesus gave the answer to go and call her husband.
- For those whose sin was known to all, like the adulteress women, Jesus gave the answer to go and sin no more.
- For those who were filled with religion, like Nicodemus, Jesus gave the answer that you must be born again.

To every person Jesus had an answer, given him by the Spirit of the LORD through the fear of God (Isa 11:2-4). To each person they heard by Jesus' answer of the Father's care as well as his awesome fear so that they might depart from iniquity. The answer of meekness and fear causes us to set before peoples' eyes: "Behold therefore the goodness and severity of God" (Rom 11:22). With meekness and fear our forerunner and example was able to answer every man for the reason of the hope that was in him. So must we learn to speak and do in both grace and fear.

The Cleansing & Preserving Power of Salt

> Bring me a new cruse, and put salt therein. And they bring *it* to him. And he went forth unto the spring of the waters, and cast the salt in there, and said, Thus saith the LORD, I have healed these waters; there shall not be from thence any more death or barren *land*. So the waters were healed unto this day, according to the saying of Elisha which he spake. 2K 2:20-22

Salt is not just a seasoning, it is also a cleansing and a preserving agent. We shall see how the fear of God preserves our heart.[121] Notice how Jesus had just finished speaking of eternal judgment and the consequences of not putting away persistent sin, when he spoke about damnation in hell.[122] Immediately following this, he exhorts his disciples to have salt in themselves – the preserving and cleansing agent that seasons everything it is added to. "Salt *is* good: but if the salt have lost his saltness, wherewith will ye season it? Have salt in yourselves and have peace one with another." Mk 9:50 What is it that preserves us from the fires of hell and allows us to be seasoned? It is none other than the salt of the fear of God. This is the salt that we must all be seasoned with. This is that seasoning which will preserve not only our lives but also those who hear us. When we speak with the fear of God, we will know how to answer every man. When we have the salt of the fear of God within us, it will cleanse and preserve our heart and other's as well.

Let us look at an Old Testament example of the cleansing and preserving power of salt. When there was no water, and the ground was barren in Jericho,

---

[121] See the chapter "Toward a More Godly, Faithful, and Perfect Heart", the section 'A Preserved Heart: A Heart of Integrity' in the book <u>Losing the Treasure of the Lord</u>.

[122] "Where their worm dieth not, and the fire is not quenched" (Mk 9:48).

men came to Elisha the holy man of God seeking help. What did Elisha do? He did the same thing (2K 2:20-22) that our Elisha, Jesus, desires to do for us today. He is looking for the new cruse, the new vessel in which he can put his salt – the fear of God. This is the same salt that seasoned Jesus' life, the fear with which he feared his heavenly Father. But first the vessel must be brought to him – speaking of lordship and discipleship – so that the vessel is in the hands of the potter. Then he would pour us out through servanthood so that the fear of God within our vessel would save and preserve the life of the church and then of the lost. Through the fear of God, the waters of people that are under the sentence of death and are barren can be healed and preserved. What a healing this would bring to the church today, if only the salt of the covenant could be freely poured out on those who are barren.

Our Fear as Children of Promise

This is why it is the greatest of tragedies that the fear of God is removed from our hearts by modern prophets and teachers. Born again believers begin with the very spirit of the fear of the LORD, being salted with the salt of the fear of God at birth (Eze 16:4). Yet soon they are taught the doctrines of men that teach them to NOT fear the LORD. By spiritual rebirth we were made children of promise and our fear ought to be the same as the fear of Isaac, yet we begin to have no fear of God. We become spoiled "through philosophy and vain deceit, after the tradition of men, after the rudiments of the world, and not after Christ." Col 2:8

God was the "fear of Isaac" (Gen 31:42,53), but is he *our* fear? "Now we, brethren, as Isaac was, are the children of promise." Gal 4:28 If we are children of promise as Isaac was, then God ought to be our fear as well! You ask, why should God be our fear if we are children of promise? Because Isaac knew, as we ought also to know, if God had not spared him, he would have been surely slain. If we had not been redeemed and forgiven, we would still be under the wrath of God, for we "were <u>by nature</u> the children of wrath" (Eph 2:3).

It is an evil and bitter thing to God that we have lost our fear of him. So God told Jeremiah of the backslidings of his own people how "*it is* an evil *thing* and bitter, that thou hast forsaken the LORD thy God, and <u>that my fear *is* not in thee</u>, saith the Lord GOD of hosts." Jer 2:19 Job warned his brethren who had dealt deceitfully with him because they had forsaken the fear of the Almighty (Job 6:14-15). Let the fear of God be in us. Let it not be lacking, let it not be forsaken or despised. Let us not come behind in this spiritual gift. Let it salt everything we do. The fear of the LORD is our highest duty, even as the conclusion of Ecclesiastes states (Ecc 12:13). John Bunyan, author of *Pilgrim's Progress* aptly stated that the fear of God is our "highest duty towards him".[123] Why does

---

[123] Bunyan, p. 2.

7 – The Door of Mercy to All Those who Fear the LORD

he call it our highest duty? "For there is no duty performed by us, that can by any means be accepted of God, if it be not seasoned with godly fear." It must be a part of everything spiritual that we do. Nothing we can do for God can be accepted by him without it.

The fear of the LORD is clean and enduring. It is what preserves our heart toward God and cleanses away our selfish desires and wants. It is what brings about the true intimacy that we desire with the Lord. The fear of God continually changes our direction by keeping us on track with his will. Without it, we will wander. With it, we will stay close to the Lord and his desire. Thus, the fear of the LORD will keep us faithfully serving him with a willing and single heart. Let us be devoted to this first work of the Spirit, this capstone of grace, the fear of God.

The fear of God must be involved in everything we do with and for the LORD. The fear of God must season all we do. Without this singular and most important attitude and preparation of the heart, nothing can be received by the LORD. He must reject any gift, any service, and any work which is not rendered unto him *with* and *in* godly fear.[124] Think on this: the fear of the LORD must precede even our obedience! "Let us hear the conclusion of the whole matter: Fear God, and keep his commandments: for this *is* the whole *duty* of man." Ecc 12:13 The obedience that is rendered in godly fear can be worked with by the LORD and received by him. The heart that fears is a heart that can be easily molded and shaped. We must fear God and then, and only then, can we keep his commandments and so fulfill the whole duty of man.

---

[124] See the section on 'A Servant's Heart' in the chapter entitled "The Way of Brokenness and God's Fear" in the book <u>Losing the Treasure of the Lord</u>.

Chapter 8. Replacing Our Many Fears with God's Singular Fear
Delivered from Fear by His Fear

"Fear not: for God is come to prove you, and that his fear may be before your faces" Ex 20:20

As the LORD does his heart surgery on us through the fear of God, his fear will increase in us. At the same time, all other fears will begin to lose their foothold and to fall away. All throughout scripture we see the command to "fear not" put side-by-side with the exhortation to "fear God". So we see Jesus tells us within 6 verses to 'fear not', 'fear him', and 'fear not' (Mt 10:26,28,31).

[1] ²⁶<u>Fear them not</u> therefore: ….
[2] ²⁸And <u>fear not them</u> which kill the body, but are not able to kill the soul:
[3] but <u>rather fear him</u> which is able to destroy both soul and body in hell.
[4] ³¹<u>Fear ye not</u> therefore, ye are of more value than many sparrows.

The first and second 'fear not' have to do with the fear of man (i.e. being afraid of what men can do to us). The fourth 'fear not' has to do with the fear of circumstances (i.e. being afraid of what may happen to us). The third 'fear' is what Jesus commands us to have, and it is to fear God. It is clear in not fearing, we must still have the fear of God. What is amazing about these verses, is that

8 – Replacing Our Many Fears with God's Singular Fear

though several different words for 'fear' in the Greek could have been used to distinguish the fear of man from the fear of God, yet only one Greek word is used in all of these verses.[125] Jesus himself is telling us, the way we fear and tremble and are afraid of men who can harm us and put us to death, is the *very* fear that we ought to have instead toward God Almighty. In fact, we should fear God much more because men can only kill our body. God, on the other hand, can not only put us to death, but can destroy both body and soul in hell! Indeed, as Jesus said, "<u>rather</u> fear him".

Natural fears and worries are to be eradicated in the life of the disciple as his trust and confidence in the Lord steadily grows and matures. We must learn to trust in the LORD with all our heart, and lean not on our own understanding (Pr 3:5-6).[126] It is time to stop leaning on our own understanding and see what is at the core of learning <u>how</u> not to fear so that we may trust in the LORD with all our heart. Consider the importance of the fear of God in this.

Jesus sets the fear of God at the very heart of knowing how not to fear men or circumstances. Jesus sandwiches, in the middle of these commands 'not to fear', the very command to fear God. It is impossible to be delivered from all our fears without the fear of the LORD possessing us. This is so clearly proven by David in Psalm 34. There he shares how the LORD delivered him from all his fears (v4), but then he goes on in the same psalm to extol the blessings of fearing the LORD (vv 7,9), and the last half of the psalm is dedicated to *teaching* us the fear of the LORD. "Come, ye children, hearken unto me: I will teach you the fear of the LORD." Ps 34:11

> Jesus himself is telling us, the way we fear and tremble
> and are afraid of men … is the *very* fear that
> we ought to have instead toward God Almighty.

At first it may seem almost schizophrenic or double-minded: we are not to fear, but we are to fear. Yet even our great hymns of the church acknowledge this: 'Twas grace that taught my heart to fear, And grace my fears relieved."[127] This is no different than God's instructions to not worship any other god, but to worship him as the true God. This is the preeminence of the Lord. He demands all our worship and should be our only fear. This is how different the fear of God is from any other fear. Natural fears are like the gods of this world; they may be real to us, but in fact are only false idols that must be cast out of

---

[125] The word used for 'fear' in these verses is *phobeo* (G5399) which means 'to *frighten*, i.e. to *be alarmed*'.

[126] Those who regularly read the Bible know Proverbs 3:5-6, yet it is often a continual struggle and rarely a reality.

[127] From the song *Amazing Grace*.

our heart. Natural fears will keep us from the true fear of God, even as idolatry keeps us from worshipping the true God.

The one thing we are to fear is the LORD. We are not to fear "death, nor life, nor angels, nor principalities, nor powers, nor things present, nor things to come, Nor height, nor depth, nor any other creature" (Rom 8:39). Neither man, nor the wicked, nor the future, nor even the unknown should cause us to be possessed with fear. But the might, power, name, word, judgments, and presence of the LORD, these ought to cause us to be possessed with fear, the fear of God. He desires only one fear to be before our faces, as he told those of the Exodus: <u>his fear</u>! We should fear nothing but God. That is sufficient. No other fears are needful or helpful. "Fear not: ... that <u>his fear</u> may be before your faces" (Ex 20:20). All other fears get in the way of the clean and enduring fear of God. Let us take a moment to consider what exactly we are not to fear.

What Not to Fear

*"Fear not: for God is come to prove you,
and that his fear may be before your faces, that ye sin not." Ex 20:20*

The establishing of God's covenant with his people has always been predicated on being set free from our enemies and that which binds us (i.e. the bondages of sin), so that we might serve God <u>without fear</u>. The opening chapter of Luke's gospel declares this. "That he would grant unto us, that we being delivered out of the hand of our enemies might serve him <u>without fear</u>" (Lk 1:74). We are free in our service of the Lord under the new covenant from the fear of our enemies. We are in the hand of the Lord and no man and no demon nor evil spirit can touch us, not even Satan himself, for "he that is begotten of God [i.e. *he who is born again*] keepeth himself, and that wicked one toucheth him not." 1Jn 5:18 We do not need to look back at past sins that are covered in the blood and worry if we will be punished for them. These have been wiped clean and forgotten by the LORD.

Neither do we fear God's retribution, <u>but</u> as a child fears their parent we still must fear the LORD's displeasure and his discipline. This is where most teachers of the word of God err in their understanding of the fear of God. For knowing that in Christ Jesus we are not under the wrath of God they are sure we needn't fear his anger. Indeed, we have been delivered, and are no longer children of wrath (Eph 2:3). This the scriptures repeatedly attest to:

> being now justified by his blood, we shall be saved <u>from wrath</u> through him. Rom 5:9
>
> *even* Jesus, which delivered us from the wrath to come. 1Th 1:10
>
> For God hath not appointed us to wrath, but to obtain salvation by our Lord Jesus Christ 1Th 5:9

8 – Replacing Our Many Fears with God's Singular Fear

Let us return again to Exodus 20:20, where God desired to put his fear before the face of all his people. At the same time he told them "Fear not." What was the fear that the Exodus people had to *not* fear? It was this fear: that if God speaks with us we will not be able to bear it and we will die. Notice the verse immediately before verse 20. "And they said unto Moses, Speak thou with us, and we will hear: but let not God speak with us, <u>lest we die</u>." Ex 20:19 This should testify powerfully to us of the utterly inconceivable majesty of his presence and the effect that it has on the soul. Many a man of God fell as if dead before the presence of the Almighty, but not one of them died because he had spoken to them. Remember, if God speaks to us it is for the purpose of life – even when it is for rebuke and correction. If we are truly his people abiding in the fear of God which we know is a fountain of life (Pr 14:27), then there can be no death in his presence – except the death of all other concerns, the death of self and being self-absorbed, and the death of our will. In the presence of God there is only one concern, one focus of attention, GOD – in his awesome presence, **he** is all-absorbing.

The fear of God and natural fears cannot peacefully coexist. Either our natural fears will keep us from having his fear, *or* his fear will drive out all other fears. Think how strange it is for David in Psalm 34, which is dedicated to teaching us the fear of God, to declare, "I sought the LORD, and he heard me, and <u>delivered me from all **my** fears</u>." Ps 34:4 David declares with praise the deliverance he had received from the LORD. He is exceedingly exultant about the deliverance he has received, but what was this deliverance? Verse 4 shows it was that he was delivered from <u>all</u> his fears. Yet right after declaring that he has been delivered from <u>all</u> his fears, he declares that this same deliverance is available to anyone who will fear God! Hear how David exhorts us all to be delivered from all our fears by the fear of the LORD.

> The angel of the LORD encampeth round about <u>them that fear him</u>, and **delivereth** them. O taste and see that the LORD *is* good: blessed *is* the man *that* trusteth in him. <u>O fear the LORD, ye his saints</u>: for *there is* no want to <u>them that fear him</u>. Ps 34:7-9

> The fear of God and natural fears cannot peacefully coexist.
> Either our natural fears will keep us from having his fear,
> *or* his fear will drive out all other fears.

As a result, David now begins to teach us the fear of the LORD. "Come, ye children, hearken unto me: I will teach you the fear of the LORD." Ps 34:11 It is clear to David, that when he says the LORD delivered him from all his fears, that that ALL did not include the fear of the LORD. How can this be? God's fear is distinctly separate from all other fears in David's mind, as it should be in ours. It is in a category all by itself. It is in fact, *not* one of our fears, but as we have shown already, it is his fear. The fear of God is as different as heavenly wisdom is different than earthly wisdom, and divine love from natural love.

The Idolatry of Other Fears versus the One Fear

Our fears are so real to us, at times we feel we can almost touch them. At times they seem so real that they seem to be alive inside us. Psychology wants us to acknowledge these fears as real. Biblical truth wants to dispel them. Man's way of thinking is to talk about them. God's ways are to take them captive and to bring them into obedience to the Word of God. Psychiatry says we need to cope with our fears. God says to deny them. Man in his wisdom would scorn and rebuke anyone who told someone who was fearful "not to be afraid." Yet this is exactly what our God commands us to do. "Be not afraid … <u>of whom ye are afraid</u>; be not afraid of him, saith the LORD: for I *am* with you to save you, and to deliver you from his hand." Jer 42:11 Did you hear that? God tells us to stop being afraid of whom we are afraid of, because of who he, the LORD, is.

Let us put Jeremiah 42:11 in context, for it is even more powerful when considering who this particular person was that they were afraid of, whom God told them *not* to be afraid of! Note what God says to the very real fear of a world ruler coming to destroy Jerusalem. "<u>Be not afraid</u> of the king of Babylon, **of whom ye are afraid**; <u>be not afraid of him</u>, saith the LORD: for I *am* with you to save you, and to deliver you from his hand." Jer 42:11 God pits our fears of the most powerful ruler or force on earth against the power and security of his deliverance. This is the revelation that David came to. In the midst of glorifying God for his deliverance from all his fears, David now turns to us to teach us the fear of God. This shows that David saw the key to being delivered from all our fears was the direct result of fearing the true God. This is proven in another psalm where, because of the fear of God, David could say "I will not fear".

> Let them now <u>that fear the LORD</u> say, that his mercy *endureth* for ever. I called upon the LORD in distress: the LORD answered me, *and set me* in a large place. The LORD *is* on my side; <u>I will not fear</u>: what can man do unto me? Ps 118:4-6

A comparison is needed to understand the true nature of our fears, and why there can only be one fear for us. We have been given one heart and one way, so that we may have one fear: the fear of God (Jer 32:39). We can be so enveloped in our own consuming fears, that we no longer see them in their proper light and perspective as the vapors of mist that they really are. On the contrary, now that we have been delivered from the god of this world and have been brought into the kingdom of God's dear son, it is easy for us to see that there are many false gods in this world – none of which are to mean anything to us any more.

> we know that an idol *is* **nothing** in the world, and that *there is* **none other God but one**. For though there be that are called gods,

8 – Replacing Our Many Fears with God's Singular Fear

whether in heaven or in earth, (as there be gods many, and lords many,) But <u>to us *there is but* one God</u> 1Co 8:4-6

Prior to the revelation of truth that comes through the new birth, the mind of the unsaved are blinded by the god of this world (2Co 4:4). In that blindness, many believe in the reality of what, in truth, are false gods. There be many that are called gods today, but there is only one true God. Now that we are saved, we know that all other gods are false gods. The same is true of natural fears. There be many that are called fears today,[128] but to us there ought to be but one fear, the fear of God! Just as there are false gods, but one true God, so there are false fears, but one true fear, the fear of God. Thus, when we give credence to our fears and allow them to rule even part of our life, it is a form of idolatry.

Eradicating the Fear of Man
"In the fear of the LORD is <u>strong confidence</u>:
and his children shall have a place of refuge." Pr 14:26

The fear of man is repeatedly dealt with in the scripture, because it can capture and paralyze men, preventing them from obeying the LORD. The Bible says, "The fear of man bringeth <u>a snare</u>: but whoso putteth his trust in the LORD shall be safe." Pr 29:25 The fear of man brings people into disobedience. The scripture records for us repeatedly that the Pharisees feared the people,[129] yet they did not fear God, even when he stood before them! They continually disobeyed the scriptures in many ways, but most significantly by continually trying to put men of God to death.[130] King Saul, after being caught by the prophet of God in his disobedience to the command of God, confessed, "I have sinned: for I have transgressed the commandment of the LORD, and thy words: <u>because I feared the people</u>, and obeyed their voice." 1Sam 15:24 The fear of man will always cause us to transgress God's commandments and to offer up partial obedience, which cannot please God.

Sometimes our departing from God is the direct result of our fears. With earthly fears (from our perspective) what we fear is what we try to avoid and to keep from having any contact with. Yet, from others' perspective it is clear that our fears, instead of being far from us, actually control us. Our fears literally master and rule over our choices, our actions, and our reasonings. The more we

---

[128] We have every phobia imaginable (at last count, that I have seen, there are over 650!) and more are being invented each year. This is yet another sign of the last days: "Men's hearts failing them <u>for fear</u>, and for looking after those things which are coming on the earth" (Lk 21:26).

[129] The fear of the people: Mt 21:26, Mk 11:18,32, Lk 20:19, 22:2.

[130] They sought to put Jesus to death repeatedly: Jn 5:18, 7:1,19,25, 8:37,40, 11:53, Mk 3:6, 11:18, 14:1, Mt 12:14, 26:4,59, 27:1,20, Lk 19:47, 22:2. They also sought to put to death John the Baptist (Mt 14:5) and even Lazarus (Jn 12:10).

try to run from our fears, the more we run directly into their control. Sadly, this is not a problem for unbelievers only. It can actually be more prevalent in children of God than in children of the devil.

A very tragic time in David's life was brought about because he gave place to his natural fears. David's fears led him to leave the covenanted promised land and to go right into the hand of the Philistines (which represents the dwelling place of the flesh). Why would David do this? Because he feared Saul and despaired of God's continued deliverance. Thus, he reasoned it out in his own mind.[131]

> And David said in his heart, I shall now perish one day by the hand of Saul: *there is* nothing better for me than that I should speedily escape into the land of the Philistines; and Saul shall despair of me, to seek me any more in any coast of Israel: so shall I escape out of his hand. 1Sam 27:1

David felt there was nothing better for him to do. Many costly errors are made by the saints when they are brought to the place of being emptied out, and they can see no other way but to take things into their own hands. When we go by only what we can see, then we have left the spiritual realm and entered the natural. We are walking by sight, not by faith. Make no mistake, friend, we cannot escape from our fears by fleeing from them. In fact, we end up running right into their arms. We think we can be delivered from our fears by avoiding contact with them and fleeing. But God himself will ensure that we come face to face with every one of our fears, for he is a jealous God and refuses to allow us to be mastered by something else. He alone wants to be the master of us – the LORD supreme.

> The fear of man will always cause us to transgress God's commandments and to offer up partial obedience, which cannot please God.

We must learn how to conquer our fears. God has called his children to be overcomers.[132] Amazingly, this natural reasoning came in David's life *immediately after* God had just miraculously delivered him for the third straight time from Saul. Thus, even the power of God's miraculous deliverances cannot keep us from being enslaved by our fears. We must learn to master them by growing in the fear of God. As Psalm 34 shows, the fear of God is the primary means by which God delivers us from our fears.

---

[131] Biblically, the mind can be shown to be a part of the heart.

[132] 7 times to 7 churches, the Spirit of God calls each to be **overcomers**: Rev 2:7, 2:11, 2:17, 2:26, 3:5, 3:12, 3:21.

8 – Replacing Our Many Fears with God's Singular Fear

Those who Stood Against the Fear of Man

We have some notable exceptions of men who, when faced with the fear of man, refused to give it place. In each case it was because of who they knew God to be. Consider Amos the prophet. Amaziah, a priest, spoke evilly of him and falsely accused him to the king. "Amaziah the priest of Bethel sent to Jeroboam king of Israel, saying, Amos hath conspired against thee in the midst of the house of Israel: the land is not able to bear all his words." Am 7:10 Amos was not moved by this treachery. He would not change what he had spoken or forsake his calling. When Amaziah told him to prophesy no more, Amos does not answer about who *he* was, but who the LORD was.

> Then answered Amos, and said to Amaziah, I *was* no prophet, neither *was* I a prophet's son; but I *was* an herdman, and a gatherer of sycomore fruit: And the LORD took me as I followed the flock, and the LORD said unto me, Go, prophesy unto my people Israel. Am 7:14-5

Amos was under a mandate from God. That settled it. No matter what man threatened, he was under the dread of the LORD to do what he had been called to do. As he himself records, "The lion hath roared, **who will not fear**? the Lord GOD hath spoken, who can but prophesy?" Am 3:8 Similarly, Jeremiah overcame the fear of man through the fear of God. He had prophesied of judgment in the courts of the LORD, yet the people were ready to kill him for it.

> Now it came to pass, when Jeremiah had made an end of speaking all that the LORD had commanded *him* to speak unto all the people, that the priests and the prophets and all the people took him, saying, Thou shalt surely die. Then spake the priests and the prophets unto the princes and to all the people, saying, This man *is* worthy to die; for he hath prophesied against this city, as ye have heard with your ears. Jer 26:8,11

Jeremiah's response, like Amos', focused not on who he was, but on who had sent him.

> Then spake Jeremiah unto all the princes and to all the people, saying, The LORD sent me to prophesy against this house and against this city all the words that ye have heard. ... As for me, behold, I *am* in your hand: do with me as seemeth good and meet unto you. But know ye for certain, that if ye put me to death, ye shall surely bring innocent blood upon yourselves, and upon this city, and upon the inhabitants thereof: for of a truth the LORD hath sent me unto you to speak all these words in your ears. Jer 26:12-15

So that we are sure not to miss the point that it is the fear of God driving out the fear of man, the book of Jeremiah continues with a contrasting story of another prophet of God. This other prophet of God is named Urijah, whose name means *flame of Jah*. When faced with the same temptation as Jeremiah of being threatened by man, Urijah fled in fear to try to save his life. Urijah ended up losing the battle in his soul to the fear of man, and ultimately lost his own life as well. Urijah was hunted down to where he had fled, brought back for judgment, and put to a shameful death. Please read his story in Jeremiah 26:20-23. Think of the dishonor that is rendered to the Lord to die this way in fear, when our forerunner himself would not flee the fear of death (Lk 13:31-33). This is why in the hall of faith those whom God has honored were those who "were tortured, not accepting deliverance; that they might obtain a better resurrection" (Heb 11:35).

> The fear of man is a powerful weapon of the enemy to shame God's servant and to make him useless. We can give no quarter to it. It must be fought and eradicated.

As Jesus warns us all, "Whosoever shall seek to save his life shall lose it; and whosoever shall lose his life shall preserve it." Lk 17:33 Jeremiah lost his life, and God saved it, while Urijah sought to save his life, and he lost it. Evil tidings will come to all of our ears through men, but we must learn to have our heart be fixed on what the LORD is saying for us to do, and not on how men would try to control us. "Praise ye the LORD. Blessed *is* the man *that* feareth the LORD, *that* delighteth greatly in his commandments. He shall not be afraid of evil tidings: his heart is fixed, trusting in the LORD." Ps 112:1,7 It is when, in the fear of God that we hold fast to his commands and delight greatly in them, that we will not be afraid of evil tidings, and our heart will be fixed and established. As we have seen with Urijah, the fear of man is a powerful weapon of the enemy to shame God's servant and to make him useless. We can give no quarter to it. It must be fought and eradicated.

As great a man as Elijah the prophet was, yet in his greatest hour of victory over the prophets of Baal and Ashtoreth, he failed! Why? Because he gave place to the fear of man. The people on Mount Carmel had witnessed the awesome hand of God to consume by heavenly fire Elijah's water-logged offering. "And when all the people saw *it,* they fell on their faces: and they said, The LORD, he *is* the God; the LORD, he *is* the God." 1K 18:39 At that time Elijah had the prophets of Baal (which were 450) and the prophets of the groves (which were 400) which ate at Jezebel's table, all put to death.[133] After a 3½ year drought, the rain was restored at the word of Elijah. Elijah even outran Ahab's chariot because "the hand of the LORD was on Elijah" (1K 18:46). It was the time set by God for revival and teaching the people the ways of the LORD again. Yet at the threatening of but one person, Jezebel, the wife of Ahab, Elijah flees for his life (1K 19:2-3). His whole witness of standing fearless against Jezebel was now

---

[133] See 1K 18:19-20,40, 19:1.

compromised, and the people immediately went back into hiding. And for this, Elijah's ministry is virtually over (except to transfer his anointing to Elisha).[134]

Nehemiah was another who had to confront the fear of man and who overcame it through the fear of God. A false prophet came and warned him that others were seeking to kill him, that he needed to save his life (Neh 6:10). Other false prophets also tried to put him in fear (v14). Nehemiah refused to give into the fear of man, because of the work he was called to do and his dedication as a servant to be serving the call of God. "Should such a man as I flee? and who *is there*, that, *being* as I *am*, would go into the temple to save his life? I will not go in." Neh 6:11

What was it that ruled Nehemiah's life, enabling him not to be moved by the fear of man? It was the fear of God. By the fear of God, Nehemiah was able to put away the paralyzing fear of man and to overcome it. As he says earlier, "so did not I, because of the fear of God." Neh 5:15 Nehemiah himself was that servant who desired to fear the name of God (Neh 1:11). As he exhorted others, so did he, "It *is* not good that ye do: ought ye not to walk in the fear of our God?" Neh 5:9

We are Commanded Not to Fear

Over 90 times in the scripture we are commanded to "fear not" or "be not afraid". If we search these out in the scriptures,[135] we see the consistent reason always centers around who God is and what **he** will do. The scriptures reveal the awesomeness of God, and so instill in us (if our heart is soft) the fear of God. The fear of God always drives out the fear of man. "So that we may boldly say, <u>The Lord</u> *is* my helper, and I will not fear what man shall do unto me." Heb 13:6 Every generation has been instructed not to fear anything but God, from the time of the patriarchs, to those of the Exodus, to the Judges (including Samuel), to those under the kings, those under the prophets, on down to Jesus' day, even down to the end of time (Revelation).[136]

---

[134] All we see of Elijah after this is (1) his proclamation of the judgment of death upon Ahab and Jezebel for killing and taking Naboth's vineyard (1K 21:17-24), (2) the proclamation of the judgment of death upon the king of Samaria for not going to the LORD for counsel but to Baal-zebub, (3) the king's vain attempt to capture Elijah (2K 1:3-4,9-14), and then (4) his ascension into heaven (2K 2). These all anticipate the end of Elijah's ministry and the beginning of Elisha's.

[135] See the appendix entitled "The Scriptures on Fearing God" in the section 'Scriptures on Not Fearing'.

[136] Thus, we see Abraham, Hagar, Isaac, Jacob, and the sons of Jacob; Moses, Joshua, and the generation of their children; David, Solomon, Jehoshaphat, … etc. ; Isaiah, Jeremiah, Joel, Zechariah, … etc.; and Zacharias, Mary, the shepherds, and those who listened to Jesus' preaching.

Why should we 'fear not' according to the scriptures? Because the LORD has promised to be our shield and our exceeding great reward. Because he hears our cry, because he *is* with us, because he fights for us against our enemies to save us, because he *will* be with us, because he will not fail us, nor forsake us, because he is the LORD our God, because it hath pleased him to make us his people, because he has promised to help us, because he redeemed us and called us by name and chose us, because we are his, because as our King he is coming, and because he is the first and the last. For all this and so much more, we have reason enough *not* to fear anything or anyone but him.

So we read in God's book of wisdom, "In the fear of the LORD *is* <u>strong confidence</u>: and his children shall have a place of refuge. The fear of the LORD *is* a fountain of life, to depart from the snares of death." Pr 14:26-27 So Jeremiah, in the fear of the LORD, departed from the snares of death. So also Nehemiah, as well as others like Hananiah, Mishael, and Azariah who feared God more than they feared the king (Dan 3). The fear of the LORD will give us a strength of refuge so that we can stand in the will of God and not be moved by the threatenings of any man – no matter whether we live or die, for our life is no longer our own.

What to Fear
"But I will forewarn you whom ye shall fear" Lk 12:5

Every sensible child **knows** to fear the anger of their father. Can we be so foolish to believe that God is not truly angered with open disobedience and defiance, especially when it is in his own children? We ought to fear, if we walk in willful disobedience and put away the conviction that would draw us to repentance through the acknowledgement of the truth. Jesus is the way, the truth, and the life. Therefore, how can we enter into eternal *life*, if we forsake the narrow *way* of the kingdom that leads us in *truth*, and if we forsake truth by putting away a good conscience? God requires that we depart from iniquity. Though we have such great promises of his mercy and grace, "<u>Nevertheless</u> the foundation of God standeth sure, having this seal, The Lord knoweth them that are his. And, Let every one that nameth the name of Christ depart from iniquity." 2Tim 2:19 Those who refuse in this life to depart from their iniquity, Jesus will openly declare he never knew them, and he will command them to depart from him. "And then will I profess unto them, I never knew you: depart from me, ye that work iniquity."[137] Mt 7:23

Is God angry with his children when they walk in disobedience? The scripture shows that God is indeed angry in these cases, even with his closest ser-

---

[137] Remember, these are those who confessed the Lord, saying "Lord, Lord" and who recognized him!

8 – Replacing Our Many Fears with God's Singular Fear

vants, such as Moses, David, Solomon, Uzzah, Peter, James, and John.[138] Why else does Paul say in reference to being subject to the higher powers (i.e. authorities) of whom God is certainly the highest, "Wherefore *ye* must needs be subject, not only <u>for wrath</u>, but also for conscience sake." Rom 13:5 We are to be subject to authority (of which God is the highest and the source), first and foremost, says Paul, because of *wrath*! Can we strip God, as the highest authority, of his rightful wrath? No. Paul also says to these same born again Romans,

> But after <u>thy</u> hardness and impenitent heart treasurest up unto <u>thyself</u> **wrath** against the day of **wrath** and revelation of the righteous judgment of God; Who will render to <u>every man</u> according to his deeds: To them who by patient continuance in well doing seek for glory and honour and immortality, eternal life: But unto them that are contentious, and do not obey the truth, but obey unrighteousness, **indignation and wrath**, Tribulation and anguish, upon every soul of man that doeth evil, of the Jew first, and also of the Gentile; But glory, honour, and peace, to every man that worketh good, to the Jew first, and also to the Gentile: For there is no respect of persons with God. Rom 2:5-11

Serving with Fear and without Fear

How can we serve God *without* fear, yet serve him *with* fear? The same way the New Testament church did. They fulfilled the promise of Luke 1:70-75 of serving God without fear, yet they still had God's fear working in them, and it was not just in a few, it was in all. "Fear came upon <u>every</u> soul" (Ac 2:43) of the believers after Pentecost. "And great fear came upon <u>all the church</u>" (Ac 5:11) after the judgment of God slew Ananias and Sapphira for lying to the Holy Ghost. Consider this, though the blood of Christ had covered the sins of Ananias and Sapphira they had committed prior to salvation and after, yet it could not cover when they lied to the Holy Ghost by denying the truth.

Remember, it is the work of the Holy Ghost to bring us to the conviction of sin (Jn 16:7-8), that we might in acknowledging the truth confess and repent and recover ourselves out of the snare of the devil (2Tim 2:25-26). Was this fear that came upon the whole church not what God wanted? Or was it in fact ex-

---

[138] Of Moses it is written, "And the anger of the LORD was kindled against Moses" (Ex 4:14). Of David it is written, "And God was displeased with this thing [*that David had done*]" (1Ch 21:7). Of Solomon, "And the LORD was angry with Solomon, because his heart was turned from the LORD God of Israel, which had appeared unto him twice" (1K 11:9). Of Uzzah, "And the anger of the Lord was kindled against Uzzah; and God smote him there for *his* error; and there he died by the ark of God." 2Sam 6:7 Jesus was clearly angry with Peter when he said unto him, "Get thee behind me, Satan: thou art an offence unto me: for thou savourest not the things that be of God, but those that be of men." Mt 16:23 Jesus was clearly angry with James and John when he rebuked them, saying, "Ye know not what manner of spirit ye are of." Lk 9:55

actly what was needed? Consider how important the presence of the fear of God is in the saints. Paul commands Timothy regarding those who would heedlessly bring up unfounded accusations against those in authority to be publicly reproved: "Them that sin rebuke before all, that others also may fear." The purpose of such public correction was for this very reason, that false accusers and whomever sides with them in the same disrespect for authority would regain the fear of God.

The writer of Hebrews calls to our attention that we **know** God judges his own people. "For we know him that hath said, Vengeance *belongeth* unto me, I will recompense, saith the Lord. And again, The Lord shall judge his people. *It is* a fearful thing to fall into the hands of the living God." Heb 10:31 This is something everyone who knows God should know, that the Lord *shall* judge his people. So then since God *does* judge his people as the scripture says,[139] how do we as God's covenant people escape the paralyzing anxiety that we are ready at any moment to be consumed by his anger? Exactly how John tells us: by the love of God. His love bears long with sin, but it does not excuse it. He is not quick to be angry, but is slow to anger. Psalms lets us know that the LORD *is* merciful and gracious, and full of compassion; slow to anger, and of great mercy (Ps 103:8, 145:8). He hates iniquity (Heb 1:9), yet is "a God ready to pardon, gracious and merciful, slow to anger, and of great kindness, and forsookest them not." Neh 9:17 In his anger he does not forsake us, but he waits for us to turn in repentance.

> And therefore will the LORD wait, that he may be gracious unto you, and therefore will he be exalted, that he may have mercy upon you: for the LORD *is* a God of judgment: blessed *are* all they that wait for him. Isa 30:18

> Therefore also now, saith the LORD, turn ye *even* to me with all your heart, and with fasting, and with weeping, and with mourning: And rend your heart, and not your garments, and turn unto the LORD your God: for he *is* gracious and merciful, slow to anger, and of great kindness, and repenteth him of the evil. Joel 2:12-13

Being Delivered from Our Fears through the Fear of God

In order to truly serve the Lord and him only we must be delivered from our natural fears. David shows us that we must desperately cry out to be delivered from all our fears. "I sought the LORD, and he heard me, and delivered me from all my fears." Ps 34:4 When God delivers us from our fears, we will also be delivered from the bondage of what we served in those fears. "And it shall come to pass in the day that the LORD shall give thee rest from thy sorrow, and from thy fear, and from the hard bondage wherein thou wast made to serve"

---

[139] See also Ps 135:14, Dt 32:36, 1Pe 4:17, Ps 7:8, 50:4, Isa 3:14.

8 – Replacing Our Many Fears with God's Singular Fear

(Isa 14:3). This is the joyful liberty of being set free from our fears. This is why Psalm 34 which documents David's great deliverance from all his fears is a great psalm of rejoicing.

> I will bless the LORD at all times: his praise *shall* continually *be* in my mouth. My soul shall make her boast in the LORD: the humble shall hear *thereof,* and be glad. O magnify the LORD with me, and let us exalt his name together. Ps 34:1-3

If we are to overcome the fear of man, we must have a strong faith, trust, and hope in the LORD God. Notice how the fear of man is put in direct contrast with our trust in God.

> The fear of man bringeth a snare: but whoso putteth his <u>trust in the LORD</u> shall be safe. Pr 29:25
>
> <u>In God have I put my trust</u>: I will not be afraid what man can do unto me. Ps 56:11

We are told by faith teachers today that faith is the opposite of fear. They say that we should be moved by faith, and our faith should move mountains. Rarely, if ever, will they speak of the fear of the LORD. Yet faith and the fear of God actually work together to perfect us. Our faith is to cooperate with the fear of God. We tend to think that the one who fears God is *not* walking in the righteousness of faith, yet as Hebrews 11:7 shows us, it is by being *moved* with fear that we become heirs of the righteousness which is by faith. No wonder in our fearless Christian thinking, our faith is so crippled – because it is devoid of the fear of God.

True faith, in fact, must be rooted in the fear of God. If faith only springs out of the love of God, eventually it will be disappointed, for we will not perceive the love of God many times in what is taking place in our life. Only the fear of God can make our faith in his word steadfast, secure, and unshakeable. Only the fear of God can justify God in all situations. Then, no matter what God takes us through, whether it be pleasant and joyful, or difficult and sorrowful, we will have a faith in him that is not waylaid by trials or troubles. But God cannot deliver us from our fears until he becomes our chief and foremost fear. This is why we must cry out to be brought into the fear of God. We must be those "who <u>desire</u> to fear thy name" (Neh 1:11) and pray toward that end. Notice repeatedly how in the very context of fearing God, we find our deliverance. God promises deliverance from our enemies, if we fear the living God.

> But the LORD your God <u>ye shall fear</u>; and he shall <u>deliver you</u> out of the hand of all your enemies. 2K 17:39
>
> Behold, the eye of the LORD *is* upon <u>them that fear him</u>, upon them that hope in his mercy; <u>To deliver</u> their soul from death, and to keep them alive in famine. Ps 33:18-19
>
> The angel of the LORD encampeth round about <u>them that fear him</u>, and <u>delivereth them</u>. Ps 34:7

If we only understood the fear of God properly, we would not have the fear of man, rather we would have a strong confidence in our God (Pr 14:26). The LORD is so sure that we should have *no* fear of man that he is utterly shocked and taken aback at such groundless fear! God wonders why we do not fear him, the eternal God, yet we fear mortal men who will pass away.

> And <u>of whom</u> hast thou been afraid or feared, that thou hast lied, and hast not remembered me, nor laid *it* to thy heart? have not I held my peace even of old, and <u>thou fearest me not</u>? Isa 57:11

God declares when we fear man and do not fear him that we make three great mistakes. First, we lie against the truth that we say we believe in – which is that God is greater than all. Second, in our thoughts and in our plans we forget God because of our earthly fear. Third, afterwards we do not truly consider the error and mistakes that we have done. This is the enslaving of our heart and the blinding of our eyes toward God that the fear of man brings.

When we consider who God is and what he has done and what he promises still to do for them that fear him, we have no grounds for the fear of man, and no grounds for fearing what man can do to us. When the fear of God lays hold of a man's heart, it will deliver him from the fear of man. Hear what the psalmist says, "I will <u>not fear</u>: what can man do unto me?" Once we see God in proper perspective, then who is man that we should fear him? For this reason, God tells Jeremiah, at the very beginning of his ministry, not to be afraid of those who would despise the word of the LORD. "Be not afraid of their faces: for I *am* with thee to deliver thee, saith the LORD." Jer 1:8

> It's either the fear of God or the fear of man
> that will possess your heart. You choose.

God instructed the judges of old not to fear men because judgment does not belong to any man, but to the LORD: "ye shall not be afraid of the face of man; for the judgment *is* God's" (Dt 1:17). Jesus similarly gives us a stern warning in the gospels, concerning whom we should fear and whom we should not fear. What is Jesus' basis for this warning of whom we fear? It is based on who we will stand before in judgment!

> And I say unto you my friends, Be <u>not afraid</u> of them that kill the body, and after that have no more that they can do. But I will forewarn you whom ye shall fear: <u>Fear him</u>, which after he hath killed hath power to cast into hell; yea, I say unto you, <u>Fear him</u>. Lk 12:4-5

The judgment day changes everything – for if we truly know God, we will know the terror of the Lord that is found at his judgment seat (2Co 5:10-11). So Jesus warns us *beforehand* whom we should fear. Jesus wants us to know <u>before</u> that great and terrible day of the Lord, whom we should fear. Matthew's ac-

8 – Replacing Our Many Fears with God's Singular Fear

count mentions that God "is able to destroy both soul and body in hell." Mt 10:28 Jesus makes eminently clear that fearing God is inconsistent with fearing man. We will either have the fear of God and no fear of man, or we will lose our fear of God and be ruled by the fear of man. It's either the fear of God or the fear of man that will possess your heart. You choose.

Chapter 9. Trust and True Faith Through Our Fear of the LORD
Walking by Faith in the Fear of God

"Then had the churches rest throughout all Judaea and Galilee and Samaria, and were edified; and walking in the fear of the Lord, and in the comfort of the Holy Ghost, were multiplied." Ac 9:31

The Faith of God & the Fear of God Growing Together
"thou standest by faith. Be not highminded, but fear" Rom 11:20

    Though natural fears ought to decrease year by year as we grow in trust and confidence in the Lord, the fear of God ought to increase year by year as we grow in intimacy, transparency, and honesty with him. This is because the fear of God births true trust and confidence and makes the securest refuge for us. "In the fear of the LORD *is* strong <u>confidence</u>: and his children shall have a place of <u>refuge</u>. The fear of the LORD *is* a fountain of life, to depart from the snares of death." Pr 14:26-27 The fear of the LORD is our strong confidence and our place of refuge. There is a strong confidence that can only come from the fear of the LORD. This confident strength in God through the fear of the

9 – Trust and True Faith Through Our Fear of the LORD

LORD is '*a refuge*, a *security*, an *assurance*', not only in our life, but also in the life of our children who observe us.

So many times we desire to show our faith and trust in the Lord, but our words are often negated by our natural fears. But as others see our life lived with the fear of God, they will see that we fear nothing, but him. It is this fearlessness through the fear of God that causes our children to have a place of refuge. The fear of the LORD in our hearts produces a continual stream of contented life. It does this through this refuge (i.e. the security and assurance it produces), so that our contentment in the Lord becomes a fountain of life which turns us away from the snares of death (i.e. from iniquity).

Without the fear of God we will be unable to trust in the LORD at all times. Fear not man and fear not the uncertainty of the future, *but* fear the LORD. The LORD questions all of us why we fear man, but don't fear him. "And of whom hast thou been afraid or feared, that thou hast lied, and hast not remembered me, nor laid *it* to thy heart? have not I held my peace even of old, and thou fearest me not?" Isa 57:11 Here we see God's law of action and reaction. When we fear man, we will not fear God. When we fear God, we will not fear man. It is because we do not remember or keep in mind who the LORD is that we fear men and forget to fear God. Thus, it is the lack of knowing the true God that explains our lack of the fear of God. The more we know him in truth according to the scriptures the more we will fear him.

All new covenant believers are partakers of the covenant of Abraham. But often we do not consider how this covenant was established, as God said, because "now I know that thou fearest God" (Gen 22:12). We cannot say Abraham did not live by faith or did not walk by faith, for he, according to the scripture, is the very *father* of faith (Rom 4:11-18). If we are to learn anything concerning faith, we ought to learn it from the *father* of faith. Abraham has been set for us as an example of faith. The 7 perfect principles of faith described in Romans 4 are all concerning Abraham's life.

And Abraham's son Isaac, the son of the covenant, the child of promise as Galatians 4:28 says, so feared God that God was known as his fear: "the God of my father, the God of Abraham, and the fear of Isaac" (Gen 31:42, also v53). We also see Joseph, who was a type of Christ in the Old Testament and who trusted God greatly, saying, "I fear God" (Gen 42:18). If we believe that we stand by faith along with the saints of old, we do well, for they believed in the LORD and feared him. But if we think we are above them and have a greater faith, a faith that delivers us from the fear of God, then we would do well to heed Paul's warning to "Be not highminded, but fear".

> Boast not against the branches. But if thou boast, thou bearest not the root, but the root thee. Thou wilt say then, The branches were broken off, that I might be graffed in. Well; because of unbelief they were broken off, and thou standest by faith. Be not highminded, but

fear: For if God spared not the natural branches, *take heed* lest he also spare not thee. Behold therefore the goodness and severity of God: on them which fell, severity; but toward thee, goodness, if thou continue in *his* goodness: otherwise thou also shalt be cut off. Rom 11:18-22

We subtly boast over the Old Testament saints because we believe our faith is greater than theirs, thinking that our faith is complete and theirs incomplete. We believe this because through the gospel we know we have:

- a better hope (Heb 7:19),
- a better testament (Heb 7:22),
- a better covenant based on better promises (Heb 8:6),
- better sacrifices (Heb 9:23), and
- better and enduring substance in heaven (Heb 10:34).

Therefore, why would not our faith be better? What do we have to boast over them? That we believe, having *seen*, when they believed, having not seen? "Jesus saith unto him, Thomas, because thou hast seen me, thou hast believed: blessed *are* they that have not seen, and *yet* have believed." Jn 20:29 "What then? are we **better** *than they?* No, in no wise" (Rom 3:9). Our faith, in the new covenant, in reality is not greater than that of the Old, but actually lesser. They did not see revealed the things which we are privileged to see in Jesus, yet they believed. They longed to see the things which we see, for they did not see Jesus, "But we see Jesus" (Heb 2:9). Jesus declared to his disciples, "Blessed *are* the eyes which see the things that ye see: For I tell you, that many prophets and kings have desired to see those things which ye see, and have not seen *them;* and to hear those things which ye hear, and have not heard *them.*" Lk 10:23-24 (also Mt 13:16-17)

Yet, the gospel is eternal (Rev 14:6). It has always been. It was preached to the Old Testament saints, as well as to us. Before the Law ever came, God preached the gospel to Abraham. "And the scripture, foreseeing that God would justify the heathen through faith, preached before the gospel unto Abraham, *saying,* In thee shall all nations be blessed." Gal 3:8 And he reaffirmed the message and purpose of the gospel through the shadows and types of the sacrificial system. God testified of the insufficiency of blood sacrifices of animals to cleanse away their sin by the fact that they continually needed to be offered (Heb 10:1-4).

The prophets confirmed and expounded even more on the gospel (Rom 10:15-19), revealing the very glory of the Lord and Saviour who was coming (Jn 12:41). Let us be assured, even those under the law heard the preaching of the gospel. "But I say, Have they not heard [*those who preached the gospel to them*]? Yes verily, their sound went into all the earth, and their words unto the ends of the world." Rom 10:18 But as it is today, only a few believed the good news of the narrow way that was preached, and even fewer endured to the end.

9 – Trust and True Faith Through Our Fear of the LORD

So what makes in reality their faith greater than ours? Two things. First, that they believed, having not seen. Every time we read the gospels we see Jesus, for they are the testimony of who he was, but they could only hear the distant thunder of the prophets as they brought forth their prophecies of him in mysteries and in "dark speeches" (Nu 12:8), proclaiming his coming. Second, the Old Testament saints had a hidden companion, or more accurately a guide, to their faith that we have lost. This guide kept their faith on the sure path of God's will. We have lost the guide of the Spirit which is the clean and enduring fear of the LORD. The fear of the LORD is the first working of the Spirit of God.

Another Faith: the Lack of the Fear of God

"By faith Noah, being warned of God of things not seen as yet, moved with fear" Heb 11:7

In Hebrews 11:7 we see Noah's faith in the warning of God caused him to be moved with fear. If we fear God, faith will be put into action. It will move. This is why the New Testament church walked, not rested, in the fear of the Lord (Ac 9:31). Rather, than ridding ourselves of fear, the Bible exhorts us to be *moved* with fear! In the true hall of faith of Hebrews 11 it is written, "By faith Noah, being ... moved with fear". If there were ever a day that we needed the faith of righteous Noah it would be today. As he stood on the brink of the judgment of the whole world, so we stand in the same way before the coming judgment of the whole world (2Pe 3:4,7). *Who* – through the fear of God – is preparing themselves in faith for these cataclysmic events? So many believe we will never see such a day, yet the scripture warns us to prepare ourselves for just such a day.

> But the day of the Lord will come as a thief in the night; in the which the heavens shall pass away with a great noise, and the elements shall melt with fervent heat, the earth also and the works that are therein shall be burned up. *Seeing* then *that* all these things shall be dissolved, what manner *of persons* ought ye to be in *all* holy conversation and godliness, Looking for and hasting unto the coming of the day of God, wherein the heavens being on fire shall be dissolved, and the elements shall melt with fervent heat? ... <u>Wherefore, beloved</u>, seeing that ye look for such things, <u>be diligent that ye may be found</u> of him in peace, without spot, and blameless. 2Pe 3:10-14

We need to learn to have the faith of righteous Noah who, being moved with the fear of God by faith, did what God commanded. Though Noah must have been mocked, jeered, and evilly spoken of for taking his stand in obedience to build an ark, yet he knew the greatness of the One who had spoken to him. When God speaks of judgment we ought to pay attention and prepare, for it will certainly come to pass. "For I *am* the LORD: I will speak, and the word that I shall speak shall come to pass" (Eze 12:25). Though we have God's promise that the world shall be consumed in fire and the very elements thereof shall melt with fervent heat, few indeed are aware on a daily basis of their duty to live in an all-encompassing holy behavior and godliness in preparation for it.

What is passed off as faith today is too often self-centered covetousness. It is believing so that we can get what we desire, rather than trusting God to become what he desires us to be and to do. We need to hear the rebuke given to Baruch, the scribe of Jeremiah: "And <u>seekest thou great things for thyself?</u> seek *them* not: for, behold, I will bring evil upon all flesh, saith the LORD: but thy life will I give unto thee" (Jer 45:5).

> **WARNING**: Baruch's faith is, in fact, the corrupt faith that is being taught so much today. It is the faith that seeks things for itself; it seeks to 'get from God'. It is founded on what <u>we desire</u>, what we want. Thus, instead of God's promises moving us by fear to prepare, instead so many ministries are trying to entice people by what 'God can do for them'. Thus the root of people's 'coming to God' is to have their carnal, selfish desires and wants fulfilled, not because they have been convicted to flee the wrath to come. This is why repentance has no place in today's modern self-centered gospel. A "me" generation has arisen in these last days and a corresponding "me"-based gospel has been produced by the mind of man in order to cater to it. Let us hear John the baptist's call, in preparation of the Lord's coming, to flee the wrath to come (Mt 3:7/Lk 3:7).

The greatest faith is the faith to do what God has commanded, to be content with what we have, and to become what he has asked of us – not to obtain what we want, nor to become what we want. Remember, the all-surpassing faith of Jesus was to put away his own ability to save his own life, and instead to take up the will of his heavenly Father. The faith of Jesus was seen in his choosing to trust God in spite of the intensity of the sufferings that he knew he would face. The faith of Jesus Christ does not "take from God", nor does it "get from God", nor does it find how to obtain what we desire or envision. Rather, it receives from him the strength to continue walking obediently in his will.

> The fear of God must be the chaperone, the escort, the governess of true faith or else that faith devolves into boasting, comparing, and lording over others ...

Another faith has developed today which is self-conceited, high-minded, and self-centered. This very thing Paul had to expose among the Roman believers. Paul exhorted the Romans in their faith not to be proud and boastful, but rather to fear God. The fear of God must be the chaperone, the escort, the governess of true faith or else that faith devolves into boasting, comparing, and lording over others (as we so prevalently see today). This is much like what happened in Jesus' day with the Pharisees. They believed God intensely, but

9 – Trust and True Faith Through Our Fear of the LORD

their fear of God was only the teachings of the precept of men, and not the circumcision of the heart. If we are going to truly believe God, we must know *his* will must be exalted in our heart, and *his* word must circumcise and cut away our flesh. Let us beware, lest we, like the Romans, begin to fall under that same conceited, smug spirit of a counterfeit faith.

> Boast not against the branches. But if thou boast, thou bearest not the root, but the root thee. Thou wilt say then, The branches were broken off, that I might be graffed in. Well; because of unbelief they were broken off, and thou standest <u>by faith</u>. <u>Be not highminded</u>, but **fear** Rom 11:18-20

This is not to say that we should not be strong in faith, for we should. Abraham, our spiritual father, was "not weak in faith … but was strong in faith, giving glory to God" (Rom 4:19-20). The scripture shows we are to grow <u>exceedingly</u> in our faith (2Th 1:3), but that faith must be properly nurtured and portered by the fear of God, so that it does not become something self-serving and wild, something which lacks discipline and order. Genuine faith does not exist when we are self-willed, and when we do as we please. Genuine faith only flourishes under authority and submission to it. This is why the greatest examples we have of great faith were always of those who understood authority, recognized the authority of Jesus' words, and placed themselves at the mercy of Jesus' command.[140] This is why the fear of God is the chaperone of faith, for true faith operates only under authority, and God's authority is only established in us through his fear.

> This is why the fear of God is the chaperone of faith, for true faith operates only under authority, and God's authority is only established in us through his fear.

Trust and the Fear of God
Walking by faith in the fear of God (2Co 5:7 & Ac 9:31)

True faith is to bring us to the place of trust. Many may believe in God. Some may have faith in God. But God is looking for those who will trust him. There can be a big difference between faith and trust. Let us illustrate it with the story of the Niagara Falls tightrope-walker Jean Francois Gravelot, known as "The Great Blondin". After successfully crossing the Niagara River on a tightrope before the crowd, he prepared to repeat his crossing, but this time while pushing a wheelbarrow before him. He called out to the crowd, "Do you be-

---

[140] This is why the centurion who was a man under authority exemplified a faith that was greater than was in **all** of Israel (Mt 8:8-10).

lieve that I, The Great Blondin, can again successfully cross over the Niagara River on this tightrope – this time while pushing a wheelbarrow?" Those watching enthusiastically answered, "We believe! We believe! We believe!" To their enthusiasm, Blondin, the master showman yelled out, "Who among you is willing to ride inside of the wheelbarrow and allow me to push you as I cross on this tightrope?" But no one was willing to put their life into the hands of the master. They considered the cost, and it was more than they were willing to risk.

This is like so many people today, both inside the church and out. Many enthusiastically say they believe in Jesus and follow him, but few are willing to follow his example. As the writer of Hebrews declares, consider Christ Jesus (Heb 3:1). Jesus is our forerunner who goes before us. He was willing to completely entrust his own life unto the will of his heavenly Father, and he has called us to follow him in all ways. Jesus trusted in God with all his heart, so it is written of him: "I will put my trust in him." Heb 2:13 (also see Mt 27:43) Trusting in the character and the authority of God is the very promise of salvation unto the Gentiles. "In his name [i.e. his *authority* & *character*] shall the Gentiles trust."[141] Mt 12:21 Are we willing to entrust our life into the Master's care and allow him to take us where he would (Jn 21:18-19)? We, like David and the Son of David, must also learn to trust God the same way.

> O my God, <u>I trust in thee</u>: let me not be ashamed, let not mine enemies triumph over me. O keep my soul, and deliver me: let me not be ashamed; for <u>I put my trust in thee</u>. Ps 25:2,20
>
> In God I will praise his word, <u>in God I have put my trust</u>; I will not fear what flesh can do unto me. <u>In God have I put my trust</u>: I will not be afraid what man can do unto me. Ps 56:4,11

But where does this trust in the LORD come from? It comes from the fear of the LORD! The fear of God leads us to trust in our God. "Who *is* among you that feareth the LORD, ... let him trust in the name of the LORD, and stay upon his God." Isa 50:10 The true fear of the LORD is designed by God to produce trust and confidence. The fear of God is our deliverance from trouble.

Thus, David in declaring his deliverance shows us that those who fear God are those that trust in him (Ps 34:7-9).[142] Why? Because the fear of the LORD is our strong confidence. As seen in Psalm 112, the man that fears the LORD has reason for rejoicing indeed, for he has been set free from the fear of man. How blessed is the man that fears God. Let him praise the LORD! He has a strong confidence. When we fear the LORD, our heart will be fixed and established, trusting in the LORD. When we fear the LORD, we will not be afraid of evil tidings or evil men. "*Oh* how great *is* thy goodness, which thou hast laid up for

---

[141] Also see Rom 15:12 and Eph 1:12-13.

[142] The same can be seen in Psalm 112:1,7-8, where our heart is established in trust through the fear of the LORD.

them that fear thee; *which* thou hast wrought for them that trust in thee before the sons of men!" Ps 31:19 Those that fear God are those that trust in him, especially before the sons of men – the unrighteous.[143] This is why we are exhorted, if we fear the LORD, to also trust in him. "Ye that **fear the LORD**, trust in the LORD: he *is* their help and their shield." Ps 115:11

When we rejoice in the face of evil tidings it will actually cause others to likewise fear God and trust in him. "And he hath put a new song in my mouth, *even* praise unto our God: many shall see *it*, and fear, and shall trust in the LORD." Ps 40:3 What greater evil report for men than the destruction of the world? Our rejoicing in God in the face of the coming judgment of the world is part of our witness to the world. We ought to have a fear of God that produces a strong confidence and a great rejoicing because of our trust in the LORD.

> **WARNING**: Today we have rejoicing and we have faith, but their source is *not* the fear of God. Consider Noah, for "as the days of [Noah] *were*, so shall also the coming of the Son of man be." Mt 24:37 Noah had faith, but he also had the fear of God. Noah walked in the righteousness which is by faith by condemning the world in his life. His faith in the coming judgment of God, caused him to be moved with God's fear of God, so that he *prepared* for that coming judgment of God by refusing to be caught up in the irreverent party spirit of his age. We live very much in Noah's day today. If we would walk in that same righteousness which is by faith, then we also must be warned of God, and by faith be moved with fear to prepare for the coming judgment of God! How few Christians today are moved by godly fear to condemn the ways of the world and the attractions of the world in their life. How few today are by the fear of God preparing today, for the coming of the Lord on the morrow.

Mercy, Hope, and the Fear of God

There is a root of hope, an earnest expectation in God that only comes from the fear of God. "Let not thine heart envy sinners: but *be thou* in the fear of the LORD all the day long. For surely there is an end; and thine expectation shall not be cut off." Pr 23:17-18 This is why those who fear God are repeatedly identified as "those that hope in his mercy." One thing that should undergird our hope in his mercy is that he takes pleasure in us when we fear him. "The LORD taketh pleasure in them that fear him, in those that hope in his

---

[143] If one will study out the term "the sons of men" [*plural*] they will see it is repeatedly put in opposition with the righteous. In Psalm 31:19 they are contrasted with them that fear and trust in God. In Psalm 4:2-3 they are contrasted with the godly. They are those who speak unrighteously (Psalm 57:4, 58:1), their heart is fully set in them to do evil (Ecc 9:3, 8:11), and they are but beasts, who without repentance will perish as beasts (Ecc 3:18-19, 9:12).

mercy." Ps 147:11 The LORD is specially watching those who fear him, that he might deliver them. "Behold, the eye of the LORD *is* upon them that fear him, upon them that hope in his mercy; To deliver their soul from death, and to keep them alive in famine." Ps 33:18-19 Is this not a source of great hope?

In both Psalm 33:18 and 147:11 where we saw the fear of God equated with hoping in God's mercies, the word used for 'hope' [H3176] means 'to *wait*; by implication to *be patient*'. It is sometimes translated 'stay, tarry, trust, and wait'. Let us in the fear of God learn to hope in his mercies and to wait on him as our sanctuary and resting place. "Sanctify the LORD of hosts himself; and *let* him *be* your fear, and *let* him *be* your dread. And he shall be for a sanctuary" (Isa 8:13-14). In the fear of God we find 'a *consecrated* place, especially a *sanctuary* or *asylum*'. The fear of God provides a secure resting place for faith to settle down and become rooted in trust. In the fear of God we are able to possess our soul so that we wait for God to move, instead of trying to make something happen on our own. Without the fear of God we will not long wait for God's promise, nor his supply. We will grow tired and soon, like King Saul, we will stretch out our hand to take it into our own hands (1Sam 13:8-10). Why? Because, like Saul, we have lost our fear of God.

> **WARNING**: There is much false hope today. Many hope that people will stop doing evil and that things will just get better, but the prophecy of scripture warns us that the days will grow more and more evil, more full of darkness. More worries and fears will encompass those whose hearts are rooted in this world and not in the kingdom of God. Without the fear of God we are not able to let go of worrying about situations that seem unfair or unjust, we are not able to let go of the senseless wickedness and destruction that we see all around the world. Yet the scripture proclaims that we should have a greater hope in these last days, not lesser! So it is written, the fear of the LORD is clean and the hope that it produces is pure. For in the fear of God there is a conviction that our expectation will not be disappointed, for our redemption draws nigh.

The Life of Trust Through the Fear of God

Our spiritual life begins when his dominion and fear reign in us. He is able to make peace in those places of our heart where we have given over control to him and where we fear only him. These are the places where he is able once again to walk with us like in the garden of old. God invites us to behold those things which cannot exist outside of him, but which within him flourish. "Behold therefore the goodness and severity of God" (Rom 11:22). David says, "I will sing of mercy <u>and</u> judgment: unto thee, O LORD, will I sing." Ps 101:1

The treasures that are with God; we could never find or re-create on our own. They can only peacefully coexist in the miraculous joining of the LORD. "Surely his salvation *is* nigh them that fear him; that glory may dwell in our land.

9 – Trust and True Faith Through Our Fear of the LORD

Mercy <u>and</u> truth are met together; righteousness <u>and</u> peace have kissed *each other.*" Ps 85:9-10 Fear enables salvation to be near. Thus, grace and fear work together as co-laborers (Heb 12:28). Righteousness and peace have intimacy only in that awesome joining of the fear of God and the salvation that is found in him. We have already seen how, though incompatible in the natural, fear and peace abide together in the presence of the LORD (i.e. the fear of the LORD and the peace of God). Similarly, we see comfort and fear walking together in perfect harmony and unity in the New Testament church (Ac 9:31).

These are the secrets of God that cannot be known apart from the wisdom that descends from above. The secrets of God that he will reveal to those who fear him are worth more than any earthly treasure, prize, or achievement. The greatest of his secrets that he reveals are his covenants. Our great God and king so desires to reveal his covenant of life and peace that was with Levi because of the fear with which he feared the LORD. Think on this. The covenant of life and peace was not only revealed to Levi, it was not only "given to him", but it was "<u>with him</u>"! O that we should long for this intimacy of peace and rest and life in walking with our God that can only come from being under his dominion and being moved by his holy fear.

"For ye shall go out with joy,
and be led forth with peace" Isa 55:12

Chapter 10. True Fellowship Flows from the Fear of the LORD
How His Fear Produces Intimacy

"Then they that feared the LORD spake often one to another: and the LORD hearkened, and heard it" Mal 3:16

We've seen how the fear of God removes the fear of man and brings peace and joy. We've seen how it also produces faith, trust, and hope, and how it is the door of mercy. Now let's see how his fear brings us into intimacy, both with him and with others, and how it opens the door to hear God's voice.

What Prevents us from Having Intimacy

"But your iniquities have separated between you and your God, and your sins have hid his face from you, that he will not hear." Isa 59:2

The intimacy we so long for with God is prevented so many times by the sin we refuse to forsake. If we would be totally honest and naked, all our sins are but a cheap substitute for intimacy. This is why the intimacy we desire with God can only be obtained through the fear of the LORD. "Having therefore these promises, dearly beloved, let us cleanse ourselves from all filthiness of the

10 – True Fellowship Flows from the Fear of the LORD

flesh and spirit, <u>perfecting holiness in the fear of God</u>." 2Co 7:1 The fear of God will cause us to cleanse ourselves from the very things that separate us from God. It is this cleansing which perfects holiness so that we may be set apart for him (2Tim 2:19-21). But what is holiness, but being separated unto God for his purposes. True holiness always produces intimacy. "Follow peace with all *men*, and holiness, without which no man shall see the Lord" (Heb 12:14). To see the Lord we must follow after or pursue both peace and holiness. Reconciliation with both God and men is our primary pursuit.

> all our sins are but a cheap substitute for intimacy.
> This is why the intimacy we desire with God can
> only be obtained through the fear of the LORD.

God cannot fellowship with sin (whether gross wickedness or just our own willfulness), nor can he fellowship with pride or self-righteousness. These separate us from our God. Often we think the great sinner, the wicked person, is the furthest from God, but the man who devotes himself to doing good and may even have a profession of Jesus Christ, but whose heart is filled with pride is just as far from the LORD God. The first is easy for us to see, especially concerning the lost, for we know God hates wickedness. "And we know that we [i.e. *those who are born again*] are of God, and the whole world lieth in wickedness." 1Jn 5:19 God is very clear, he hates those who are wicked.

> A froward heart shall depart from me: I will not know a wicked *person*. Ps 101:4
>
> For thou *art* not a God that hath pleasure in wickedness: neither shall evil dwell with thee. Ps 5:4-5
>
> … thou <u>hatest</u> all workers of iniquity. … the wicked and him that loveth violence his soul <u>hateth</u>. Ps 11:5

But it is not only the lost, the sinner, who finds themselves separated from God because of their sins. The saved when they walk in sin will also feel this same separation, if they do not come to repentance. God said, "But your iniquities have separated between you and your God, and your sins have hid *his* face from you, that he will not hear." Isa 59:2 Let us put this in context. God was not speaking to the lost heathen, but to his own people. This is why we must keep a good conscience with the Lord through the fear of God. We often think of acts of wickedness as far more evil in God's eyes than the pride of man. We can ignore the proud man, but God cannot. God mentions pride as a greater evil even than those who do wickedness. Notice how he mentions them first in line for the day of destruction!

> For, behold, the day cometh, that shall burn as an oven; and <u>all the proud</u>, yea, and all that do wickedly, shall be stubble: and the day that

cometh shall burn them up, saith the LORD of hosts, that it shall leave them neither root nor branch. Mal 4:1

God hates the pride of man's heart more than he does those who do wickedly. Until we know the heart of God, it is difficult for us to see pride as God sees it, but hear what the scriptures reveal about God's despising of it.

- God will not dwell with the proud, nor will he help them.
- Neither will he know them or be intimate with them.
- He has no respect for the proud of heart (Ps 40:4).
- He will not suffer them, but will cut them off.[144]
- The proud in heart are an abomination to him.
- He has rebuked them, for they're cursed (Ps 119:21).
- He promises that they shall not go unpunished (Pr 16:5).
- Even a proud look is 1 of the 6 things that God hates (Pr 6:17)!
- He will judge them by destroying their house (Ps 31:23, 94:2, Pr 15:25).

Notice how the proud look, the proud heart, and the work of the wicked are all equally sin in God's eyes. Yet the first that God always exposes is pride. "An high look, and a proud heart, *and* the plowing of the wicked, *is* sin." Pr 21:4 Is it any wonder, then, that God does not have any intimacy with us when we walk in pride. Therefore God has promised to resist the proud (Jam 4:6, 1Pe 5:5). This word resist is *antitassomai* (G498) and means 'to *oppose*'. It comes from the roots *tasso* and *anti* which respectively mean 'to *arrange* in an orderly manner' and '*opposite* or against'. God will arrange himself and circumstances to be opposite or against us when we walk in pride.

As his people we must flee pride, for it is the very thing that consumed Lucifer and brought about his downfall: the pride that comes from the loss of the fear of God. If we would have any intimacy with the Almighty God, clearly, we must humble ourselves and put pride far from us. "Though the LORD *be* high, yet hath he respect unto the lowly: but the proud he knoweth afar off." Ps 138:6 The greatest examples of pride in the Bible were always from the servants of God who began to err in their hearts from God's authority and no longer were able to hear God's warnings or corrections.

- Consider the penultimate example of pride, Satan who was one of God's own angels. As Lucifer he was the anointed cherub, the chief of God's servants who day and night served the living God.
- Consider the godly kings of Judah.[145] Many of them knew the LORD and served him for years, but pride got a foothold and took them captive to do the devil's will.

---

[144] He cuts off the proud: Ps 101:5, 12:3, Isa 2:12.

10 – True Fellowship Flows from the Fear of the LORD

- Consider the Pharisees of Jesus' day, whom the people considered righteous men and servants of the most high God. They were models of (external) righteousness, but they could not enter into the kingdom of God.

So the pride of the servant of God is not uncommon throughout history, and it is certainly not lacking in this generation. The Spirit of God has prophesied to us that in these last days we will see this spirit of pride increase – and where so? In the hearts of them that call themselves Christians and ministers of the gospel. "This know also, that in the last days perilous times shall come. For men shall be lovers of their own selves, covetous, boasters, proud, blasphemers, disobedient to parents, unthankful, unholy" (2Tim 3:1-2).[146] So we must especially search our own hearts today, for this spirit is increasing greatly as we approach the coming of the Son of Man in his glory.

> The pride of man can *only* be kept in check
> by the fear of God.

The fear of the LORD, as we have seen, cannot co-exist with the pride of man. The effect of possessing the fear of the LORD is to have our pride continually exposed, and if we are willing to repent, our pride (in that area) is removed. Through repentance, the axe is laid to the root of our pride, but first pride must be exposed and revealed by the fear of God. Without the fear of God or God's authority, which brings forth the fear of God, our pride often stays concealed. Notice how John the Baptist ties in the bringing forth of bad fruit with the pride of self-righteousness ("We have Abraham to *our* father"), and the answer is the axe needs to be laid unto the root (Lk 3:8-9).

The pride of man can *only* be kept in check by the fear of God. Pride is the wall of separation that prevents relationship and destroys intimacy. Sin is the eternal problem and the root of all of our problems, yet Jesus has dealt such a blow to sin. "To wit, that God was in Christ, reconciling the world unto himself, not imputing their trespasses unto them" (2Co 5:19). Because of Christ's sacrificial death, God no longer imputes or takes account of our trespasses. By becoming sin for us (v21), Christ Jesus has removed our sin. "Verily I say unto you, All sins shall be forgiven unto the sons of men, and blasphemies wherewith soever they shall blaspheme" (Mk 3:28). Glory, Hallelujah!

---

[145] This is detailed in the section entitled 'Warnings from Good Kings Gone Bad' in the chapter "Why We Forsake the Fear of the LORD" in Losing the Treasure of the Lord.

[146] Note the lost have always been this way. The last days warning is that God's *own* people will be this way!

Fellowship with One Another
"Let those that fear thee turn unto me" Ps 119:79

We will look later at how the fear of the LORD develops an intimacy with our Master, but first let us see how to follow peace with all men. The fear of the LORD produces true intimacy with all them that call on the name of the Lord out of a pure heart. How does it do this? The removal of our pride through the fear of God opens a great door to intimacy with others in the kingdom of God. The fear of the LORD joins our vertical and horizontal relationships into what God has always desired for us. When a true fear of the LORD is present in the heart, it will draw those who are likeminded together around the things of God.

The fear of God enables true fellowship to occur since pride is removed and there is mutual *submission* in the Lord, and none will be in the body for themselves. Mutual submission to the same commander and the development of the same heart produces an intimacy of fellowship with those of our spiritual family who are like-minded and like-hearted. This is why Paul speaks of the unity that can only come from being "perfectly joined together in the same mind and in the same judgment." 1Co 1:10

Let us examine the analogy of marriage. When we think of intimacy between two people we can think of no greater intimacy than the intimacy of the God-given covenant relationship of husband and wife when the two are fulfilling God's heart for them. What is the biblical basis for intimacy in marriage? Notice how right before going into the understanding of marriage in the spiritual and in the natural, Paul joins the threefold cord of the giving of thanks, submission, and the fear of the Lord:

> Giving thanks always for all things unto God and the Father in the name of our Lord Jesus Christ; Submitting yourselves one to another in the fear of God. Eph 5:20-21

The fear of God will cause us not only to submit to the Lord, but also to submit to one another in his fear. [147] Mutual submission with thanksgiving unto God[148] provides the foundation for true intimacy. This is why *before* Paul speaks the greatest verses on the intimacy of marriage in Ephesians 5:22-33, he states that we must submit ourselves to one another in the fear of God (v21).

---

[147] Along with the lack of the word of God, the lack of mutual submission in the fear of God is the greatest problem I repeatedly see in Christian marriages today. Yet it is clear from the placement of this verse immediately preceding *all* of Paul's instruction on marriage (Eph 5:22-33) that mutual submission is the very foundation of marriage!

[148] Submission *without* thanksgiving, on the other hand, is like a trap or a prison. It is thanksgiving unto God that reveals our faith in God's good purpose for submission and that keeps our heart set on his purpose.

10 – True Fellowship Flows from the Fear of the LORD

To walk with the Lord in the fear of God is to depart from iniquity. As we depart from the lust of this world it will cause us to hunger and thirst more and more for righteousness. Evil communications or worldly talk will have no place in us, nor will we want to be around it. This new found hunger and thirst for righteousness will cause us to seek out pure and holy fellowship with those who are like-minded. Thus, the result of the fear of the Lord is to draw us together with others who are likewise trying to maintain a pure heart before God. "Flee also youthful lusts: but follow righteousness, faith, charity, peace, <u>with them</u> that call on the Lord out of a pure heart." 2Tim 2:22 When we begin to depart from iniquity (i.e. from a wrongful character) as a result of the fear of God working in us, the Lord begins to draw us together with those who have the same heart.

Let us focus on this, for if we still enjoy ungodly or worldly relationships or conversations, then it is patently clear we are not pursuing a pure heart, nor is the fear of God being allowed to work within us. Through the fear of the LORD we are brought together with others who also fear him. It is unavoidable. David says, "Let those that fear thee **turn unto me**, and those that have known thy testimonies." Ps 119:79 When our relationship with one another is undergirded by the fear of the LORD, it will produce an intimacy that natural friendship and earthly religion cannot match. The fear of God will not only draw us together, it will also *keep* us together. Notice how Malachi records for us that those that feared the LORD spoke <u>often</u> to one another. "Then they that feared the LORD spake often one to another: and the LORD hearkened, and heard *it*" (Mal 3:16).

This 'speaking often to one another' refers not only to the depth of their fellowship around the things of the Lord, but also to the fact that they repeatedly and regularly fellowshipped together. There is a pure desire to gather together around the things of God and to share what the Lord is doing in our lives. Notice also how the LORD hearkened and heard! These two words hearkened and heard, respectively mean 'to *prick up* the ears' and 'to *hear* intelligently (often with the implication of attention)'. God is present when those that fear him speak together, for he loves to dwell in their midst. This should be no surprise, for he has promised, "For where two or three are gathered together in my name [i.e. *authority, character*], there am I in the midst of them." Mt 18:20 Thus, the fellowship of those who fear the Lord is made all the sweeter by the attendance of the Lord himself who intently listens to their conversation. This is the beauty of the fear of the Lord. It opens the door of spiritual fellowship and intimacy with one another and with the Lord.

Truly indeed, when we gather in his name, under his authority, "Deep calleth unto deep at the noise of thy waterspouts" (Ps 42:7). God begins to speak and to minister to us when he is allowed to rule and reign. As the water of God's word springs forth from us, as a waterspout, the deep cry of the Spirit that dwells within us calls out to the depths of the Spirit of God in others. Our spirit man longs for such spiritual fellowship and intimacy, and hence those who fear the Lord will speak often to each other. We are driven to it. David declares how he was the "companion of <u>all</u> *them* that fear thee, and of them that keep thy precepts." Ps 119:63 If someone feared God, then David desired to be their companion. This word 'companion' is translated 'knit together' in Jdg 20:11, where it says, "So all the men of Israel were gathered against the city, <u>knit together</u> as one man." So it should be with everyone that is walking in the fear of the Lord. In the fear of God, we ought to be knit together in following our captain. When the spirit of the fear of the Lord in them is answered by the same spirit in another, a knitting together will take place as soon as they meet. This is none other than what formed the intimacy of New Testament fellowship, that the saints would be "knit together in love" (Col 2:2).

Another reason why the fear of the Lord brings about an intimacy amongst those who hunger and thirst for righteousness is that we long to be strengthened by those who go through the same battles as we do, yet are holding fast to the same hope of our profession (Heb 10:23).[149] "They that fear thee will be glad when they see me; because I have <u>hoped</u> in thy word." Ps 119:74 The fear of the Lord plants deep within our being the intense desire to be an overcomer. We long for it, hope for it, pray for it, endure for it, and suffer for it. When another is an example to us of pursuing the calling of God to walk as a chaste virgin of Christ, it stirs up the holy flame of passion within us to diligently continue. Their hope, in God's word in the midst of their trial, sparks us and vice versa. A great joy and gladness arises in our hearts that another is winning the race and fighting the good fight of faith and enduring through their trials and afflictions. So Paul echoes this kinship.

> Therefore, brethren, we were <u>comforted</u> over you in all our affliction and distress by your faith: For <u>now we live</u>, if ye stand fast in the Lord. For what <u>thanks</u> can we render to God again for you, for all the <u>joy</u> wherewith we <u>joy</u> for your sakes before our God 1Th 3:7-9

Fellowship with the Almighty

"Oh how great is thy goodness, which thou hast laid up for them that fear thee; which thou hast wrought for them that trust in thee before the sons of men! Thou shalt hide them in the secret of thy presence" Ps 31:19-20

Let us now turn to our intimacy with the Lord. In human relationships it is a well-known experience that natural fear completely inhibits intimacy. If I fear what another will do to me, I will never open up to be vulnerable. Yet this, as with all spirituals, is how the kingdom of God turns everything upside down. The promise of scripture is that "the secret of the LORD *is* with them that fear him; and he will shew them his covenant." Ps 25:14 This itself shows us a depth of intimacy with the Lord that does not exist elsewhere, for only the clos-

---

[149] The word 'faith' in Heb 10:23 is the only time (out of 47 times) that this word is not translated 'hope' but 'faith'.

10 – True Fellowship Flows from the Fear of the LORD

est of friends will share their secrets. Throughout scripture we see God sharing the secrets of his covenants only with those who were closest to him, those who truly were his friends, those who had the fear of God. The fear of the Lord enables us to become the friend of God. We begin to hate what he hates and to depart from iniquity. The fear of God brings about the humble and perfect heart that he can work with and speak to.

Our Intimacy with God: His fear

The beautiful nugget in Psalm 25:14 is hidden in the word 'secret'. In the Hebrew this word means 'by implication *intimacy*'. Thus, God is letting us know that the intimacy of the Lord *is* with them that fear him! There is no greater blessing than intimacy with the Lord. His presence and friendship are more to be desired than all else; nothing can be compared with these. Notice how Job refers to this same secret intimacy with the Lord. "As I was in the days of my youth, when the <u>secret</u> [i.e. the *intimacy*] of God *was* upon my tabernacle; When the Almighty *was* yet <u>with me</u>" (Job 29:4-5). Notice how Job says that the secret of God was 'the Almighty being with him'! This is the intimacy of the fear of God – God with us. The new covenant of "Emmanuel, God with us" can never be completely fulfilled in our life without the fear of the Lord. This is because, as we have seen already, the new covenant is a covenant of grace and fear. Only grace and fear can bring us to the intimacy with the Lord that we yearn for.

> There is no greater blessing than intimacy with the Lord. His presence and friendship are more to be desired than all else; nothing can be compared with these.

Thus, the secret of the Lord also speaks of taking counsel, so it is translated several times as follows.

> We took sweet <u>counsel</u> together, *and* walked unto the house of God in company. Ps 55:14
>
> For who hath stood in the <u>counsel</u> of the LORD, and hath perceived and heard his word? who hath marked his word, and heard *it*? But if they had stood in my <u>counsel</u>, and had caused my people to hear my words, then they should have turned them from their evil way, and from the evil of their doings. Jer 23:18,22

We have seen already that the fear of God enables us to hear and to receive his good counsel. This produces intimacy with the Lord. Maybe now we can better understand why it is written, "Surely the Lord GOD will do nothing, but he revealeth his <u>secret</u> unto his servants the prophets. The lion hath roared, who will not fear? the Lord GOD hath spoken, who can but prophesy?" Am 3:7-8 Why does God particularly reveal the intimate things of his heart to his

More Abundant Life

servants the prophets? Because they walk in his fear, and they are used to hearing the lion roar without fleeing or turning away. Many will not endure the hard sayings of the word of God. They will not endure the chastening of the Lord and his rebuke (Heb 12:5-6).

We have seen already the intimacy that we have with one another through the fear of the LORD from Malachi 3:16. Now let us look further at this passage and see how the fear of the LORD also produces an intimacy with God himself.

> Then they that feared the LORD spake often one to another: and the LORD hearkened, and heard *it*, and a book of remembrance was written before him for them that feared the LORD, and that thought upon his name. And <u>they shall be mine</u>, saith the LORD of hosts, in that day when I make up my jewels; and I will spare them, as a man spareth his own son that serveth him. Mal 3:16-17

God states, concerning those who both fear him and who fellowship with those who fear him, that he '*pricks up* the ears to hear and listens attentively' to what they say. Is this not the first mark of intimacy, that we are able to hear and that we care enough to take the time to listen to what another has to say? There is no intimacy in one doing all the talking or in monologues or even in one continually teaching another. No, even Jesus made himself available to answer the questions of his disciples, and to find out what they were thinking by asking them questions. This is the beauty of the intimacy we can have with the LORD through the fear of God, and that we ought to have with one another if we truly fear God. The fear of God changes both how we speak to one another and how we listen to one another. This is especially true of our relationship with the LORD. We shall see that the fear of God radically transforms how we pray to him.[150] The fear of God in us causes God to now listen to us, and in turn to speak to us. When we fear him he will share his secrets with us in intimacy and will guide us with his counsel.

How the fear of Almighty God produces, not distance but unity and intimacy, is the difference between the natural realm of the fear of man and the spiritual realm of the fear of God.[151] Let us look closer at what is the effect of fear. Fear always causes us to be absorbed in the object of our fear. Whatever we fear, our thoughts will gravitate and begin to fixate on. This is true of both fearing situations and fearing a person/persons. John Bunyan wrote of this very issue, saying,

---

[150] Refer to the section 'The Test of How We Pray' in the chapter entitled "The Testings of the Fear of the LORD" in the book <u>Losing the Treasure of the Lord</u>.

[151] This is where so many completely misconstrue the fear of God, for they look at it from a natural and not a spiritual perspective. Thus, they force the fear of God to be something else and change it to become but respect, awe, and reverence.

10 – True Fellowship Flows from the Fear of the LORD

> All fear, good and bad, hath a natural propensity in it to incline the heart to contemplate the object of fear, and though a man should labour to take off his thoughts from the object of his fear, … yet do what he could, the next time his fear had any act in it [i.e. was aroused], it would return again to its object.[152]

This is why every natural fear brings us into bondage and cripples our life. This is also why God hates natural fears in our life and continually exhorts us to "fear not" (50+ times) and to "be not afraid" (24 times).[153] Yet at the same time, can we now see why it is that he so desires for us to fear him? As a jealous God he would have us continually meditating and thinking about him and what he has spoken. He desires for our thoughts and concerns to continually be upon him. Only the fear of the LORD can keep our hearts and minds stayed on him. Only the fear of the LORD can open the secret of his presence.

WARNING: This is the most overlooked part of the parable of the labourers. Those who were first hired agreed to work for a day's wages, but they were grieved when they were paid what they agreed to work for. Why? Because they got their eyes on others who, having come later, received the same pay as them, and they compared themselves with them which the Bible says it is not wise to do (2Co 10:12). Were they thankful? No, for "they supposed that they should have received more; … And when they had received [*their originally agreed upon wages*], they <u>murmured against</u> the goodman of the house, Saying, … thou hast made them **equal** unto us" (Mt 20:10-12). They considered themselves *better* than those who came later. Thus, they resented being treated as equals.

Greed, covetousness, comparing, and envy are blinding plagues that pollute our heart so that we cannot see what we do have. What was the reward that those who had labored all day for the "goodman of the house" should have been blessed with? It was none other than the fellowship of whom they had labored for! Did they come to know the goodness of the goodman of the house? No. O how we miss God's greatest plan for our life which is, in all we do, to <u>know</u> him (Php 3:10, Jn 17:3)!

This is the great goodness of God, his great reward for those who fear him: the secret of his presence (Ps 31:19-20). So often we look for an external reward, but the true reward of our service is just that we were able to be at his side. Think about Jesus' first and foremost call: "follow me."[154] Think about his first calling of the twelve. What was it? "And he ordained twelve, that they should be <u>with him</u>" (Mk 3:14). It was a call to be with the Master. The greatest

---

[152] Bunyan, p. 84-85.

[153] See the appendix entitled "The Scriptures on Fearing God" in the section 'Scriptures on Not Fearing'.

[154] Just looking at Matthew's gospel alone we see it 5x: Mt 4:19, 8:22, 9:9, 16:24, 19:21.

reward for the disciples of Jesus was not the miracles they experienced or the works they were privileged to do, but the time they had to spend with him.

After Jesus' ascension these are what they treasured more than any other thing on earth. Remember what Jesus prophesied unto them, "And he said unto the disciples, The days will come, when ye shall **desire** to see <u>one of the days of the Son of man</u>, and ye shall not see *it*." Lk 17:22 They would long for the days they had with the Son of man and being able to walk with him and talk with him and ask him questions. Is this what you long for more than anything else – the all-sufficiency of his presence? Are not all our idolatries but poor substitutes for what our spirit truly craves? Intimacy with our spiritual husband.

The testimony of those who were intimate with God

When we look to the testimony of those who truly knew God and were intimate with him, we see they had the greatest fear of God. Consider Jesus, the only begotten Son of the Father. "For the Father loveth the Son, and sheweth him all things that himself doeth" (Jn 5:20, also 3:35). No man knew the heavenly Father better than he. This was his own claim: "As the Father knoweth me, <u>even so</u> know I the Father" (Jn 10:15). "O righteous Father, the world hath not known thee: <u>but I have known thee</u>" (Jn 17:25). Jesus claimed a unique knowledge of God, and part of why he came was to declare who the Father is and what he is like, how he thinks, and most of all how we may in turn know him: "neither knoweth any man the Father, save the Son, and *he* to <u>whomsoever the Son will reveal *him*</u>." Mt 11:27 Jesus invites us to have the same intimacy that he has with the Father when he prays that we might be one even as the Father and he are one.

> That they all may be one; as thou, Father, *art* in me, and I in thee, that they also may be one in us: … that they may be one, even as we are one: … I in them, and thou in me, that they may be made perfect in one … that the love wherewith thou hast loved me may be in them, and I in them. Jn 17:21-23,26

Yet it was Jesus who taught us about the fear of God (Lk 12:5, 18:2-6) and who lived it (Heb 5:7). If we claim to be Jesus' followers, we must hearken to his warnings to fear God and to walk in the same fear which he himself did. "He that saith he abideth in him ought himself also so to walk, even as he walked." 1Jn 2:6 We have 'a moral duty', we are *'under obligation'* to walk like Jesus. We must fear God even as he feared God. Why would we even think that we can so love God (who hates sin) that we do not *have* to fear him who <u>ought to be feared</u>? Remember, we have fallen short of the glory of God through repeated willful sin. Why would we think we need not fear God, when Jesus taught us that we ought to fear God? Why would we think we need not fear

10 – True Fellowship Flows from the Fear of the LORD

God, when Jesus who was without sin[155] and who was not an adopted son, but God's only begotten son,[156] himself feared his heavenly Father?

We cannot draw nigh to God and have any intimacy with him without the fear of God. It is the fear of God that brings us to a place of humility before him so that we can draw near. It is his fear that prepares our heart for him and opens our ears to hear. "Dominion and fear *are* with him" (Job 25:2). If dominion and fear are with him, then we cannot come near him without these in us, for that is what he has told us are with him. If we would be with Jesus, then let us get back his dominion and his fear! This is why we cannot be saved without confessing him as Lord (because dominion is with him), and we cannot be with him without the fear of God (because fear is with him).

There was no one quite so intimate with the LORD in the Old Testament as Moses. "And there arose not a prophet since in Israel like unto Moses, whom the LORD <u>knew face to face</u>" Dt 34:10 Let us look at his life. Taken as a baby from his loving godly parents, he was taken into Pharaoh's court and raised as an adopted son to be one of the most powerful, best-educated men in all the world, who at the side of Pharaoh was next in line to rule the known world. But he forsook all the riches, pleasures, and power of Egypt just to be with God's people.

> Choosing rather to suffer affliction with the people of God, than to enjoy the pleasures of sin for a season; Esteeming the reproach of Christ greater riches than the treasures in Egypt: for he had respect unto the recompence of the reward. By faith he forsook Egypt, not fearing the wrath of the king: for he endured, as seeing him who is invisible. Heb 11:25-27

Moses, the servant of God, went from the height of earthly glory to the epitome of insignificance (in man's eyes), as he tended sheep on the backside of the desert. But it was here, in the brokenness of the desert, not in the courtroom of kings, that God met him and first revealed himself, especially his holiness. As a result of encountering God, the scripture records, "Now the man Moses *was* very meek, above all the men which *were* upon the face of the earth."[157] Nu 12:3 Moses had encountered God's glory, God's holiness, God's presence. He was intimate with the Lord GOD like few other men in all the Bible, yet he feared God greatly (Heb 12:21).

---

[155] Sinless Jesus: 2Co 5:21, 1Pe 2:22, Jn 8:7, Heb 4:15, 9:28.

[156] The only begotten of the Father: Jn 1:14,18, 3:16,18, 1Jn 4:9. The express image of God: Heb 1:3.

[157] The significance of this is that this is the very first time the word 'meek' is ever used in the scripture.

Moses taught the people continually to fear God,[158] because it is what he had learned. When he picked men to be at his side in spiritual leadership, he picked men that were, like him, men who feared God (Ex 18:21). This was *the* most important requirement for leadership in "the church in the wilderness" (Ac 7:38) – even as it ought to be today. May we learn to have incredible intimacy, face to face intimacy with God through the fear of the LORD.

Let us look also at Abraham whom the Bible calls the father of all them that believe (Rom 4:11). Abraham is not only the father of faith, but he is also the model for discipleship. He left family, friends, nation, people, and possessions behind for the sake of following the call of God. In particular, let us look at his life, for he was specially called the "Friend of God" (Jam 2:23). Note, it does not say "friend of God" with a small 'f'. Rather it says "Friend of God" with a capital 'F'. This is because Abraham was the friend of all friends to God.

> The fear of God fashioned Abraham's heart so that he was willing to give up everything in order to be obedient to the LORD. This is what made him the Friend of God.

Abraham is our example that God sets before us of everything that God is looking for in a friend. He was a man that forsook all in his life to follow the God of glory. The LORD appeared to him and spoke with him face to face. Abraham received covenants and blessings because of his willingness to do exactly as God commanded. Abraham had an intimacy and a walk with God that is to be desired and sought after. The Bible declares that we are to be those who "also walk in the steps of that faith of our father Abraham" (Rom 4:12). Yet, when we investigate <u>when</u> Abraham became the friend of God, it was *not* when he first believed (as many suppose), but years later!

James informs us that Abraham was called the friend of God "<u>when</u> he had offered Isaac his son upon the altar" (Jam 2:21). What is so significant about this time is that this was exactly when the angel of the LORD said to him, "now I know that <u>thou fearest God</u>, seeing thou hast not withheld thy son, thine only *son* from me." Gen 22:12 Abraham only came to the revelation of God as Jehovah Jireh, God our supplier AFTER he was willing to give up everything – especially that which was most precious to him. The fear of God fashioned Abraham's heart so that he was willing to give up everything in order to be obedient to the LORD. This is what made him the Friend of God. On the mount, we see the joining of all the necessary parts of an intimate walk with God:

---

[158] Moses taught extensively on the fear of the LORD (25x): Ex 15:11, 20:20; Lev 19:14,32, 25:17,36,43; Dt 4:10, 5:29, 6:2,13,24, 8:6, 10:12,20, 13:4,11, 14:23, 17:13,19, 19:20, 21:21, 28:58, 31:12-13. Moses himself recorded for us all these warnings to fear God because he knew how important they were for us as God's people.

- the hearing and following of God's voice,
- the faith & trust in God to know he has more than can be seen with the eyes (Heb 11:19),
- the obedience and great sacrifice given to God without murmuring or complaining.

But what did God see in Abraham on the mount? God saw the fear of God in motion. It was the fear of God that moved Abraham, much like Noah, to walk by faith and obey God, no matter what it cost him. Thus, the fear of God is what will produce intimacy with God like nothing else can. It is the fear of God in responding to his voice that enables us to be like-minded with him so that we may walk agreed with him. Without the fear of God it is impossible to walk together with him for long. Are you ready, like Abraham, to give up that which is most precious to you in order to know the living God? Are you ready to let the fear of God lead you into an intimacy with God that you could never have dreamed of? God has promised us, once we come to understand the fear of the LORD, then we will find the knowledge of God (Pr 2:5). O what a reward the fear of the LORD brings!

The Fear of God: the Key to Knowing the LORD

*"Then shalt thou understand the fear of the LORD,
and find the knowledge of God." Pr 2:5*

The treasure of the LORD is his presence with us. I pray we know this with all our heart. There is no greater treasure we could ever hope to obtain than to know our Maker and to know his heart. The presence of God is what so many saints seek today, yet so few find. So many saints cry out for an intimate knowledge of God, having never been taught that "the secret [the *intimacy*] of the LORD *is* with them that fear him" (Ps 25:14). At the end of Proverbs chapter one and leading to chapter two verse five, God is warning about a people who will call upon the LORD, but he will not answer (Pr 1:27). They will seek him early, but they shall not find him (Pr 1:28). Why will people call upon him and not hear from him, and seek him but not find him? "For that they hated knowledge, and did not choose the fear of the LORD: They would none of my counsel: they despised all my reproof." Pr 1:29-30

Loving knowledge and choosing the fear of the LORD will cause us to receive his counsel and to welcome his reproof. David, who not only had the fear of God, but taught it to us, said, "Let the righteous smite me; *it shall be* a kindness: and let him reprove me; *it shall be* an excellent oil, *which* shall not break my head" (Ps 141:5). How far we have diverged from Biblical humility. David saw correction and reproof from the righteous as a kindness and as the oil of anointing. The anointing with oil Biblically was often to bring comfort and refreshment, to soothe dry skin.[159] How can David see reproof and correction as comforting and refreshing? Because it would bring him back into proper relationship with the LORD, with him who is our peace (Eph 2:14).

The two greatest reasons why we do not hear from God are hidden here in Proverbs 1:29. First, we do not love knowledge above all other things, and hence we do not seek after it as for silver and gold. We are often busy seeking after so many other things that we are too busy to regularly and diligently seek after our heavenly Father. If we would be brutally honest, we would know that we do not seek him as we ought to and which he is worthy of. Why? Simply because of a lack of desire, a lack of loving his knowledge. Second, when we do receive the knowledge of his person and the knowledge of his will, we do not receive it with the fear of God. Paul continually prayed for this very thing amongst the church. "For this cause we also, since the day we heard *it*, do not cease to pray for you, and to desire that ye might be filled with the knowledge of his will in all wisdom and spiritual understanding" (Col 1:9).

You say what does this have to do with the fear of God? We need to be filled with the knowledge of his will, but how? It says, "in all wisdom and spiritual understanding". "Behold, the fear of the Lord, that *is* wisdom; and to depart from evil *is* understanding." Job 28:28 To depart from evil *is* understanding, but it is by the fear of the LORD *men* depart from evil (Pr 16:6). Therefore, the fear of the LORD is understanding and it is wisdom! If we are to be filled with the knowledge of his will, the way God wants us to be, then it needs to be in the fear of God. We see the only way we can be filled with the knowledge of his will in all wisdom and spiritual understanding is through the fear of God. It is the willingness to hear correction and reproof by choosing the fear of the LORD that will cause us to understand the fear of the LORD *and* appreciate its inestimable value, for the fear of the LORD is what enables us to be filled with the knowledge of his will.

When we lose our fear of God, we lose our access to him and our ability to hear his guidance and counsel. We may still see the words in the Word of God and hear the words a man of God speaks to us, but we do not really hear them – not if our heart is not set on complete obedience in the fear of God. This is the danger of seeking counsel from men of God or even the word of God, when we already have made up our mind on what we will do. Such counsel will fall on ears that are in truth deaf, and all the wisdom and insight of God will fall to the ground wasted.[160] When we regain the fear of the LORD we will see it is

---

[159] So we see the good Samaritan (Lk 10:34) binding up and dressing the wounds of the man on the side of the road. And what is used, but wine for cleansing and oil to soothe and heal.

[160] Contrast Samuel, he feared God, and concerning the words of God it is written of him, "And Samuel grew, and the LORD was with him, and did let none of his words fall to the ground." 1Sam 3:19

10 – True Fellowship Flows from the Fear of the LORD

clean, and as such it prepares us to meet with the LORD. It does this by cleansing our heart and opening our ears to hear. The fear of God opens our ears by making ready our heart to obey his will. This is the key. Our ears cannot hear what our heart will not receive, nor what our soul will not choose to do. This is why we must love knowledge and choose the fear of the LORD.

> The knowledge of God secures us *where we are*, while the wisdom of God secures us in *where we are going*. And both of these come through the fear of God.

When we fear God, God is able to reveal himself and his ways to us. What we know of the LORD profoundly affects our life. When the fear of the LORD is our treasure, we shall clearly receive knowledge and wisdom, and these shall become unto us the stability of our times. "And wisdom and knowledge shall be the stability of thy times, *and* strength of salvation: the fear of the LORD *is* his treasure." Isa 33:6 Nothing so secures the heart as having the knowledge and the wisdom of God. The knowledge of God secures us *where we are*, while the wisdom of God secures us in *where we are going*. And both of these come through the fear of God. In knowing God, we come to know he knows us and cares for us intimately. In knowing his wisdom, we come to know his purposes and his heart. His wisdom then teaches us that his will is perfect – there is nothing better than the will of God.

Finding the Knowledge of God

Would you find the knowledge of God, dear reader? Then choose the fear of the LORD, for "The fear of the LORD *is* the beginning of knowledge: *but* fools despise wisdom and instruction." Pr 1:7 As we have shown before, the order of Isa 11:2 is clearly in reverse order from our perspective. The Spirit of God always begins with us with the fear of the LORD. Then he is able to reveal to us his knowledge. Take notice, it is **his** knowledge. Not until we come in the fear of God, can we truly receive his truth and the knowledge of who he is.

We play the fool when we despise the wisdom and instruction of the Almighty. The person who has no fear of God, according to the scriptures, has no true knowledge or experience of God. When we lose the fear of God, the Bible indicates this is the same as being a fool before him.[161] The LORD alone knows the path laid out for us and the steps that we should take. "The steps of a *good* man are ordered by the LORD: and he delighteth in his [i.e. in the LORD's] way." Ps 37:23

---

[161] Note how having the fear of the LORD is <u>contrasted</u> with being a fool in both these scriptures: Pr 1:7 and 14:16.

There is a great lack today in knowing God in truth and knowing his will in all spiritual understanding. Both of these are revealed to whosoever would come with a humble heart and drink of the waters of the voice of God through the Spirit contained in the Bible. It is the book of life into which our life and our name must be written. We must come, as Moses did, to have a face to face encounter with the LORD. We must come to know not only about the LORD as the Exodus people did by knowing his acts, but also his ways. And what were these ways of God that Moses knew? None other than the knowledge of God himself. As Moses himself cried out, "Now therefore, I pray thee, if I have found grace in thy sight, shew me now <u>thy way</u>, that I may <u>know thee</u>, that I may find grace in thy sight" (Ex 33:13).

The ways of God are how we may know him and how we may find yet more grace! This is the greatest grace or gift of all: the knowledge or experience of the LORD himself. When God could give no greater gift he gave his Son (Rom 8:32). Knowing God is eternal life. As Jesus said, "And this is life eternal, <u>that they might know thee</u> the only true God, and Jesus Christ, whom thou hast sent." Jn 17:3 Yet how shall we know God in truth, and not after the making of our own image, as so many did even in Jesus' day and in Paul's day? The key to knowing God, as we have seen, is the fear of the LORD. If we would truly know him we must fear him.

Just remember, no fear of God, then no enduring knowledge of God. No fear of God, then no intimacy with him. But if we know the fear of the LORD, we will certainly come to know the LORD intimately. If we know the fear of the LORD, we will certainly have life through him, for "The fear of the LORD *tendeth* to <u>life</u>" (Pr 19:23). And again, "The fear of the LORD *is* a fountain of <u>life</u>, to depart from the snares of death." Pr 14:27 In the fear of the LORD we will find the life of God and the intimacy with him that we so desire. When he could give nothing greater, he gave *himself!* Take the time now to truly pray for the fear of God to consume your being, that you may come to know the intimacy of the LORD, for this is his great treasure, his very presence.

10 – True Fellowship Flows from the Fear of the LORD

Chapter 11. Recapturing the Purity of the Fear of the LORD
Finding the Capstone of Grace

"Sanctify the LORD of hosts himself; and let him be your fear, and let him be your dread." Isa 8:13

So how do we recapture the fear of God? The fear of God does not come naturally, nor are we naturally born with it. The Bible declares as children of wrath, without God, without Christ, without hope in the world, we were also without the fear of God. One of the defining characteristics of the unsaved is there is no fear of God before their eyes (Ps 36:1, Rom 3:17-18). This, then, is *the* fault that God finds against his very own people and against his church – that there is no fear of God before their eyes, just like the lost! This is why we must take it very seriously when we have no fear of God continually before our eyes, for we are in very bad company.

When we are begotten again unto a lively hope the Spirit of God is given to us as a deposit. We have seen that the Spirit of adoption which we have received as a result of the new birth is none other than the Spirit which came upon Christ Jesus, which is the Spirit of the fear of the LORD (Isa 11:1). Thus, from the moment of our spiritual conception we have the fear of God planted in us

11 – Recapturing the Purity of the Fear of the LORD

by his Spirit. This deposit of grace by the gift of God through the Holy Spirit is a grace that we cannot afford to put away. This is why we should not ask, "How do we gain the fear of God?" (as if we never had it). Rather, we must ask, "How do we recapture the fear of God, that we have let slip and which we have lost?" Our answer is the same as that which was given to the Hebrews who once had the fear of God, but had begun to fall back from what they had once heard and believed. "Therefore we ought to give the more earnest heed to the things which we have heard, lest at any time we should let *them* slip." Heb 2:1 Let us turn back to the foundation of the word of God.

Choosing the Fear of the LORD
"they hated knowledge, and did not <u>choose</u> the fear of the LORD" Pr 1:29

The fear of the LORD comes several ways. But first and foremost, the fear of the LORD is a choice. No one can force you or coerce you into the enduring fear of the LORD. Neither can anyone make you fearful enough to gain it. God's reproof of those he calls fools is "that they hated knowledge, and did not <u>choose</u> the fear of the LORD: They would none of my counsel: they despised all my reproof." Pr 1:29-30. At the very root of possessing the fear of God is loving the knowledge of God and his ways and choosing it over our ways. We have discussed this already with regard to the necessity for born again Christians to be willing and open to receive correction and godly counsel without being offended. We are always called as children of God to be able to receive correction and admonishment and to measure it by the word of God. When we cannot do this, it is a grave sign of the hardness of our heart.

We ought always be able to acknowledge truth, for once we enter into the way, it is the truth that is to guide us. This is the true humility that God has always looked for amongst his people, but even more so today because of the adulterous and sinful generation we live in (Mk 8:38). Acknowledging the truth is the only way we "may recover [our]selves out of the snare of the devil" (2Tim 2:26). The ability to receive correction is the only way that the elect will escape being deceived (Mt 24:24-26). Repentance, the willingness to change the way one thinks, always precedes the coming of the kingdom of God (Mt 3:2, 4:17, Mk 1:15). We must be willing to change, especially the way we think about things, in order to enter into the rule and reign of our King Jesus. Thus, as we have said before, repentance and seeking must precede the fear of God. Without these we will never find where we have lost the fear of God.

The spiritual man who desires to be led of the Spirit will hunger and thirst for the fear of the LORD. The natural man resists and refuses the fear of the LORD. Those who are self-willed, who love their own pleasures more than they love God (2Tim 3:4), who still maintain control over their own life and have not given up their life, will despise and hate the fear of the LORD. This is all of our problem to some extent, that we do not desire the fear of God as we ought.

Why do we not desire it more? Because we still love what is in God's eye evil. It may be something good, very good in fact, but we love it more that God. The fact that we love anything more than God is what makes sin so exceeding sinful. The Bible declares that the will of God is "good, and acceptable, and perfect" (Rom 12:2). Because of our carnality (i.e. our being conformed to this world), we do not always see his will this way. Therefore, we are exhorted to be transformed by the renewing of our mind, so that we may be able to test and approve that God's will is as he says it is.

Let us not continue in deception and entertain the excusing and accusing pattern that are a part of our sinful nature and which Adam and Eve immediately produced after the fall. No one makes us or forces us to sin. We choose to sin. We can blame no one else. But why do we choose to sin? Because we love and desire something temporal and selfish, instead of that which is good, acceptable, and perfect! Sin is the fruit, the evidence, that reveals our sinful nature and the unrighteousness of our heart. That we would choose what we desire, over what the Almighty God and loving Father has chosen for us – this is the great crime of sin. We have this fact that the will of God is '*intrinsically* good', it is 'acceptable (i.e. *fully agreeable* and well pleasing)', and it is 'perfect and *complete*'. We have an assurance from all of scripture that there is nothing better than his will, yet we still choose our will over his in complete unbelief and selfishness.

Our faith needs to be rooted in the fear of God and not in our desires. We must learn to crucify our desires so that we may desire to do his will, more than our own. We must set before our heart that one needful thing (Lk 10:42): the yearning for intimacy, the desire to sit before the Master and learn of him. This will change us more than anything else, that we have been with Jesus (Ac 4:13). We must remember the door of intimacy is opened with the key of God's fear.

Without God's fear we will never win the battle of temptation and sin. Often in our battle against sin, we only want the fear of God a little, here and there. Therefore we do not *often* choose it. Ultimately, we will only choose what we truly desire. Though Jesus did not desire to die, yet his desire to submit to his heavenly Father and to do his will was greater. We know what gave him the strength to overcome temptation were these three fountains of help:

1. **the Sword of the Spirit**, which is the word of God (Eph 6:17)
2. **the Power of the Spirit**, which is the baptism in the Holy Ghost & the subsequent refillings[162]
3. **the Cry of the Spirit**, which is the effectual fervent prayer of a righteous man that availeth much[163]

---

[162] Baptism in the Holy Ghost: Zec 4:6 – Mic 3:8, Lk 4:14, Rom 15:19, 1Co 2:4, 2Tim 1:7

11 – Recapturing the Purity of the Fear of the LORD

So by the word of God, by the power of the Spirit, and by prayer, Jesus overcame the greatest of all natural fears, the fear of death. It was a battle for Jesus, even as it is for us. But we forget what it was that stabilized his soul and strengthened his heart in all of this. For we may see the word and know we ought to do it, we may desperately pray to do it, and wait for the Spirit's strength to fulfill it, but if we do not truly desire to do the will of God in the depth of our heart in a particular area, then all these other founts will dry up. We must serve him with a <u>willing</u> mind (1Ch 28:9). But where, or rather in what, is our willingness rooted?

The Joy of the LORD is our Strength

"Looking unto Jesus the author and finisher of our faith;
who for the <u>joy that was set before him endured</u> the cross,
despising the shame, and is set down at the right hand of the throne of God." Heb 12:2

Our willingness to do anything is rooted in our joy, or more precisely, in what we joy in. This is why we see the greatest times of giving and offering unto the LORD were always those done in joy and in rejoicing. David says of one of these times, "and now have I seen with joy thy people, which are present here, to offer willingly unto thee." 1Ch 29:17 The people's joy to bring gifts to build God's house is what made them offer willingly.[164] We are to "bring the sacrifice of praise into the house of the LORD." Jer 33:11 We <u>must</u> have joy in doing God's will. Without the joy of the LORD our offerings are not acceptable unto him. Thus, God prescribes that when we offer unto him it must be done with joy! In the house of the LORD the people were "to offer the burnt offerings of the LORD, as *it is* written in the law of Moses, <u>with rejoicing and with singing</u>" (2Ch 23:18). So it is in the New Testament also.

> Every man according as he purposeth in his heart, *so let him give;* not grudgingly, or of necessity: for God loveth a cheerful giver. 2Co 9:7

> For if there be first a willing mind, *it is* accepted according to that a man hath, *and* not according to that he hath not. 2Co 8:12

God prophesied ahead of time that when his people lost their joyfulness in serving him, they would find themselves the captives of their enemies and end up serving them instead. "Because thou servedst not the LORD thy God with <u>joyfulness</u>, and with <u>gladness of heart</u>, for the abundance of all *things;* Therefore shalt thou serve thine enemies" (Dt 28:47-48). Without joying in God's will, our soul will never run the way of God's commandments. It will be as a dead weight

---

[163] Fervent prayer: Col 4:12, Jam 5:16. Ceaseless prayer: Ac 12:5, 1Th 5:17, 2Tim 1:3. Praying always: Eph 6:19, Lk 18:1, 21:36, Rom 1:9, Php 1:4, Col 1:3, 1Th 1:2, 2Th 1:11, Phm 1:4, Ac 10:2.

[164] It also produced joy in David himself as he watched the people.

which must be continually dragged and pushed, and eventually we will run out of strength to do his will. Remember, God will not accept an unwilling offering.

Moses was instructed to gather offerings unto the LORD "whosoever [*was*] of a willing heart" (Ex 35:5).[165] "For if there be first a willing mind, *it is* **accepted**" (2Co 8:12). The same is true even of men (Phm 1:14, 1Co 9:17). God has always desired for us to delight in his will and to take great joy in it. Thus, when God restores his "house of prayer" and brings us back to it, he says that he will make us joyful there, and **then** "their burnt offerings and their sacrifices *shall be* **accepted** upon mine altar" (Isa 56:7). Even the offering of Paul's own life "upon the sacrifice and service of your faith" for the sake of the Philippians had to be done in joy (Php 2:17).

Even his Spirit will not strengthen us for long to do what we do not truly want to do. He will strengthen us for a while by faith to see if we delight in doing God's will, but if there is no change, then he will turn us over to our true desire. Then our soul will indeed begin to serve its enemies (i.e. the lusts of this world). This is why we must renew, not only our thoughts but also our desires through God's word. Without the joy of doing God's will we will have no strength to continue doing it, "for the joy of the LORD is your strength." Neh 8:10

> When we see spiritually what God works by our obedience and willing submission to his will, then joy supernaturally arises and our hearts leap to become willing.

The renewing of our desires in the word of God, so that we have joy in offering unto God what he asks for, is done by beholding the goodness of the LORD and the perfectness of his will. First, we must renew our mind so that we come to know his will. We must freshly and daily have his will written upon the tables of our heart. "I delight to do thy will, O my God: yea, thy law *is* within my heart." Ps 40:8 Then we must learn to love his will by seeing why it is better than anything else. When we see spiritually what God works by our obedience and willing submission to his will, then joy supernaturally arises and our hearts leap to become willing. Even Jesus had to do this, and this was his victory over being able to die to his own will, when it was not his own desire.

> Looking unto Jesus the author and finisher of *our* faith; who for the joy that was set before him endured the cross, despising the shame, and is set down at the right hand of the throne of God. For consider him that endured such contradiction of sinners against himself, lest ye be wearied and faint in your minds. Heb 12:2-3

---

[165] For a willing heart see also Ex 35:21-22,29, 25:2, 1Ch 29:6,9,14,17.

11 – Recapturing the Purity of the Fear of the LORD

His often overlooked and unseen source of victory was the joy that was set before him. His joy enabled him to choose what he, of his own desires, would never have chosen. This is how God enlarges our hearts so that we have the strength, not only to go the way of his commandments, but also to run in them! "I will run the way of thy commandments, <u>when thou shalt enlarge my heart</u>." Ps 119:32 Our heart must be enlarged so that we can see what God desires to do in every situation. We must see by faith the vision of what the LORD of Glory has in store for us (i.e. how we will glorify him by the death of our will). We need this so that we can not only walk where we do not want to go (Jn 21:18-19), but even run. Was this not Abraham's strength to not delay in the sacrifice of his own son? Was this not why he was able to rise up early and go to the mount of sacrifice to offer that which was most precious to him (Gen 22:3)? The psalmist puts it this way, "O send out thy light and thy truth: let them lead me; let them bring me unto thy holy hill, and to thy tabernacles. Then will I go unto the altar of God, unto <u>God my exceeding joy</u>" (Ps 43:3-4).

When once God's light and truth go before us to show us the way unto his glory (i.e. the place where he is glorified), then we are ready to go to the altar of God and sacrifice whatever he has asked for with "exceeding joy"! O let us renew our mind to see as God sees, so that we are no longer blinded by despair or weariness. But as it is written, Eye hath not seen, nor ear heard, neither have entered into the heart of man, the things which God hath prepared for them that love him. But God hath revealed *them* unto us by his Spirit: for the Spirit searcheth all things, yea, the deep things of God." 1Co 2:9-10

We need to allow God's Spirit to reveal to us the things which we cannot see, nor are in our hearts, but which he has prepared for us. As soon as David saw the light and salvation of the LORD (Ps 27:1) and how destruction was not the end, but honor, then he was able to say, "therefore will I offer in his tabernacle <u>sacrifices of joy</u>" (Ps 27:6). Why is joy necessary to choose the fear of the LORD? To choose the fear of the LORD we must rejoice in it. It must become the joy and delight of our heart. It is like any good gift of God, he will not give it to us unless we sincerely and earnestly desire it. God will not baptize anyone in the Holy Ghost who does not want it and who fears it with natural, earthly fears. So we are exhorted,

> But <u>covet earnestly</u> the best gifts 1Co 12:31
>
> Follow after charity, and <u>desire</u> spiritual *gifts* 1Co 14:1
>
> If ye then, being evil, know how to give good gifts unto your children: how much more shall *your* heavenly Father give the Holy Spirit <u>to them that ask him</u>? Lk 11:13

So it is with the grace of the fear of God. We must earnestly ask for it, because we know we absolutely need it, knowing what a truly good and perfect gift it is. The fear of the LORD must become the treasure of our heart.

The Treasure of Our Heart

*"For where your treasure is, there will your heart be also.
Let your loins be girded about, and your lights burning"* Lk 12:34-35

Sanctifying the LORD of hosts prepares our heart to choose the fear of the LORD. "Sanctify the LORD of hosts himself; and *let* him *be* your fear, and *let* him *be* your dread." Isa 8:13 Why do we particularly sanctify the "LORD of hosts"? Because he is the one who *brings* judgment[166] and who is *exalted* in judgment (Isa 5:16) and before whom we must all stand (1K 18:15, 2K 3:14). Setting the LORD of hosts apart as holy and exalted in our heart opens the door for the fear of the LORD to easily enter in. "But <u>sanctify the Lord God</u> in your hearts: and *be* ready always to *give* an answer to every man that asketh you a reason of the hope that is in you with meekness <u>and fear</u>" (1Pe 3:15). If we have set apart the LORD as holy in our heart, then he and what he desires will be what we desire most.

Jesus assured us that our heart will always be on that which we treasure. "For where your treasure is, there will your heart be also." Mt 6:21 This is why the fear of the LORD needs to be our great treasure. "And wisdom and knowledge [i.e. *the fruits of the fear of the LORD*] shall be the stability of thy times, *and* strength of salvation: <u>the fear of the LORD *is* his treasure</u>." Isa 33:6 The scriptures show us that the fear of God is more valuable and of more worth than great treasure, and exhorts us to seek it as for hidden treasure. "Better *is* little with the fear of the LORD than great treasure and trouble therewith." Pr 15:16

The fear of the LORD is to be our great treasure. This great treasure will keep us from great trouble. Once we treasure the fear of God as it is – the root and foundation of the kingdom of God, the capstone of all grace, and the missing underpinning of the new covenant, the covenant of grace *and* fear – only then will we seek it as for buried treasure and sell all we have in order to obtain it. "Again, the kingdom of heaven is like unto treasure hid in a field; the which when a man hath found, he hideth, and for joy thereof goeth and selleth all that he hath, and buyeth that field." Mt 13:44 The treasure of the kingdom of God is none other than the fear of God. In finding it and hiding it in our heart, we will find great abundant joy. We will "rejoice with trembling" (Ps 2:11).

The question is, "Are you convinced that you <u>need</u> the fear of God more than anything else in life? Is it the greatest treasure you can imagine? Or is there something else that you are willing to let take its place, some poor substitute of your will and desires?" The wisdom of Proverbs instructs us that not until we seek after the fear of the LORD as for silver and search for it, not just as treasure, but as for <u>hidden treasures</u>, only then will we come to understand it.

> My son, if thou wilt receive my words, and hide my commandments with thee; So that thou incline thine ear unto wisdom, *and* apply thine

---

[166] Jer 11:17,20 19:15, 20:12, 25:29, 26:18, 29:17, Mal 1:8, 2:2, 3:5, …

heart to understanding; Yea, if thou criest after knowledge, *and* liftest up thy voice for understanding; If thou seekest her as silver, and searchest for her as *for* **hid treasures**; Then shalt thou understand the fear of the LORD, and find the knowledge of God. Pr 2:1-5

Remember, our search for godly knowledge, understanding, and wisdom is none other than a search for the fear of the LORD itself, for the fear of the LORD is the source of all of these.[167] The Spirit of the LORD which has been given unto those who are born again is the spirit of the fear of the LORD, the spirit of understanding, and the spirit of wisdom. The Spirit which we have received of God will make us "of quick understanding in the fear of the LORD" (Isa 11:3). But we will experience none of the life of the Spirit that he wants to bring if we do not diligently seek and pursue after it – for we are in a warfare over the affections and attention of our heart. Where our heart is, there will our treasure be (Mt 6:21). We must seek those things which are above and set our affections on things above (Col 3:1).

Uniting our Heart
through the Word to Fear the LORD
*"Teach me thy way, O LORD; I will walk in thy truth:
unite my heart to fear thy name." Ps 86:11*

"But covet earnestly the best gifts: and yet shew I unto you a more excellent way." 1Co 12:31 The greatest gift is the gift of the Spirit himself. If we allow the Spirit to work in us he will bring forth the characteristics of his nature, the perfectness of his character, namely, the fear of the LORD, knowledge, might, counsel, understanding, wisdom, and love (Isa 11:2, 2Tim 1:7). The first of these, as we have discussed is the fear of the LORD. The end or goal of these is love. This is why when Paul speaks of the "more excellent way" of obtaining the best gifts in 1Corinthians chapter 13, he speaks all about love. To grow and properly exercise any of the gifts of the Spirit we must follow a more excellent way, the way of love. We must love the LORD with all our heart, soul, mind, and strength, but this love must be according to his word. This is the simplicity (i.e. the *singleness*) that is in Christ (2Co 11:3). Thus, it is the divided heart that keeps us from the fear of God.

A divided heart stands in the way of us obtaining the fear of God. As long as our heart is divided we cannot walk in the fear of God, and we cannot fulfill God's will. Jesus' greatest struggle was in Gethsemane where he had to lay down his soul, his mind, will, and emotions, to do his Father's will. In essence, he had to get back to a united heart, to only desiring the will of God. Once his heart was united it was no longer a question of his will versus the will of God.

---

[167] We have looked at these before, but for reference see Ps 111:10, Pr 9:10, 1:7.

Now it was "thy will be done" (Mt 26:42). Without a united heart we cannot have much of the fear of God. So David prays, "Teach me thy way, O LORD; I will walk in thy truth: <u>unite my heart to fear thy name</u>." Ps 86:11

It is the singleness of heart that enables us to serve God in the fear of God. Without our heart being united and single in seeking and desiring his will and not our own for our life, we will not be able to walk in the treasure that the fear of God is. Properly valuing the fear of the LORD is the only way we will desire to recapture it. Notice how Paul in the kingdom Epistles of Ephesians and Colossians reveals that we must have a singleness of heart in order to serve God in the fear of God.

> Servants, be obedient to them that are *your* masters according to the flesh, <u>with fear and trembling, in singleness of your heart, as unto Christ</u> Eph 6:5

> Servants, obey in all things *your* masters according to the flesh; not with eyeservice, as menpleasers; but <u>in singleness of heart, fearing God</u> Col 3:22

The first step to obtaining a singleness of heart is to acknowledge that we do desire something other than what the LORD would have for us. Without acknowledging the truth of the compromise that is already going on in our heart, we will never begin to fight the battle that is set before us. Our heart *is* divided. We must see that our heart is in this condition. But once we see that we do not desire the things of God as we ought to, how do we begin to get our desires rightly aligned with his?

This is the great treasure of God's word and why it must be our daily bread. The manna of the word of God, like freshly baked bread, awakens our tastes for spirituals and reminds us of our eternal reward, laid up for us in heaven. If we are ever to walk in the fear of the LORD, then we must stay close to his word. It must lay upon our heart like the dew of the morning which feeds the grass. "My doctrine shall drop as the rain, my speech shall distil as the dew, as the small rain upon the tender herb, and as the showers upon the grass" (Dt 32:2). If our heart is ready to receive the dew of his doctrine, by acknowledging truth, by being willing to change, and by submitting to the authority of his word, then it will produce in us the fear of the LORD.

> Now these *are* the commandments, the statutes, and the judgments, which the LORD your God commanded <u>to teach you</u>, that ye might do *them* in the land whither ye go to possess it: <u>That thou mightest fear the LORD thy God</u>, to keep all his statutes and his commandments, which I command thee, thou, and thy son, and thy son's son, all the days of thy life; and that thy days may be prolonged. Dt 6:1-2

The Word of God, if our heart is pliable, will cause us to learn his fear (Dt 6:1-2, 17:18-19). In turn, "The fear of the LORD *is* a fountain of life, to depart from the snares of death." Pr 14:27 The fear of God causes us to have a heart

11 – Recapturing the Purity of the Fear of the LORD

which turns from the snares of death. Sin is the snare of death, for if unrepented of, it always leads to death. Our will must be subjugated to his perfect will, for Jesus said, "If any *man* will come after me, let him deny himself, and take up his cross daily, and follow me." Lk 9:23 Once we fall in line with God's will and put aside our will, God's spiritual dynamics of life begin to be put in motion, and we are on our way to growing up in him, "precept ... upon precept, precept upon precept; line upon line, line upon line; here a little, *and* there a little" (Isa 28:10). But it must start with the Word of God, the revealing of his way. So David prays, "Teach me <u>thy way</u>, O LORD; I will walk in <u>thy truth</u>: unite my heart to fear <u>thy name</u>." Ps 86:11 The necessity of having the foundation of the word of God as our daily bread cannot be overstressed. John Bunyan in his excellent book "The Fear of God" wrote,

> For as a man drinketh good doctrine into his soul, so he feareth God. If he drinks it in much, he feareth him greatly; if he drinks it in but little, he feareth him but little; if he drinks it not drink in at all, he feareth him not at all.[168]

There can be no stability, no real maturing in the things of God, no growth in grace or spiritual knowledge without daily studying to show ourselves approved unto God (2Tim 2:15). Such is the importance of what the word of God supplies, that God commanded the kings of Israel to daily take it up. They were to have their own personal copy, and to read therein all the days of their life so that they would **learn** to fear the LORD their God (Dt 17:19-20). No king and no man, can properly govern his own life or even hope to properly take oversight to other's lives, much less his own family, without the continual input and light and life that the scriptures bring through the fear of God. The daily study of the scriptures brought forth many fruits: wisdom, insight, the fear of God, humility, faithful obedience to God's commands, and even the promise of lengthening not only one's own life, but even the lives of one's children! How can we afford today to be without our daily bread?

The Pattern of the Church in the Wilderness: The Lively Oracles of God

After the people had experienced the fear of the LORD at Mount Horeb, God wanted them to ever have his fear working in them. To secure this he commanded them to gather them together to be taught his word. Sadly, so many are gathered weekly in churches, but are not taught both judgment and truth, and hence the fear of God is not being learned.

> Gather me the people together, and **I will make them hear my words**, <u>that they may learn to fear me</u> all the days that they shall live upon the earth, and *that* they may teach their children. Dt 4:10

---

[168] Bunyan, p. 74.

> Gather the people together, men, and women, and children, and thy stranger that *is* within thy gates, <u>that they may hear</u>, and <u>that they may learn</u>, and <u>fear the LORD your God</u>, and <u>observe to do</u> all the words of this law: And *that* their children, which have not known *any thing*, may hear, and learn to fear the LORD your God, as long as ye live in the land whither ye go over Jordan to possess it. Dt 31:13

Get this deep within your spirit: to keep the flame of the fear of God alive within you, it must continually be fed by the pure oil of the Word. We must have the scriptures continually set before us to keep us in the fear of God. God said he *needed* to make us hear his words. Without them we will certainly drift from a holy dread of his power, authority, and presence. When the word of God is set before us it cannot be diluted by man's sentimentality and a love-and-comfort-only gospel. It must speak, yes of the love of God and his unfathomable forgiveness, but it must also dwell on God's holiness and his judgments, even against his own people, even as every New Testament apostle did.

> Get this deep within your spirit: to keep the flame of the fear of God alive within you, it must continually be fed by the pure oil of the Word. We must have the scriptures continually set before us to keep us in the fear of God.

The hearing of the scriptures is designed by God to cause us to learn of him and his ways, which in turn should cause us to fear him and to observe to do his ways. This is why the psalmist says, "Blessed *is* the man *that* feareth the LORD, *that* delighteth greatly in his commandments." Ps 112:1 If we lose our love for the word of God (i.e. our delighting in his commandments), we will not remain in the fear of God. Notice how despising or disrespecting the word of God is equated with the lack of the fear of God: "Whoso despiseth the word shall be destroyed: but he that feareth the commandment shall be rewarded." Pr 13:13 It is utter self-deception for a believer in the Lord today to think that they fear God if they do not daily read his word and seek to obey that which they see and hear by its light. We are put to the test daily concerning whether we will do his word or not. As God did with the Israelites so he does with us.

> And thou shalt remember all the way which the LORD thy God led thee these forty years in the wilderness, <u>to humble thee</u>, *and* <u>to prove thee, to know what *was* in thine heart</u>, **whether thou wouldest keep his commandments, or no**. And <u>he humbled thee</u>, and suffered thee to hunger, and fed thee with manna, which thou knewest not, neither did thy fathers know; **that he might make thee know** that man doth not live by bread only, but by every *word* that proceedeth out of the mouth of the LORD doth man live. Dt 8:2-3

God allows us to suffer hunger and to be humbled so that he may prove us and know what is in our heart, whether we will obey him or not. Then he feeds us with the manna of his word so that he can make us to know that our real life is found in the words that proceed out of his mouth. By God's command, their daily sustenance came. God knows the power that is in his word to change us, if we only continually partake of it and maintain a good conscience while hearing it. Our purposing to do the will of God is essential. God exhorted his people as they were ready to enter into the promised land that they should "observe to do all the words of this law that are written in this book, that thou mayest fear this glorious and fearful name, THE LORD THY GOD" (Dt 28:58).

> God allows us to suffer hunger and to be humbled so that he may prove us and know what is in our heart, whether we will obey him or not.

The New Testament Pattern: the Apostles' Doctrine

The New Testament church reveals the same pattern as that of the "church in the wilderness" (Ac 7:38). The newly saved believers continued steadfastly in the apostles' doctrine (Ac 2:42). The word of God was their daily meat. Out of this was born their fellowship, their breaking of bread, and their prayers. So often the modern church tries to build off of fellowship or even prayer, but the foundational pattern is that the word of God ought to precede all things, even prayer![169] This is why God's people must flee the doctrines of selfishness that are being taught today (of how to get from God what we want), and return to the foundational pattern of obedience to God.

What was the result of this apostolic pattern which we have lost? What was the fruit of the apostles' doctrine which was continued in steadfastly? The fear of God came upon every soul. Did you hear that? Within every soul was birthed the fear of God!

> And they continued stedfastly in the apostles' doctrine and fellowship, and in breaking of bread, and in prayers. And **fear came upon every soul**: and many wonders and signs were done by the apostles. And all that believed were together, and had all things common; And

---

[169] Many times people will try to prove that the church was birthed in prayer and that the word of God follows prayer. They will give Acts 1 as the preeminent example of how the disciples prayed for 10 days before Pentecost came and *then* the preaching of the word followed powerfully. The only problem is, this was not their decision to pray. The word of the Lord Jesus had already preceded this. He had commanded them to wait (Ac 1:4). This was his idea, not theirs. His word had clearly preceded all their prayers. For forty days by the Holy Ghost, he "had given commandments unto the apostles" (Ac 1:2). So the word or command of Jesus *preceded* the prayers of the 120. Without his word we do not even know what to pray for.

sold their possessions and goods, and parted them to all *men*, as every man had need. And they, continuing daily with one accord in the temple, and breaking bread from house to house, did eat their meat with gladness and <u>singleness of heart</u>, Praising God, and having favour with all the people. And the Lord added to the church daily such as should be saved. Ac 2:42-47

This phrase 'came upon' is *ginomai* (G1096) and means 'to *cause to be ("gen"-erate)*, i.e. (reflexive) to *become (come into being)*'. The apostles' doctrine causes the fear of God to come into being in the souls of the saints. This is why we so desperately need the authority of the word of God which manifests through the apostles' doctrine.[170] Let us look now at what that apostolically generated fear of God produced. That fear produced a completely changed heart with a new set of priorities. In the fear of God they "had all things common", and they took care of each other's needs. Their life was focused around the house of God and fellowshipping with one another, and not around the entertainment of the day or on living their individual, separate lives. They truly had a singleness of heart as evidenced by their lives – it was the word of God, the house of God, and the saints of God. This singleness is often one of the most tell-tale signs that the fear of God is alive within us. Contrariwise, the lack of a love for the word of God, for the house of God, or for the saints of God is a sure sign we are lacking the fear of God. Without a singleness of heart we can have no real fear of God for it prepares the way and produces this three-fold fruit of love.

---

[170] Refer to the definition of 'The Apostles' Doctrine' in the appendix entitled "Definition of Some Biblical Terms" for a better understanding of exactly what this is.

11 – Recapturing the Purity of the Fear of the Lord

Chapter 12. Having a Heart to Learn the Fear of the LORD
Preparing the Heart for His Fear

"that thou mayest learn to fear the LORD thy God always." Dt 14:23

We must thread another fine line in learning the fear of God, but first let us establish the fact that we **must** LEARN the fear of God. God's first desire for the children of the Exodus who knew nothing was for them to learn the fear of God. The fear of God does not come naturally. We must learn the fear of the LORD by hearing and learning to obey the Word of God.[171]

> Gather the people together, men, and women, and children, and thy stranger that *is* within thy gates, that they may hear, and that they may learn, and fear the LORD your God, and observe to do all the words of this law: And *that* their children, which have not known *any thing*, may hear, and learn to fear the LORD your God Dt 31:12-13
>
> *Specially* the day that thou stoodest before the LORD thy God in Horeb, when the LORD said unto me, Gather me the people together, and I will make them hear my words, that they may learn to

---

[171] This is the same process a disciple must undergo: to learn to obey.

12 – Having a Heart to Learn the Fear of the LORD

<u>fear me</u> all the days that they shall live upon the earth, and *that* they may teach their children. Dt 4:10

And it [i.e. the copy of the scriptures] shall be with him, and he shall read therein all the days of his life: <u>that he may learn to fear the LORD his God</u>, to keep all the words of this law and these statutes, to do them Dt 17:19

In so many areas of our life we have a worldly mentality in wanting to "go it alone" and "do it my way", yet that is never God's prescribed pattern. We cannot reject learning the fear of God from others, for it is through God's ordained authorities that God will put us to the greatest tests concerning whether we fear God or not. That is not to say that there are not serious pitfalls when trying to learn the fear of God from men. But it is settled in God's heart already that we **must** learn the fear of God from those he puts in our life as spiritual overseers.

One trouble from man's perspective lies in the fact that all men fall short of the glory of God, and therefore it is easy to find fault with the life of any teacher. If the man now justifies his sin and continues in it, then the fear of God becomes lost in that man's life. But if there is acknowledgement of truth and true repentance[172] so that he is set free from the snare of the devil (2Tim 2:25-26), then the fear of God is restored in a most wonderful way.

Contrary to what many would think, we may actually learn **more** from that fallen and restored man than we may learn from others who have never fallen (outwardly) and yet believe they are better because of it. Remember, no man is as blind as he who cannot see his own sin, yet despises such things in others. It is the brokenhearted and those who are contrite in spirit that the LORD is near to (Ps 34:18, Isa 57:15). This is why of all people in the Bible, the one we learn the fear of God most from is he who lost the fear of God and fell in the most outward, dramatic way: David, the king who committed adultery, added to that lying and deceiving, and 'covered it' with murdering the innocent. Yet once repentance was complete, he is now the vessel through which the only recorded extended teaching on the fear of God is recorded for us in Psalm 34.

---

[172] Repentance is a term that will be used repeatedly in this book – for without it there can be no fear of God. Repentance is the key to entering into the kingdom of God, for repentance always *precedes* the kingdom. So we must define what we mean by repentance for many speak of it incorrectly as merely the acknowledgement or the confession of our sins. That is the doctrine of men which originates with the Catholic church and is rooted in the earthly priesthood of men who wear collars. Sadly, it has infected most of the Protestant church.

Repentance according to the Bible is turning away from our way, turning back unto the Lord, and changing our way of thinking to be in agreement with God's thinking. See the more detailed explanation of 'Repentance' in the appendix entitled "Definition of Some Biblical Terms".

> Come, ye children, hearken unto me:
> I will teach you the fear of the LORD.
> What man *is he that* desireth life, *and* loveth *many* days,
> that he may see good? Ps 34:11-12

Let us find hope and courage in David's words, "Come, ye children, hearken unto me: I will teach you the fear of the LORD." Ps 34:11 Though David lost the fear of God and paid dearly for it, yet through repentance he recaptured the fear of God and became a man after God's own heart. This is the awesomeness of how through restoration grace and fear work together as co-laborers in our heart to perfect and keep us, and why earlier they were referred to as fraternal twins. The grace of God teaches our heart to fear, and the fear of God keeps our heart in his grace.

What Must We be Taught to Learn His Fear?
"I will make them hear my words, that they may learn to fear me" Dt 4:10

We have seen that we must hear the Word of God and learn to do his commandments in order to learn the fear of God, but what specifically must we be taught? Do we have a pattern in scripture to follow? Yes, we do! In Psalm 34 a pattern has been left for us to follow. David had lost his fear of God and was walking in the fear of man. It had all begun right after David had been miraculously delivered from Saul by God the third time. Instead of being strengthened in his assurance of God's repeated provision and deliverances and growing in his fear and trust of God, he reasoned within his heart and forsook these. As a result, he lost his fear of God and was overtaken by the fear of man. It is recorded for us thus,

> And David said in his heart, I shall now perish one day by the hand of Saul: *there is* nothing better for me than that I should speedily escape into the land of the Philistines; and Saul shall despair of me, to seek me any more in any coast of Israel: so shall I escape out of his hand. 1Sam 27:1

This was man's understanding and man's plan, not the leading of the Holy One. It denied the LORD and his power to providentially, as well as miraculously, preserve those who trust in him. This is why David said, "there is nothing better for me", when in fact, there *is* something better! This is what the fear of God gives us: a better hope than what we can see with our natural eyes! So David in fear of Saul, and forsaking the fear of God, left the promised land and the covenant of God and fled, of all places, for refuge right into the enemy's camp![173]

---

[173] To think that we can escape out of a situation by our own scheming and doings is foolishness as the scriptures repeatedly show. Though our clever workings may appear

12 – Having a Heart to Learn the Fear of the LORD

This is how our adversary would have it for all of us who name the name of the Lord – to so convince us that we can find rest, security, and protection in the very thing God has declared will be our downfall: the power of the flesh. When we lose our fear of God, we will make the most spiritually foolish decisions of our life. Our God takes special delight in delivering his servants time and again,[174] yet we, like David, will trade our trust in God's mighty hand for temporal relief, for earthly peace, and for a path that we can see with our own eyes, rather than continuing to walk by faith. As soon as we flee to the land of the Philistines – that is, the dominion of the flesh – the authority of God's protective plan is removed. We have no 'business' dwelling in the camp of the Philistines (i.e. in the strength of our abilities and wisdom). We have no inheritance or part there, and we will not find deliverance there, only more fear, more bondage, more hardship, and more heartbreak.

So David would find out, for this is when he was encompassed with the fear of man. Psalm 34 marks the moment when he finally, as a prodigal son, came to his senses and began to awake from the deception of such a false trust. What a rude awakening it was, as he realized he was where he *never* should have been! God had not led him there, his own thinking had. In Psalm 34 David shares with us how he was delivered from all his fears (v4). Yet this is the marvel of God's grace, to redeem our willful disasters and through repentance to turn them into blessings. God's great forgiveness and miraculous deliverance from the very hand of the chief of the Philistines is what restored the fear of the LORD in David. God's fear, in turn, delivered him from all his fears. We can be assured that the restoration of the fear of God in David's heart was the key for his deliverance, for this is the testimony of the rest of Psalm 34 and why David exalts the fear of the LORD three times:

- v7: The angel of the LORD encampeth round about them that <u>fear him</u>, and delivereth them.
- v9: O <u>fear the LORD</u>, ye his saints: for *there is* no want to them that <u>fear him</u>.
- v11: Come, ye children, hearken unto me: I will teach you the <u>fear of the LORD</u>.

What is so remarkable about this passage is, it is the only one in which the teaching of the fear of the LORD is laid out for us step by step. In fact, the remainder of Psalm 34 from verse 11 on is all about *how* we learn the fear of God. As God's prescribed manual on the fear of the LORD, we will use it as an out-

---

to have worked (for a time), they only remove us from one set of external circumstances to another, which in the end will always prove more difficult. We go 'from the frying pan into the fire.'

[174] David's life is a clear example of this, for he did not just escape from death or disaster once or twice, but repeatedly.

line to learn how to recapture the fear of God. Let us look at the last half of this psalm in detail.

Psalm 34 teaches us how to gain the fear of the LORD

¹¹Come, ye children, hearken unto me: I will teach you the fear of the LORD. ¹²What man *is he that* desireth life, *and* loveth *many* days, that he may see good? ¹³Keep thy tongue from evil, and thy lips from speaking guile. ¹⁴Depart from evil, and do good; seek peace, and pursue it. ¹⁵The eyes of the LORD *are* upon the righteous, and his ears *are open* unto their cry. ¹⁶The face of the LORD *is* against them that do evil, to cut off the remembrance of them from the earth. ¹⁷*The righteous* cry, and the LORD heareth, and delivereth them out of all their troubles. ¹⁸The LORD *is* nigh unto them that are of a broken heart; and saveth such as be of a contrite spirit. ¹⁹Many *are* the afflictions of the righteous: but the LORD delivereth him out of them all. ²⁰He keepeth all his bones: not one of them is broken. ²¹Evil shall slay the wicked: and they that hate the righteous shall be desolate. ²²The LORD redeemeth the soul of his servants: and none of them that trust in him shall be desolate. Ps 34:11-22

First, let's summarize the points before we speak of each in detail. We will deal only with the first one in this chapter and the others we will look at in subsequent chapters.[175]

Table 12-1   Recapturing the Fear of God – David's Outline

1. **We must come as children to learn from men of God who will teach us** (v11): Here we will look at the willing spirit, the humble spirit, & the teachable spirit.

2. **We must know his fear is the key to life, both its length and its quality** (v12): Here we will investigate the great treasure that the fear of God is to be in our life.

3. **We must keep our tongue from evil and our lips from speaking guile** (v13): Here we will look at a perfect heart and pleasing God.

   ----

4. **We must depart from evil & do good, we must seek peace & pursue it** (v14): Here we will look at holiness, righteousness, & faithfulness.

5. **We must cry out unto him, knowing that he both hears and delivers** (v15-17): Here we will look at the root of worship & the fruit of giving.

---

[175] The items below the dashed line are covered in the next book <u>Losing the Treasure of the Lord</u>.

6. **We must put our unwavering trust in the One who can redeem us** (v20-22): Here we will look at the testings of the fear of the LORD.
7. **We must be willing to be broken hearted and to be contrite in spirit** (v18-19): Here we will look at brokenness, serving, & the fear of God.

A Willing Spirit to Seek after the Fear of God
We must come to learn and listen as children to men of God who will teach us (Ps 34:11)

David says we must first of all 'come' (Ps 34:11). We must have a **willing** spirit to come and be taught the fear of God. We must have a heart that yearns and seeks after the fear of God. The fear of God is the door to the blessings of God. If we would eat of the good of the land we must be willing, in addition to being obedient. "If ye be willing and obedient, ye shall eat the good of the land" (Isa 1:19). We will never obtain the fear of the LORD by waiting for it to 'arrive' or letting it 'come to us'. The wisdom of Proverbs exhorts us that until we seek after the fear of God as for silver and gold, as for hidden treasures, we will never come to understand it. If we are not actively seeking after the fear of God as the treasure that it is, then we have little understanding of its tremendous value or how much it will guide us in our walk with God.

> My son, if thou wilt receive my words, and hide my commandments with thee; So that thou incline [to *prick up* the ears, i.e. *hearken*] thine ear unto wisdom, and apply thine heart to understanding; Yea, if thou criest after knowledge, and liftest up thy voice for understanding; If thou seekest her as silver, and searchest for her as for hid treasures; Then shalt thou understand the fear of the LORD, and find the knowledge of God. Pr 2:1-5

If we are not actively seeking after the fear of God as the treasure that it is, then we have little understanding of its tremendous value

---

Seeking after the fear of God and treasuring its value more than silver and gold will require a different valuation in our heart of our priorities. In our seeking there will have to be repentance, for repentance and seeking must precede the fear of God. If there be no willingness to change, the fear of God can never be revealed to our heart. God has always been looking for those who would repent, and seek him, and find the fear of God. This in fact is God's promise especially for those who live in the last days. "Afterward shall the children of Israel return [i.e. repent], and seek the LORD their God, and David their king; and shall fear the LORD and his goodness in the latter days." Hos 3:5 'Seek' 'seek' means 'to *search* out (by any method, specifically in worship or prayer); by implication to *strive after*'.

The Fear of God and Coming Together as God's People

The first step to obtaining the fear of God is a willing spirit: a spirit willing to change and to search after the LORD. That willing spirit will continually urge and compel us to gather together in 'the assembly of the LORD' as we seek him. We must be willing to be gathered together to hear his words, "Not forsaking the assembling of ourselves together, as the manner of some *is*" (Heb 10:25). When we gather to hear God's instruction it keeps our heart alive to the fear of God because we are continuing to seek his instruction and put it before us, rather than our own desires. God promises that his fear will greatly arise in our hearts through our corporate seeking of him – if the LORD and his commands are truly being glorified. Then, "God is greatly to be feared in the assembly of the saints, and to be had in reverence of all them that are about him." Ps 89:7

When we begin to forsake the house of God, we lose the fear of God in two ways. First, we lose it because we have lost his way through disobedience. This is the price we always pay for disobeying his will – the loss of his presence. He has called us to gather together and not forsake our assembling together in the house of God. If we are truly his servants, then we must follow him to his Father's house. "If any man serve me, let him follow me; and <u>where I am, there shall also my servant be</u>: if any man serve me, him will *my* Father honour." Jn 12:26 Note what Jesus said: 'Where he is, there will his servant be.' We so often expect God to be with us where we go, but he says, if we are his servants, we will follow him and be where he goes. And we *know* where Jesus will be: in his Father's house (Lk 2:45-49), singing praises to the Father and declaring his Name unto his brethren "in the midst of the church" (Heb 2:11-12).

> <u>**WARNING**</u>: A sure sign one is falling back in their walk with God and losing the fear of God is a lessening of their attendance to the house of God. We cannot be growing in his fear and falling away from the house of God at the same time. They are incompatible. If we truly desire the Lord, we will truly desire his people, "for he that loveth not his brother whom he hath seen, how can he love God whom he hath not seen?" 1Jn 4:20 The local church is not man's idea, it is God's. "But now hath <u>God</u> set the members every one of them in the body, <u>as it hath pleased him</u>." 1Co 12:18 This word 'set' means 'to *place* in a passive or horizontal posture' and is also translated 'ordain'! God has ordained that we be in a local body and that we learn to lay our lives down there.

Remember, the local church does not exist to serve us. We exist to serve the local body. The local body, if it is truly built on the kingdom of God, is under the direct headship of Jesus – and no man. Jesus is the head of the church. We are but his body, and we have life in order to serve him, not to be served. This was what Jesus had to correct even the apostles about. "Even as the Son of man came <u>not to be ministered unto</u>, but to minister, and to give his life a ransom for many." Mt 20:28 Notice Jesus said, "Even as", because we are to be "Even as the Son of man" in serving others.

> **WARNING**: This is the two-fold spiritual disaster of the seeker-sensitive movement which tries to cater to the desires of the seeker. First, the holy commands of God to repent are not being set before them, but instead they are kept them focused on *their* desires, and <u>using</u> God to get those desires met. Hence, the fear of God is being literally put away for our wants and desires. Instead of denying ourself and our desires so that we might follow the Lord (Mt 16:24, Mk 8:34, Lk 9:23), instead we give place to our desires and learn how to get what we want from God. Second, this leads naturally to the second error of coming to God to be served, rather than to serve. Thus, God serves *our* purposes, instead of us serving his. In our pleasure-based society, we have forgotten why we were created, which is NOT for our pleasure, but for his. "Thou art worthy, O Lord, … for thou hast created all things, and for <u>thy pleasure</u> they are and were created." Rev 4:11

In being where Jesus is, the Father will honor us with his presence. Thus, when we leave the house of God by forsaking it, we will lose much! Most of all we will lose the fresh experience of his holiness that produces the fear of God, for we are not encountering him in his holy house. This is the anointing that continually takes us aback and removes us from the realm of the natural, 'baptizing us into his presence'. This we cannot afford to lose, for it is what keeps our heart soft, fresh, and alive in him.

Second, we lose the strength, sustenance, and exhortation that we could have had from our brethren when we forsake the house of God. We so often forget that we are part of Christ's body, but that body cannot function without a tangible manifestation called the local body. This is the testimony of the book of Acts. The apostolic work was never done with a mystical universal body of Christ. It was always done with the local churches. The church was always those who assembled (Ac 11:26), those who were gathered together (Ac 14:27). "If therefore the whole church be come together into one place" (1Co 14:23) and "when ye come together in the church" (1Co 11:18). The church is a body, so when we willingly withdraw from the body which God has planted us in, then we are removing ourselves from the life-flow of the body. We are then out of joint. We will therefore lose that which every joint supplies (Eph 4:16).

Our planting in the house of the LORD is so that we might flourish in the courts of our God (Ps 92:13-14)! We are still to be bringing forth fruit in old age there, rooted, planted, and not moved away. But our planting is not as it pleases us; it is as it pleases him! Rarely, do those who leave a local fellowship consider the depth of what they are doing spiritually. They are in the realm of the spirit breaking joints and marrow.[176] God gave a clear prescription to Moses to gather the people, both those who were willing and those who were strangers (i.e. *those who might be unwilling*), that they may both hear the instructions of God that they might learn to fear the LORD and observe to do the word of God (Dt 31:12).

It is the marrow of our bones which produces the blood. It is the blood which is the life of our soul. Our relationship to the individual members of Christ's body is through joints and marrow. It is our brethren, in the local body that we are a part of, through whom God often desires to bring strength to us. The brethren that know us, among other things, are called by God to daily exhort us to submit to God's voice by obeying the scriptures. They are to help encourage us to keep our hand to the plow of the kingdom of God, and not to look back. This is how the fear of God is kept alive in our hearts.

We often fail in receiving such intimate, godly exhortation as the writer of Hebrews warns us, "To day if ye will hear his voice, harden not your hearts, as in the provocation." Heb 3:15 It is when we enter into provocation with the servant of the Lord sent to us, that our heart becomes hardened. We then refuse to hear God's voice, and we lose our fear of God. This word 'provocation' means 'to be provoked or *irritated*, to be *embittered alongside*, i.e. (figurative) to *exasperate*'.[177] Come, let us be willing to be taught the fear of God through the word of God by humble and obedient servants of God, who themselves also fear God. Our willingness to come and listen must also include our own commitment to study the scriptures for ourselves. This we have seen already. Let us also do this so that our heart may be protected from being lifted up above our brethren and from turning aside from God's commandments (Dt 17:19-20). We cannot be the priests of God ourselves (as we are called to be in the new covenant)[178] without this two-fold willingness:

1. <u>a corporate willingness</u> to gather as a royal priesthood, a holy nation, to hear his voice *corporately* and to minister to one another, as well as
2. <u>an individual willingness</u> to come before the LORD *individually* to hear his voice and to minister unto him.

We have a corporate ministry to each other, and we have a private ministry unto God. Each ought to confirm and strengthen the other. We cannot be complete in Christ without both callings being fulfilled in our life. With no private

---

[176] Joints and marrow (Eph 4:16, Col 2:19, Heb 4:12) is a powerful teaching often lacking in the body of Christ. It defines the intimacy of our relationships in the body of Christ and how they give us life. As Hebrews 4:12 shows us, our spiritual versus our soulish joints and marrow can only be revealed by the sword of the word of God.

[177] You will observe this is what always happens, both with others and with yourself, that the exhortation to depart from sin and to be obedient to God's word <u>when refused</u> always causes 'irritation' in the one who rejects their brother/sister's counsel.

[178] Priests of the Lord: 1Pe 2:5,9, Rev 1:6, 5:10.

time in the scriptures, we will end up receiving the words of men and (whether we realize it or not) following men. With no corporate time in the church of the firstborn, we will end up following our own ways, our own self-important thoughts, our private interpretations of the scripture, and we will no longer receive the words of correction from men of God who represent the LORD and are anointed of him to perfect us.[179]

The Fear of God: Walking with the Lord

As we have seen in Psalm 34:11, we must come with a willingness to learn the fear of God. Interestingly enough, the Hebrew word for 'come' in this case means 'to walk'. If we would learn the fear of God, we cannot remain motionless and wait for it to 'come to us'. We must walk in and toward the things of the LORD. The fear of the LORD is repeatedly linked with walking in his ways.[180] Let us look at one of these verses that shows this link very clearly. "And now, Israel, what doth the LORD thy God require of thee, but to fear the LORD thy God, to walk in all his ways, and to love him, and to serve the LORD thy God with all thy heart and with all thy soul" (Dt 10:12). Here in Deuteronomy 10, God defines for us the fear of God as 'walking in his ways'. Note how it is written, for it is easy to overlook. God requires us to fear him, *and* to love him, *and* to serve him. Thus, "to walk in all his ways" is the only one without an 'and', and hence is clearly a parenthetical thought describing what it is to fear him.

The scripture repeatedly shows that walking with God *is* walking in his fear. Solomon defines walking in uprightness as one who is fearing God. "He that walketh in his uprightness feareth the LORD" (Pr 14:2). He also says, "That they may fear thee, to walk in thy ways" (2Ch 6:31). 'To fear God' and 'to walk in his ways' are often synonymous in scripture. This is because God's fear always begets a walking in God's ways. We see this equivalence in Psalms, "Blessed *is* every one that feareth the LORD; that walketh in his ways." Ps 128:1

The fear of God itself is not a resting – this is what too much of Christianity has focused on for too long: resting. Salvation is our rest, but discipleship is our walk. We find our salvation in rest. "For thus saith the Lord GOD, the Holy One of Israel; In returning [i.e. in *repentance*] and rest shall ye be saved" (Isa 30:15). Salvation is ceasing from our works and entering into his finished work. "For he that is entered into his rest, he also hath ceased from his own works, as God *did* from his." Heb 4:10 It is by faith that we enter into God's rest (Heb 4:3). Yet Christianity some times has been like the man at the gate beautiful. His life is established around the things of God, he is always around the house of God, and knows the people of God, yet he never arises to go and do God's ap-

---

[179] The work of servants of God to perfect us: Eph 4:11-12, Col 1:28-29, 1Th 3:10-11.

[180] Scriptures which link the fear of God to walking in his ways: Dt 8:6, 13:4, Ps 86:11, Isa 50:10, Jer 44:10.

pointed work. Instead, he always rests in the assurance that God will take care of his need and so continually begs. It is not until the apostolic anointing comes that he is set free.

> Christianity some times has been like the man at the gate beautiful. His life is established around the things of God, he is always around the house of God, and knows the people of God, yet he never arises to go and do God's appointed work.

God, indeed, takes pleasure in saving us, but he takes no pleasure in our life *remaining* unfruitful (2Pe 1:8-10, Tit 3:14). He, in fact, as an expert gardener expects us in due season to bear fruit, and fruit in abundance. So he has re-created us "in Christ Jesus unto good works, which God hath before ordained that we should walk in them." Eph 2:10 God has a work for each of us to do, which we can fulfill only as we walk with him. That work we will never know *how* to do or *be able* to do without being cured from our lameness, taking us by the hand, and causing us to arise in Jesus' name. This is what discipleship in the fear of God does for us. It teaches us how to walk with God and fulfill his vision for our life – the very vision that was, by grace through salvation, procured for us.

> **WARNING**: Walking is something infants are not yet capable of doing. This is why the fear of God is not for infants or for babes who need still to be coddled and rocked to sleep. The fear of God is for the child which is weaned and which is ready to be taught doctrine (Isa 28:9). It is specifically for those who would learn to walk. The word 'walking' in Ac 9:31 in the Greek means 'to *traverse*, i.e. *travel* (especially to *remove* [figurative *die*], *live*, etc.)'.
>
> When we walk in the fear of God we are on a journey with the Lord. To walk in the fear of God is to begin an exodus, to be removed from the old familiar death of the slavery of sin and to move toward the life of self-denial that leads to the promises of God. The fear of God will require that we die to all that we once knew and that we take up his commandments, his counsel, and his ways as the manna from heaven. His will must become our meat – over are the days of eating the fleshpots of Egypt (Ex 16:3).

We talked earlier about the pillar of faith which rests upon the pedestal of God's fear and which brings forth the fruit of righteousness in our life.[181] We mentioned that this missing pillar is not primarily for resting in the Lord, but is for walking in the Lord. Now, there *is* a 'rest' to faith, and we do need to rest at times in our walk with God. But the scripture shows the fulfillment of faith is

---

[181] See the chapter entitled "Understanding the New Covenant of Grace & Fear".

12 – Having a Heart to Learn the Fear of the LORD

not found in forever resting. Faith begins as a baby, sleeping much. So we must be taught how to rest in the Lord. We must learn to rest and then to stand before we can learn to walk. But as our faith grows and we develop in the Lord, our faith is to be exercised and is to cause us to rise up and walk. Thus, we must learn to stand by faith and then by faith to walk.[182] So the scripture, concerning faith, speaks often of walking with God. "For we walk by faith" (2Co 5:7), and we are to "walk in the steps of that faith of our father Abraham" (Rom 4:12). God's call to Abraham our spiritual father was not to rest, but to walk before him (Gen 17:1).

The maturing of faith is 'trust', and so we see it also in connection with walking with God. David declares that he walked in his integrity and trusted in the LORD (Ps 26:1). In his trust toward God, he desired for God to show him "the way wherein [he] should walk" (Ps 143:8). Solomon reveals that he that puts his trust in the LORD walks wisely before God (Pr 28:25-26). Finally, "Who *is* among you that <u>feareth the LORD</u>, that obeyeth the voice of his servant, that <u>walketh *in* darkness</u>, and hath no light? <u>let him trust</u> in the name of the LORD, and stay upon his God." Isa 50:10 Those who fear the LORD are those who walk in darkness, not seeing by their natural eye how things will unfold, but trusting in the name (i.e. the character and authority) of the LORD.

The fear of God throughout scripture is a walk, a walk before God and a walk with God. We are called to go on a journey with a purposeful destination, like the good Samaritan. Jesus called his disciples to rest at times, but his primary call to them was always to follow.[183] Even the most famous verse on rest is in the very context of taking up a yoke and following him!

> Come unto me, all *ye* that labour and are heavy laden, and I will give you rest. <u>Take my yoke upon you</u>, and learn of me; for I am meek and lowly in heart: and ye shall find rest unto your souls. For my yoke *is* easy, and my burden is light. Mt 11:28-30

A yoke is not for standing still. It is for pressing forward as one plows. Make no mistake, Jesus' first and primary call to the disciples was not to rest, but to follow him. Jesus laid it down as a requirement that if we were unwilling to die and to follow him, we were not worthy of him. "And he that taketh not his cross, and <u>followeth after me</u>, is not worthy of me." Mt 10:38 To the rich young ruler who was willing to be obedient and keep the commandments, Jesus said he still lacked one thing, "If thou wilt be perfect, go *and* sell that thou hast,

---

[182] Stand by faith: 2Co 1:14, 1Co 16:13, Rom 11:20.

[183] Over and over Jesus called us to follow him: Mt 4:19, 8:22, 9:9, 16:24, 19:21; Mk 2:14, 5:37, 6:1, 8:34, 10:21; Lk 5:27, 9:23,59, 18:22; Jn 1:43, 10:4,27, 12:26, 13:36-37, 21:19,22. Only thrice does Jesus speak positively of taking rest: Mt 11:28-29; Mk 6:31. Even unto the end of his earthly ministry, Jesus was still calling his disciples to continue following him, even as he does to this very day (Jn 21:19,22).

and give to the poor, and thou shalt have treasure in heaven: <u>and come *and* follow me</u>." Mt 19:21 Jesus said that his true sheep will follow him (Jn 10:27).

We must learn to walk in the fear of God. Without it, we bring shame, because the heathen will see our open disobedience and disrespect for our God. Nehemiah, the Old Testament disciple of the Lord and a shadow and type of the New Testament apostle warns, "It *is* not good that ye do: ought ye not to <u>walk in the fear of our God</u> because of the reproach of the heathen our enemies?" Neh 5:9 Knowing that the New Testament church consisted of the heart of disciples who desired to glorify their Father in heaven, we would expect to see the church continually following the Lord Jesus and walking in the fear of God. That is in fact what we see (Ac 9:31).

A Humble Spirit: Having a Heart to Draw Near
"By humility and the fear of the LORD are riches, and honour, and life." Pr 22:4

Related to having a willing spirit to come and learn the fear of God is the attitude with which we come. David says we must come not as scholars or as experts, but rather as children to learn. "Come, <u>ye children</u>, hearken unto me: I will teach you the fear of the LORD." Ps 34:11 We must come as children and humble ourselves to learn the fear of God. Without childlikeness we will never enter into the kingdom of God, and we will never be able to be taught his fear. Jesus said, "Verily I say unto you, Except ye be converted, and become as little children,[184] ye shall not enter into the kingdom of heaven." Mt 18:3 Only the child comes to learn the fear of God, for only child-like faith receives the things of God with simple innocence.[185]

Solomon himself was one who was taught the fear of God as a child by his father David. Thus, this same exhortation to learn the fear of God as a child is echoed by Solomon in the wisdom of Proverbs.

> <u>My son</u>, fear thou the LORD and the king Pr 24:21

> The fear of the LORD *is* the beginning of knowledge: *but* fools despise wisdom and instruction. <u>My son</u>, hear the instruction of thy father, and forsake not the law of thy mother Pr 1:7-8

---

[184] It is interesting to note that Jesus in this verse did not use the word for 'children', which means *a new-born babe* (i.e. *brephos*), nor did he use the word for *an infant*, which is still on the milk and cannot yet speak (i.e. *nepios*). Rather, he uses the word which represents a weaned child (i.e. *paidion, weaned*)! This is a child 1 to 4 years old) who begins to both speak and walk.

[185] This is why scholars may debate it yet in the eyes of God know nothing of it, because they will not humble themselves as children to receive it. The doubting of the scholar is often challenging and scoffing in nature, for they would justify themselves, rather than God through repentance and acknowledging of the truth (Lk 10:29, 2Tim 2:25-26).

12 – Having a Heart to Learn the Fear of the LORD

Notice in Proverbs 1:7-8 how the fear of the LORD immediately leads into being *willing* to hear the instruction of a father. In our pride we will never come to understand the fear of the LORD. Our pride is a dam that holds back the cleansing waters of the fear of God. It is not until our soul can be humbled and weaned of having its way that we can behave and quiet ourselves enough to be taught the fear of God.

> LORD, my heart is not haughty, nor mine eyes lofty: neither do I exercise myself in great matters, or in things too high for me. Surely I have behaved and quieted myself, as a child that is weaned of his mother: my soul *is* even as a weaned child. Ps 131:2

We must become children again in attitude, and in doing so we must put away the haughtiness of what we already know. The LORD has much still to teach us. None of us has the right to think we have arrived – for that truly is an evil that we must depart from. The wisest man warn us, "Be not wise in thine own eyes: fear the LORD, and depart from evil." Pr 3:7 Pride is a great evil that we must continually depart from. Thus, we need not only a willing spirit, but also a **humble** spirit. Without a humble spirit we will never have the ear to hear the things of the Spirit – especially when he demands us to change.

Pride stands directly opposed to both his knowledge and to his fear. To learn the fear of God we must humble ourselves. "Boast not … <u>Be not highminded</u>, but fear" (Rom 11:18,20). "They are <u>not humbled</u> *even* unto this day, <u>neither have they feared</u>, nor walked in my law, nor in my statutes" (Jer 44:10). God is repeatedly asking us to come as children unto him. So Proverbs repeatedly refers to us as children,[186] exhorting us to hear. In all the following verses in Proverbs (as well as the one in Psalm 34:11), the words for hearken/hear are *shama* (H8085) which means 'to *hear* intelligently (often with implication of attention and obedience)'.

> <u>Hear</u>, ye <u>children</u>, the instruction of a father, and attend to know understanding. Pr 4:1

> <u>Hear me now</u> therefore, O ye <u>children</u>, and depart not from the words of my mouth. Pr 5:7

> <u>Hearken unto me now</u> therefore, O ye <u>children</u>, and attend to the words of my mouth. Pr 7:24

> <u>Now therefore hearken unto me</u>, O ye <u>children</u>: for blessed *are they that* keep my ways. Pr 8:32

---

[186] The following verses in Proverbs are all addressed to us as "my son": 1:8,10,15; 2:1; 3:1,11,21; 4:10,20; 5:1,20; 6:1,3,20; 7:1; 23:15,19,26; 24:13,21; 27:11. In so doing, God is speaking to us as his own children.

A Teachable Spirit: Having Ears to Hear

"Come and hear, all ye that fear God, and I will declare what he hath done for my soul." Ps 66:16

We must have a willing spirit, a humble spirit, and a **teachable** spirit. A teachable spirit is ready to listen attentively with the purpose of obeying. David invites us to hear him as a seasoned man of God with wisdom. "Come *and* hear, all ye that fear God, and I will declare what he hath done for my soul." Ps 66:16 Remember that 'not choosing the fear of the LORD' is rooted in hating knowledge, not receiving his counsel, and rejecting all God's reproof (Pr 1:29-30). We must be willing to hearken and to be taught.

> **WARNING**: There can be no fear of God without the desire to learn knowledge.[187] "The fear of the LORD *is* the beginning of knowledge: *but* fools despise wisdom and instruction." Pr 1:7 The way of our old nature is to grow more and more set in our own ways and less and less willing to receive instruction, correction, and reproof. This is why we need to be sitting under the apostolic anointing that will build us off the very foundation of Jesus Christ, the chief cornerstone (Eph 2:20). So many reject the work of the apostle today, yet it is the very one the church needs for there is so much disorder. Apostles were those who built the saints strong in kingdom order and authority through the wisdom of God. Planter apostles, like Paul, were the wise master builders who laid in the saints the foundation of Jesus Christ (1Co 3:10, 2Pe 3:15), which foundation we still need laid in the hearts of the saints today.

Even the context of understanding the fear of God (Pr 2:5) is that of having a teachable spirit – one that loves knowledge (Pr 1:29), that desires God's counsel and does not despise his reproof (Pr 1:30), that receives God's words (Pr 2:1), that inclines their ear unto wisdom and applies their heart to understanding (Pr 2:2). Look at it again, "My son, if thou wilt receive my words, and hide my commandments with thee; … Then shalt thou understand the fear of the LORD, and find the knowledge of God." Pr 2:1,5 Solomon goes directly from those who hated knowledge and did not choose the fear of the LORD and who would not receive the counsel of wisdom, despising its reproof, right into an exhortation to receive the words of wisdom as children so that we may come to understand the fear of the LORD.

Teachers who can No Longer be Taught

---

[187] It is not coincidental that the seventh verse of Proverbs (*the* book of Wisdom) makes this link, even in its first chapter, for seven speaks of perfection.

12 – Having a Heart to Learn the Fear of the LORD

Sadly, my experience as a man of God is that the older a person is in the Lord the less likely they are to hear the word of God when it disagrees with what they think or what they want to do. Though this should never be the case, yet it is the overwhelming norm and pattern. The marks of maturity are clearly not stubbornness, hardness of heart, and dimness of spiritual insight.[188] They do not reflect maturity, but selfishness and immaturity. Why is there such a contradiction among those who ought to (by their spiritual age in the Lord) be mature? Because of the lack of the foundation of the doctrine of Christ being either laid in the lives of God's people or maintained through apostolic oversight. Remember, we cannot go on unto perfection, or maturity, without that singular foundation, according to the scriptures themselves (Heb 6:1-3).

The kingdom of God that is designed by God to come into every new believer's life can only come with the preaching of repentance, for repentance always precedes the kingdom. This is why one of the doctrine of baptisms, and the first and surely most important of them that we need to know, is the baptism of repentance.[189] The saint of God ought to be continually immersed in repentance – the changing of our way of thinking to agree with God's word. Without this foundation we are doomed to be stunted in our growth, lame in our walk with the Lord, on a road toward spiritual deafness and hardness of heart, growing further and further from the fear of God.

For this very reason, mature men of God need the fear of God <u>more than</u> the young do. "Whoso despiseth the word shall be destroyed: but he that feareth the commandment shall be rewarded." Pr 13:13 The more mature we grow in the Lord, the more his word ought to have all our attention. How rare are men of God who are more than a few years old in the Lord who will gather together with other men of God and reason using the scriptures, when it ought to be their very heart. This is an astounding tragedy. It explains why so many diverse doctrines of men exist among those who claim to be born again: because they cannot sit down and spiritually reason from the Word of God with other men of God. Why? Because of the pride of man and holding fast to the comfortability of what we know.

Think of the amazement and utter shock, though, that this must be to God himself who has humbled himself more than any man by inviting mere men to reason with him!! "Come now, and let us reason together, saith the LORD" (Isa 1:18). The mark of Paul's maturity was that he was able to do this very thing, to reason from the scriptures with others. In fact, it was a trademark of Paul's. This was Paul's very manner and custom. He always started by reasoning out of

---

[188] These are in fact spiritual blemishes that are exemplified for us in Eli the priest.

[189] See the sub-section 'Baptism of Repentance' in the appendix entitled "Definition of Some Biblical Terms" for information on its validity and necessity today.

the scriptures[190] with those who claimed God was their Father. We see this beginning with Paul's second journey and on into his third. We see it in Thessalonica, in Corinth, in Ephesus, even in prison in Caesarea! "And Paul, **as his manner was**, went in unto them, and three sabbath days <u>reasoned with them out of the scriptures</u>" (Ac 17:2).[191] Think of all the experts in the law who could not hear the word of truth spoken by Paul, even though he reasoned with them from the very scriptures that they supposedly based their life on.

If we are to be taught the fear of God we must be willing to be taught. We must all come the same way (i.e. being taught, so that we might teach others).[192] We must be correctable. We must be able to receive rebuke and reproof and to truly search our heart to see if there is any truth to what is being spoken to us. This is the only way to ensure ourselves that we are truly under authority, and not an authority unto ourselves, walking in the spirit of pride. We ought therefore never to lose our teachableness, for that is our beginning. Without being teachable, we could never have learned the fear of God in the first place. How then can we teach others the fear of God, if we put away the means by which we gained it for ourself? That would be hypocrisy embodied – for we must all be taught the fear of God (Dt 4:10, 31:12-13).

A humble and teachable spirit will always be put to the test in regards to our willingness to receive reproof and correction. The word David uses in Psalm 34:11 for 'teach' when he says "I will teach you the fear of the LORD" means 'to *goad*, i.e. (by implication) to *teach* (the rod being an Oriental *incentive*)'. God puts our love to the test the same way. "As many as I love, I rebuke and chasten: be zealous therefore, and repent." Rev 3:19 Let us be eager 'to *reconsider* and to change our way of thinking'.

---

[190] Note this reasoning cannot be from **our** understanding or **our** thinking, for our thoughts and our ways are not his ways and his thoughts (Isa 55:8). It must be "out of the scriptures"!

[191] See also Ac 18:4,19, 24:25.

[192] We are all called to teach (Mt 28:19-20, Heb 5:12, Tit 2:3-4, Rom 12:7), though not all in the office of the teacher (1Co 12:28-29, Eph 4:11; 1Tim 2:7, 2Tim 1:11, Rom 11:13; 1Tim 1:7), just as we are all called to prophesy (1Co 14:24,31), but not all are called to be in the office of the prophet.

Chapter 13. The Inestimable Treasure of God's Fear
Properly Valuing the Fear of God
"the fear of the LORD is his treasure." Isa 33:6

We have looked at Psalm 34:11 at how David, the man of God, invites us to learn the fear of God. We have seen that we must come as children to learn, and we must learn it from men of God who know it and walk in it. We have seen how our heart must be prepared if we are to acquire the fear of God. We must come with a willing spirit to learn, a humble spirit to hear, and a teachable spirit which receives correction. Once we come with a prepared heart, now David invites us to know the great treasure of the fear of the LORD. He asks, "What man *is he that* desireth life, *and* loveth *many* days, that he may see good?" Ps 34:12 The fear of God is a fountain of life within us that will satisfy our deepest desire for life.

Let us consider this greatest of treasures, this fountain of life: the fear of the LORD. Let us look at how David came to know this true treasure and how it sprang up in his life. The Bible says of the fear of God that it is an heritage (i.e. an inheritance) which is given by God himself (Ps 61:5). Psalm 61 specially groups these blessings into three time frames. The blessing of the fear of the LORD covers our past, present, and future.

1. what he has done for us – His Protection
2. what he will do for us – His Provision
3. what he is doing for us – His Presence

The Past Heritage of those who Fear Him: His Protection

"For thou, O God, hast heard my vows: thou hast given me the heritage of those that fear thy name." Ps 61:5

Let us first consider the past blessings which are shown us in Psalm 61:3, "For thou hast been a shelter for me, *and* a strong tower from the enemy." So often we struggle in our battles against the enemy of our soul without the strength, strong defense, or place of protection which the LORD has created and prepared for us in the fear of the LORD. When we have the fear of the LORD in our lives we will see how God has been a shelter, a place of refuge for us, and a defense against the enemy: a "strong tower from the enemy." When we have been wearied and emptied and needed a shelter, through the fear of the LORD he has been that shelter. When we were threatened and/or attacked and needed a safe place of defense from which to fight, through the fear of the LORD he has been that strong defense.

The fear of the LORD is a strong defense against the enemy, keeping us from being overtaken. "Surely his salvation [i.e. *deliverance*] *is* nigh them that fear him" (Ps 85:9). This is why the enemy so wants to destroy the fear of the LORD in us.[193] This is what the serpent in the garden as a master surgeon was so precisely able to extract out of Eve's heart: the fear of the LORD. The blessings of God, we shall see, are attached to the fear of God because it allows the promises of God's word to come to pass in us. Thus, we can say the fear of God, from our side, is what causes God's word to be endued with power. No fear of God = no power in the word of God within our heart. God's word is the fuel. It is the power of God, but the fear of God is as the flame and the trigger that lights the explosiveness of it in our life.

The Future Heritage of those who Fear Him: His Provision

"yet surely I know that it shall be well with them that fear God, which fear before him" Ecc 8:12

There is also a future heritage to them that fear him: "I <u>will abide</u> in thy tabernacle for ever: I will trust in the covert of thy wings. Selah." Ps 61:4 So

---

[193] He will either try to remove it altogether or to replace it with the false fear of God. Refer to "An Epilogue: Enduring Fear of God" to see why Satan so hates the true.

Solomon shares the blessing to come for those who fear God, "yet surely I know that <u>it shall be well</u> with them that fear God, which fear before him" (Ecc 8:12). It *shall* be well for those who fear God. If we look to the future heritage that arises from the fear of the LORD, we see his awesome presence and protection set before us. "The angel of the LORD encampeth round about them that fear him, and delivereth them." Ps 34:7 With these we can be secure and safe from the natural fears which would try to overwhelm us. Many a Christian knows the grace of God well, yet is still captured by their fears. When the fear of the LORD is set before us, it is able to deliver us from the ravages of natural fear. Only the fear of God can keep us from falling prey to the innate bondage that is a part of every other fear.

So many have sought the LORD to be delivered from their fears, yet they flee from or ignore the fear of the LORD. As a result, many find no deliverance from their enslaving fears. Only God's fear gives us the assurance of his encampment about us and his deliverance. Only God's fear causes us to know that his provision will be there when it is most needed. This is why only the fear of the LORD can deliver us from all our fears. Without it being restored to its proper place in our life we will ever battle and fall prey to our fears.

It is his encampment around us for deliverance and his provision that are shown also in Psalm 61 to be part of the heritage of those that fear the LORD. There we find in verse 4 that the heritage of the fear of the LORD is 'the abiding place of his tabernacle and the covert of his wings'. The abiding place of his tabernacle is *his continuing presence* in our lives, first through the indwelling of the Holy Ghost, and second by our heart being laid out before the throne of God. There can be no greater reward than the presence of our Father with us when we are pleasing unto him. It is the fear of the LORD that prepares us for his Son's coming, making us acceptable and pleasing in his sight. The fear of God also draws us nigh unto him today and brings him near to our senses.

O "the riches of the glory of his inheritance in the saints" (Eph 1:18)! And we have more, we have not only his presence, but also *his protection*. We have the covert of his wings. The covert of his wings is how he gathers us close to him for protection. This gathering together is not unto any 'thing', but unto the hearkening of his word! He would gather us, but so often his own people would not be gathered unto his voice. God promised the Exodus people, just as Jesus did to his disciples, that if they would hearken to his voice they would become his special people.

> Ye have seen what I did unto the Egyptians, and *how* I bare you on eagles' wings, and brought you unto myself. **Now therefore**, if ye will <u>obey my voice</u> indeed, and keep my covenant, then ye shall be a peculiar treasure unto me above all people: for all the earth *is* mine: And ye shall be unto me a kingdom of priests, and an holy nation. Ex 19:4-6

13 – The Inestimable Treasure of God's Fear

Observe how Moses immediately follows up God bearing the people on eagles' wings with continuing to walk in obedience to God's voice. So it was even when Jesus came, he came as humility personified, as a servant, as one who did not strive, nor cry out in the streets, but as a gentle lamb that would not break the bruised reed, nor quench the smoking flax (Mt 12:19-20). But he came with authority also, the very authority of heaven, yet the word of his Father could not be heard and his people would not be gathered. Jesus himself cried out to his own people, yet they did not receive him (Jn 1:10-11),

> O Jerusalem, Jerusalem, *thou* that killest the prophets, and stonest them which are sent unto thee, how often would I have gathered thy children together, even as a hen gathereth her chickens under *her* wings, and ye would not! Mt 23:37

Why wouldn't his *own* people be gathered? Because they would not submit to the Word of God. Let us be careful today that we are not as those chicks, for a great judgment is coming. The fear of God enables us to escape the wrath to come (Rev 11:18, Pr 14:27), but who is hearkening to the correction of the Son?

The Present Heritage of those who Fear Him: His Presence

"From the end of the earth will I cry unto thee,
when my heart is overwhelmed: lead me to the rock that is higher
than I. For thou, O God, hast heard my vows: thou hast given me
the heritage of those that fear thy name." Ps 61:2,5

The LORD is not just a help in times past, nor only for the times to come, but he is "our refuge and strength, a very <u>present</u> help in trouble." Ps 46:1 The LORD God is not just the great God of our forefathers and of those who have gone before us, but he is the living God who would be with us today, if we would be with him. His promise of deliverance and protection covers the past and the future, but is also manifest in our workings and dealings with him today. The fear of God produces stability in the life of those who have it. "Fear before him, all the earth: <u>the world also shall be stable</u>, that it be not moved." 1Ch 16:30 Notice the command "Fear before him", followed by the consequence of fearing before him, namely, our world shall be stable and immovable. All things may fall apart around us, but the fear of God will keep our heart steady in the way of God.

Today is the day of salvation, the day of being delivered from all our fears and brought into the safety of fearing God and him alone. Today is the day we may either enter into his deliverances by hearkening to his voice, *or* we may harden our hearts and provoke him to anger. We may provoke God by not listening to his voice or we may please him by hearkening to it. It is our choice: reject the word of the LORD or receive the fear of the LORD – which is to hearken to his word. How shall we see his strength, deliverance, and protection? Only by his leading. This is always how he has guided and kept safe his people:

by his voice. If we will not hearken to the voice of his word, we cannot be protected from the enemy. Why?

1. Because we do not allow him to guide us to our desired haven.
2. Because we do not hear his cries to turn from danger.
3. Because we provoke him to anger, and he himself *must* become our enemy! "But murmured in their tents, *and* <u>hearkened not</u> unto the voice of the LORD. **Therefore** he lifted up his hand against them, to overthrow them in the wilderness" (Ps 106:25-26).

> **WARNING**: America is more like the nation of Judah during Jeremiah's day than any truly know.[194] Evil is pronounced against this land of promise, even as it was against the promised land of Israel, but none could hear it then, and none can hear it now. God cries out, "Therefore **now** amend your ways and your doings, and <u>obey the voice of the LORD</u> your God; and the LORD will repent him of the evil that he hath pronounced against you." Jer 26:13
>
> America has forsaken the blesser, yet still with conceit believes she is worthy of the blessings. The only blessing any man may truly find in this day is in obeying the voice of the LORD. It is promised that the wickedness of our days will grow into a gross darkness, which covers the whole land, and so we have seen it come to pass. As Jeremiah urged Judah's fearful king, "<u>Obey</u>, I beseech thee, <u>the voice of the LORD</u>, which I speak unto thee: so it shall be well unto thee, and thy soul shall live." Jer 38:20

But who can hear God's voice, if they will not hear God's word? The psalmist declares that he had taken God's word as his heritage for ever. "Thy testimonies have I taken as an heritage for ever: for they *are* the rejoicing of my heart. I have inclined mine heart to perform thy statutes alway, *even unto* the end." Ps 119:111-112 We can have no inheritance without holding fast to the word. So many have deceived themselves to think that they can reject the word of God, or in their minds merely ignore the parts they would not listen to, and yet still have the reward of God, which is eternal life with him. Yet how may we dwell with him whom we will not hear? "Can two walk together, except they be agreed?" Am 3:3

---

[194] Jeremiah lived during a day of great apostasy which exactly foreshadows our day. The people of Jeremiah's day laid down in shame and confusion covered them. Why? Because they sinned against the LORD their God. How? As it is written, "we and our fathers, from our youth even unto this day, ... have <u>not obeyed the voice of the LORD</u> our God." Jer 3:25 This was indeed God's judgment against them, that they were "a nation that <u>obeyeth not the voice of the LORD</u> their God, nor receiveth correction: truth is perished, and is cut off from their mouth." Jer 7:28 (See also Jer 40:3, 42:21, 44:23.)

13 – The Inestimable Treasure of God's Fear

We must hear and obey in the fear of God to inherit what he has for us. There is sorrow and suffering enough laid up for the just in this life because of the wicked. Let us not add to it by provoking the LORD because we will not hear his voice. "Wherefore as the Holy Ghost saith, To day if ye will hear his voice, <u>Harden not your hearts</u>, as in the provocation, in the day of temptation in the wilderness: ... While it is said, To day if ye will hear his voice, <u>harden not your hearts</u>, as in the provocation." Heb 3:7-8,15

> We may provoke God by not listening to his voice or
> we may please him by hearkening to it. It is
> our choice: reject the word of the LORD or receive
> the fear of the LORD – which is to hearken to his word.

As wickedness increases in the earth and the love of many waxes cold because "iniquity shall abound" (Mt 24:12), we need ever more the present heritage of fearing the LORD, which is the ability to hear his voice. Notice this is the very <u>first</u> heritage spoken of in Psalm 61 of those who fear him: "From the end of the earth will I cry unto thee, when my heart is overwhelmed: <u>lead me</u> to the rock *that* is higher than I." Ps 61:2 The leading of his voice is worth more than all the treasures and pleasures of life that man could imagine. His heritage to them that fear him is to lead them to the rock that is higher than them. God is our portion and our exceeding great reward, our rock of salvation and our high place. The Father desires to lead us to the rock of our salvation, Jesus Christ. He is our inheritance, and nothing is sweeter to the lover of God than to hear the voice of their beloved calling them! So sings the woman of the Song of Songs, "The voice of my beloved! behold, he cometh ..." (SS 2:8).

When we are wakened by the moving of his Spirit to hear his voice in his word, let us arise to his call and open our hearts to him who alone deserves to dwell in undisputed lordship over our heart. "I sleep, but my heart waketh: *it is* the voice of my beloved that knocketh, *saying*, Open to me, my sister, my love, my dove, my undefiled" (SS 5:2). Ought we not to so desire to hear his voice that we cry out as the Shulamite woman for her King, "Thou that dwellest in the gardens, the companions <u>hearken to thy voice</u>: <u>cause me to hear</u> *it*." SS 8:13

An Understanding Spirit: A Fountain of Life
We must know that the fear of God
is the key to life, both its length and quality (Ps 34:12)

Through the fear of God, the Spirit will lead us to the rock that is higher than us. There at the rock of Jesus, he will satisfy us "with honey out of the rock" (Ps 81:16, Dt 32:13). So many are seeking satisfaction in life and not finding it – sadly even Christians. So many seek for a fountain of life today. You will see advertisements for special healthy water, miracle herbs, balanced diets, power foods, anti-aging compounds, fitness programs, holistic methods, special meditations, and a panary of philosophies, all with the promise of rejuvenating or renewing your life. But the fountain of youth or fountain of life, which so many desire, is not found in this world – it is found in our relationship with the LORD through the fear of God. Man searches for the power of life here on the earth (i.e. "under the sun"), yet denies the very *source* of life, the very giver of life, the Almighty God.[195]

Ponce de León, as well as many other explorers, once searched the Americas for the fountain of life, but none ever found it. America is again filled with this same spirit of lust. In these last days, people have again taken up the vain search for the key to natural eternal life. The fool-hardy pattern has been repeated hundreds of times in history, but mankind is ever so remiss to learn from these tragic lessons. Hundreds of years before such explorers came and went and wasted their time, Solomon, the wisest of men, was caught up in an intense search that equally proved as fruitless. He had all the riches, all the wisdom, all the women, all the wine, all the parties, all the laughter, all the pleasures, and all the pastimes that anyone could ever desire, but all this was not enough to fill his empty heart, a heart that lacked the fear of God. Here was his warning,

> I have seen all the works that are done under the sun; and, behold, all *is* vanity and vexation of spirit. Ecc 1:14
>
> Then I looked on all the works that my hands had wrought, and on the labour that I had laboured to do: and, behold, <u>all *was* vanity</u> and vexation of spirit, and *there was* no profit under the sun. Ecc 2:11

The fullness of life cannot be found under the sun. So where is it to be found, according to the wisest of men? What was his conclusion? What do we learn from his great wisdom? Of all the pleasures the world has to offer, all of which were in Solomon's grasp, what ought we to seek? What is it that will truly satisfy? It is none other than the fear of God, which we are seeking:[196]

> Though a sinner do evil an hundred times, and his *days* be prolonged, yet <u>surely I know</u> that it shall be well with them that <u>fear God</u>, which <u>fear before him</u> Ecc 8:12
>
> Let us hear the conclusion of the whole matter: <u>Fear God</u>, and keep his commandments: for this *is* the whole *duty* of man. Ecc 12:13

---

[195] Job 33:4, Ecc 5:18, 8:15, 9:9, Mt 20:28, Jn 4:14, 6:27,51, 10:28, 17:2, Ac 17:25, 2Co 3:6, 2Pe 1:3, 1Jn 5:11,16, Rev 2:7; Ecc 7:12 [wisdom].

[196] This is why Solomon taught us so much concerning the fear of God – because he learned it was the key to a completed life. As he wrote, "*he that hath it* shall abide satisfied" (Pr 19:23).

God has promised to freely give us to drink of the water of life. So often we only think of believing on Jesus when we think of drinking of the water of life. That is truly the beginning, but let us learn more about how we continue to drink of this water of life especially *after* we have believed on Jesus for salvation. We learn much by seeing where this water of life comes from? "And he shewed me a pure river of water of life, clear as crystal, proceeding out of the throne of God and of the Lamb." Rev 22:1 Where else could the water of life to sustain us come from, but from the very throne of authority? The water of life flows from the authority of God and of the Lamb, the Word of God. As we have seen, God's authority and God's word are the source of the fear of God.

Man looks in all the wrong places, yet the *one* place it is to be found is in the fear of the LORD. "The fear of the LORD *is* a fountain of life" (Pr 14:27). What do we *need* to drink of this fountain? God does not charge us, but is ready freely to let us drink. He only asks that we thirst for it. Jesus said, "I will give unto him that is <u>athirst</u> of the fountain of the water of life **freely**." Rev 21:6 Sadly, so many have no thirst or desire for what God would give freely, yet those who know of its refreshing vigor urge us to drink, "the Spirit and the bride say, **Come**. And let him that heareth say, **Come**. And let him that is athirst **come**. And whosoever will, let him take the water of life **freely**." Rev 22:17

Why does the scripture say "The fear of the LORD *is* a fountain of life" (Pr 14:27)? Because the fear of the LORD produces life in us. What is the fear of the LORD in us, but our confidence, our hope, and the uprightness of our ways in him! "*Is* not *this* thy fear, thy confidence, thy hope, and the uprightness of thy ways?" Job 4:6 God's fear will keep our heart single, selfless, and dedicated to pleasing him. The fear of the LORD will enlarge our heart (Isa 60:5) and fill it with compassion. It keeps our heart soft, humble, and open before him. It will keep our heart fixed on the things of God and not on the things of this world, which are passing away. So the fountain of youth does exist, in a sense – not in making us forever young again[197] – but in lengthening our life. God's promise to the kings of Israel was if he learned "to fear the LORD his God, to keep all the words of this law and these statutes, to do them" (Dt 17:19), then the end would be that he would "prolong [i.e. to make long] *his* days in his kingdom, he, and his children, in the midst of Israel." Dt 17:20

This is the promise of the fear of God for us all. "The fear of the LORD <u>prolongeth days</u>: but the years of the wicked shall be shortened." Pr 10:27

---

[197] Forever living or re-living our youth would be a curse indeed. We cannot forget once we are saved our goal, our eternal home is no longer this earth, rather it is heaven. Hence, no blessing from God would give us eternal life to be lived in the foolishness of youth here in this cursed world. No, the blessing is to give us a little more time in the maturity of wisdom to be able to reach a few more for his kingdom, and to pass a solid foundation of obedience onto the next generation. "So teach *us* to number our days, that we may apply *our* hearts unto wisdom." Ps 90:12

Here, the word 'prolongeth' means 'to *add* or *augment*' and in context is contrasted with 'shortened' which means 'to *dock* off, i.e. *curtail*'. Notice the LORD will add <u>days</u> to those who fear him, but will cut off <u>years</u> from those who are wicked (i.e. those who lack the fear of God). So God exhorted his people as he brought them into the promised land that he desired to prolong their days and the days of their children.

> That thou mightest fear the LORD thy God, to keep all his statutes and his commandments, which I command thee, thou, and thy son, and thy son's son, all the days of thy life; and <u>that thy days may be prolonged</u> [i.e. to *make long*]. Dt 6:2

The fountain of life of the fear of God increases our spiritual life not only in quantity, but also in quality. We were created to be in fellowship and relationship with the Creator of all life, but that fellowship and life that comes from him is so often disrupted by *our* disobedience. Nothing will satisfy the saint whose heart is possessed with the fear of the LORD, but the approval of God. "The fear of the LORD *tendeth* to <u>life</u>: and *he that hath it* shall <u>abide satisfied</u>; he shall not be visited with evil." Pr 19:23 A deep, continuing satisfaction settles in the heart of the saint of God who possesses the fear of the LORD. With it he or she is able to attend unto the Lord without distraction (1Co 7:35). With it our ears are attentive to his voice and our heart is prepared to honor him and love him by keeping his commandments. There is an inherent blessing in fulfilling our god-given roles of being in willing submission to his will.

The Fear of the LORD: A Storehouse of Blessings
"the fear of the LORD is his treasure." Isa 33:6

The fear of the LORD is the door to so many of God's blessings in our life. The fear of the Most High brings the knowledge of the holy so that the chambers of 'our house' or vessel are filled with great treasures. So many times we see God's promises in the Word, but either do not partake of them or are unable to keep them in our life, because we are not walking in the fear of God. Isaiah tells us that the fear of the LORD is to be our treasure. This word 'treasure' here in Hebrew means 'a *depository*'. It is the same word used for the treasury of the house of the LORD (Jos 6:19,24, 1Ch 9:26). The precious things of God for the service of him were stored in the treasury of the house of the LORD. Now, we are that house that God is building, and the treasure that is to be stored within us for his service is the fear of the LORD. Is the fear of the LORD your treasure? Is it your storehouse? Is it that which you draw strength and supply from?

Let's look at this treasure house of the fear of the LORD. God's blessing in the scriptures was seen over and over again to be bestowed on them who feared him enough to be different than the world around them, for "he honoureth them that fear the LORD" (Ps 15:4). The midwives of Moses' day "feared God, and did not as the king of Egypt commanded them …. And it came to pass, because the midwives feared God, that he made them houses." Ex 1:17,21 The manifold blessings of the fear of the LORD in the believer's life are many indeed. May you be truly awed by the goodness of God, and not be polluted as so many are today to think evil or lowly of the fear of God. Men mock the idea that we should 'tremble at his word', yet the Bible tells us that the fear of God is "for the good of them, and of their children after them", that he may do us good (Jer 32:39-40). The scriptures repeatedly declare the blessing of the fear of the LORD:

> Blessed *is* the man *that* feareth the LORD, *that* delighteth greatly in his commandments. Ps 112:1
>
> Blessed *is* every one that feareth the LORD; that walketh in his ways. Ps 128:1
>
> He will bless them that fear the LORD, *both* small & great. Ps 115:13

Through the fear of the LORD he is able to make us complete. Our life finds its satisfaction in him and not in substitutes, which always become idols. Let us see how blessed we are when we fear the LORD. Let us "consider how great *things* he hath done for [us]" that we may fear him and serve him in truth with all our heart (1Sam 12:24).

The fear of the LORD is the door to so many of the blessings of the LORD. We will look at many of these in detail in other chapters, but to establish in our hearts why the fear of the LORD should be our great treasure, let us summarize them here:

- mercy
- salvation
- protection
- deliverance
- a whole heart
- answered prayer
- approval from God
- intimacy with the LORD
- fellowship with the saints
- the leading of the Spirit
- faithfulness
- humbleness
- obedience
- wisdom
- worship
- blessing
- service
- giving

13 – The Inestimable Treasure of God's Fear

Table 13-1   The Blessings of the LORD on those who Fear Him

The Blessings Abounding on those who Fear Him[198]

"*Oh* how great *is* thy goodness, which thou hast laid up" Ps 31:19

- His eye will be upon us (**Ps 33:18**) & his ear will hear our cry (**Mal 3:16**)
- God will show us his covenant and his secret will be with us (**Ps 25:14**)
- By humility and the fear of the LORD *are* riches, honour, life (**Pr 22:4**) [199]
- It *is* a fountain of life to depart from the snares of death (**Pr 14:27**)
- It causes us to make spiritual, not natural judgments (**Isa 11:3-4**)
- It is the way of peace that many have not known (**Rom 3:17-18**)
- It brings forth wisdom (**Pr 15:33, 9:10, Ps 111:10, Job 28:28**)
- Healing will arise and we shall go forth & grow up (**Mal 4:2**)
- It prolongeth days (**Pr 10:27**) and *tendeth* to life (**Pr 19:23**)
- God will teach us the way he has chosen for us (**Ps 25:12**)
- He gives the covenant of life and peace to us (**Mal 2:5**)
- The LORD shall be for a sanctuary to us (**Isa 8:13-14**)
- We shall not be visited with evil (**Pr 19:23, Ps 34:7**)
- So great is his mercy toward us (**Ps 103:11,13,17**)
- Happy *is* the man that feareth always (**Pr 28:14**)
- The LORD taketh pleasure in us (**Ps 147:11**)
- There *is* a <u>strong confidence</u> (**Pr 14:26**)
- He *is* our help and shield (**Ps 115:11**)
- He will fulfill our desire (**Ps 145:19**)
- We shall abide satisfied (**Pr 19:23**)
- It enlarges our heart (**Isa 60:5**)
- *there is* no want to us (**Ps 34:9**)
- We depart from evil (**Pr 16:6**)

"Behold, that thus shall the man be blessed that feareth the LORD." Ps 128:4

There is a great reward indeed to those who fear God enough to fear his commandments. The scripture says, "Whoso despiseth the word shall be destroyed: but he that feareth the commandment shall be rewarded." Pr 13:13 The word 'rewarded' here means 'to be *safe* (in mind, body, or estate); to be or make *completed*; by implication to be *friendly*'. Through the fear of the LORD, God will keep us safe in mind, body, and estate. He is able to easily warn us through the fear of the LORD and to keep us from vain and prideful ways of thinking. When we walk in his fear, God is able to show himself friendly to us because we begin to have a humble heart, a listening ear, and eyes that see spiritually instead of naturally.

---

[198] Also see the appendix entitled "The Scriptures on Fearing God" under the section 'Key Scriptures on the Fear of God'.

[199] Honor and praise will come to the woman that fears the LORD (Pr 31:30).

Where is the Fear of GOD? Finding the Treasure of the Lord

The Blessing Laid up for Those who Fear God

The fear of the LORD is its own reward, but these rewards do not come overnight. The scripture states it takes time, but it is sure. As we endure through our struggles and disappointments and the testings of God, we ought to be assured and know that it will be well for us if we continue in the fear of God.

> Though a sinner do evil an hundred times, and his *days* be prolonged,
> yet <u>surely</u> I know that it shall be well <u>with them that fear God,</u>
> <u>which fear before him</u>:
> But it shall not be well with the wicked,
> neither shall he prolong *his* days, *which are* as a shadow;
> <u>because he feareth not before God</u>. Ecc 8:12-13

Notice it does not say that "it has been well" or even "it is well". Rather, it says, "it <u>shall</u> be well", meaning the blessings are forward looking. They will grow in time. They are a result of faithfully walking in the fear of God. It will be well with those who fear God and who keep his commandments. This is God's promise, not only for the one who has the fear of God, but also for their children (Dt 5:29). The fear of God lays up so many wonderful blessings in the future for us, not only in our life, but also in others who will watch and behold. "God shall bless us; and all the ends of the earth shall fear him." Ps 67:7 The great storehouse of blessings await those who will fear before him.

The blessing is sure, but will we be sure and bold in proclaiming truth? As we patiently wait for the blessings of God, we ought to declare openly unto others our hope in the LORD. This brings about the greatest opportunity for bringing about righteousness in those who watch our life. So many want to blend in with the world to "win the world", but God would have us be his peculiar people who stand apart from the world and call them to repentance. In the vanity of this world and the pursuit of pleasure that has captured the heart of the nations, ought not we, along with Solomon, declare that it shall *not* be well with the sinner or the wicked, but it *shall* be well with them that fear God, that fear before him.

This sets the ground for the testimony of the LORD to truly be seen. Then when God brings these assured blessings because we fear him, it will cause all the ends of the earth to be humbled and to see that God's word is sure, that there is a spiritual realm that cannot be seen by natural eyes. Was not this the life of Elijah? "And when all the people saw *it,* they fell on their faces: and they said, The LORD, he *is* the God; the LORD, he *is* the God." 1K 18:39 When we acknowledge that these blessings are not of our own making, but are the gift of God unto all that fear him, they in turn will be deeply moved to fear him. There is no investment a person can make that is more secure than devoting oneself to the fear of God. David prays to God for the promises of God's word to be manifested and secured in his life on the singular basis that he was devoted to the fear of God: "Stablish thy word unto thy servant, who *is devoted* to thy fear." Ps 119:38

The Effect of the Fear of God: Pleasing God
"Then they that feared the LORD spake often one to another: and the LORD hearkened, and heard it" Mal 3:16

Having a pure heart is what enables us to have intimacy with the LORD, for we can only approach the LORD with clean hands and a pure heart. Thus, the psalmist asks who may come into God's presence. "Who shall ascend into the hill of the LORD? or who shall stand in his holy place? He that hath clean hands, and a pure heart; who hath not lifted up his soul unto vanity, nor sworn deceitfully." Ps 24:3-4 So it is echoed and amplified in the New Testament when Jesus said, "Blessed *are* the pure in heart: for they shall see God." Mt 5:8 Take note that a pure heart is not a heart that has not sinned, but rather a heart that humbly acknowledges the truth. Thus, the repentant tax collector, though he were a sinner in the eyes of men, yet in God's estimation he had a pure heart and so went home *justified*. How did the tax collector obtain this pure heart? Clearly through the fear of God that led him to "repentance to the acknowledging of the truth" (2Tim 2:26).

God takes great pleasure when we fear him. Let the wicked mock and ridicule for the self-restraint we have through the fear of the LORD to depart from iniquity and to do *only* that which pleases God. We have God's approval on our side! "The LORD taketh pleasure in them that fear him" (Ps 147:11). "As a man takes pleasure in his wife, in his children, in his gold, in his jewels; so the man that fears the Lord is the object of his delight."[200] The word God uses for 'pleasure' here means 'to *be pleased with*; specifically to *satisfy* a debt'. Through the fear of the LORD, he is able to show his loving kindness and compassion to us as a father does for his children. "Like as a father pitieth *his* children, *so* the LORD pitieth them that fear him." Ps 103:13 A special intimacy of a father to his tender children exists between the LORD and those who love him in truth through the fear of the LORD.

> Note that 'pitieth' here is not the exact equivalent of our modern word 'pity'. Rather, it is the Hebrew word which means 'to *fondle*; by implication to *love*, especially to have compassion upon'. Thus, it speaks of a much deeper intimacy, closeness, and affection than does our modern English word 'pity'.

It is fascinating that this word 'pleasure' (in Psalm 147:11) also means 'to satisfy a debt', for we have a debt of love that we are to pay. The two greatest commandments are to love God with all our heart, mind, soul, and strength,

---

[200] Bunyan, p. 112.

and to love our neighbor as ourself. We are to "Owe no man any thing, but to love one another: for he that loveth another hath fulfilled the law." Rom 13:8 As we maintain the fear of the LORD and walk in it, we fulfill our debt of love toward God, and our heart becomes perfect before him!

An Honest Spirit: Keeping our Tongue from Evil
We must keep our tongue from evil and our lips from speaking guile (Ps 34:13)

We have already looked at how the fear of the LORD will teach us to be in proper relationship with authority and how to have a proper fear of authority. We must not speak evil of authority, for it is forbidden by God. As David himself was such a model of this, he has the full right to teach us the fear of God, "Keep thy tongue from evil, and thy lips from speaking guile. Depart from evil, and do good; seek peace, and pursue it." Ps 34:13-14 As David was hunted and persecuted by King Saul, David continually had to keep his tongue from evil and his lips from speaking guile. He had to repeatedly depart from evil. Though we are evil spoken of or evilly treated (which we certainly shall be),[201] we cannot render evil for evil. We are to "Recompense to no man evil for evil. Provide things <u>honest</u> in the sight of all men." Rom 12:17 Paul prays this for the Corinthians. "Now I pray to God that ye <u>do no evil</u>; not that we should appear approved, but that ye should do that which is <u>honest</u>" (2Co 13:7).

Isn't it amazing that God's answer to our propensity to do evil is to "do that which is honest". We cannot walk in the fear of God and allow evil to abide in our heart. "The fear of the LORD *is* to hate evil: pride, and arrogancy, and the evil way, and the froward mouth, do I hate." Pr 8:13 The fear of the LORD is clean. It is not soiled or dirty, and it will make us clean by continually convicting us of attitudes and choices that dishonor the LORD. God is looking for truth in our inward parts. "Behold, thou desirest truth in the inward parts: and in the hidden *part* thou shalt make me to know wisdom." Ps 51:6

To obtain the fear of God we must learn how to maintain an honest and good heart. Let us look at honesty, for without honesty we can never maintain a good heart. Honesty is what opens our eyes to be able to behold truth. Honesty is the first requirement of a good conscience. God desires truth in the inward parts (Ps 51:6). It will take honesty to acknowledge to our own heart that many, many times we truly do not want to come before God. Often we do not pray simply because we do not want to pray. Notice how a good conscience is linked to living honestly <u>in all things</u>. "Pray for us: for we trust we have a good conscience, in all things willing to live honestly." Heb 13:18

Honesty is what helps us to not deceive ourselves and to acknowledge our transgression. Honesty continually reminds us that he sees and knows all things:

---

[201] Those who walk with the Lord will be evil spoken of: Ps 41:5, 109:20, 1Pe 3:16, 4:4.

"but all things *are* naked and opened unto the eyes of him with whom we have to do." Heb 4:13 Honesty reminds us that we must always answer to authority. Paul shares how he and his fellow laborers commended themselves "to every man's conscience in the sight of God" by renouncing the hidden things of dishonesty and "not walking in craftiness, nor handling the word of God deceitfully" (2Co 4:2).

Willing to live honestly in all things is the key to a good conscience. What is a good conscience, but living in agreement with the truth. Guile is deception or feigned speech. It is trying to act and come across as if our heart toward someone is one way when in fact, it is another altogether. Thus, guile is the killer of a good conscience, and it will keep us from the fear of God. The fear of the LORD is to keep our tongue from evil and our lips from speaking guile. Truth cannot dwell in our inward parts when we allow guile to operate through us, for truth cries out to be known. Even the truth of our failures and our sins, God is able through his redemptive bounty to transform into his glory, for where sin abounds, grace does much more abound (Rom 5:20).

Speaking Evil of No Man

We are "to speak evil of no man" (Tit 3:2). What is worse, is to *think* evil of another and to speak pleasantly to that person, for that is lying and deception. "But if ye have bitter envying and strife in your hearts, glory not, and lie not against the truth." Jam 3:14 Guile is lying against the truth of what is in our heart. We cannot glory in our sin by giving place to the anger that is bitterly working in us, nor can we lie against the truth and say it is not there. Rather, we are called to confess it as sin and put it far from us. "Wherefore putting away lying, speak every man truth with his neighbour: for we are members one of another." Eph 4:25 Guile and evil speaking must be purged from the child of God by continually laying down our judgments and our desire for revenge.

> Speak not evil one of another, brethren. He that speaketh evil of *his* brother, and judgeth his brother, speaketh evil of the law, and judgeth the law: but if thou judge the law, thou art not a doer of the law, but a judge. Jam 4:11

As the people of God, we are called to bear witness, not of our hurt, but to the truth. Such was the testimony of Jesus to Pilate. "To this end was I born, and for this cause came I into the world, that I should bear witness unto the truth." Jn 18:37 Jesus did not speak of the mockery of his trial or his beatings or how he had been mistreated. He did not cry out for justice on his own behalf. No, he spoke of the truth that he was sent to witness of, even as we are also sent to bear witness of. If we will be obedient to the truth, which has saved us, then we will have a pure, fervent, and unfeigned heart of love and compassion for others. "Seeing ye have purified your souls in obeying the truth through the Spirit unto unfeigned love of the brethren, *see that ye* love one another with a pure heart fervently: Being born again" (1Pe 1:22-23).

God calls us to live in agreement and in open declaration of the truth that has saved us and that will preserve us – if we hold fast to it. David was evil spoken of AND evilly treated (Ps 41:5), but he would not speak evil in return. David, like you and I, must provide things honest in the sight of all men. We must depart from evil and do good. We must seek peace and pursue it (Ps 34:14). This is a critical part of the fear of the LORD that must be established in us in order to get beyond the continual defeat of taking things into our own hands. When we are hurt, it is so easy for any one of us not to depart from evil and not to do good. We justify our anger, and say, "But you do not know what they have done to me." Yet we are warned strictly in scripture concerning this, "Dearly beloved, avenge not yourselves, but *rather* give place unto [*His*] wrath: for it is written, Vengeance *is* mine; I will repay, saith the Lord." Rom 12:19

> **WARNING**: At a first reading Romans 12:19 may seem to contradict itself when it says "avenge not yourselves", but then it says "give place unto wrath". This confusion is quickly cleared up when we understand exactly *whose* wrath it is that we are giving place to. I have added the parenthetical 'His' before wrath, because it is clearly God's wrath, not ours, that we must give place to. When we avenge ourselves, *our* wrath is being satisfied, and we prevent God from doing what he sees is best.
>
> When we do not avenge ourselves, we are not giving place to our wrath, but we are giving place to God's wrath. Now he is able to do what he sees is best – whether it *is* to bring judgment, or even in his great wisdom, if it is to be merciful and to bless the other. For though we may not always understand this, sometimes his wrath is actually poured out in overwhelmingly abundant blessings and not (initially) in destruction. Consider when the people wept for meat and God gave them meat for a whole month – until it came out of their nostrils (Nu 11:18-20)! "Or despisest thou the riches of his goodness and forbearance and longsuffering; not knowing that the goodness of God leadeth thee to repentance?" Rom 2:4

Dearly beloved, God knows. Rest sufficient in that, and do not nurture a wounded spirit – for that is the way of destruction that consumed King Saul. In the final analysis, is what you are experiencing at the hands of sinful men or women any *greater* than what our Lord went through, who was completely without sin? "For consider him that endured such contradiction of sinners against himself, lest ye be wearied and faint in your minds."[202] Heb 12:3 Is it any won-

---

[202] The deceptiveness of our own heart should **never** be underestimated. A few times in my life when exhorting another to love God and to continue in good deeds, I have had to ask the person to compare their struggles and sufferings with those of David, the

der that right after Paul exhorts Titus, his son in the faith, to remind the people to be subject to authorities, that Paul then must remind the people to speak evil of no man? "Put them in mind to be subject to principalities and powers, to obey magistrates, to be ready to every good work, To speak evil of no man, to be no brawlers, *but* gentle, shewing all meekness unto all men." Tit 3:1-2

We can never afford evil to take a foothold within us, for then the old leaven of malice and hatred begins to work within us and to fill our wretched heart. These are of the old nature and reflect how the unsaved man or woman responds to offense. They are contrary to how we were saved and how we are to live. If we only understood that such things as bitterness and anger and evil speaking grieve and *distress* the Holy Spirit with whom we are sealed, we might be more ready to put away such things.

> And grieve not the holy Spirit of God, whereby ye are sealed unto the day of redemption. Let all bitterness, and wrath, and anger, and clamour, and evil speaking, be put away from you, with all malice: And be ye kind one to another, tenderhearted, forgiving one another, even as God for Christ's sake hath forgiven you.
>
> Be ye therefore followers of God, as dear children; And walk in love, as Christ also hath loved us, and hath given himself for us an offering and a sacrifice to God for a sweetsmelling savour. Eph 4:30-5:2

We must continually purge ourselves from malice and all desires to do or to think evil. Just as the Jews naturally had to cleanse their entire house of any leaven in preparation for the Passover, so we must cleanse our entire heart from the leaven of malice and wickedness. What is the Passover feast for us, but our fellowship with the Lord and with his people. Therefore, when we fellowship with our God or with his people we must "keep the feast, not with old leaven, neither with the leaven of malice and wickedness; but with the unleavened *bread* of sincerity and truth." 1Co 5:8 God's exhortation to us to prevent the leaven of malice and wickedness from growing in our heart is to have our heart purged from these things, and then to keep it full of sincerity and truth.

---

man of God, or even with Jesus our Lord, in order to get a proper perspective. This must be done when we see our pain as greater than any one else's, when we begin to excuse our actions with, "Well, you just don't understand the depth of my pain, and why I *had* to do this." No man *has* to sin against God.

Amazingly on a few occasions the deception was so great the individual actually tried to explain how their sufferings compared with that of David and Jesus and were in fact greater! Whenever this happens, friend, know that we have lost sight of reality and proper perspective. It is then that our problems must be brought down to the size they actually are. We can easily make the same mistake of the 10 Exodus spies who magnified their enemies beyond measure and excluded God's ability to fulfill his promise.

The Effect of the Fear of God:
The Intimacy of God's Leading
"Surely thou wilt fear me, thou wilt receive instruction" Zep 3:7

An honest and good heart, one that is ready to obey, opens our hearts to be able to hear the Master's voice. Jesus was always looking for those who truly had ears to hear.[203] Without open ears that can hear his voice, it is impossible to be led forth with peace, for we cannot hear which way he wants us to go. This brings great distress, for now we turn to the right, the next moment we turn to the left. Only the sure voice of the Lord can provide stability. The fear of God enables us to tremble at his word and to truly have that ear to hear what he is saying and to take it soberly and diligently. Through the fear of the LORD we learn to hearken to his commandments. The scripture promises that if we hearken to God's commandments that our peace will be as a river (Isa 48:18, 66:12). Therefore we can know that the fear of God will produce great peace in our life, even peace as a river! So much in our life waits for the establishment of the fear of God within us. "By humility *and* the fear of the LORD *are* riches, and honour, and life." Pr 22:4

We have seen that the fear of the LORD will bring about a soft, humble, and pure heart that is able to hear the Word of God. The fear of the LORD also produces a single, willing, and obedient heart that desires to do the will of God. The ability to hear and the desire to do combine to make it easy for God to now lead us through the fear of the LORD. Thus, the fear of the LORD prepares the heart to receive God's instruction. "I said, Surely thou wilt fear me, thou wilt receive instruction" (Zep 3:7). This will produce an intimacy with the LORD that cannot be achieved any other way. The LORD promises to take those who fear him and to teach them his ways. "What man *is* he that feareth the LORD? him shall he teach in the way *that* he shall choose." Ps 25:12 This is the instruction of the fear of the LORD. It should be no surprise, then, how easy it is for us to now hear the LORD and to be led by his Spirit. God is especially ready to speak to those who fear him, for he knows they will listen with a heart to obey.

What it is to be Led of the Spirit

Today, so many who believe in the Charismatic gifts think that being led of the Spirit is but an ecstatic experience. The problem with ecstatic experiences is that so often, without proper correction and oversight, they degenerate into unrestrained emotionalism, to self-centeredness, and to spiritual pride. This is the record of scripture, especially as evidenced in 1Corinthians, but this is a different spirit than the one which we received. The true Spirit of God will lead us into:

---

[203] Ears to hear: Mt 11:15, 13:9,15-16,43; Lk 14:35.

13 – The Inestimable Treasure of God's Fear

- doing all things decently and in order (1Co 14:40),
- being subject one to another in the fear of God (Eph 5:21), and
- doing all things for the sake of others, not for ourselves or our enjoyment.

As it is written, "But he that prophesieth speaketh unto men *to* edification, and exhortation, and comfort." 1Co 14:3 The Spirit of God is not trying to take us on a joy ride. Rather, he is trying to prepare us for the coming of the LORD of Hosts in all soberness. The Spirit of God is actually trying to bring us into a greater and greater discipline of our lives so that we may serve the Lord and others more effectively and powerfully.

We need to learn to hear his voice from all the other voices out there, including our own. The fear of God is a protection that keeps us from following after two deceptive dangers. The first is the multitude of dreams which we may follow after. The second is the vanities of those who speak many words (Ecc 5:7). Without the fear of God, all of us have an innate tendency to wander in our walk with the LORD and to begin to go our own way (Isa 53:6), but this is what the LORD wants to deliver us from.

Putting Away Many Words and Many Dreams

The instruction of the Lord also keeps us from following the multitude of dreams and the diverse vanities of men's words. "For in the multitude of dreams and many words *there are* also *divers* vanities: but fear thou God." Ecc 5:7 Many a saint has been led astray by their own desires and dreams who easily could have been kept from straying and erring from truth, if *only* they had the fear of God. Remember, it is the fear of God that keeps us humble and teachable. If we lose the fear of God, then pride subtly slips in, and pride keeps us from being able to hear correction. Pride hardens our heart, and in this way deceives us. "The pride of thine heart hath deceived thee" (Ob 1:3).

On the contrary, when the fear of the Lord is working within us, we are very conscious of our need to be in submission to authorities. "Wherefore *ye must needs be subject*, not only for wrath, but also for conscience sake." Rom 13:5 When we fear God we see ourselves as *needing* to be in subjection for the sake of maintaining a good conscience. It is this necessity to be in subjection that keeps us in a safe and submissive place with the Lord and with the spiritual authorities he has put us with.

The fear of the LORD is not only an instruction and a protection, it is also a warning. Noah was moved with fear "being warned of God of things not seen as yet" (Heb 11:7). The fear of God enabled Noah to hear the voice of God even though it was contrary to everything he had ever known or experienced in his life. God has a way that he has chosen for us. It is different from anything we have ever known or experienced. It is the life of the kingdom rule of his Son. He has pre-ordained the good works that we are to walk in (Eph 2:10). We do not choose them for ourself. It is God's choice and we must receive it, for we are no longer our own (1Co 6:19, 2Co 13:5). The LORD desires that we come to know his will so we may do the works which he has chosen for us. Through the fear of the LORD he will teach us these.

> The instruction of the fear of the LORD will teach us the deep things of God – the spiritual meat of the Word

When we are first born again we are but babies that need to feed only on the milk of the Word (1Pe 1:23, 2:2). As we grow up through the maturing process from being spiritual babes and infants to those who no longer require milk, we come to the place where we are able to eat strong meat (Heb 5:12-14, 1Co 3:1-2). The instruction of the fear of the LORD will teach us the deep things of God – the spiritual meat of the Word (1Co 10:3). God is especially able to do this for those who fear him, for it is written, "He hath given **meat** unto them that fear him: he will ever be mindful of his covenant." Ps 111:5 Clearly, the fear of God is integral to growing up in the LORD – because those who are mature, those who can handle the meat of the word, are those who have the fear of God.

The Revelation of His Covenants

The LORD not only reveals his will to the man or woman that fears him, but he also reveals his covenant. "The secret of the LORD *is* with them that fear him; and he will shew them his covenant." Ps 25:14 In particular, God will reveal his part of the covenant, that is, what God will do for that man or woman. God promises to show his covenant to those who fear him. This is fulfilled most surely in the exercise of the new covenant. Hear Paul's words to those who feared God on his first apostolic journey, "Men *and* brethren, children of the stock of Abraham, and whosoever among you feareth God, to you is the word of this salvation sent." Ac 13:26

Thus, even the new covenant, the word of salvation, is shown particularly to those who fear God. The fear of God is what opens the ears to hear and enables the heart to change. This is why we see so many blessings associated with the fear of God. Because "the LORD taketh pleasure in them that fear him" (Ps 147:11), he shares his good pleasure with us (i.e. the goodness of his will), by revealing the secrets of his kingdom with us! He has "made known unto us the mystery of his will, according to his good pleasure" (Eph 1:9).

And what is his good pleasure? "it is your Father's good pleasure to give you the kingdom." Lk 12:32 God is able to entrust those who fear him with the secrets of the kingdom of God! He is able to make it known best to those who fear him. Through the fear of God our ears become open to hear what he has

13 – The Inestimable Treasure of God's Fear

to say with a readiness to do it. God takes great pleasure in revealing the awesomeness of his kingdom and how it works. Remember, it is the very reason Jesus came to this earth – to establish his kingdom in the earth (Isa 9:6-7). This is why Jesus told so many parables concerning the kingdom of God to his disciples, for disciples have an ear to hear what their master is instructing them. Disciples commit themselves to follow and to obey, and this prepares the way for the Father's good pleasure to be revealed.

This pattern is also foreshadowed for us in the Old Testament. This is why when we see Levi and the priests respecting God's holiness and growing in the fear of God, God was able to specially reveal his covenant to them. "My covenant was with him of life and peace; and I gave them to him *for* the fear wherewith he feared me, and was afraid before my name." Mal 2:5

The tribe of Levi had become priests upon the terrible disobedience of the people with the golden calf. Thus, they well knew what it was to truly fear God and to depart from iniquity. When Moses had come down from the Mount having been in the presence of God for 40 days and nights, God was angry with the people for they had sinned a great sin of idolatry. Moses broke the two tablets containing the word of God. "Then Moses stood in the gate of the camp, and said, Who *is* on the LORD'S side? *let him come* unto me. And all the sons of Levi gathered themselves together unto him." Ex 32:26 Because the Levites were willing to be obedient to God and to fear God and not man, God chose them to be his priests. The intensity of their fear of God and being afraid of God's name was evidenced by their willingness to sacrifice even their own brethren, companions, and neighbors to be obedient to the voice of God (Ex 32:27).

> **WARNING**: We must *not* take up the natural sword of Peter of political resistance. Protesting, marches, and any other form of political resistance must always end up in the shedding of blood and the cutting off of someone's ear, so they can no longer hear the message of the truth! Sadly, it is often the Christian's ear that is no longer able to hear in this case. Now the Christian ends up being involved in natural conflicts that he has no permission from our Lord being in, yet he feels convinced (by his own thinking) that he *has* to be in. Jesus' kingdom is not of this world, which is why we do not use natural means to fight for it. Remember, this whole event *impeded* Christ's going to the cross, which had been ordained by God. Thus, Jesus had to rebuke Peter with the severest warning,[204] that if he did not stop such actions he would **surely perish**, "for all they that take the sword shall perish with the sword." Mt 26:52

---

[204] Jesus' response also shows that those who take up the sword of political resistance think situations are out of his control. "Thinkest thou that I cannot now pray to my Father, and he shall presently give me more than twelve legions of angels? But how then shall the scriptures be fulfilled, that thus it must be?" Mt 26:53-54

Jesus asks nothing less of us today in the realm of the spirit. We must be willing to forsake all others (family, friends, brethren, even our own ways) in order to follow him. We must take up the sword of the word of God and cut down any thought which exalts itself against the knowledge of God, whether it be in ourself, our neighbors, our companions, our family, or even our own Christian brethren. "If any *man* come to me, and hate not his father, and mother, and wife, and children, and brethren, and sisters, yea, and his own life also, he cannot be my disciple." Lk 14:26 As a result of "the fear wherewith he feared [God], and was afraid before [God's] name" God gave him a covenant of life and peace.

Search the scriptures and you will find those with the fear of the LORD were also those with whom it was easy for God to both speak to and to lead and who had the closest relationship with him. Abraham who was called the friend of God is the perfect example of this in the Old, and in the New we see Jesus who had an intimacy with the Father we all long for. Those who feared God greatly were those who repeatedly heard God's voice. Similarly, those who lost their fear of God, lost their relationship with the LORD and the ability to hear his voice. Thus, we see many a man who once heard the voice of God and enjoyed his presence, crying out for God to again lead them. King Saul is a noticeable example of one who lost his relationship with the LORD and the ability to hear from God because he lost his fear of God.[205]

> And Samuel said to Saul, Why hast thou disquieted me, to bring me up? And Saul answered, I am sore distressed; for the Philistines make war against me, and <u>God is departed from me, and answereth me no more</u>, neither by prophets, nor by dreams: therefore I have called thee, that thou mayest make known unto me what I shall do. Then said Samuel, Wherefore then dost thou ask of me, seeing <u>the LORD is departed from thee</u>, and <u>is become thine enemy</u>? … **Because thou obeyedst not the voice of the LORD** …, therefore hath the LORD done this thing unto thee this day. 1Sam 28:15-18

On the other hand, we see that the LORD invites those that tremble at his word to hear his word: "Hear the word of the LORD, ye that tremble at his word" (Isa 66:5). Will you be such a man, a man who can hear God's leading, because you tremble at his word? If we will fear him, God promises that he will teach us in the way that he shall choose. God will divinely reveal his will to those who fear him.

This is why so many Christians struggle knowing and hearing the will of God for their life – for the simple fact that they are not wholly committed to doing his will, no matter what it is or what it costs. Yet this is exactly what made Abraham, our father in the faith, one whom God could so freely speak to – the

---

[205] The loss of the fear of God in King Saul's life is evidenced by the fact that he no longer had a respect for God's commandments.

fact that he feared God and sacrificed everything to obey God's will. The most common word for 'obey' in the Old Testament, *shama`* (H8085), means 'to *hear* intelligently, often <u>with the implication of attention and obedience</u>'! This is why God rarely directly speaks to those whose hearts are set on doing their own will, or who have a heart of compromise to only do part of God's will and to leave the other part undone. He, of course, will not speak at all (except in rebuke and condemnation) to the stubborn hearted, for he knows they will not listen and they refuse to change.[206]

Maturity and the Fear of the LORD

"But unto you that <u>fear my name</u> shall the Sun of righteousness arise with healing in his wings; and ye shall go forth, and <u>grow up</u> as calves of the stall." Mal 4:2

God wants our hearts to be the good ground which brings forth good fruit. "But that on the good ground are they, which in an <u>honest</u> and <u>good</u> heart, having heard the word, keep *it,* and bring forth fruit with patience." Lk 8:15 We cannot remain in the fear of God, nor can we find it in the first place, if we do not maintain an honest spirit that does not continually put away evil and guile. If we find ourselves shading the truth or allowing someone to believe a situation is one way, when we know it to be another, then we must take warning for we are losing our fear of God and speaking with guile. But as we allow the fear of God to continually clothe us with the belt of truth that girds our loins (Eph 6:14), we will grow up in maturity. When we grow up in the fear of God, particular changes will begin to occur.

A Time for Correction

Babies do not fear their tender and loving parents. Neither do babies walk or eat meat. But as we begin to grow, changes are to take place, both in us *and* in our relationship with our father and mother. We must learn to walk and be weaned of the milk and begin to partake of solid food. Eventually meat is to be a part of our diet. As children grow and come to understanding, they must also learn to fear the voice of authority that resides in the office of their parents.

> Speak unto all the congregation of the children of Israel, and say unto them, Ye shall be holy: for I the LORD your God *am* holy. Ye shall

---

[206] This again is evidenced by Saul's life, and why he finally went to the witch at Endor (1Sam 28:6-7). It is frightening in the realm of the Spirit how many 'believers' who are older in the Lord are in such a state, where they are set in their ways and will not change. This is why it is so important to understand the baptism of repentance for today. We need to be continually immersed and washed in changing our way of thinking to agree with the word of God, for repentance *always* precedes the kingdom of God, that is, his rule and reign in our life.

<u>fear</u> every man his mother, and his father, and keep my sabbaths: I *am* the LORD your God.[207] Lev 19:2-3

It is a commandment from God that every child is to learn to fear their parents. Are we to think God would require such of children toward their earthly, natural fathers and not toward the church's spiritual fathers? Or even more so toward the heavenly Father himself? Surely, he does require it and so he sharply asks, "if then I *be* a father, where *is* mine honour? and if I *be* a master, where *is* my fear? saith the LORD of hosts unto you, O priests, that despise my name." Mal 1:6 This is why it falls to the authority of the home, the father, to raise his children and to implant in them the fear of the Lord. "And, ye fathers, provoke not your children to wrath: but bring them up in the nurture and <u>admonition of the Lord</u>." Eph 6:4

As children begin to understand admonition or correction, then they become ready to learn the weightier principles of responsibility. Once the child is old enough to understand why they are being corrected and to respond with understanding, they are at the place where the principles and covenants of the Word of God can now be sown into their spirits with great impartation. Spiritually as we mature in the fear of God, he is able as we respond correctly to admonition[208] to be able to impart unto us the admonition and instruction of the fear of the Lord. Spiritual meat can then begin to be chewed and swallowed. The fear of the Lord now begins to warn us of things to come.

> By faith Noah, <u>being warned of God of things not seen as yet</u>, **moved with fear**, prepared an ark to the saving of his house; by the which he condemned the world, and became heir of the righteousness which is by faith. Heb 11:7

> And if we have not *rather* done it **for fear** of *this* thing, saying, <u>In time to come</u> your children might speak unto our children, saying, What have ye to do with the LORD God of Israel? For the LORD hath made Jordan a border between us and you, ye children of Reuben and children of Gad; ye have no part in the LORD: so shall your children make our children <u>cease from fearing the LORD</u>. Jos 22:24-25

---

[207] Some may say "But this was spoken to Israel, not to those of the new covenant", yet it *is* spoken to those of the new covenant. Note how Peter parallels the two ideas of being holy and fearing our father, when he says: "But as he which hath called you is holy, so be ye holy in all manner of conversation; Because it is written, Be ye holy; for I am holy. And if ye call on the Father, who without respect of persons judgeth according to every man's work, pass the time of your sojourning *here* in fear." 1Pe 1:15-17 Concerning whether we are to keep the Sabbath, if we are in Jesus Christ and have ceased from our own works of righteousness (Heb 4:10), then we *are* keeping the sabbaths spiritually, for Jesus *is* our sabbath.

[208] Note, an admonition is a 'mild *rebuke* or *warning*'.

The Fruit of Balance

God hates a false balance. "Divers weights *are* an abomination unto the LORD; and a false balance *is* not good. Man's goings *are* of the LORD; how can a man then understand his own way?" Pr 20:23-24 Without the Lord coming into our life and setting the false balances of our life into a true balance, how can we know our own way, and where it will lead? We must allow God to measure our life on the true balance of justice and judgment, of mercy and truth. If we only allow the Lord to measure us with mercy and justice, we will never find the true balance in our life, and we will never understand our way. This is the perfect balance that only the fear of God can add to grace. Bunyan said of this:[209]

> For, this fear keeps a man, even in his words and judgment of things. It may be compared to the ballast of the ship, and to the poise of the balance of the scales, it keeps all even, and also makes us steer our counsel right with respect to the things that pertain to God and man.

God longs to be gracious unto us, but often he must wait until he can bring correction unto us first. If he cannot bring us back into his way, then how can he heal us with his mercy and loving kindness? Before we can be raised in newness of life, we must first die to the old. Paul who lived the greatest life of the apostles in newness of life said, "I die daily." 1Co 15:31

We cannot be healed, when we are in error, without being 'smitten' with correction. So we read the LORD had to smite his people *before* he could heal them. "Come, and let us return unto the LORD: for he hath torn, and he will heal us; he hath smitten, and he will bind us up." Hos 6:1 Without his correction, we cannot even know that it is the LORD who is healing us. The LORD speaking of his people when they were young and when he dealt with them gently and not with correction says, "but they knew not that I healed them." Hos 11:3 Thus, there comes a time in all of our lives spiritually and naturally when we grow up, that discipline, chastening, and admonishing must be administered by our fathers. So fathers are to bring up their children "in the nurture and admonition of the Lord." Eph 6:4

Envy's Cure and Avoiding Extremes

Sometimes our missing God does not take the path of deliberately choosing to do evil, but just of getting our eyes on what others have, or rather what we think they have. Remember, the great commandment that showed Paul's guiltiness before God was not "thou shalt not lie" or "thou shalt not steal" (Ex 20:15-16), rather it was the last of the ten commandments, "thou shalt not covet" (v17). Of all the commandments this is the one that is a snare to all of us in these last days of merchandising, "thou shalt not covet." This was the com-

---

[209] Bunyan, p. 72.

mandment which convicted Paul of sin, and showed him that he was "sold under sin" (Rom 7:7,14).

So Solomon warns us, "Let not thine heart envy sinners: but *be thou* in the fear of the LORD all the day long." Pr 23:17 Being in the fear of the LORD "all the day long" is what keeps us from getting out of balance in our life, and seeking after things that are not what the Lord would have for us. The fear of the Lord will rein in our passions and desires and keep us from covetousness and lusting after things that will all perish with the using. Thus, men who fear God are men of truth who hate covetousness (Ex 18:21). Abiding in the fear of the LORD specifically keeps us from envying and desiring what the disobedient have. We need to avoid many other pitfalls and excesses, such as being overly righteous or self-righteous, being overly wise, and being foolish, but the fear of God will deliver us from *all* these.

> Be not righteous over much; neither make thyself over wise: why shouldest thou destroy thyself? Be not over much wicked, neither be thou foolish: why shouldest thou die before thy time? *It is* good that thou shouldest take hold of this; yea, also from this withdraw not thine hand: for he that feareth God shall come forth of them all. Ecc 7:16-18

Thus, true balance in our life is ensured by the fear of God continually operating in our heart. Let us desire God's perfect balance and get the fear of God in our heart. It will keep us from a host of troubles and extremes, and it will prepare God a dwelling place.

Preparing a Habitation for the LORD

"Thus saith the LORD, The heaven is my throne, and the earth is my footstool: where is the house that ye build unto me? and where is the place of my rest?" Isa 66:1

So how do we come to know God's holiness, when we have not encountered him in his holiness as those before Mount Horeb did? How do we come to know God's holiness, when we are, in our thoughts and actions unholy? We must begin by preparing a *habitation* for the Lord GOD. This is what David set in his heart to do. It was his priority, to prepare a habitation for the LORD. "I will not give sleep to mine eyes, *or* slumber to mine eyelids, Until I find out a place for the LORD, an habitation for the mighty *God* of Jacob." Ps 132:4-5 Our God has always wanted us to build him a habitation, but not one built by the hands of men. Rather, he would have one built by the Spirit in our heart.

> Thus saith the LORD, The heaven *is* my throne, and the earth *is* my footstool: where *is* the house that ye build unto me? and where *is* the place of my rest? For all those *things* hath mine hand made, and all those *things* have been, saith the LORD: **but to this *man* will I look**, *even* to *him that is* poor and of a contrite spirit, and trembleth at my word. Isa 66:1-2

13 – The Inestimable Treasure of God's Fear

The house or habitation where God has always longed to dwell is not a cathedral built of stone or glass. It is not a place where thieves break through and steal, or where rust corrodes. Hear what he says in Isaiah, where will he look for his habitation? He will look for his habitation in the man who "*is* poor and of a contrite spirit, and <u>trembleth</u> at [his] word." Isa 66:2 The one who trembles at God's word, the one whose heart fears God's commands, is the one in whom God finds a resting place, a place to settle down and dwell in. The fear of God is the key, without it God cannot make his dwelling place in us.

God's habitation is holy, and he only dwells in a holy place. His is a habitation of holiness and glory (Isa 63:15).[210] So Isaiah exhorts us, "Sanctify the LORD of hosts himself; and *let* him *be* your fear, and *let* him *be* your dread." Isa 8:13 We allow the fear of God to come into our heart when first we sanctify him there. This is where the LORD must be set apart as holy: in our heart. So Peter says, "But sanctify the Lord God <u>in your hearts</u>" (1Pe 3:15). This is truly enlightening, because he is exhorting born again believers who are *already* sanctified by faith in Christ Jesus.[211] His exhortation clearly is not to be saved again. It is to grow in personal sanctification, by setting the Lord apart in our heart.

This is what Moses sang also in his song after the Red Sea deliverance. "The LORD *is* my strength and song, and he is become my salvation: he *is* my God, and <u>I will prepare him an habitation</u>" (Ex 15:2). Notice how *after* God has become our salvation we must now prepare him a habitation! Sanctifying the Lord GOD in our hearts will bring in his holiness, and his holiness will birth his fear. It is the pattern of scripture, whenever a place was set apart for him, according to his perfect standards and built according to the pattern which he revealed (through his word), then he inhabited that place with his glory, his holiness was then known, and his people bowed in fear before him.

---

[210] His habitation is repeatedly seen as holy (Zec 2:13, Jer 25:30). It is also a "mountain of holiness" (Jer 31:23).

[211] At salvation we are *positionally* sanctified (1Co 1:2, 6:11, Heb 2:11, 10:10,14,29, Jude 1:1), but God still wants to work in our life to bring about *personal* sanctification so that we might bring him glory as he is glorified through us.

Chapter 14. Experiencing the Genuine Fear of God
The Event that Forever Changes You

*"Fear not: for God is come to prove you,
and that his fear may be before your faces, that ye sin not." Ps 25:12*

What if we observed and studied all the members of a family, categorizing their inter-relationships so that we might understand what a family was. We might come to know much scientific knowledge, but if we had never experienced being part of a family ourself, we would still be lacking the depth of the foundation upon which to properly frame such information. It would be like analyzing every inch of a house from the outside, even looking in through the windows and trying to understand what a beautiful treasure that a home really is to those who live in it.

Can anyone understand the intimacy and transforming power of prayer, if they have never experienced it or if they rarely pray? Can anyone understand the change and insight that is added to the disciple's spirit through fasting, if they never fast? Understanding the value of something cannot be done merely from the outside. To understand anything spiritually, it must be spiritually discerned.

14 – Experiencing the Genuine Fear of God

But what if what we are trying to discern spiritually, changes us so that we obtain more spiritual discernment? Then there is no way we can completely discern it, until we receive what God has commanded us to receive. This is why once one knows they need salvation, or the baptism of the Holy Ghost, or the fear of God, then the search for knowledge concerning that work of God must undergo a change in purpose. The search for knowledge now must be subjugated to only that which either shows us how to obtain it or further arouses in us a holy desire to obtain it. This is where knocking, seeking, and asking for the gift must now begin in earnest through prayer, repentance, patience, and if necessary, fasting. The gifts of God are given to all who humble themselves and cry out for them and who receive them by faith. So it is with the fear of God, you must experience it to begin to see it and know it as it really is.

> The gifts of God are given to all who humble themselves and cry out for them and who receive them by faith.

Entering into the Promise

*"That ye be not slothful, but followers of them
who through faith and patience inherit the promises." Heb 6:12*

It is one thing to talk about the fear of the LORD. It is an entirely different thing to experience it. Let us compare it with the other grace of the Lord. Salvation must be preached and explained so that the foundation is sure. So the fear of the LORD must also be taught and exhorted. But salvation must be experienced before it can ever truly be understood by the receiver. The baptism in the Holy Ghost can only be understood by those who have first experienced it. The same is equally true of the fear of God. Without the singular experiences of salvation, being baptized with the Holy Ghost, and receiving the fear of the LORD, when we study them (even in the perfection of the Word) we are still only looking "through a glass, darkly", and we still need to see face to face (1Co 13:12).

This is the danger of learning the knowledge of anything spiritual. If we remain in our natural state, we will forget what manner of man we are. We will deceive ourselves, thinking we have truly understood and profited from such knowledge, when Jesus would still see us as naked, poor, and blind (Rev 3:17) for we have not put on the truth, which he has set before us. Spiritual truth profits us nothing until it opens our eyes, enriches our heart, and clothes us with a new walk with God. Until we learn to put on the truth and do that which is true, we will never be free. "For if any be a hearer of the word, and not a doer, he is like unto a man beholding his natural face in a glass: For he beholdeth himself, and goeth his way, and straightway forgetteth what manner of man he was." Jam 1:23-24

Once we have the experience and look through the looking glass of the Word, then we shall know, even as we are known (1Co 13:12). As we grow up through the Word and in obedience to it, our mind becomes renewed in spirit. Through spiritual maturity we become a man or woman of understanding, then we are able to put away the childish ways of thinking concerning salvation, baptism in the Holy Ghost, the fear of the LORD, and so many other things (1Co 13:11). Spiritual knowledge, obedience, and experience now combine to make a three-fold cord of transformation that will produce godly change and maturity.

The Importance of Experiencing the Fear of the LORD

There was a singular mountain-top experience that God's people had that brought the fear of God alive to them. It took place at Mount Horeb[212] which the scripture calls "the mount of God".[213] Its significance in scripture is great. God's presence at the mount was so important that it was the primary thing that God referred his people back to, even after forty years. He wanted them to *always* remember this singular event: when he came down from heaven upon the holy mount and placed the fear of God before their faces that they might not sin against him. Thus, the LORD gave them special instructions on how to keep themselves in the things of God and how to keep their souls from straying, so that they would not forget what he had shown them concerning his glory.

> Only take heed to thyself, and keep thy soul diligently, lest thou forget the things which thine eyes have seen, and lest they depart from thy heart all the days of thy life: but teach them thy sons, and thy sons' sons; *Specially* the day that thou stoodest before the LORD thy God in Horeb, when the LORD said unto me, Gather me the people together, and I will make them hear my words, that they may learn to fear me all the days that they shall live upon the earth, and *that* they may teach their children. Dt 4:9-10

God was forever bringing them back to the remembrance of this place, because of the importance of this event (Neh 9:13, Ps 68:8,17, Dt 5:2, 18:16, 29:1, Mal 4:4). It is the *only* place ever called the mount of God. Thus, it represents where and how we may approach God, so that we may know him in intimacy. God declared concerning this event that he wished the fear of God that had come into the heart of his people here would *always* be in the hearts of his people (Dt 5:29)! God desires every generation of his children to spiritually come to the mount of God in their life to experience his intimacy, encounter his fear, and to depart from iniquity through it. If we know that God desires this experience for each of his children, then we must also know he has assuredly left a spiritual pattern for us to follow, that we also might fear him in this same way.

---

[212] Most people are more familiar with the name Mount Sinai, but it was only called this because it was in the wilderness of Sinai (Ex 19:1-2,18-23).

[213] It is called the mount of God as follows: Ex 4:27, 18:5, 24:13, 1K 19:8.

14 – Experiencing the Genuine Fear of God

> **WARNING**: Of all things that God would particularly have his people not forget, it was this day, when God descended on the mount. It was "specially the day" when God would teach them the fear of God by showing them his own presence.[214] Once we experience his fear face to face we ought never to let such things depart from our heart all the days of our life. It is what we should teach our natural and spiritual sons (Dt 4:10), even as David did to his sons (both natural and spiritual), as we have seen in Psalm 34. We must learn to fear God all our days and to teach it to our children and never forget it.

Let us therefore look symbolically *when* this took place. It was after their salvation from sin via Passover and the shedding of blood for the remission of their sins (Ex 12). It was after their deliverance from the world (Ex 13, i.e. from Egypt). It was after their water baptism in the Red Sea, their incorporation into a spiritual body, and after they had been baptized unto Moses in the Sea to now trust godly leadership (Ex 14).[215] It was after God had revealed and healed their ingratitude of heart at the testing of the bitter waters (Ex 15).

The experience of the fear of God was also after they had been brought to the place of refreshment in the desert where "they encamped there by the waters." Ex 15:27 Here there were 12 wells of water and 70 palms, which speaks of the house of God with apostles and elders.[216] They continued in the refreshing provision of sound doctrine, by abiding in the type and shadow of the house of God. It was after God had given them their daily allotment of manna from heaven (Ex 16). This represented the discipline of daily reading the word of God for themselves. It was after the rock was struck and poured forth water for them all to drink (Ex 17), representing "before whose eyes Jesus Christ hath been evidently set forth, crucified among you" that they should learn to obey the truth (Gal 3:1). It was after their victory over Amalek (Ex 17), which speaks of overcoming pride and selfish independence. It was after the appointment of "able men, such as fear God, men of truth, hating covetousness; and place *such* over them, *to be* rulers" to be judges over the people (Ex 18:21).

God had now fully established the government of God – his leadership – with men that feared God. God was now ready to visit his people and to instill in them the fear of God, only one thing remained. In order to make them into a "kingdom of priests, and an holy nation" (Ex 19:6), he must first secure the

---

[214] The purpose of that day in Exodus 19 and 20, which is also talked about in Deuteronomy 5, is being referred to here also in Deuteronomy 4.

[215] This represents the foundation of a set man and the willingness to trust in and submit to spiritual authority ordained by God.

[216] Twelve always represents the government of God (i.e. the foundation apostles lay). There are 12 gates and 12 foundations in the New Jerusalem related to the 12 apostles (Rev 21). Seventy in the Bible represents the fullness of eldership oversight for there were 70 elders (Ex 24:1, 24:9; Nu 11:16,24-25) in the church in the wilderness (Ac 7:38).

purposing of their heart to obey him by a covenant of discipleship to be a set apart people who learn to obey.[217]

> Now therefore, if ye will obey my voice indeed, and keep my covenant, then ye shall be a peculiar treasure unto me above all people: for all the earth *is* mine: And ye shall be unto me a kingdom of priests, and an holy nation. And all the people answered together, and said, All that the LORD hath spoken we will do. Ex 19:5-6,8

As soon as the people committed themselves to be his special, called-out people, to obey God's voice and to keep his covenant, it was now time to prepare the people for the visitation of the LORD. So the LORD instructs Moses to tell the people to sanctify themselves "to day and to morrow, and let them wash their clothes, And be ready against the third day: for the third day the LORD will come down in the sight of all the people upon mount Sinai." Ex 19:10-11 God in his unfathomable wisdom chose at this time not to come down with comfort or in peace or rejoicing. He did not ask for sacrifice or offerings or praise or worship or singing or dancing – there were none of these things. The people were only to stand still and behold the glory of their God. How did the LORD come down this specially prepared time? He came down with the display of his *power*, with thunderings and lightnings, with a thick cloud, and the blast of the trumpet exceeding loud.

> And it came to pass on the third day in the morning, that there were <u>thunders</u> and <u>lightnings</u>, and a <u>thick cloud</u> upon the mount, and the <u>voice of the trumpet exceeding loud</u>; so that all the people that *was* in the camp trembled. …
>
> And all the people saw the <u>thunderings</u>, and the <u>lightnings</u>, and the <u>noise of the trumpet</u>, and the <u>mountain smoking</u>: and when the people saw *it*, they removed, and stood afar off. And they said unto Moses, Speak thou with us, and we will hear: but let not God speak with us, lest we die. And Moses said unto the people, Fear not: for God is come to prove you, and that his fear may be before your faces, that ye sin not. Ex 19:16, 20:18-20

This event is repeatedly described throughout the scriptures, both in the Old Testament and in the New. Concerning it, the Bible says "the mountain burned with fire unto the midst of heaven, with darkness, clouds, and thick darkness."[218] Dt 4:11 Also at this time, "The earth shook, the heavens also dropped at the presence of God: *even* Sinai itself *was moved* at the presence of God, the God of Israel." Ps 68:8 God chose to particularly reveal his fear before the faces of his people.

---

[217] A disciple is one who learns to obey.

[218] The fact that the mount burned with fire is noted several times in scripture (Dt 4:11, 5:23, 9:15; Heb 12:18), indicating the uniqueness and awesomeness of this terrible event.

14 – Experiencing the Genuine Fear of God

In speaking of this event in the book of Hebrews, we see that the effect was not merely a startling or the fear of surprise. No, it was the extreme fear that is the very dread of God. "And <u>so terrible</u> was the sight, *that* Moses said, I <u>exceedingly fear and quake</u>" (Heb 12:21).[219] So *'frightful'* and *formidable'*, so terrible was the sight that Moses saw, that he quaked in fear, being *terrified* by the presence of God. Moses exceedingly feared![220]

> **WARNING:** It is this singular fact – the lack of the experiential fear of God – that betrays so many popular ministers of the gospel today and their "real" stories of seeing Jesus firsthand. If the Jesus of the scripture had visited all those that claim he has, then they would possess the fear of God in great measure, and many of the antics and entertainment done in the name of Christ by them would no longer be done! Repentance would be seen and holiness would manifest. But "Because they have no **changes**, therefore they fear not God." Ps 55:19 Therefore, neither do they have great intimacy with our holy God, and he has *not* spoken to them what they claim he has.

Standing on this side of that great event we cannot truly fathom the intensity and the depth of what they saw, felt, and experienced that caused such great fear – we can only know by what is recorded that it was a fear, greater than any other fear! But we at least have another reference point of when some others in the New Testament experienced this same quaking. This word 'quake' in Hebrews 12:21, which is used to describe Moses' exceeding fear, is used only one other time. It is when Peter, James, and John were with Jesus on the mount of transfiguration (Mk 9:6). There it is translated 'sore afraid'. This occurs right before they are overshadowed by the cloud and the voice of God said, "This is my beloved Son: hear him." Mk 9:7

> Standing on this side of that great event we cannot
> truly fathom the intensity and the depth of what they saw,
> felt, and experienced that caused such great fear –
> we can only know by what is recorded
> that it was a fear, greater than any other fear!

---

[219] The Greek word for 'quake' in Hebrews 12:21 is *entromos* (G1790) whose root words mean 'in trembling'. Similarly, the Greek word for 'exceedingly fear' is *ekphobos* (G1630) which means '*frightened out* of one's wits'.

[220] And people are so sure in themselves that God does not want his people to fear him. God indeed would have us fear him, for he himself has chosen to reveal himself this way.

Significantly, both references have to do with God's people being <u>on the mount</u> when God appears to them. Together they encompass both covenants, yet they are both recorded for us in the New Testament (thus, in the same language, i.e. in Greek). Because of this we can be assured it was the <u>very</u> <u>same</u> <u>fear</u> in both cases. In both of them we see God's people being sore afraid of the awesome presence of God. We have a two-fold witness, then, that this is the expected reaction of God's people to God's near presence. By this we can be assured his dread and exceeding fear is very real, especially to those who know him. Thus, the greater our depth of experiencing intimacy with the LORD, the greater our experiencing of the fear of God we ought to know.

God's Pleasure

The greatest need for God's people today is to find the fear of the LORD. When God revealed Himself unto his people as a people, his primary revelation was that of this awesomeness. His eternal purpose was so that his fear would be <u>before their faces</u>. The fear of God before our faces is what God knows we need more than anything else to turn us away from sinning (Ex 20:20).

So many today teach that the LORD was disappointed with his people's request that day, that they actually turned away from the LORD and turned toward religion. Thus, they suppose that the priesthood was born – a priesthood which stands between God and man (in a negative sense). Nothing could be farther from reality! God was actually *pleased* with his people's response to fear him and desires that every generation would have the same heart. How do we know this? Forty years later as Moses is recounting the experiences of their wilderness wanderings so they will remember them, he lets us know God's response to that unique event.

> The LORD our God made a covenant with us in Horeb. The LORD made not this covenant with our fathers, but with us, *even* us, who *are* all of us here alive this day. The LORD talked with you face to face in the mount out of the midst of the fire Dt 5:2-4

After this Moses repeats the giving of the 10 commandments which were spoken in Exodus 20:1-17. God spoke these words "out of the midst of the fire, of the cloud, and of the thick darkness, with a great voice" (Dt 5:22). Again we have the testimony of the people's promise to hear men of God speak the word of God and their purposing to obey the will of God. This was a 'covenant of discipleship' to follow the LORD.

> And ye said, Behold, the LORD our God hath shewed us his glory and his greatness, and we have heard his voice out of the midst of the fire: we have seen this day that God doth talk with man, and he liveth. Go thou near, and hear all that the LORD our God shall say: and speak thou unto us all that the LORD our God shall speak unto thee; and we will hear *it,* and do *it*. Dt 5:24,27

14 – Experiencing the Genuine Fear of God

Was this, as men say, the formation of religion and the priesthood to substitute direct and intimate relationship with God? On the contrary, O how pleased God was with this! **All** that they spoke was pleasing to him, so much so that he wishes there would *always* be such a heart in his people to fear him and keep his commandments. Notice how God was pleased with **all** that they had spoken![221]

> And the LORD heard the voice of your words, when ye spake unto me; and the LORD said unto me, I have heard the voice of the words of this people, which they have spoken unto thee: they have well said all that they have spoken. O that there were such an heart in them, that they would fear me, and keep all my commandments **always**, that it might be well with them, and with their children **for ever!** Dt 5:28-29

Man's Rejection

Even today, the LORD is still desiring his people by adoption through the new birth to fear him and to keep his commandments. Many through the serpent's plan are robbing men of the true fear of God, either by eliminating it altogether or so altering it that it is powerless to bring about a willing obedience to God. As a result, many times people are brought into the bondage of the doctrines of men which strip them from the fullness of the word of God. You say, "How so?" When scholars and teachers today say, "That's in the Old Testament, that's not for us." Just know, these are the Sadducees that only take the parts of the word of God that they choose, yet God says,

> All scripture *is* given by inspiration of God, and *is* profitable for doctrine, for reproof, for correction, for instruction in righteousness: That the man of God may be perfect, throughly furnished unto all good works. 2Tim 3:16-17

> It is written, Man shall not live by bread alone, but by every word that proceedeth out of the mouth of God. Mt 4:4

> Now these things were our examples, to the intent we should not lust after evil things, as they also lusted. Now all these things happened unto them for ensamples: and they are written for our admonition, upon whom the ends of the world are come. 1Co 10:6,11

> Think not that I am come to destroy the law, or the prophets: I am not come to destroy, but to fulfil. For verily I say unto you, Till heaven and earth pass, one jot or one tittle shall in no wise pass from the law, till all be fulfilled. Whosoever therefore shall break one of these least commandments [i.e. *in the Old Testament*], and shall teach men so, he shall be called the least in the kingdom of heaven: but whosoever shall do and teach *them*, the same shall be called great in the kingdom of heaven. Mt 5:17-19

---

[221] Note God's pleasure is witnessed twice, once here and later again in Dt 18:16-17.

> **WARNING**: Do not be deceived by the Sadduceean spirit that takes the Old Testament scripture and discards it saying "That's not for today." God's word does not change, nor does God change. What has been written is for all time. It is not seasonal, nor is it dispensational, nor will it ever pass away. Some parts have been specifically fulfilled, but these are called out clearly. We do not keep a natural Sabbath or natural feasts for the scripture makes clear Jesus is our rest and he is our Passover (i.e. he is the fulfillment of all the feasts). When we come to salvation, then the Law has fulfilled its purpose so that we are no longer under the ordinances of the law but are now under faith, for so it is written, "Wherefore the law was our schoolmaster *to bring us* unto Christ, that we might be justified by faith. But after that faith is come, we are no longer under a schoolmaster." Gal 3:24-25 But we do not throw away the truth and the principles that are found in the Old for they are reflected, perfected, and amplified for us in the New.

Spiritual truth is eternal and does not change from one generation to the next. Salvation has always been by grace through faith. Jesus Christ is the word made flesh. Therefore, what can be said of Jesus Christ can be said of the eternal word of God, for in the beginning he was and ever more shall be the word of God.[222] So when we read "Jesus Christ the same yesterday, and to day, and for ever" (Heb 13:8), we know that the Word of God is "the same yesterday, and to day, and for ever". It has not changed, nor will it change. This is why the very next verse says, "Be not carried about with divers and strange doctrines." Heb 13:9 It is the unchanging nature of the word of God that is to keep us from new and strange doctrines.

Neither Jesus, nor any of the apostles cast away the Old Testament, rather they used it to show what God was doing. Everything in the New is built off of the Old. If we know little of the Old our depth of understanding the foundation of the New will be small. The Old Testament prophets[223] pointed to the Messiah and the work that he would do. "But now the righteousness of God without the law is manifested, being witnessed by the law and the prophets" (Rom 3:21). In fact, the eternal gospel is preached first in the Old. "And the scripture, foreseeing that God would justify the heathen through faith, preached before the gospel unto Abraham" (Gal 3:8). Let us be instructed in both Testaments. "Therefore every scribe *which is* instructed unto the kingdom of heaven is like unto a man *that is* an householder, which bringeth forth out of his treasure *things* new and old." Mt 13:52 But some may say, in supposed agreement with the writer of Hebrews,

---

[222] Jesus, the Word of God: Jn 1:1,14, 1Jn 5:7, Rev 19:13.

[223] The Law and the prophets: Mt 5:17, 7:12, 11:13, 22:40; Lk 16:16; Jn 1:45; Ac 13:15, 24:14, 28:23; Zec 7:12.

> For ye are not come unto the mount that might be touched, and that burned with fire, nor unto blackness, and darkness, and tempest ... But ye are come unto mount Sion, and unto the city of the living God, the heavenly Jerusalem, and to an innumerable company of angels Heb 12:18,22

But what do these verses in Hebrews mean? That we are under grace, and sin may abound? Scripture says, "God forbid" (Rom 6:1-2)! Do they mean that God will understand and ignore our disobedience? But how can God understand that we fear him less or obey him less, when we have been forgiven more, and the forgiveness of God is to lead us to both repentance (Rom 2:4) and the fear of God (Ps 130:4)? Do they mean that because of grace we are not as accountable as Old Testament saints? No. We are in fact far <u>more</u> accountable.

So what do these verses in Hebrews 12:18-22 mean? They were brought to an earthly mountain of God, but we have been brought to the heavenly mountain of God. They were brought to a mountain that could be touched and burned with fire (i.e. it was natural). But we have been brought to a mountain that is in heaven (i.e. it is spiritual). God has brought us of the new covenant so much closer to him than those of the old. We have been brought to the spiritual reality which is the fulfillment of all that was hoped for in the old. Let us not forget, then, that "Dominion and fear *are* with him" (Job 25:2), so the closer we approach God, the more fear we shall experience.

Remember, we are coming to God the judge of all (v23). "See that ye refuse not him that speaketh. For if they escaped not who refused him that spake on earth, <u>much more</u> *shall not* we *escape*, if we turn away from him that *speaketh* from heaven" (Heb 12:25). The writer of the Hebrews does not say, "much less", rather he says, "much more"! Let us learn to fear God much more than they of the old covenant, because we have a better covenant, established upon better promises (Heb 8:6) which ought to produce a *stronger* and better fear of God and a *stronger* and better obedience.[224]

As important as obedience is, the fear of the LORD is **more** important. Obedience without godly fear is incomplete in God's eyes, for it does not satisfy his holy eyes. This is why fear must precede obedience. It is always 'fear' and then 'keep',[225] and it is 'fear' and then 'obey'.[226] "Let us hear the conclusion of

---

[224] The partakers of the old covenant did not receive the over-abundance of grace which we have received in the New (see Jn 1:16). It is the grace of God which we have received which makes us more accountable and which God expects will make us more obedient! Grace was not given to us so that we may fall into sin more in Christ. It was given so that we may fall into sin less in him. As Peter lets us know, "I have written briefly, exhorting, and testifying that this is the true grace of God <u>wherein ye stand</u>." 1Pe 5:12 The grace of God is given to us so that we might stand, "that ye may be able to withstand in the evil day, and having done all, to stand." Eph 6:13

[225] Lev 19:3, Dt 5:29, 6:2, 8:6, 13:4, 17:19, Ps 119:63, Ecc 12:13.

the whole matter: Fear God, and keep his commandments: for this *is* the whole *duty* of man." Ecc 12:13 As any parent knows, obedience may be done by their child with a total heart of despising and in rebellion – and such obedience will not long last. Such incomplete obedience does not fulfill the purpose of the command. It is one thing to obey God's command. It is quite another to *fulfill* them. As it is written, "Now the end [i.e. *goal, conclusion, result,* or *purpose*] of the commandment is charity out of a pure heart, and *of* a good conscience, and *of* faith unfeigned" (1Tim 1:5), for "love *is* the fulfilling of the law." Rom 13:10 (see also Gal 5:14)[227] Thus we see Barnabas and Paul, who walked in the fear of God, <u>fulfilled</u> the work which they had been sent to do (Ac 14:26).

> Hypocrite! be admonished that there is no obedience accepted of God where the heart is destitute of this grace of fear. Keeping the commandments is but one part of the duty of man, and Paul did that, even while he was an hypocrite. ... to "fear God" goes before the command to keep his commandments; and if thou dost not fear God first, thou transgresseth instead of keeping the commandments.[228]

As important as obedience is, the fear of the LORD is more important. Obedience without godly fear is incomplete in God's eyes, for it does not satisfy his holy eyes.

Preparing for the Fear of the LORD

"And the LORD said unto Moses, Go unto the people, and sanctify them to day and to morrow, and let them wash their clothes,
And be ready against the third day: for the third day the LORD will come down in the sight of all the people upon mount Sinai." Ex 19:10-11

The need for the sanctification of obedience, as the children of God (not to *become* the children of God, but because we *are* the children of God by faith in Christ Jesus), has all but been lost in today's Christianity. We are focused more on the blessings than on the responsibilities of being in covenant with God. Yet Paul's whole purpose was "to make the Gentiles obedient, by word and deed" (Rom 15:18). To the Corinthians he writes "For to this end also did I write, that I might know the proof of you, whether ye be <u>obedient in all things</u>." 2Co 2:9 He exhorted them to bring "into captivity every thought to the <u>obedience of Christ</u>" (2Co 10:5). Paul instructs Titus to teach those servants of Crete

---

[226] 1Sam 12:14, 15:24, Isa 50:10.

[227] It is clear from the context in 1Tim that some knew and taught the commandments, but the purpose of them was escaping these false teachers. It is the fear of God alone that brings about these 3 ends: a pure heart, a good conscience, and an unfeigned faith.

[228] Bunyan, p. 172.

to be <u>obedient</u> unto their own masters, *and* to please *them* well in all *things;* not answering again; Not purloining, but shewing all good fidelity; that they may adorn the doctrine of God our Saviour in all things. Tit 2:10

Think of this saint, obedience *adorns* the doctrine of God. The word 'adorn' in Greek also means to *'put in* proper *order'*. Is this what you are being regularly taught? That the teaching about God is put in proper order in the eyes of those who see our lives, *when* we obey him. May we not forget, obedience is our calling as children of God. So Peter exhorts us, "As obedient children" (1Pe 1:14).

How did God sanctify and prepare his people for this momentous event, this intensity of experiencing the fear of the LORD that would change their lives forever? First, he had to teach them about the lamb that needed to be shed and to cover their lives. Without the proper understanding of the finished work of Jesus Christ and his sacrificial atoning death on the cross, we cannot draw near to God. Salvation is first and foremost. Sadly, most believers never go beyond this point in their life and hence their salvation is weak and sickly. As Paul says, because the Corinthians were not growing up in their salvation but were remaining as babies (1Co 3:1) who were "not discerning the Lord's body. For this cause many *are* weak and sickly among you, and many sleep." 1Co 11:29-30 That is, they were weak and sickly spiritually and some were spiritually dying!

But let us go on unto maturity, for as soon as each family had a lamb which was slain, immediately it was time for God to move his people onward. They were not to spend even one night in Egypt – once the blood was shed and the angel of death had passed over their sin. Immediately, God had to remove them from the world system and their Egyptian style of life. In leaving the land of their bondage, they were to put all that they knew of life behind. Once we are born again and cleansed by the blood of the spotless lamb of Christ, God will have us on the move as an exodus people. In order to leave the old behind, the LORD immediately brought them to a 'crossing over' (i.e. a water baptism) for the open declaration that they would never go back to Egypt (i.e. the world). Those who once had fleshly rule, authority, and enslavement over God's people were no more. They were now drowned, never again to be seen (Ex 14:13).

This was a time of great rejoicing for the people of God. The joy of their salvation was manifested in the songs and praises, the timbrels and the dances unto God, which they sang on the far side of the Red Sea. But God also brought them into a spiritual baptism, the baptism unto Moses in the sea (1Co 10:2), where they not only believed in the LORD and in his power, but they also believed in Moses, the man of God who was sent of God. "And Israel saw that great work which the LORD did upon the Egyptians: and the people feared the LORD, and believed the LORD, and his servant Moses." Ex 14:31

This was the people's first experience with, their first installment of, the fear of the LORD. This fear comes from experiencing God's mighty acts of deliverance, especially that of salvation. The Exodus Israelites at the Red Sea had seen what God could do, but not the glory of who God was. We, likewise, are to fear God for two reasons. First, we are to fear God because of his wondrous deliverances in our life, the greatest of which is saving us from sin and from the world. Second, we are to fear God because of who he is. Unfortunately, this first experience with the fear of God often proves to be all too short lived.

Though we ought always to remember the works of the LORD, rarely as human beings do we. This is why we need a deep encounter with not just the mighty acts of God, but also with the awesome person of God. The LORD is so great that not even his works, as great as they are, can compare with his eternal Godhead, his divine and glorious being. It is one thing to experience the deliverances of God. It is yet quite another to experience the holy presence of God.

> It is one thing to experience the deliverances of God. It is yet quite another to experience the holy presence of God.

David knew God's multitudinous deliverances, yet he still earnestly craved God's presence. The same was true for Moses. Think of all the things that Moses saw, yet what enabled him to persevere through all the questionings, doubtings, complainings, challenges, rebellion, and disappointments? It was not the mighty acts of God, but the awesome presence of him that enabled him to endure. "By faith he forsook Egypt, not fearing the wrath of the king: for he endured, as seeing him who is invisible." Heb 11:27 This was Moses' heartbeat, that God's presence would go with him (Ex 33:13,15-16).

The Effect of the Fear of God: Change
"Because they have no changes, therefore they fear not God." Ps 55:19

If we would but humble ourselves under the mighty hand of God and choose the fear of the LORD, he would then draw us nigh to Himself and speak to us (Jam 4:7). God promises if we have the fear of God that it will change us (Ps 55:19). But because of the hardness and impenitence of our heart, we store up God's wrath against ourselves (Rom 2:5). We must be willing to change and commit to holding fast to the change the LORD wants to work in us. The importance of having a heart to obey (which truly only comes from the fear of the LORD) cannot be over-emphasized. You may read the word of God all you want, and you may pray continually, but without the fear of the LORD you will never change.

The fear of the LORD is the catalyst which ignites the word and prayer in your life to produce the flames of fervency and true change. Without a change in the course of our life to be continually corrected by the LORD and kept on the narrow path of the kingdom of God, we are actually drifting from God and from his ways. We are rudderless, and this is when we truly need to fear, for then there is no fear of God working within us, and there can be no lasting victory or safety. "Because they have no **changes**, therefore they fear not God." Ps 55:19 Men speak of the purpose-driven life, but there is no purpose acceptable to God without the fear of God. God is looking for the life that is driven by the fear of God. This is why God worked so marvelously through Noah to bring salvation to man, because he was moved, he was propelled and driven with fear (Heb 11:7)!

You may think, "Surely studying the word of God daily, praying faithfully, and mixing it with faith will produce the life of God?" No, not unless they be encompassed and undergirded with the fear of the LORD. Let me give you an example from my youth. I grew up in a hard-working home of immigrant Germans. By watching dad and mom, I believed that anything could be accomplished merely by persistent hard work. In high school on the tennis team I noticed a fellow team mate that practiced more than all of us. After we all left, he would continue to practice on his own hitting against the wall. No one could fault him for lack of effort, yet in all the time I knew him and watched him, his game never improved. He continued to make the same errors in the same situations.

Why? He practiced, he put in the time, he had the dedication and the discipline, but something was missing. Instead of getting better he actually got worse, for he got more ingrained into his bad habits. In the end, the result was that he was practicing his mistakes, and there was no forward progress. He lacked the ability to step back, to see what he was doing, and to make the appropriate changes. He is like many Christians; we are practicing our mistakes, with great diligence, and we have them down quite well. We try so hard to improve, but no real change occurs in our life. We study the Bible daily, commit ourselves to prayer, and serve in ministries, yet inside we are changed but little. Our scent remains the same, and we cannot understand why we do not see greater progress, for we believe with diligence and hard work and dedication that we ought to change, for we are called to it. Paul instructs Timothy, "Meditate upon these things; give thyself wholly to them; that thy profiting may appear to all." 1Tim 4:15 This word 'profiting' means '*progress* or *advancement*'.

So where does the problem lie? How come with all our dedication, devotion, and hard work there is no progress or advancement? The problem was that at his heart he was on his own and not a member of a team that needed to function together in subjection to a coach. All of the instruction of the coach or even insight from other more experienced team players fell on deaf ears. He had his own way of doing things (as we all do). The great failing of doing things our way is that we *all* are blind to ourselves. Like the tennis player, all of us by nature do not want to risk making things worse temporarily in order to fix things to make them better in the long run. This is why so many fear the plow of the kingdom of God and flee from it, because it comes with repentance "to root out, and to pull down, and to destroy, and to throw down" in order that it might build and plant our lives (Jer 1:10). The change of repentance will always turn our life upside down and will always initially bring disorder and greater weakness, before it can ever bring in new order and greater strength.

All of us, in the areas where we are most weak, have this same inability to step back and to see what needs to be changed in our own life – how to truly deal with the root of the issue. And even when we do see, we always under estimate the depth of the change that God is asking for and the severity of it. At the same time we always also over estimate our own ability, strength, and wisdom to be able to handle it. This is innately human as a result of the fall – the complete inability to see ourselves accurately in the light of truth.

> But be ye doers of the word, and not hearers only, deceiving your own selves. For if any be a hearer of the word, and not a doer, he is like unto a man beholding his natural face in a glass: For he beholdeth himself, and goeth his way, and straightway forgetteth what manner of man he was. Jam 1:22-24

The change of repentance will always turn our life upside down & will always initially bring disorder & greater weakness, before it can ever bring in new order & greater strength.

This is why James likens the word of God to a mirror (i.e. a looking glass), and warns us of the danger of not doing that which we hear. We may see ourselves face to face in the mirror of the Word, and yet we do not believe that is the way we truly are. And even if we do accept that we are like that, we often make no immediate plan to change and to address the problem, and hence we soon forget that we are that way, for we do not take it as seriously as God does.

WARNING: Sin has a dangerous way of deceiving us to think that it is not such a big problem as others make it out to be. But remember, sin is *always* a bigger problem than we realize. The Bible speaks of the "deceitfulness [i.e. the *delusion*] of sin" (Heb 3:13). Consider this next time you minimize sin: it took the ultimate sacrifice, the death of God's very own Son, Jesus Christ, to pay for and remove our sins. We had to be born again and become a completely new creation to escape the corruption that sin caused, and even still we must continually be transformed by the renewing of our mind so that by the engrafted word our souls may be saved (Jam 1:21).

James shows us that whenever the word of God is brought to us it reveals our state and who we really are. But if there is no real purposing to change, if we still 'go our own way', such revelation of truth is all in vain, for straightway (i.e. *at once, immediately*) we will forget what we are really like. Then what we have seen produces nothing – but a harder heart. We need a coach, an instructor to come along side and bring in correction and reinforce truth, holding us to it. This is why we <u>must</u> be willing to hear that instruction, to change, and to put it into practice. So it really comes down to respecting the words of the instructor more than our own thoughts and perceptions. Without submission to authority, no teacher anywhere can help us. Once again, we see the need to have the fear of the LORD to open our ears to hear.

Remember who our primary instructor that has been given to us is. He is the Spirit of truth who will guide us into all truth (Jn 16:13), but don't forget who that Spirit is. Yes, he is the Spirit of wisdom, but he is first and foremost the Spirit of the fear of the LORD (Isa 11:2)! God will send us messengers and servants to bring correction and reproof to us to protect us. These are his witnesses and messengers whom we are called to receive with fear and trembling (2Co 7:15). Remember Jesus' words, "As many as I love, I rebuke and chasten: be zealous [i.e. have *warmth* of feeling for, <u>desire</u>] therefore, and repent." Rev 3:19 He will always put us to the test as his people, even as he did to the Jews throughout the scriptures. He will send human imperfect vessels to bring his reproof and correction through, to see if we will receive the authority of his command that comes through his messengers.

Since God is the source of all authority (Rom 13:1), part of the fear of the LORD is the proper response to authority. This is why the Bible speaks of a trembling at his word (Isa 66:2,5), because one's promise, command, or word reflects one's measure of authority. Our response to his authority will always be tested by how we respond and how we treat his messengers and servants. This is why Jesus taught the parable of the husbandman[229] who sent his servants which were beaten and killed, and then finally his son. The husbandman received these as personal attacks against himself – which they clearly were.

Are We Ready for the Fear of the LORD?

"Now therefore perform the doing of it; that as there was a readiness to will, so there may be a performance also out of that which ye have." 2Co 8:11

Next in this journey, God had to test why his people were following him. Was it just to be blessed, or was it truly to grow in obedience unto him to whom they owed everything? The LORD must deal with why we are following him, before he can show us his fear that will keep us from sinning. This is the key to faithfulness. If we are following to get the blessings of God, then we will never arrive at our hoped for destination. We will be as the children of the Exodus that perished in the wilderness for murmuring and complaining, because things will not go as we desire them to, and because of the lack that we will all be tested by.

---

[229] See Mt 21:33-44/Mk 12:1-11/Lk 20:9-18.

> But with many of them God <u>was not well pleased</u>: for they were overthrown in the wilderness. Now these things were our examples, to the intent we should not lust after evil things, as they also lusted. … <u>Neither murmur ye</u>, as some of them also murmured, and were destroyed of the destroyer. Now all these things happened unto them for ensamples: and they are written for our admonition, upon whom the ends of the world are come. Wherefore let him that thinketh he standeth take heed lest he fall. 1Co 10:5-6,10-12

Avoiding Bitterness: Do All Things without Murmurings and Disputings

Think of where God led his people. He purposefully brought his people to a place not of plenty, but to a wilderness, a place of severe lack, to see if they would still trust in him and not complain. They failed the test, as we often do, and became bitter. The people murmured against Moses (and against God) at a place called Marah [i.e. *bitter*], because the waters were bitter (Ex 25:23-24). How did God show Moses how to heal the bitter waters – which represent the complaining hearts of his people? "The LORD <u>shewed him a tree</u>, *which* when he had cast into the waters, the waters were made sweet: there he made for them a statute and an ordinance, and there he proved them" (Ex 15:25).

God was able, even then, to heal their grumbling and murmuring through the cross.[230] When we suffer, even wrongfully,[231] we must learn not to complain. Bitterness, anger, and evil speaking – all fruits of complaining – grieve the Holy Spirit (Eph 4:30-31). Such bitterness must be healed by looking upon the cross. Only this will turn our sour spirit into sweet waters. You may find yourself even now at a place where you are in great desperate need. Will you complain and become bitter, or will you trust in Jehovah Jireh, the LORD your provider?

> *Let your* conversation *be* without covetousness; *and be* content with such things as ye have: for he hath said, I will never leave thee, nor forsake thee. So that we may boldly say, The Lord *is* my helper, and I will not fear what man shall do unto me. Heb 13:5-6

To be healed of grumbling and murmuring, we must get our eyes back on the cross, both on what Jesus did there, as well as, how he would have us follow him daily bearing our own cross. We must focus on the example left for us to follow. Jesus suffered on our behalf in order to follow God and do the Father's will. We must do the same if we would be his disciples.

> For this *is* thankworthy, if a man for conscience toward God endure grief, suffering wrongfully. … but if, when ye do well, and suffer *for it*, ye take it patiently, this *is* acceptable with God. For even hereunto

---

[230] This is none other than the tree upon which our Lord was crucified, and *why* scripture calls it a tree: Ac 5:30, 10:39, 13:29.

[231] That is, when we do not deserve it.

14 – Experiencing the Genuine Fear of God

> were ye called: because Christ also suffered for us, leaving us an example, <u>that ye should follow his steps</u>: Who did no sin, neither was guile found in his mouth: Who, when he was reviled, reviled not again; when he suffered, he threatened not; but committed *himself* to him that judgeth righteously[232] 1Pe 2:19-23

We are all proved by God through the lack he causes us to endure. Now maybe you can understand the following passage a little better and why God's charge to them immediately after he had healed the bitter waters was,

> If thou wilt diligently hearken to the voice of the LORD thy God, and wilt do that which is right in his sight, and wilt give ear to his commandments, and keep all his statutes, I will put none of these diseases upon thee, which I have brought upon the Egyptians: for I *am* the LORD that healeth thee. Ex 15:26

The other thing God had to prove his children on was whether they would challenge or reject his authority by disputing or arguing with his ordained servants. Thus, we are called not only to do all things without murmurings or complainings, but we are also to learn how to do all things without disputings (Php 2:14). This word 'disputings' (dialogismos, Greek 1261) means to debate and is also translated as 'imagination, reasoning'. Before God can show us his fear, he must also bring us under his delegated spiritual authority, and we must learn how not to dispute with the authorities he sets over us.

The Foundation of the Government of God

Note how immediately after removing bitterness and bringing them into eldership oversight, the manna began to flow to each individual person (Ex 15:27 → 16:12-24). Through the crucified life, victories were now being won over the flesh (i.e. over Amalek) that couldn't be won before. God waits for our commitment to fully obey his word and to keep his covenant. God will begin to woo us by his Spirit by reminding us of all the things he has done for us. Then he will prick our heart, not to be foolish any longer, but to prepare ourselves to meet the Lord: "we know that, when he shall appear, we shall be like him; for we shall see him as he is. And every man that hath this hope in him <u>purifieth himself</u>, even as he is pure." 1Jn 3:2-3 If we truly believe that he shall appear, then we must 'purify ourselves, <u>even as</u> he is pure.' As a people who truly want to come to know the fear of God firsthand, we must sanctify ourselves today and tomorrow, in preparation for his coming.

---

[232] 'Thankworthy' is the Greek word for 'grace' (charis, Greek 5485) used throughout the New Testament! Its definition is 'the divine influence upon the heart, and its reflection in the life; including *gratitude*'.

We see the same pattern in Acts. Once the church was set in divine order, both in government (with apostles and elders)[233] and in helps (with deacons), immediately the word of God increased in the lives of the saints. The manna began to freely flow, as it is written, "and the word of God increased; and the number of the disciples multiplied in Jerusalem greatly; and a great company of the priests were obedient to the faith." Ac 6:7

> **WARNING**: This is why the local body of Christ is so vital, for only there can proper correction be brought and our response be proved. We *must* be brought into a spiritual home called the church, not some mystical "universal body of Christ" that exists out there 'in the spirit', but has no responsibilities, no accountability, no family relationships, no authority, no submission, and no call to faithful ministry. No! We must be planted in the true church, a local body of believers which have Christ as their head, and where the Word of God has preeminence.
>
> We must be rooted in the church as revealed not in America or some other nation, but as revealed in the scripture; a church not with Senior Pastors and Associate Pastors which exists no where in scripture, but a church built off of the government of God. We must be brought into a church founded on the word of God where a plurality of elders take spiritual oversight and feed the flock, as the scriptures say (Ac 20:17,28, 1Pe 5:1-2), and where apostles are received who will set foundational and governmental order.[234]

As the word of God increased in the lives of the saints and their obedience to it as disciples, so the Lord Jesus was set forth even more evidently as crucified in their lives. As a result, even some of the priests of the old covenant, were finally getting born again and becoming obedient to the faith (i.e. to the word of God). Let us meditate on this. It is not until the church is set in divine order in regard to both government and helps that those who are entrenched in traditions, bound in their thinking to the doctrines of men, and in the grip of religion, will be set free. This is why the government of God being set in its proper order is so important.

that the LORD God might Dwell among them

---

[233] In the beginning of the church, the apostles must also have functioned as elders. See the sub-section 'Development of Elders in the New Testament' under the description of 'Bishops & Pastors: Understanding the Office & Function' in the appendix entitled "Definition of Some Biblical Terms" in the book Losing the Treasure of the Lord.

[234] Remember, this was what was revealed even in the church in the wilderness (Ac 7:38): the word of apostles and elders, Moses being that Old Testament apostle and with him the 70 elders.

14 – Experiencing the Genuine Fear of God

God desires to dwell amongst his people today, even as he did in the church in the wilderness and in the church of Acts. The problem is he cannot dwell in our midst because of our unholiness, our worldliness, and our open disrespect for the authority of his word. So as then, he must establish "bounds" to bring back his holiness, and thus rekindle his fear in our hearts. The necessity to obey God's commands must be set strongly in our life in the form of *bounds*. This is why bounds were set for the people (Ex 19:12-13). These were very serious and brought the judgment of death to anyone who transgressed them.

> God establishes these bounds of respect for his holiness by setting before us the fear of God & the fear of his judgment.

Think on the seriousness of these bounds that God established for the people. They were so important that God in the *midst* of meeting with Moses told him to go back down to the people and warn them *again* not to violate these bounds, even though they had already been established and the people warned (vv21-25)! God would not continue in intimacy with Moses or in visiting his people until these bounds were absolutely secure. God would not have his holiness overrun by inquisitive seekers. God establishes these bounds of respect for his holiness by setting before us the fear of God and the fear of his judgment. God *would* be sanctified before his people, either through the warning of his fear that would keep them from death or through the penalty of death.

God would not fill the tabernacle of Moses, nor the temple of Solomon, nor the church of Jesus Christ until all was set in divine order and everyone was in their proper place. Let us learn submission to God's order and authority so that we will see his glory come down again upon his people. God "gave gifts unto men" (Eph 4:8). As seen in Ephesians 4:11, these gifts are the mantles of the apostles, prophets, evangelists, shepherds, and teachers. Paul is quoting from Psalm 68 where, according to prophecy,

> Thou hast ascended on high, thou hast led captivity captive: thou hast received gifts for men; yea, *for* the rebellious also, that the LORD God might dwell *among them*. Ps 68:18

Thus, in Psalm 68 we see the purpose of the office gifts. God desires to dwell among his people. But he cannot, nor will not do it until we begin to "cleanse ourselves from all filthiness of the flesh and spirit, perfecting holiness in the fear of God." 2Co 7:1 This requires the inward work of the fear of God in maintaining a good conscience to walk before the Lord in holiness. This will also take the outward work of the fear of God which is rendered unto men of God, whose spiritual authority we faithfully submit to. The five-fold ministry, of apostles, prophets, evangelists, shepherds, and teachers, have a work to do, and we must let them do that work.[235]

For God to dwell among us two things must take place. First, we must come and be separate from the world (2Co 6:16-18). Second, we must come into the church and be under spiritual authority, for the five-fold ministry has a work to do in our life to prepare us for his presence.[236] How does the five-fold ministry prepare us so that God might dwell among us? They have been given to the church "For the perfecting of the saints, for the work of the ministry, for the edifying of the body of Christ" (Eph 4:12).

The Need for Experiencing the Fear of God

The time for the fear of the LORD is now. God always exhorts his people to choose *now* the fear of the LORD. So Moses, when reviewing the last forty years of their wilderness journeyings to the Exodus people, and desiring to show them how not to fall away from the LORD, proclaims the urgency of fearing God: "And **now**, Israel, what doth the LORD thy God **require** of thee, but to fear the LORD thy God" (Dt 10:12). When Joshua is ready to pass on and would similarly warn the people on how not to fall away in their hearts from the LORD, he proclaims, "**Now** therefore fear the LORD, and serve him in sincerity and in truth" (Jos 24:14). Years later when Jehoshaphat wanted to bring the people of the kingdom back to the LORD their God, he proclaims, "Wherefore **now** let the fear of the LORD be upon you; take heed and do *it*" (2Ch 19:7).

The fear of God is not for us to delay or to choose tomorrow. It is always for us to choose now. We in the new covenant have the same calling to **choose** the fear of God. So Paul writes to his beloved Philippians, who were his joy and his crown (Php 4:1). He writes to them on how to "so stand fast in the Lord"; exhorting them, "**now** ... work out your own salvation with fear and trembling." Php 2:12

The last days that we are living in so reflect the days of Jeremiah. God's judgment against his own backsliding people in Jeremiah's day is an amazement that his people do not *now* choose to fear him. "Fear ye not me? saith the LORD: will ye not tremble at my presence ... Neither say they in their heart, Let us **now** fear the LORD our God" (Jer 5:22,24). If we know these things, then let us choose today the fear of God by being willing to change. Let us get on our knees now and commit ourselves to do what he asks of us. Let us take heed and

---

[235] But *first* we must see such men prepared through discipleship, servanthood, and the process of brokenness to be set in such callings and offices. We must see them prove themselves worthy of such honor and trust, being found faithful to the truth of God's word. "Moreover it is required in stewards, that a man be found faithful." 1Co 4:2

[236] As proved by Psalm 68:18 and Ephesians 4:7-12.

do it, before our heart deceives us again. "Wherefore **now** <u>let the fear of the LORD be upon you; take heed and do *it*</u>: for *there is* no iniquity with the LORD our God, nor respect of persons, nor taking of gifts." 2Ch 19:7

Remember, if we do not fear him, God will not favor us just because we are his children, for he has no respect of persons. "A wise servant shall have rule over a son that causeth shame, and shall have part of the inheritance among the brethren." Pr 17:2 God will not excuse us because we have given him great and precious gifts – whether of time, energy, labor, possessions, or even prayer. God's exhortation to us first is to allow the fear of God to come upon us *now*. We must with diligence allow and permit the fear of God to be in our heart. We must stop casting it aside, for it is the very first fruits of the Spirit which we have received of God!

The Conclusion of the Matter

"Come and hear, all ye that fear God,
and I will declare what he hath done for my soul." Ps 66:16

"Only fear the LORD, and serve him in truth with all your heart:
for consider how great things he hath done for you." 1Sam 12:24

Have corrupt men destitute of the truth who despise the fear of God stolen from you the awesome blessing and foundation of the fear of the LORD? Has false teaching twisted the true fear of God into something that it is not, so that you no longer *hear* the warning of God, and hence are no longer "moved with fear" to prepare as holy men of the past did? Have the strangleholds of religion with its doctrines and traditions of men removed the cutting edge of the fear of God from your heart so that it has no power to change you through fear and trembling to hate iniquity and to depart from evil? Has the spirit of entertainment and showmanship that infects much of the growing church today kept you so satisfied or at least so occupied that you have not even desired or sought after the fear of God in a long, long time?

Isn't it time to get back to God's desire for us? Isn't it time for the true church to "Awake to righteousness, and sin not; for <u>some have not the knowledge of God</u>: I speak *this* to your shame." 1Co 15:34 Isn't it high time to prepare ourselves for the Lord's coming through the fear of God? If we would not be found to be the five foolish virgins who are shut out from the presence of the Lord, then we must recapture the fear of God in our heart. Only the fear of God will keep us desiring to have our life prepared by being set in order according to God's pattern.

We must learn to work out our salvation in fear and trembling through the fear of God. Remember, our salvation is *not* worked out in grace. It is worked out (i.e. finished, strengthened, and matured) in the fear of God. We must recapture the missing pillar of truth, the fear of God, so that we have strength to finish the course. Only the fear of God can properly ground and secure our faith in the truth. It is that which we must fight to maintain, lest it be stolen by the scheming and deceitfulness of false teachers. We must desire it, choose it, seek it, learn it, keep it, and be devoted to it.

God has desired every generation to have the true fear of God working in them. It is the primary and the first thing he requires of us. "And now, Israel, what doth the LORD thy God <u>require of thee</u>, **but to fear the LORD thy God**, to walk in all his ways, and to love him, and to serve the LORD thy God with all thy heart and with all thy soul" (Dt 10:12). Note, this is none other than the first and greatest commandment. "Thou shalt love the Lord thy God with all thy heart, and with all thy soul, and with all thy mind. This is the first and great commandment." Mt 22:37-38 The fear of the LORD will affect every area of our life. It is the very essence of the spirit which we received from God, when we first become a new creation in Christ Jesus. We were literally fashioned in fear (Ps 139:14), so it is the essence of our spiritual life.

We must humble ourselves as children and be taught *how* to fear the LORD. It is the beginning of spiritual knowledge, the understanding of the holy, and the beginning of God's wisdom. It searches and plumbs the depth of our heart and our conscience and keeps both clean. The fear of the LORD will prepare and transform our heart into a soft heart, a humble heart, a willing heart, a united heart, a pure heart, an enlarged heart, a servant's heart, an obedient heart, a faithful heart, and a perfect heart.

We can have no good heart without the fear of God. It keeps us from those great corrupting influences of the heart: from hypocrisy, from dishonesty, from covetousness, and from all idolatry. It is the keeping of a good conscience before God and man. It is the way of peace (Rom 3:17-18) and the source of healing (Mal 2:5). It is clean and enduring and will never pass away. The fear of the LORD is not for this life only, but carries a future reward to them that fear him (Ps 61:5, Rev 11:18). It warns us of things to come, and keeps us from following vanities, empty dreams, and all extremes (Ecc 7:16-18). It gives us an urgency to persuade others to be reconciled to God (2Co 5:11, Jude 1:23).

The fear of the LORD is our treasure (Isa 33:6)! The fear of God is for our good (Jer 32:39), and enables us to have one heart and one way (Jer 32:39-40). It removes from us a divided heart and makes us single toward the Lord. It tends toward life, keeping us from the snares of death (Pr 14:27, 19:23). When the LORD truly desires to bless a man or a woman he gives them his fear. "*Oh how great is thy goodness, which thou hast laid up for them that fear thee!*" Ps 31:19 The treasure of the fear of God fashions our obedience and forms our worship and service of the living God. We are to obey in fear and trembling. We are to worship in fear. Through it, we depart from iniquity and evil.[237] The fear of the LORD moves us to obey (Heb 11:7).

God's fear is the key to our faithfulness and the door to his mercies. The fear of the LORD is what it means to walk with God, and it is what undergirds and establishes our relationships with both others, authorities, and with God himself. It is a banner of truth that is displayed in our life before others. The fear of the LORD is what brings both division in ungodly relationships and true intimacy and unity in godly relationships. Thus, it is the key to friendship with God, and the fulfillment of our life, for he fulfills the desire of those who fear him (Ps 145:19), and *there is* no want to them that fear him (Ps 34:9)! Those who seek the LORD in the fear of God "shall not want any good *thing*" (v10). He that has the fear of the LORD "shall abide satisfied" (Pr 19:23).

> We cannot exhaust the depth of the riches of the fear of the LORD for it is our heritage from God and our reward (Ps 61:5 & Rev 11:18)!

To fear him will cause us to hope in his mercy and to change (Ps 55:19). It is how we *perfect* holiness (2Co 7:1). It is what enables us to hear (Ps 66:16) and to wait (Ps 130:4-6).[238] We have good reason to wait on him in the fear of the LORD, for so great is his mercy toward them that fear him.[239] God is able to reveal his secrets and his covenants to those who fear him, and to show them his ways (Ps 25:12,14). He honors them and does them much good that have the fear of the LORD (Ps 15:4, Jer 32;39-40), so that it will be well with those forever who have it (Dt 5:29). Those that fear God's commandments will be doubly rewarded (Pr 13:13).

We cannot exhaust the depth of the riches of the fear of the LORD for it is our heritage from God and our reward (Ps 61:5, Rev 11:18)! But we have seen more than enough to know that without it we cannot be overcomers. The fear of the LORD must be at the very core and heart of every follower of the Lord. In fact, it is the very heartbeat and desire of God for his people. The LORD truly takes pleasure in us when we have it (Ps 147:11) – this more than anything else should spur us on to recapture it in our life. As God himself said when they stood fearful and quaking before him for his awesome wonders at Horeb as they were to receive the commandments of God, "O that there were such an heart in them, that they would fear me, and keep all my commandments always, that it might be well with them, and with their children for ever!" Dt 5:29

---

[237] Departing from iniquity: Pr 16:6, 14:16, 3:7.

[238] Note also Psalm 147:11 where 'hope' in the Hebrew means 'to wait'.

[239] His mercy is toward those who fear him: Ps 103:11,13,17.

So some forty years later God is still bringing that same significant event to their remembrance. O that we would fear God always and for ever! Each of us needs to come to that same mountain top experience of being face to face with the fear of God. We are truly blessed if we have the fear of the LORD (Ps 112:1, 128:1), and truly destitute if we are void of it. O how "Happy *is* the man that feareth always" (Pr 28:14). How can we thank God enough for this wonderful grace of the fear of God? Dare we discard it? Dare we despise it, or deny it? God forbid. "Let us now fear the LORD our God" (Jer 5:24) and never let anyone steal from us again the treasure of the fear of the LORD that God himself has given to us as part of our new covenant inheritance. Only by the fear of the LORD will we ever see fulfilled the intimacy that he desires.

14 – Experiencing the Genuine Fear of God

Appendix I. Definition of Some Biblical Terms

The kingdom of God will always turn the world upside down (Ac 17:6). It must, because God's ways are not our ways and God's thoughts are not our thoughts (Isa 55:8) – even after we are born again as illustrated by the Corinthians to whom Paul says, "And I, brethren, could not speak unto you as unto spiritual, but as unto carnal, *even* as unto babes in Christ." 1Co 3:1 This is why in Jesus' first recorded teaching in Matthew chapters 5, 6, and 7, over and over again he must distinguish between what they had heard that was contrary to the truth[240] from what he was telling them.[241] The spirit of the Pharisees that Jesus was dealing with in no way has diminished in the earth but has in fact increased. Therefore, the same must be done today before we can properly understand the kingdom of God. Hence, the following terms must be defined according to God's word and not man's usage.

1. The Bible: Reasons for Holding to the King James Bible

You have heard it said that the newer versions are more accurate, but I tell you nay. You have heard it said that it doesn't matter which translation of the scriptures you use, they all say the same thing, but I tell you nay. If there is one truth, one way, and one life as the scriptures teach (Jn 14:6, Jer 32:39), and if we are all called to speak the same thing, have the same mind and be in the same judgment, with no divisions among us (1Co 1:10), then how can we have multiple versions of the Bible in the same language which say *different* things, with *different* judgments, and which most certainly have divisions among them, seeing they contradict each other in numerous places?

Remember, according to the scriptures themselves we are not called primarily to know and obey "truth", we are called rather to know and obey "the truth" (Jn 8:32, Gal 5:7). We are not sanctified through truth, but through "the truth" (Jn 17:17,19). When God gave us his truth in the Bible we needn't look for it in twelve different versions, only one.

All of the modern versions disagree among themselves in hundreds of places. They cannot all be correct, without error, and thereby be the inspired, inerrant word of God. There is one version, and one version only which God will ordain as "his truth" (Ps 100:5, 57:3) at any one time, and put into our hands, and judge us by (Ps 96:13). We must find that one which God has ordained by his Holy Spirit and put away all others. We are never allowed by God to come to different versions of the Bible – as so many do today – to determine what is truth for us and to pick and choose which one we like. What is and what

---

[240] "Ye have heard that is was said": Mt 5:21,27,31,33,38,43.

[241] "But I say unto you": Mt 5:18,20,22,26,28,32,34,39,44; 6:2,5,16,25,29.

I – Definition of Some Biblical Terms

is not the word of God is NOT for our choosing. That is nothing other than partaking from the tree of the knowledge of good and evil which can only produce spiritual death through deception.

> We are never allowed by God ... to pick and choose ... what is and what is not the Word of God

The King James Bible has not been pieced together by well-meaning scholars from a multitude of different sources. No, you have a complete Bible based on a single Old Testament text and a single New Testament text. That is something all the modern versions cannot boast of, for in their wisdom they have rejected bible preservation.

> The words of the LORD *are* pure words: *as* silver tried in a furnace of earth, purified seven times. Thou shalt keep them, O LORD, thou shalt <u>preserve</u> them from this generation for ever. Ps 12:6-7

God has promised to preserve his words – which he has purified seven times! – from the wicked of this generation. He has '*guarded* them, *protected* them, *maintained* them, and *concealed*' them from this present evil generation. Sadly, the modern versions, by the very foundational texts which they use, prove they do not believe the Word of God. By the very texts which the modern versions use they prove that they do not believe the Bible is preserved, for the "older and better" manuscripts which they use have corrections ad nauseam and even missing chapters and books. Do not buy into the deception that the new versions are more accurate than the King James, for this is an outright lie. Their typical line of reasoning goes as follows:

> We have older manuscripts than the King James translators had and these older manuscripts (1) by the very fact of being older therefore are more accurate. Knowledge has increased since then and (2) with knowledge therefore so has truth. We have used (3) better manuscripts, (4) better translators, and (5) better translation techniques, therefore we have a better translation.

Each of these suppositions by careful study can be proven false.[242] The modern versions have not used better manuscripts, better translators, or even better translation techniques. In fact, their manuscripts are inferior to those used by the King James translators – and even the King James translators witness to this fact.[243] The very fact that the modern versions rely on commentaries

---

[242] For an excellent book on this subject please read, <u>Defending the King James Bible</u> by D. A. Waite, published by The Bible For Today Press, 1999.

[243] For instance, that the Septuagint was not a good source manuscript, they say, "It is <u>certain</u>, that that Translation [i.e. the Septuagint] was not so sound and so perfect, but it <u>needed in many places correction</u>." They also had access to Codex Vaticanus (the partial

of the scriptures rather than the original scriptures themselves shows their lack of respect for the word of God and its preservation. They have followed in the same error as the scribes of Jesus' day. They trust in what men say *about* the scriptures more than what the scriptures themselves say.

This along with the use of inferior manuscripts and inferior translation techniques (such as Dynamic Equivalence) explains where much of the inaccuracies of the new versions arise. This is the complete irony and lie of the modern versions. They use "older manuscripts" because they claim they are thereby more accurate, yet in fact by studying and comparing these "older manuscripts" it is patently obvious to anyone who believes in Bible preservation they are not preserved manuscripts at all and are *not* more accurate, but less. In addition to that, they do not stick to even their "older, more accurate manuscripts" but turn often to commentaries on the scriptures. Thus, they have no solid foundation at all on which to stand for proper translation of the word of God.

The King James Bible alone is untainted by modern inferior translation techniques. It alone is uncorrupted by recently discovered faulty manuscripts which are supposedly older, and by the presumption of scholars therefore more accurate, yet which are clearly full of errors and corrections and reveal a Bible which has not been preserved by God. The modern versions are all based on an ungodly mixture of pseudo-scriptural sources for the basis of the Word of God, such as men's commentaries on what the scripture says or the writings not from the original Hebrew Old Testament[244] nor from the Greek New Testament (examples abound such as the use of the Samaritan Pentateuch, the Septuagint,[245] and the Latin Vulgate).

Is there any Version which is More Accurate than All the Rest?

There are many proofs to confirm the superior accuracy of the King James, but one simple one will suffice to prove the point that none of the modern versions in use are as accurate in comparison. What Bible version maintains the singular versus plural pronoun distinction that is in both the Biblical Hebrew and Greek languages? Any of the many versions of the NIV? No. How about

---

Bible found in the Vatican archives), upon which all the modern versions are based, but rejected it as being unworthy.

[244] Small portions of the Old Testament are also in Aramaic and Syriack, but they are integrated into the text.

[245] So many modern scholars think so highly of the Septuagint, because it is easy to translate the Old Testament from Greek rather than from Hebrew. The problem is God did not preserve the Septuagint. He preserved the Old Testament, not in Greek, but primarily in Hebrew. The King James translators witness to the fact of the inferiority of the Septuagint in their preface 'The Translators to the Reader'.

I – Definition of Some Biblical Terms

the "accurate" NAS? No.[246] Only the King James Bible maintains this distinction. Did the King James translators maintain this distinction because it was the common language in vogue, as so many claim? No. The distinction of singular pronouns (i.e. "thee", "thou", "thine") versus the plural pronouns (i.e. "ye", "you", "your") had vanished over a 100 years before.

Though Shakespeare uses both types of pronouns in his writings, and he is a clear contemporary of the time the King James Bible was translated, yet he uses them only to distinguish between formal speech (such as to a superior or stranger) and casual (i.e. familiar) references. Shakespeare does not use them to distinguish between singular and plural. In contrast, the King James Bible never uses the pronouns to denote respect or familiarity,[247] but always uses the pronouns in their antiquated, outdated, and archaic forms to distinguish between singular or plural.

Why did they purposefully translate a Bible into the vulgar [i.e. common] tongue using <u>archaic</u> language? Isn't this counter-productive?[248] They did this for one reason: for <u>accuracy</u>, because they needed to preserve the distinction that was in the original manuscripts as much as possible – even if they had to sacrifice readability or sales! O that men would learn from their example. If you want the most accurate Bible there is, take the King James Bible. It is without equal. It has been the standard for over 400 years – that is stability and accuracy you can count on!

2. <u>The Apostles' Doctrine: The Doctrine of Christ</u>

The apostles' doctrine is recorded for us in the New Testament so that one can accurately say the New Testament *is* the apostles' doctrine. Yet the kingdom of God is a mystery that escapes many a teacher of the Word. One could know

---

[246] The NAS appears to preserve the "thee's" and "thou's" but does so inconsistent with the source manuscripts. They use them only to artificially distinguish formal versus informal, using the "thee's" and "thou's" to refer to God. This distinction does not exist in the original manuscripts. Thus, they are found to add to the word of God! They do this to pick up the common usage in Shakespeare's day, but miss why the King James translators used them in the first place. Modern versions seeing this inconsistency of the NAS remove the "thee's" and "thou's" altogether. Thus, they are found to take away from the word of God that which was originally useful and purposefully there!

[247] Evidence of this fact is also seen in that pronouns are not capitalized even when it is clear in context that they refer directly to God. For example, the phrase "thou art my God" is always with a small 't' in 'thou' (e.g. Ps 22:10, 63:1, 143:10, Isa 25:1), <u>unless</u> it begins the sentence or the quote (e.g. Ps 31:14, 118:28, 140:6, Hos 2:23).

[248] Using archaic language certainly doesn't sell more Bibles, as the present sales rates of all the modern Bibles are showing. But back then, accuracy was more important than ease of use. Sorry, but if you want the undiluted word of God you must endure the archaic thee's and thou's.

the New Testament backwards and forwards and yet have no real understanding of the apostles' doctrine. This is because the apostles' doctrine is focused around the work of an apostle which is to set order to the church based on the doctrine of Christ. Thus, without insight into the apostolic order of foundations one cannot see these things unless they are taught to him.

This is exactly what had to be done for Apollos (in Ac 18), they had to be taught to him. Aquila and Priscilla who had been taught by Paul, a wise master builder, came and instructed Apollos "in the way of God more perfectly." Ac 18:26 This they had to do because Apollos was a waterer apostle, while Paul was a planter apostle (1Co 3:6-8), and it is the planter apostle who lays the foundation of the kingdom in people's lives. Because Aquila and Priscilla had been at the side of Paul for 18 months they were in turn able to teach Apollos the foundation of the kingdom, which they themselves had received from Paul. We should not be offended by this, for even Apollos who was mighty in the scriptures and was himself an apostle could not see these things.

The apostles were commanded to teach only those things which Jesus had commanded them. The apostles were clearly commissioned to teach others "to observe all things whatsoever I have commanded you" (Mt 28:20). Yet we know from the epistles there are many things which Jesus did not specifically address that the apostles did. So how did the apostles fulfill this command? Understanding the answer to this helps us understand something about the apostles' doctrine. All of what the apostles taught is based on the foundational principles of the doctrine of Christ of what he taught. In this way, the apostles' doctrine is none other than the doctrine of Christ because it is founded on the same elementary principles. These are the very ones which the writer of Hebrews was trying to bring the Hebrews back to, "the principles of the doctrine of Christ" (Heb 6:1). Once we understand "the foundation of repentance from dead works, and of faith toward God, Of the doctrine of baptisms, and of laying on of hands, and of resurrection of the dead, and of eternal judgment" (Heb 6:1-2), then we will see how all that the apostles taught rests on this singular foundation.

Sadly, so few truly preach the apostles' doctrine today because they have never been trained in it, nor do they know it. So many "know" the Bible but contradict the apostles' doctrine in their preaching. Of those who are behind pulpits few indeed know what it is or its foundational importance. This alone shows the great need for the apostolic mantle in the church today. How shocking that a "minister" may graduate from Bible College and know nothing of the foundation of the apostles' doctrine! How sad that the body of Christ is not being taught these things when the writer of Hebrews has to chasten them for forgetting this essential foundation, and let them know that without God's permission, they could not go on unto maturity without these (Heb 6:1,3).

I – Definition of Some Biblical Terms

> If a man has never known or has fallen back from "the first principles of the oracles of God", which are the doctrine of Christ (Heb 6:1), then he is in the eyes of God a baby and has no right to be teaching other believers.

When a man has forgotten or, worse yet, has never known "the first principles of the oracles of God", then they are "such as have need of milk, and not of strong meat. For every one that useth milk *is* unskilful in the word of righteousness: for he is a babe." Heb 5:12-13 If a man has never known or has fallen back from "the first principles of the oracles of God", which are the doctrine of Christ (Heb 6:1), then he is in the eyes of God a baby and has no right to be teaching other believers. Sad, but true. Such is the judgment of the word of God, friends, and it is a serious matter. You have seen God's word on this issue, not the word of any man.

3. <u>Repentance: The Foundational Stone of our Salvation</u>

The importance of repentance cannot be overstressed. Volumes could be written on repentance for it is **the** most important biblical doctrine. Of the doctrine of Christ, which is to be the foundation of every believer and without which no man can go on unto perfection or maturity, repentance is first and therefore most important. Repentance is therefore more important than even faith toward God, for the latter is second in order and thus in importance.

> Therefore leaving the principles of the doctrine of Christ, let us go on unto perfection; not laying again the foundation of repentance from dead works, and of faith toward God Heb 6:1

Without repentance we cannot enter or even perceive the kingdom of God. Notice how John the Baptist preached repentance in order to prepare the people for the kingdom of God that was coming, saying, "Repent ye: for the kingdom of heaven is at hand." Mt 3:2 Jesus preached the exact same message of repentance. "From that time Jesus began to preach, and to say, Repent: for the kingdom of heaven is at hand." Mt 4:17 Even after John was imprisoned Jesus continued to preach this same message. "Now after that John was put in prison, Jesus came into Galilee, preaching the gospel of the kingdom of God, And saying, The time is fulfilled, and the kingdom of God is at hand: repent ye, and believe the gospel." Mk 1:14-15 Thus, preaching the gospel of the kingdom of God is none other than the preaching of repentance! This is what the gospel of Luke ends with: "And that repentance and remission of sins should be preached in his name among all nations, beginning at Jerusalem." Lk 24:47

Men today ignore repentance by and large. They put exclusive emphasis on faith, yet the Bible teaches that repentance must precede faith and that without it such faith is vain and weak, having no proper foundation. Jesus tells the

Pharisees they could *not* believe because they would not repent! "For John came unto you in the way of righteousness, and ye believed him not: but the publicans and the harlots believed him: and ye, when ye had seen *it,* repented not afterward, that ye might believe him." Mt 21:32 Remember, the gospel of the kingdom of God which Jesus preached was "repent ye, and believe the gospel." Mk 1:15 Thus, repentance precedes Biblical faith. Paul went everywhere "Testifying both to the Jews, and also to the Greeks, repentance toward God, and faith toward our Lord Jesus Christ." Ac 20:21

> Jesus did not come to call sinners to faith, as so many do today. Rather, Jesus came to call sinners to repentance.

Repentance is required to escape eternal damnation. God is "not willing that any should perish, but that all should come to repentance." 2Pe 3:9 What keeps us from perishing is repentance. Jesus himself says twice to those he spoke with, "I tell you, Nay: but, except ye repent, ye shall all likewise perish." Lk 13:3,5 Jesus did not come to call sinners to faith, as so many do today. Rather, Jesus came to call sinners to repentance.[249] It is the missing foundation in the church. The apostles themselves equated the salvation of Cornelius and his whole family, not with believing on the Lord, but with being "granted repentance unto life." Ac 11:18 The Bible does not say that the angels rejoice over one sinner who believes. Rather, it says they rejoice "over one sinner that repenteth, more than over ninety and nine just persons, which need no repentance." Lk 15:7 (also v10) This shows us that salvation and being justified with God comes first and foremost by repentance. Thus, it was prophesied by the prophet, "For thus saith the Lord GOD, the Holy One of Israel; In returning [i.e. in repentance[250]] and rest shall ye be saved; in quietness and in confidence shall be your strength: and ye would not." Isa 30:15 So many know the 'rest' of faith needed for salvation, but know nothing of the returning of repentance, which must precede it.

Repentance is the command of God. "And the times of this ignorance God winked at; but now commandeth all men every where to repent" (Ac 17:30). God no longer wants us to be in the ignorance of ignoring the absolute need to repent. In fact, Jesus said we need to go and learn about repentance and why it is so important, for it is the very key to mercy.

---

[249] Sadly the "more accurate" modern translations of the Bible (such as the NAS and NIV) twice do not tell us what Jesus came to call sinners to, for they leave off the words "to repentance" in both Matthew 9:13 and Mk 2:17 (without any footnotes). Why? Because their supposedly older and better manuscripts do not have these words.

[250] The word for 'returning' is *shuwbah* (Hebrew 7729). It comes from *shuwb* (Hebrew 7725), which we shall see is the Old Testament word used for 'repent'. Thus, in repentance and rest (i.e. ceasing from our works – Heb 4:10) is salvation.

I – Definition of Some Biblical Terms

> But go ye and learn what *that* meaneth, I will have mercy, and not sacrifice: for I am not come to call the righteous, but sinners <u>to repentance</u>. Mt 9:13

When those who were pricked in their hearts besought the apostles what they should do to be saved, Peter's clarion call at Pentecost and first gospel invitation was not 'to believe' but 'to repent' (Ac 2:38). This was how they were to save themselves from this crooked and perverse generation (v40). This is how we must indeed save ourselves from this generation which is even *more* crooked and perverse than Peter's. Over and over again repentance is the revealed key to the forgiveness of sins.[251] Jesus' call to 5 of the 7 churches is to repent.[252] The telltale sign of the last days is that people will not repent! The last four times (four, speaking of the fullness of the earth) 'repent' is used in the Bible, they are all referring to those who "repented not of their deeds" – even after the terrible judgments of God against them (Rev 9:20-21, 16:9,11).

Definition of Repentance

So what is Biblical repentance? Men say it is merely the acknowledgement or the confession of our sins. Others say it is being sorry for our sins. A typical dictionary definition of repentance is "to feel pain, sorrow, or regret for something one has done or left undone; to be conscience-stricken."[253] Confession is not repentance. Sorrow and tears are not repentance, in general. Repentance will involve all of these, but these by themselves do not make repentance. Repentance according to the Bible is two-fold. First, it is turning away from our way back unto the Lord. Second, it is changing our way of thinking to agree with God's thinking (i.e. with his Word).

Let's start with the New Testament and work our way back. In this case it will be easier to understand, for there are two different kinds of repentance in the scripture. The primary Greek word for 'repent' is *metanoeo* (G3340). It is used 32 times and means 'to *think differently* or *afterwards*, i.e. *reconsider* (moral *feel compunction*)'. It is a compound word which comes from two roots:

1. *meta* (G3326) means *succession* or change
2. *noieo* (G3539) means 'to *exercise* the *mind* (*observe*), i.e. (figurative) to *comprehend*, *heed*'. It is translated 'consider, perceive, think, understand'

---

[251] Repentance precedes not only faith, but not surprisingly, therefore, also forgiveness: Ac 2:38, 3:19, 5:31, 8:22, Lk 3:3, 17:3, 24:27, Eze 18:30.

[252] See Rev 2:5,16,21-22, 3:3,19. Only the churches of Smyrna (which was enduring the fiery trials of tribulation) and Philadelphia (which had kept his word and not denied his name) are not commanded to repent.

[253] Webster's New Universal Unabridged Dictionary, Deluxe Second Edition, Dorset & Baber, 1979, p.1533.

Thus, the repenting that God desires and commands of us is to change our mind, by changing the way we perceive, think, and understand. This is why we see true repentance brings us to the acknowledging of the truth (2Tim 2:25-26). If we are sorry for what we have done, but continue to desire to do it, then we have not come to true repentance. The word for 'repentance' (i.e. the act of repenting) is similar. It is *metanoia* (G3341) and is used 24 times. It means '*compunction* (for guilt, including *reformation*); by implication *reversal* (of a decision)'. It comes from our previous word for 'repent' *metanoeo*.

True Repentance versus Sorrow and Regret

There is another type of repentance mentioned in the New Testament, but it is definitely not the one that God wants of us. We may call it 'regret' or worldly sorrow, for it does not produce spiritual restoration or life. It is the word *metamellomai* (G3338) which means 'to *care afterwards*, i.e. *regret*'. It comes from *meta* (G3326) which we have already seen and the middle of *melo* (G3199) which means 'to *be of interest* to, i.e. to *concern* (only third person singular presumed indicative used impersonal *it matters*)'. It is translated '(take) care'. This repentance, *metamellomai*, is used only 6 times and truly represents the regret that comes from man.

Regret or worldly sorrow also results in changing one's actions, but it does not result in turning back to the Lord's authority like true repentance. We are still in control of our actions and operating under our own authority. This is the word used of Judas' repentance. He returned the blood money and acknowledged his sin and had sorrow of heart, but he could find neither forgiveness, nor peace for his soul with this kind of repentance. "Then Judas, which had betrayeth him, when he saw that he was condemned, repented himself, and brought again the thirty pieces of silver to the chief priests and elders" (Mt 27:3). Why? Because Judas was still in control of his own life, as evidenced by his own decision to take his life by committing suicide. This is a repentance to be repented of (as we see Paul doing in 2Co 7:8),[254] whereas *metanoeo* is a repentance not to be repented of (from God's perspective). We never need to be sorry for godly repentance.

Paul contrasts these two types of repentance when he explains to the Corinthians the difference between godly sorrow and worldly sorrow. Paul did not rejoice that they sorrowed, for he knew that sorrow, being alone, does not bring forth true repentance. "Now I rejoice, not that ye were made sorry, but that ye

---

[254] The other uses of regret involve (1) the repentance or lack thereof of the Pharisees who should have repented after they had seen others receive the witness of John (Mt 21:29,32), (2) Paul's repentance which he repented of (2Co 7:8), and (3) the LORD who will not repent concerning his choice to make Jesus a priest after the order of Melchisedec (Heb 7:21).

sorrowed to repentance: for ye were made sorry after a godly manner, that ye might receive damage by us in nothing." 2Co 7:9 This proves sorrow and repentance are not the same.

God is not looking for tears when we sin, as the story of Esau so poignantly reveals. "For ye know how that afterward, when [Esau] would have inherited the blessing, he was rejected: for he found no place of repentance, though he sought it carefully <u>with tears</u>." Heb 12:17 Tears do not make true repentance to God, no matter how much we seek it with them. The phrase 'sought carefully' in the Greek means to '*search out*, i.e. (figurative) *investigate, crave, demand,* (by Hebrew) *worship*'. We can worship all we want, search and seek all we want, crave it from God, even demand it of him, but he is not moved by worldly sorrow that brings forth no promise of fruits worthy of true repentance. God's sorrow brings about restoration through godly change, mercy, and comfort. Man's sorrow on the contrary often brings forth no change, no life, and only worldly regret. Such is not worthy of heaven.

There was a godly sorrow that Paul was looking for that worked repentance to salvation. "For godly sorrow worketh repentance to salvation not to be repented of: but the sorrow of the world worketh death." 2Co 7:10 There we see such godly sorrow or true repentance is not to be repented of, whereas the worldly sorrow or regret is to be repented of. In other words, we need to change the way we think about merely being sorry for our sin. Being sorry about our sin, but not changing, brings no pleasure to God at all. This, even more than the sin, is what we should be truly sorry for. But when we change the way we think about our sin to see it the way God sees it, that, we will never need to be sorry for, nor to repent of, or change the way we think about it. Then, it is an eternal change that brings forth salvation or deliverance from the error that we were walking in.

This godly sorrow which brings forth true repentance is what God is looking for. Why? Because true repentance always produces fruits meet or appropriate for it. True repentance was always put to the test by the harvest it brought forth. Thus, John demands fruit from repentance. "Bring forth therefore fruits meet for repentance" (Mt 3:8). This word 'meet' in the Greek means '*deserving, comparable* or *suitable* (as if *drawing* praise)'. This is why God delights in true repentance, because it brings forth fruit deserving and suitable to it. Such fruit draws forth God's praise when he sees it. Paul also, as a spiritual father, had great rejoicing in the fruits of repentance that manifested from the Corinthians.

> For behold this selfsame thing, that ye **sorrowed after a godly sort**, what carefulness <u>it wrought in you</u>, yea, *what* clearing of yourselves, yea, *what* indignation, yea, *what* fear, yea, *what* vehement desire, yea, *what* zeal, yea, *what* revenge! In all *things* <u>ye have approved yourselves</u> to be clear in this matter. 2Co 7:11

Godly sorrow produces true repentance which in turn brings forth fruit, meet or suitable for it. Hear what Paul says. It wrought *in* them. This word 'wrought' means 'to *work fully*, i.e. *accomplish*; by implication to *finish, fashion*'. Repentance will fully work in us to accomplish a change in us that is in agreement with the truth. This is our rejoicing, "the testimony of our conscience" which brings forth fruits meet for repentance "in simplicity and godly sincerity, not with fleshly wisdom, but by the grace of God". The end result? We have "our conversation in the world, and more abundantly to you-ward." 2Co 1:12 We begin to live our life not for ourselves (in self-centeredness), but for the sake of others. Repentance is the way of the kingdom of God *and* the way of righteousness (Mt 21:32). If we would follow Jesus, we must walk in repentance.

Repentance in the Old Testament

Now that we have gained the clarity of the two different types of repentance, we will see the Old Testament follows a very similar pattern. The difference will be that the Old Testament will focus on the external change, rather than the internal transformation, as is so often the case with the Old. The Old does indeed have two different types of repentance. The word most often translated into English as repent(ing) is not the word we would expect though. It is *nacham* (Hebrew 5162) and it means 'to *sigh*, i.e. *breathe* strongly; by implication to *be sorry*, i.e. (in a favorable sense) to *pity, console* or (reflex.) *rue*; or (unfavorably) to *avenge* (oneself)'.

Additionally, over 60 times *nacham* is translated 'comfort' (or a variation thereof).[255] This word is also used of the LORD repenting and changing his mind on what he will do, often because of the sorrow he feels at the suffering that would take place.[256] By no means coincidentally is *nacham* used of man exactly 6 times, for 6 is the number of man (Rev 13:18)![257] This is not the primary

---

[255] Some examples include: Noah who would bring comfort (Gen 5:29); Isaac was comforted after his mother's death (Gen 24:67); Boaz comforted Ruth (2:13); David comforted Bath-sheba (2Sam 12:24); God's rod and staff comfort us (Ps 23:4); his word comforts us (Ps 119:50); and God himself comforts us (Ps 86:17, Isa 49:13, 51:3,12, 52:9, 61:2, 66:13, Zec 1:17). The foreshadowing of the Comforter (Lam 1:6) also uses this same word.

[256] It is used of the LORD 34x (i.e. 2x17!) in regard to him repenting or not repenting, as follows: Gen 6:6-7, Ex 32:12,14, Nu 23:19, Dt 32:36, Jdg 2:18, 1Sam 15:11,29,35, 2Sam 24:16, 1Ch 21:15, Ps 90:13, 106:45, 110:4, 135:14, Jer 4:28, 15:6, 18:8,10, 20:16, 26:3,13,19, 42:10, Eze 24:14, Joel 2:13-14, Am 7:3,6, Jonah 3:9-10, 4:2, Zec 8:14. Two additional words, both which come from *nacham* (H5164), also refer to the LORD repenting. We see repentance in Hos 13:14 is *nocham* (H5164) and repentings in Hos 11:8 is *nichuwm* (H5150).

[257] The following scriptures using *nacham* are in regard to man repenting or not repenting: Ex 13:17 (1st word only), Jdg 21:6,15, Job 42:6, Jer 8:6, 31:19.

I – Definition of Some Biblical Terms

repentance of the new covenant that man is to partake of. This is regret or sorrow for one's actions. Thus, it corresponds to our Greek word for sorrow or regret (*metamellomai*). It perfectly describes God's choice to not bring forth his judgments that he planned, but to show mercy instead. But it does not describe the repentance that God is looking for in us after we have already sinned.

The one other Old Testament word for 'repent' is *shuwb* (Hebrew 7725) which means 'to *turn* back (hence, away), (not necessarily with the idea of *return* to the starting point); generally to *retreat*'. It is translated 'repent' only three times, but each time it is of man repenting and turning from their sin and idolatry.[258] This word is a very common word and is translated into English over 90 different ways, many of which do not relate to repentance at all. Many times when *shuwb* is translated as 'turn' or 'return' in English it is in line with the new covenant meaning of 'repent'. In the following verses each time a word is *shuwb*, it has been underlined in order to give an example of how this word carries with it the idea of repenting (even though not always translated into English as such).

> *Yet* if they shall <u>bethink</u> themselves in the land whither they were carried captives, and **repent**, and make supplication unto thee in the land of them that carried them captives, saying, We have sinned, and have done perversely, we have committed wickedness; And *so* <u>return</u> unto thee with all their heart, and with all their soul, … and pray unto thee … Then hear thou their prayer and their supplication in heaven thy dwelling place, and maintain their cause, And forgive thy people that have sinned against thee and all their transgressions wherein they have transgressed against thee 1K 8:47-49

> This is the repentance we need today – not just tears, not just the acknowledgement of our sin, not just confession, but the changing of our way of thinking to agree with God's Word and to change our direction toward him.

The previous passage employing *shuwb* is God's promise to hear the cry of his people who are in bondage and slavery and to bring them back into God's covenant provisions. When will he do this? If they will repent or turn from their ways and pray, acknowledging their sins, perversity, and wickedness. If they will turn unto God with all their heart and all their soul, God will hear and maintain their cause and forgive their sin. Similarly, in the next two passages where *shuwb* is translated as 'repent', they have the context of turning away from idolatry, abominations, and transgressions.

---

[258] The following scriptures using *shuwb* are translated 'repent': 1K 8:47, Eze 14:6, 18:30. We will not explore those here, for that would be part of a larger work on repentance.

> Therefore say unto the house of Israel, Thus saith the Lord GOD; **Repent**, and <u>turn</u> *yourselves* from your idols; and turn away your faces from all your abominations. Eze 14:6
>
> **Repent**, and <u>turn</u> *yourselves* from all your transgressions; so iniquity shall not be your ruin. For I have no pleasure in the death of him that dieth, saith the Lord GOD: wherefore <u>turn</u> *yourselves*, and live ye. Eze 18:30,32

Putting Old and New Together

Let us now put together the repentance of the Old with that of the New. We have seen that the old covenant focuses on an external change in our *direction* with an emphasis on bringing forth fruits to demonstrate our <u>turning away</u> from carnality and idolatry. This is why John the Baptist who was the last of the Old Testament prophets demanded fruits worthy of repentance. The new covenant focuses on an internal change in thinking with an emphasis on acknowledging the truth to demonstrate our <u>turning toward</u> the living God. Thus, the Old is to turn away from our disobedience and the New is to turn toward our God. The beauty of this two-fold cord which along with the Spirit of God is not easily broken can be seen in two New Testament passages. When Peter and John, at the hour of prayer, are at the Gate Beautiful (a picture of the door of the kingdom of God!), they encounter a lame man whom they heal in the name of Jesus. Many people gather about wondering what has happened. Peter preaches to them, saying,

> <u>Repent</u> ye therefore, and be <u>converted</u>, that your sins may be blotted out, when the times of refreshing shall come from the presence of the Lord Ac 3:19

Peter shares they must repent and be converted. Let us take a look at this word 'converted' since it is paired with 'repent'. This word 'converted' is the Greek word *epistrepho* (G1994) which comes from the two roots:

1. *epi* (G1909) means *towards*,
2. *strepho* (G4762) means 'to *twist*, i.e. *turn* quite around or *reverse*'.

Therefore, *epistrepho* means to <u>turn quite around towards</u>. It is a complete U-turn. Peter perfectly joins the New Testament repentance with the Old. He says in effect, change your way of thinking [*the New part of repentance*] and be one who is turned away from your old life and your sins [*the Old part of repentance*]. Paul echoes this cry of turning away from our way and toward the living God by changing our way of thinking to agree with God's word. This, in fact, was what he preached everywhere, as he witnesses to King Agrippa.

> But shewed first unto them of Damascus, and at Jerusalem, and throughout all the coasts of Judaea, and *then* to the Gentiles, that they should <u>repent</u> and <u>turn to God</u>, and do works meet for repentance. Ac 26:20

I – Definition of Some Biblical Terms

The underlined word 'turn' is again this same word *epistrepho* that we have looked at, 'to be converted or to turn quite around towards'. Notice again how changing our way of thinking and turning completely away from our way unto God, along with bringing forth the fruits that are worthy of such a true repentance, is all that God is requesting of us in salvation. This is the repentance we need today – not just tears, not just the acknowledgement of our sin, not just confession, but the changing of our way of thinking to agree with God's Word and to change our direction toward him.

Baptism of Repentance: A Continual Immersing in Change

Many, many reject the baptism of repentance saying this is John's baptism and it is not for today, but was only for the preparatory time and now is no longer needed since Jesus has come. The scripture soundly refutes any such Sadduceean theory. [Remember, the Sadducees were those who removed things from the scriptures, saying they were not for today (Ac 23:8).] The baptism of repentance, though called the baptism of John, was not in any way from John, nor has it passed away. Jesus said it was for the purpose of bringing forth "the way of righteousness" (Mt 21:32) into the earth, and he challenged the hypocrisy of the Pharisees, demanding to know of them whether it was of God or not (Mt 21:25).

Jesus asks us the same question today as he asked the chief priests of his day, "The baptism of John, was it from heaven, or of men?" Lk 20:4 What will you say? May you believe like the publicans and harlots who found the kingdom of God and not be as the lawyers and chief priests who "when ye had seen *it*, repented not afterward, that ye might believe him." Mt 21:32

> Jesus asks us the same question today as he asked the chief priests of his day, "The baptism of John, was it from heaven, or of men?" Lk 20:4

Consider what the scripture says of Apollos. We see he was an apostle, and he was mighty in the scriptures (Ac 18:24). "This man was instructed in the way of the Lord; and being fervent in the spirit, he spake and taught diligently the things of the Lord, underline{knowing only the baptism of John}." Ac 18:25 Let us hear this again. Apollos was instructed in the way of the Lord *and* he taught diligently the things of the Lord, yet, he **only** knew John's baptism! John's baptism *is* the baptism of repentance as seen in several scriptures.[259] But the remarkable truth we learn from this passage in Acts is the baptism of repentance IS the way of the Lord.

---

[259] John's baptism is the baptism of repentance: Mk 1:4, Lk 3:3, Ac 13:24, 19:4.

The baptism of repentance is to be continually immersed into repentance (i.e. the changing of our way of thinking to agree with God's word). It is the way of the Lord which leads us to righteousness. It is because this baptism is not taught or maintained, that God's people as they get older in the Lord often unknowingly grow old, cold, and hard. This is the effect of men's doctrine and empty religions, so that few who are five or more years old in the Lord have an ear to hear truth! This is the same as Jesus' day, for those days will be replicated in the last days preceding the coming of the Son of Man. Without the baptism of repentance and the preaching of the kingdom of God which demands change, anyone will become more and more set in their ways rather than continually being emptied out to go from glory to glory (through weakness). The baptism of repentance is what will maintain a soft heart of flesh which God's Spirit can easily convict and lead (Eze 36:26).

I – Definition of Some Biblical Terms

Appendix II.   The Scriptures on Fearing God

I. Key Scriptures on the Fear of God

The following is a summary list of the most important scriptures related to the fear of God, which are grouped by category. These scriptures are key to the fear of the LORD and are listed here with a few notes on why they are so important. These are essential if you would understand the inestimable value of God's holy fear and the great gift it is. You would do well to keep them in your heart.[260]

1. <u>Its Endurance</u>: The fear of God will endure throughout all generations.
    a. It is for every generation.
        The fear of the LORD *is* clean, <u>enduring for ever</u> Ps 19:9
        They shall fear thee as long as the sun and moon endure, <u>throughout all generations</u>. Ps 72:5
        Afterward shall the children of Israel return, and seek the LORD their God, and David their king; and shall fear the LORD and his goodness <u>in the latter days</u>. Hos 3:5
    b. God desires it always to be in our heart.
        O that there were such an heart in them, <u>that they would fear me</u>, and keep all my commandments <u>always</u>, that it might be well with them, and with their children for ever! Dt 5:29
        that thou mayest learn to fear the Lord thy God <u>always</u>. Dt 14:23
        Happy *is* the man <u>that feareth alway</u> Pr 28:14

2. <u>Its Importance</u>:
    a. God takes pleasure in us.
        The LORD <u>taketh pleasure in them</u> that fear him, in those that hope in his mercy. Ps 147:11
    b. Everything God does, he does so that we will fear him.
        I know that, <u>whatsoever God doeth</u>, it shall be for ever: nothing can be put to it, nor any thing taken from it: and God doeth *it*, <u>that *men* should fear before him</u>. Ecc 3:14
    c. The whole duty of man is to fear God & keep his commandments.
        Let us hear the conclusion of the whole matter: Fear God, and keep his commandments: for <u>this *is* the whole *duty* of man</u>. Ecc 12:13
    d. God honors and blesses those who fear him.

---

[260] A comprehensive list of all scriptures relating to the fear of God is in the appendix entitled 'The Scriptures on Fearing God' in the book <u>Losing the Treasure of the Lord</u>.

but he honoureth them that fear the LORD Ps 15:4

He will bless them that fear the LORD, *both* small and great. Ps 115:13

3. Its Effect:

   a. Causes us to depart from sin.

   The fear of the LORD *is* a fountain of life, to depart from the snares of death. Pr 14:27

   By mercy and truth iniquity is purged: and by the fear of the LORD *men* depart from evil. Pr 16:6

   Fear not: for God is come to prove you, & that his fear may be before your faces, that ye sin not. Ex 20:20

   b. Causes us not to depart from him.

   And I will make an everlasting covenant with them, that I will not turn away from them, to do them good; but I will put my fear in their hearts, that they shall not depart from me. Jer 32:40

   c. Gives us strong confidence and a place of refuge.

   In the fear of the LORD *is* strong confidence: and his children shall have a place of refuge. Pr 14:26

   d. Enables us to draw near to God.

   Dominion and fear *are* with him, he maketh peace in his high places.[261] Job 25:2

4. Its Protection and Supply:

   a. God supplies the need of those who fear him.

   O fear the LORD, ye his saints: for *there is* no want to them that fear him. Ps 34:9

   b. God watches over those that fear him.

   Behold, the eye of the LORD *is* upon them that fear him, upon them that hope in his mercy; Ps 33:18

   And the LORD commanded us to do all these statutes, to fear the LORD our God, for our good always, that he might preserve us alive, as *it is* at this day. Dt 6:24

   He hath given meat unto them that fear him: he will ever be mindful of his covenant. Ps 111:5

   c. It delivers us from our enemies (especially from the fear of man) and from harm.

---

[261] We cannot draw near to God without the fear of God because "Dominion and fear *are* with him". This is why we cannot be saved without confessing him as Lord (because dominion is with him) and we cannot draw nigh to him without the fear of God.

The angel of the LORD encampeth round about them that fear him, <u>and delivereth them</u>. Ps 34:7

The fear of the LORD *tendeth* to life: and *he that hath it* shall abide satisfied; <u>he shall not be visited with evil</u>. Pr 19:23

Ye that fear the LORD, trust in the LORD: <u>he *is* their help and their shield</u>. Ps 115:11

   d. It keeps us from all extremes.

   It is good that thou shouldest take hold of this; yea, also from this withdraw not thine hand: for he that feareth God <u>shall come forth of them all</u>. Ecc 7:18

5. <u>Its Value</u>:

   a. It is our great treasure and our heritage.

   And wisdom and knowledge shall be the stability of thy times, *and* strength of salvation: the fear of the LORD *is* <u>his treasure</u>. Isa 33:6

   For thou, O God, hast heard my vows: thou hast given *me* <u>the heritage</u> of those that fear thy name. Ps 61:5

   Oh how great *is* thy goodness, which <u>thou hast laid up for them</u> that fear thee; Ps 31:19

   b. It causes us to abide fulfilled and satisfied in life.

   He will <u>fulfil the desire</u> of them that fear him: he also will hear their cry, & will save them. Ps 145:19

   The fear of the LORD *tendeth* to life: and *he that hath it* <u>shall abide satisfied</u>; Pr 19:23

   By humility *and* the fear of the LORD *are* riches, & honour, & <u>life</u>. Pr 22:4

   c. All will go well with them that fear God, but it shall not go well with them that do not.
   Though a sinner do evil an hundred times, and his *days* be prolonged, yet surely I know that <u>it shall be well with them that fear God</u>, which fear before him: But <u>it shall not be well with the wicked</u>, neither shall he prolong *his* days, *which are* as a shadow; <u>because he feareth not before God</u>. Ecc 8:12-13

   d. God will show his will to those who fear him.

   What man *is* he that feareth the LORD? him <u>shall he teach in the way *that* he shall choose</u>. The secret of the LORD *is* with them that fear him; and he will <u>shew them his covenant</u>. Ps 25:12,14

   e. God will hear the cries of those who fear him.

   Then they that feared the LORD spake often one to another: and the LORD hearkened, and heard *it,* Mal 3:16

II – The Scriptures on Fearing God

6. <u>Its Life-Giving Properties</u>:
   a. It is a fountain of life.

   The fear of the LORD *is* a <u>fountain of life</u>, to depart from the snares of death. Pr 14:27

   The fear of the LORD *tendeth* to <u>life</u> Pr 19:23

   b. It brings healing and growth.

   Be not wise in thine own eyes: fear the LORD, and depart from evil. It shall be health to thy navel, and marrow to thy bones. Pr 3:7-8

   But unto you that fear my name shall the Sun of righteousness arise with healing in his wings; and ye shall go forth, and <u>grow up</u> as calves of the stall. Mal 4:2

   c. It brings great mercy.

   For as the heaven is high above the earth, <u>so great is his mercy toward them that fear him</u>. Like as a father pitieth *his* children, *so* the LORD pitieth them that fear him. Ps 103:11,13

   But the mercy of the LORD *is* from everlasting to everlasting <u>upon them that fear him</u>, and his righteousness unto children's children; Ps 103:17

   And his mercy *is* on them that fear him from generation to generation. Lk 1:50

   Let them now that fear the LORD say, that <u>his mercy *endureth* for ever</u>. Ps 118:4

   Surely <u>his salvation *is* nigh</u> them that fear him; that glory may dwell in our land. Ps 85:9

   d. It is the way of peace.

   And the way of peace have they not known: There is no fear of God before their eyes. Rom 3:17-18

   My covenant was with him of <u>life</u> and <u>peace</u>; and I gave them to him *for* the fear wherewith he feared me, and was afraid before my name. Mal 2:5

   e. It produces godly change in our life.

   God shall hear, and afflict them, even he that abideth of old. Selah. Because they have no **changes**, therefore <u>they fear not God</u>. Ps 55:19

7. <u>Its Insight</u>: To know anything spiritually, we must have God's fear.
   a. It is the key to knowledge.

   The fear of the LORD *is* <u>the beginning of knowledge</u>: *but* fools despise wisdom and instruction. Pr 1:7

   b. It is the key to understanding.

   by the fear of the LORD *men* depart from evil. Pr 16:6

Behold, the fear of the Lord, that *is* wisdom; and to depart from evil *is* understanding. Job 28:28

    c. It is the key to wisdom.

        The fear of the LORD *is* <u>the beginning of wisdom</u> Pr 9:10/Ps 111:10

        The fear of the LORD *is* <u>the instruction of wisdom</u>; and before honour *is* humility. Pr 15:33

        Behold, the fear of the Lord, <u>that *is* wisdom</u>; and to depart from evil *is* understanding. Job 28:28

II. <u>Scriptures on Not Fearing</u>

The fear of God is to be the *only* fear in our heart. It should drive all other fears out. The following scriptures are a partial list of the many which exhort us on what we ought not to fear. These specifically have been chosen because they show us why we ought not to fear everything outside of God. Most of them are the direct result of how we know and understand the LORD God. [Usage note: The commands to "fear not", "be not afraid", etc. are <u>underlined</u>, while the focus on the LORD is shown in **bold**.]

1. After these things the word of the LORD came unto Abram in a vision, saying, <u>Fear not</u>, Abram: **I *am* thy shield, *and* thy exceeding great reward.** Gen 15:1

2. And God heard the voice of the lad; and the angel of God called Hagar out of heaven, and said unto her, What aileth thee, Hagar? <u>fear not</u>; **for God hath heard** the voice of the lad where he *is*. Gen 21:17

3. And the LORD appeared unto him the same night, and said, I *am* the God of Abraham thy father: <u>fear not</u>, **for I *am* with thee, and will bless thee, and multiply thy seed** for my servant Abraham's sake. Gen 26:24

4. And he said, Peace *be* to you, <u>fear not</u>: **your God, and the God of your father, hath given you treasure in your sacks**: I had your money. And he brought Simeon out unto them. Gen 43:23

5. And he said, **I *am* God, the God of thy father**: <u>fear not</u> to go down into Egypt; for **I will there make of thee a great nation**: Gen 46:3

6. Behold, **the LORD thy God hath set the land before thee**: go up *and* possess *it,* as the LORD God of thy fathers hath said unto thee; <u>fear not</u>, neither be discouraged. Dt 1:21

7. Then I said unto you, <u>Dread not, neither be afraid of them</u>. **The LORD your God which goeth before you, he shall fight for you**, according to all that he did for you in Egypt before your eyes; Dt 1:29-30

8. Thou shalt <u>not be afraid</u> of them: *but* shalt well **remember what the LORD thy God did** unto Pharaoh, and unto all Egypt; Dt 7:18

II – The Scriptures on Fearing God

9. When thou goest out to battle against thine enemies, and seest horses, and chariots, *and* a people more than thou, <u>be not afraid</u> of them: **for the LORD thy God *is* with thee**, which brought thee up out of the land of Egypt. Dt 20:1

10. And shall say unto them, Hear, O Israel, ye approach this day unto battle against your enemies: let not your hearts faint, <u>fear not</u>, and do not tremble, neither be ye terrified because of them; **For the LORD your God *is* he that goeth with you, to fight for you against your enemies, to save you.** Dt 20:3-4

11. Be strong and of a good courage, <u>fear not</u>, nor be afraid of them: for **the LORD thy God, he *it is* that doth go with thee; he will not fail thee, nor forsake thee.** Dt 31:6

12. And the LORD, **he *it is* that doth go before thee; he will be with thee, he will not fail thee, neither forsake thee**: <u>fear not</u>, neither be dismayed. Dt 31:8

13. Have not I commanded thee? Be strong and of a good courage; <u>be not afraid</u>, neither be thou dismayed: for **the LORD thy God *is* with thee** whithersoever thou goest. Jos 1:9

14. And the LORD said unto Joshua, <u>Fear not</u>, neither be thou dismayed: take all the people of war with thee, and arise, go up to Ai: see, **I have given into thy hand** the king of Ai, and his people, and his city, and his land: Jos 8:1

15. And Joshua said unto them, <u>Fear not</u>, nor be dismayed, be strong and of good courage: for **thus shall the LORD do to all your enemies against whom ye fight.** Jos 10:25

16. And the LORD said unto Joshua, Be <u>not afraid</u> because of them: for to morrow about this time will **I deliver them up** all slain before Israel Jos 11:6

17. And I said unto you, **I *am* the LORD your God**; <u>fear not</u> the gods of the Amorites, in whose land ye dwell: but ye have not obeyed my voice. Jdg 6:10

18. And Samuel said unto the people, <u>Fear not</u>: ye have done all this wickedness: yet turn not aside from following the LORD, but serve the LORD with all your heart; ... **For the LORD will not forsake his people for his great name's sake: because it hath pleased the LORD to make you his people.** 1Sam 12:20,22

19. Thus saith the LORD, Be <u>not afraid</u> of the words which thou hast heard 2K 19:6/Isa 37:6

20. And David said to Solomon his son, Be strong and of good courage, and do *it*: <u>fear not</u>, nor be dismayed: for **the LORD God, *even* my God, *will be* with thee; he will not fail thee, nor forsake thee**, until thou hast finished all the work for the service of the house of the LORD. 1Ch 28:20

21. And he said, Hearken ye, all Judah, and ye inhabitants of Jerusalem, and thou king Jehoshaphat, Thus saith the LORD unto you, Be <u>not afraid</u> nor dismayed

by reason of this great multitude; for **the battle *is* not yours, but God's**. 2Ch 20:15

22. Ye shall not *need* to fight in this *battle:* set yourselves, stand ye *still,* and see the salvation of the LORD with you, O Judah and Jerusalem: <u>fear not</u>, nor be dismayed; to morrow go out against them: for **the LORD *will be* with you**. 2Ch 20:17

23. And I looked, and rose up, and said unto the nobles, and to the rulers, and to the rest of the people, <u>Be not ye afraid</u> of them: **remember the Lord**, *which is* great and terrible, Neh 4:14

24. <u>Be not afraid</u> of sudden fear, neither of the desolation of the wicked, when it cometh. For **the LORD shall be thy confidence**, and shall keep thy foot from being taken. Pr 3:25-26

25. Say to them *that are* of a fearful heart, Be strong, <u>fear not</u>: behold, **your God will come *with* vengeance, *even* God *with* a recompence; he will come and save you**. Isa 35:4

26. <u>be not afraid</u>; say unto the cities of Judah, **Behold your God!** Isa 40:9

27. For I the LORD thy God will hold thy right hand, saying unto thee, <u>Fear not</u>; **I will help thee**. <u>Fear not</u>, thou worm Jacob, *and* ye men of Israel; **I will help thee**, saith the LORD, and thy redeemer, the Holy One of Israel. Isa 41:13-14

28. But now thus saith the LORD that created thee, O Jacob, and he that formed thee, O Israel, <u>Fear not</u>: for **I have redeemed thee, I have called *thee* by thy name; thou *art* mine**. Isa 43:1

29. <u>Fear not</u>: for **I *am* with thee**: I will bring thy seed from the east, and gather thee from the west; Isa 43:5

30. Thus saith the LORD that made thee, and formed thee from the womb, ***which* will help thee**; <u>Fear not</u>, O Jacob, my servant; and thou, Jesurun, whom I have chosen. Isa 44:2

31. <u>Be not afraid</u> of their faces: **for I *am* with thee to deliver thee**, saith the LORD. Jer 1:8

32. <u>Be not afraid</u> of [idols]; for they cannot do evil, neither also *is it* in them to do good. Forasmuch as *there is* none like unto thee, O LORD; thou *art* great, and thy name is great in might. Jer 10:5-6

33. Therefore <u>fear thou not</u>, O my servant Jacob, saith the LORD; neither be dismayed, O Israel: for, lo, **I will save thee from afar**, and thy seed from the land of their captivity; and Jacob shall return, and shall be in rest, and be quiet, and none shall make *him* afraid. Jer 30:10

34. <u>Be not afraid</u> of the king of Babylon, of whom ye are afraid; <u>be not afraid</u> of him, saith the LORD: **for I *am* with you to save you, and to deliver you** from his hand. Jer 42:11

35. But <u>fear not</u> thou, O my servant Jacob, and be not dismayed, O Israel: for, behold, **I will save thee from afar off**, and thy seed from the land of their cap-

II – The Scriptures on Fearing God

tivity; and Jacob shall return, and be in rest and at ease, and <u>none shall make <i>him</i> afraid</u>. Jer 46:27

36. And thou, son of man, <u>be not afraid</u> of them, <u>neither be afraid</u> of their words, ...: <u>be not afraid</u> of their words, nor be dismayed at their looks, Eze 2:6

37. <u>Fear not</u>, O land; be glad and rejoice: for **the LORD will do great things**. Joel 2:21

38. O house of Judah, and house of Israel; **so will I save you**, and ye shall be a blessing: <u>fear not</u>, *but* let your hands be strong. Zec 8:13

39. But the angel said unto him, <u>Fear not</u>, Zacharias: for **thy prayer is heard**; and thy wife Elisabeth shall bear thee a son, and thou shalt call his name John. Lk 1:13

40. And the angel said unto her, <u>Fear not</u>, Mary: for **thou hast found favour with God**. Lk 1:30

41. And the angel said unto them, <u>Fear not</u>: for, behold, **I bring you good tidings of great joy**, which shall be to all people. Lk 2:10

42. But when Jesus heard *it*, he answered him, saying, <u>Fear not</u>: believe only, and **she shall be made whole**. Lk 8:50

43. But even the very hairs of your head are all numbered. <u>Fear not</u> therefore: **ye are of more value than many sparrows**. Lk 12:7

44. <u>Fear not</u>, little flock; for **it is your Father's good pleasure to give you the kingdom**. Lk 12:32

45. <u>Fear not</u>, daughter of Sion: behold, **thy King cometh**, sitting on an ass's colt. Jn 12:15

46. Then spake the Lord to Paul in the night by a vision, <u>Be not afraid</u>, but speak, and hold not thy peace: **For I am with thee, and no man shall set on thee to hurt thee** Ac 18:9-10

47. Saying, <u>Fear not</u>, Paul; thou must be brought before Caesar: and, lo, **God hath given thee all them that sail with thee**. Ac 27:24

48. And when I saw him, I fell at his feet as dead. And he laid his right hand upon me, saying unto me, <u>Fear not</u>; **I am the first and the last**: Rev 1:17

Appendix III.   Words Used with Fearing God

The following are the Hebrew and Greek words used in connection with the fear of God (including dread, terror, and trembling). They are generally arranged by usage, the most common being listed first, although root and derivative words are grouped together. Hebrew words are put first, followed by Greek. Words are arranged from reverential fear to great fear and trembling. Some scripture references are included in some cases which are illustrative. Underlining has been used to call to attention those which specifically show the fearfulness (i.e. the trembling) of the fear of God. After the arrow (→), brackets ([ ]) give information about the context and parentheses show the word translated.

<u>Hebrew Words</u>

da'ag, **H1672**, a primitive root; *be anxious* :- be afraid (careful, sorry), sorrow, take thought. → Isa 57:11, Jer 2:12

yare', **H3372**, a primitive root; to *fear*; moral to *revere*; causative to *frighten* :- affright, be (make) afraid, dread (-ful), (put in) fear (-ful, -fully, -ing), (be had in) reverence (-end), × see, terrible (act, -ness, thing).

> yare', **H3373**, from H3372; *fearing*; moral *reverent* :- afraid, fear (-ful).

> yir'ah, **H3374**, feminine of H3373; *fear* (also used as infinitive); moral *reverence* :- × dreadful, × exceedingly, fear (-fulness).

> mowra', **H4172**, *mo-raw'*; or **mora'**, mo-raw'; or **morah**, mo-raw'; (Ps 9:20), from H3372; *fear*; by implication a *fearful* thing or deed :- dread, (that ought to be) fear (-ed), terribleness, terror.

pachad, **H6342**, a primitive root; <u>to *be startled* (by a sudden alarm)</u>; hence to *fear* in general :- be afraid, stand in awe [Ps 119:161], (be in) fear, <u>make to shake</u>. → Pr 28:14 [always], Hos 3:5 [last days], Job 23:15 (afraid)

> pachad, **H6343**, from H6342; <u>a (sudden) *alarm*</u> (properly the object feared, by implication the feeling) :- <u>dread</u> (-ful), fear, (thing) great [fear, -ly feared], <u>terror</u>. → Ps 36:1 [no fear], 119:120 [trembles], Job 25:2, 13:11 (dread), Gen 31:42,53 [Isaac's fear], 1Sam 11:7 [King Saul], 2Ch 19:7 [judges],

> pachdah, **H6345**, feminine of H6343 (pachad); *alarm* (i.e. *awe*) :- fear. → Jer 2:19 [bitter]

ba`ath, **H1204**, a primitive root; to *fear* :- affright, be (make) afraid, <u>terrify</u>, trouble. → terrify: Job 7:14 [visions], 9:34 [rod]; afraid: 1Ch 21:30 [sword], Job 13:11 [excellency], 13:21 [dread]

> bi`uwthiym, **H1161**, masc. plural from H1204; <u>*alarms*</u> :- <u>terrors</u>. → Job 6:4

III – Words Used with Fearing God

'eymah, **H367,** or (shortened) **'emah**, ay-maw'; from the same as H366 ('ayom); *fright*; concrete an *idol* (as a bugbear) :- dread, fear, horror, idol, terrible, terror. → Job 9:34 (fear), 13:21 (dread)

bahal, **H926,** a primitive root; to *tremble* inwardly (or *palpitate*), i.e. (fig.) *be* (causative *make*) (suddenly) *alarmed* or *agitated*; by implication to *hasten* anxiously :- be (make) affrighted (afraid, amazed, dismayed, rash), (be, get, make) haste (-n, -y, -ily), (give) speedy (-ily), thrust out, trouble, vex. → Job 23:15-16 (troubled)

ragaz, **H7264,** a primitive root; to *quiver* (with any violent emotion, especially anger or fear) :- be afraid, stand in awe, disquiet, fall out, fret, move, provoke, quake, rage, shake, tremble, trouble, be wroth. → Joel 2:1 (tremble), Ps 99:1 [he reigns], 4:4 (stand in awe)

`arats, **H6206,** a primitive root; to *awe* or (intrans.) to *dread*; hence to *harass* :- be affrighted (afraid, dread, feared, terrified), break, dread, fear, oppress, prevail, shake terribly. → Isa 29:23

charad, **H2729,** a primitive root; to *shudder* with terror; hence to *fear*; also to *hasten* (with anxiety) :- be (make) afraid, be careful, discomfit, fray (away), quake, tremble. → Am 3:6 [trumpet]

dᵉchal, **H1763,** (Chaldee); corresponding to H2119 (zachal); to *slink*, i.e. (by implication) to *fear*, or (causative) *be formidable* :- make afraid, dreadful, fear, terrible. → Dan 6:26

chathath, **H2865,** a primitive root; properly to *prostrate*; hence to *break* down, either (literal) by violence, or (fig.) by confusion and fear :- abolish, affright, be (make) afraid, amaze, beat down, discourage, (cause to) dismay, go down, scare, terrify. → Mal 2:5

chittah, **H2847,** from H2865; *fear* :- terror.

chuwl, **H2342,** or **chiyl**, kheel; a primitive root; properly to *twist* or *whirl* (in a circular or spiral manner), i.e. (specific) to *dance*, to *writhe* in pain (especially of parturition) or fear; fig. to *wait*, to *pervert* :- bear, (make to) bring forth, (make to) calve, dance, drive away, fall grievously (with pain), fear, form, great, grieve, (be) grievous, hope, look, make, be in pain, be much (sore) pained, rest, shake, shapen, (be) sorrow (-ful), stay, tarry, travail (with pain), tremble, trust, wait carefully (patiently), be wounded. → fear: 1Ch 16:30, Ps 96:9; tremble: Jer 5:22, Ps 114:7, 97:4, Hab 3:10

guwr, **H1481,** a primitive root; properly to *turn* aside from the road (for a lodging or any other purpose), i.e. *sojourn* (as a guest); also to *shrink, fear* (as in a strange place); also to *gather* for hostility (as *afraid*) :- abide, assemble, be afraid, dwell, fear, gather (together), inhabitant, remain, sojourn, stand in awe [Ps 33:8], (be) stranger, × surely. → afraid: Job 19:29 [sword] [262]

GREEK WORDS

eulabeia, **G2124,** from G2126 (eulabes); properly *caution*, i.e. (religiously) *reverence* (*piety*); by implication *dread* (concrete) :- fear (-ed). → Heb 5:7 [Jesus]

eulabeomai, **G2125,** middle from G2126 (eulabes); to *be circumspect*, i.e. (by implication) to *be apprehensive*; religiously, to *reverence* :- (moved with) fear. → Heb 11:7

phobos, **G5401,** from a primary **phebomai** (to *be* put in *fear*); *alarm or fright* :- be afraid, + exceedingly, fear, terror. → Php 2:2 [salvation], 1Pe 2:18 [subject to masters], 1:17 [pass our time], Rom 3:18 [before our eyes], 13:17 [whom due], 2Co 7:1 [holiness], 7:11 [repentance], 7:15 [receive Titus], 5:11 (his terror)

>phobeo, **G5399,** from G5401; to *frighten*, i.e. (passive) to *be alarmed*; by analogy to *be in awe* of, i.e. revere :- be (sore) afraid, fear (exceedingly), reverence. → Rom 11:20, 13:3, Col 3:22, Heb 4:1, 1Pe 2:17, Rev 11:18, 19:5, 14:7, 15:4

>phoberos, **G5398,** from G5401; *frightful*, i.e. (object) *formidable* :- fearful, terrible. → Heb 13:21 [in his hands], 12:21 (terrible [sight])

>emphobos, **G1719,** from G1722 (en) and G5401; *in fear*, i.e. *alarmed* :- affrighted, afraid, tremble.

>ekphobos, **G1630,** from G1537 (ek) and G5401; *frightened out* of one's wits :- sore afraid, exceedingly fear. → Mk 9:6 (sore afraid), Heb 12:21 (exceedingly fear)

tremo, **Greek 5141,** strengthened from a primary **treo** (to "*dread*", "*terrify*"); to "*tremble*" or *fear* :- be afraid, trembling. → Ac 9:6 [Saul], 2Pe 2:10 [the unjust are not afraid!]

>tromos, **G5156,** from G5141; a "*trembling*", i.e. quaking with *fear* :- + tremble (-ing). → 2Co 7:15 [received Titus], Eph 6:5 [servants], Php 2:12 [salvation]

>>entromos, **G1790,** from G1722 (en) and G5156; *terrified* :- × quake, × trembled. → Ac 7:32, Heb 12:21 (quake)

---

[262] The remaining uses are all of the fear of man: Nu 22:3, Dt 1:17, 18:22, 32:27, 1Sam 18:15, Job 41:25, Jer 22:25, Hos 10:5.

III – Words Used with Fearing God

Content Index: Finding A Specific Topic

A

Abraham
    covenant, 155
    feared God, 177, 236
    Friend of God, 68, 176
    gospel preached to, 156

afraid of God, 82, 83, 106
    as father, 108
    David, 84
    excellency of God, 88
    holiness, 107
    Job, 88
    judgment, 86, 89
    safety, 108
    sovereignty of God, 88

America
    education, 50
    like Nineveh, 55
    past greatness, 52

anger of God
    his servants, 149
    Uzzah, 84

apostasy, 13

apostles
    doctrine, 271
    pattern, 193

authority, 42
    faith, 159
    false, 25
    fear, 105, 257
    not speak evil of, 228

    of a father, 108
    removed, 74
    respect, 42, 51
    submit to, 95, 149, 261

avenge not, 230

avoiding extremes, 240

awe, 75

B

banner of truth, 67

baptism of
    repentance, 281
    way of the Lord, 281

beginning
    grace & fear, 120
    in the garden, 106
    of fear, 104
    of new covenant, 70
    teachable, 212
    work of the Spirit, 58

Bible
    King James, 268, 270
    mirror, 256
    reasoning from, 211
    standard of law, 52

bitterness, 258

blessings
    abounding, 225
    take time, 226

    testimony, 226

body of Christ
    local, 260
    universal, 203

brokenness
    priceless, 48

Bunyan, John
    & obedience, 252
    balance, 239
    fear Creator, 81
    good doctrine, 191
    growth in, 316
    highest duty, 136
    much word, 191
    object of fear, 172, 227

C

characteristics of the Spirit
    counsel, 62
    reverse order, 62

chastening, 38, 83
    analogy of fear, 107
    despise not, 45, 103
    purpose of, 44

children
    Greek words, 208
    of promise, 136

church, 202, 203

comfort
    oil of, 177
    repent, 278

Content Index: Finding a Specific Topic

coming of the Lord, 19, 101, 113, 233
   fear of God, 161, 263
   prepare, 106, 313
   Son of Man, 17, 167

comparing, 173

complaining. *See* murmuring

confidence, 154

conscience, 122, 148, 165, 228, 233, 264

consuming fire, 110

contentment, 155

correction
   in early church, 15
   receiving, 14, 183
   rod of, 109
   time for, 238

counsel
   desiring, 210
   ignoring, 85
   receiving, 171, 177
   rejection of, 42
   wise, 62

covenant
   everlasting, 115
   revealed to, 234

covetousness, 173, 240
   Baruch, 158

D

danger of
   many words, 233

David, 84

delivered, 141
   fear of man, 144

discipleship, 19

disputings, 259

dominion, 93, 95, 110, 175

dread of God, 100

dreams
   multitude of, 233

duty, 136

E

envy's cure, 239

evil
   not speaking, 228

excellence of God, 36, 78

F

faith, 154
   boasting, 156
   covetous, 158
   false, 158
   father of, 155
   patience, 87
   trust, 159

false
   balance, 239
   comfort, 133
   fear of God, 122
   fears, 142

fear
   born in, 63
   controls, 143
   delivered from, 150
   effect of, 172
   first, 104
   idolatry, 142

   inhibits intimacy, 170
   moved with, 157
   natural, 141
   not, 141, 147
   of Isaac, 136
   of man, 143, 152
   of parents, 238
   one fear, 142
   paralyzing, 150

fear of God
   blessings, 223
   both covenants, 248
   cannot find him out, 78
   change, 116, 254
   choice, 177, 183
   circumcision, 65
   companions
      loving & serving God, 24
   creation witnesses, 80
   David, 197
   deliverances, 254
   desiring, 31
   detectable, 69
   dominion, 95
   Elihu, 77
   exceeding, 72, 78
   experiencing, 244
   exposes pride, 167
   faithfulness, 257
   for whom, 26
   forever, 65, 67
   fulfillment, 64
   glory, 50
   God's pleasure, 248
   greatly, 314
   growing in, 313
   guide, 157
   heritage, 214
   his, 92
   his excellency, 29, 77
   his presence, 216

More Abundant Life

how to answer, 133
in motion, 177
intensity of, 247
intimacy. *See* intimacy
joy, 24, 110
knowing him, 109
last days, 66, 312
learning, 196, 198
loss of, 310
master key, 11
maturity, 64, 237
new covenant, 70
no respect of persons, 77
now, 262
passages on, 307
patience, 68
precedes obedience, 137
prepares the heart, 232
present help, 217
protection, 103, 215
recapturing, 200, 201, 245
refuge of, 215
required, 29
response to authority, 257
salvation, 81, 130
sanctification, 31
sanctifying the Lord, 188
Satan hates, 307
seek after, 33, 201
spirit of, 59
spiritual birthright, 58
storehouse, 223
victory, 11
walk uprightly, 205
walk with God, 207
warning of, 233
why needed, 22

with him, 92
fellowship, 169
 one another, 168
 with him, 173
forgiveness, 30, 31
 births his fear, 81, 129
 covenant, 115
 false, 123
fountain of life, 214, 219, 223

G

gifts of God, 243
God
 father, 108
 judge, 39, 46, 109
 power, 78, 79
 wrath, 41, 87, 149
God-fearers, 130
gospel
 Abraham, 156
 eternal, 156
 everlasting, 113
 lordship, 113
 repentance, 113
grace
 frustrated, 122
 position, 116
growing up, 234

H

habitation
 holy, 241
 preparing, 240
hearing his voice, 16
 ears to hear, 232
 fear of God, 233
 refusing, 204
 Shulamite, 219
 treasure, 219

heart
 deceptive, 230
 humble, 208
 pure, 227
 single, 194
 united, 189
heritage, 123
 future, 215
 past, 215
 present, 217
holiness, 165
 early church, 109
 fear of, 107
 knowing, 240
 respect for, 261
hope, 161
house of
 Israel, 114

I

inheriting promises, 23, 58, 218
 Esau failed, 87
intimacy
 God's leading, 232
 marriage, 168
 prevented by, 165
 with brethren, 168
 with God, 171

J

Jeremiah's day
 apostasy, 218
 backslidings, 136, 262
 correction, 46
 know no judgment, 44
 latter days, 41
 new covenant, 114
 not afraid, 83

Content Index: Finding a Specific Topic

Jesus
- door, 94
- Jesus' day, 16

Job, 37, 68, 102, 107, 171
- character, 88, 307

joy, 185
- despite evil, 161
- for repentance, 274, 277
- set before, 187
- with trembling, 74

judgment
- day, 152
- eternal, 105
- for whom, 36
- hear & fear, 42
- mercy, 40
- of God, 37
- preserve us, 44
- seat of Christ, 105
- with him, 39

K

kingdom of God
- impact of, 13
- need, 93

knowing
- God, 179
- God's will, 236

L

last days
- fear of God, 312

leading of the Spirit, 232

learning fear of God
- as a child, 208
- gather & hear, 192

lordship, 29

M

marriage, 95, 168

marrow, 204

mercy
- fear of God, 123
- floodgates, 128
- salvation, 130

ministers
- correction, 69
- Eli, 211
- Levi feared God, 68
- seeing Jesus, 247

Moses
- intimate with God, 68
- knew face to face, 175

mount of God, 244
- sanctified for, 253

mount Sion, 251

murmuring, 257
- healed through cross, 258
- removal brings manna, 259

N

Nehemiah, 31, 69, 128, 147, 208

new covenant
- better hope, 156
- grace & fear, 114
- two pillars, 117

no fear in love, 33

no fear of God, 34
- before eyes, 182
- disobedience, 121
- evil, 136
- God amazed, 28
- judgment, 316

no intimacy
- pride of man, 165
- wickedness, 165

Noah
- ark, 126
- faith, 157
- Noah's day, 17, 161
- righteousness, 68

O

Obadiah, 315

obedience
- Levites, 235
- our calling, 253
- voice of Lord, 218

offering
- heave, 132

Old Testament
- for warning, 38

overcomers, 144

overcoming
- temptation, 184

P

parable
- labourers, 173

paradox
- fear & no fear, 63
- trembling & joy, 110

parallelism, Hebrew, 128

peace, 110
- great, 232

pillar of
- Boaz, 117
- Jachin, 117

More Abundant Life

pleasing God, 227

politics
   resistance, 235

practicing mistakes, 255

predestinated, 27

pride, 165, 166, 167, 209
   deceives, 233

promise of God, 32

prophets
   accused, 145

proved through lack, 258

R

reconciliation, 164

repentance, 197
   commanded, 274
   converted, 280
   definition, 275
   escape hell, 274
   foundational stone, 273
   Old Testament, 278
   precedes
      faith, 273
      the kingdom, 211
   unto life, 274
   versus regret, 276

rest, 111

return of the Lord. *See* coming of the Lord

reverence, 72

S

salt of the covenant, 132
   preserves, 135

salvation, 94
   Noah & ark, 126
   with fear, 65

save with fear, 64

scholars, 208

secret of the LORD, 234
   taking counsel, 171

seeker-sensitive movement, 203

serve
   acceptably, 132
   without fear, 140

service, 223

specially the day, 245

speech
   seasoned with salt, 133

spirit
   honest, 228
   humble, 208
   led of, 232
   of love, 60
   of pride, 167
   Sadducee, 249, 250, 281
   teachable, 210
   willing, 201, 202

stirring up God's fear, 315

storehouse, 223

T

terror of God, 101, 102

testimony, 12

treasure
   leading of his voice, 219
   new & old, 123
   of our heart, 188
   wisdom & knowledge, 179

trembling, 66, 98
   at his word, 82, 99
   at presence, 96
   men of God, 96

trust, example, 159

truth
   acknowledging, 183, 190
   the, 268

U

unbelievers, 28

W

weightier matters, 15

willingness, 204
   renewing, 186
   rooted in joy, 185

wisdom, 62
   hidden, 309

worldly methods, 84

Content Index: Finding a Specific Topic

Treasures from Within

The following quotes are from this book concerning the fear of God. They are provided here in summary to help punctuate the importance of God's fear. They are especially useful for rereading on occasion to see if the fear of God is still being treasured in your heart.

All of the Old Testament judgments are written for our admonition, not our dismissal! Consider this, Paul in writing the Greek, non-Jewish believers in Corinth used the Old Testament destructions in order to warn them of what would happen if they continued in the way they were headed. 38

As we are not to despise the chastening of the Lord (Pr 3:11), neither let us despise the fear of the Lord as so many do, for it is for our deepest protection and ultimately the doorway to our deepest intimacy with the God who dwells in unapproachable light (1Tim 6:16). 104

As we maintain the fear of the Lord and walk in it, we fulfill our debt of love toward God, and our heart becomes perfect before him! 228

Clearly, the fear of God is integral to growing up in the Lord – because those who are mature, those who can handle the meat of the word, are those who have the fear of God. 234

Consider this, the fear of the Lord is so important to God that everything he does is to awaken in us his fear. 80

Dominion and fear are with the Lord. If we would approach him we must submit to his rule and to his fear. To come any other way is to come disrespectfully and dishonorably. 93

Faith enables us to reach forward for what he has, but the fear of God enables us to leave the old behind. The fear of God is what enables us to depart from the iniquity we still desire and to exchange our selfish, sinful desires into a longing for his perfect, selfless will. 32

Fearing God, loving God, and serving God are not strangers at all in the pages of scripture, but in fact, are covenant companions. 24

Find a person with no fear of God and you will find a person who is not under Christ's lordship, one who at the root serves the Lord as they see fit, and not per his authoritative command. 95

God does not look at the fear of God as something we can do with or without. To God losing the fear of God is a manifest form of backsliding and forsaking him. 23

God has promised to "fulfil the desire of them that fear him" (Ps 145:19). How then can we ever find our true fulfillment without the fear of God? 64

God's word is the fuel. It is the power of God, but the fear of God is as the flame and the trigger that lights the explosiveness of it in our life. 215

His power and judgments are to bring us to a place of brokenness so that we may fear him. In our fear we are able to more deeply worship him, not in song only, but now with a heart that is circumcised and exposed to his inspection. 39

If we are not actively seeking after the fear of God as the treasure that it is, then we have little understanding of its tremendous value or how much it will guide us in our walk with God. 201

If we have received more abundant grace and the overflowing of forgiveness in the new covenant, ought we not to fear God more than any Old Testament saint? 31

If we would see our salvation worked out in our lives, then we must have the fear of God working in us. So we need faith for salvation and fear for growth and obedience. 65

It is because we do not consider God's sovereign right to do as he pleases that we do not fear him more! 89

It is because we do not see how high and how holy God is compared to our small selves that we do not fear him as he ought to be feared (Ps 76:11)!.. 88

It is in fact a curse from God, a judgment of his anger expressed toward us because of the hardness of our hearts, that we do not have the fear of God working within us. 317

it is through God's ordained authorities that God will put us to the greatest tests concerning whether we fear God or not. 197

It is utter self-deception for a believer in the Lord today to think that they fear God if they do not daily read his word and seek to obey that which they see and hear by its light. 192

Jesus himself is telling us, the way we fear and tremble and are afraid of men who can harm us and put us to death, is the very fear that we ought to have instead toward God Almighty. In fact, we should fear God much more because men can only kill our body. God, on the other hand, can not only put us to death, but can destroy both body and soul in hell! 139

Many through the serpent's plan are robbing men of the true fear of God, either by eliminating it altogether or so altering it that it is powerless to bring about a willing obedience to God. 249

Maybe the reason the fear of God is so much less in our generation, more than any other, is because we take so little time to consider what he has done. . 79

Nothing will satisfy the saint whose heart is possessed with the fear of the Lord, but the approval of God. 223

Religious men wonder why men fear God when "God is loving and merciful", but God himself wonders why we do NOT fear him for those very same reasons!.. 32

Satan challenges this singular virtue: the fear of God that is in a man's heart. 309

Since God is the source of all authority (Rom 13:1), part of the fear of the Lord is therefore the proper response to authority. 257

The fear of God must be the chaperone, the escort, the governess of true faith or else that faith devolves into boasting, comparing, and lording over others 158

the fear of the Lord prepares the heart to receive God's instruction................ 232

The goodness of God reflected in his great mercy to forgive us is his divine highway prepared to lead us to the fear of God. If we would truly understand the depth of his forgiveness, we would indeed fear him as David the man of God did before us... 122

The grace of God teaches our heart to fear, and the fear of God keeps our heart in his grace. 198

the Old Testament saints had a hidden companion, or more accurately a guide, to their faith that we have lost. This guide kept their faith on the sure path of God's will. We have lost the guide of the Spirit which is the clean and enduring fear of the Lord. The fear of the Lord is the first working of the Spirit of God. 157

The scripture shows us time and again that the one who is not afraid of God is the one who does not know God. 76

There be many that are called gods today, but to us there is but one God. The same is true of natural fears. There be many that are called fears today, but to us there ought to be but one fear, the fear of God! Just as there are false gods, but one true God, so there are false fears, but one true fear, the fear of God. 143

There is nothing so securing to the heart as having the knowledge and the wisdom of God. The knowledge of God secures us where we are, while the wisdom of God secures us in where we are going. And both of these come through the fear of God. 179

This is why the fear of God is the chaperone of faith, for true faith operates only under authority, and God's authority is only established in us through his fear. 159

This, then, is the fault that God finds against his very own people and against his church – that so often there is no fear of God before their eyes, just like the lost!.. 182

Though many despise it, think evil of it, try to stamp it from existence, or twist it into their own making, yet God has established his fear, like his word, to endure forever (Ps 19:9) 308

Thus, if we are lacking power in our walk with God it can often be traced back to a loss of the fear of the Lord! 60

Thus, it is the lack of knowing the true God that explains our lack of the fear of God. The more we know him in truth according to the scriptures the more we will fear him. 155

Thus, not only our spiritual birth was in the fear of God, but even our natural birth was in the fear of God! So from beginning to new beginning, God has orchestrated his fear to be in us. 63

To fear God is to receive instruction, warning, reproof, and chastisement. To reject any of these, and not to have an ear to hear, is to reject the fear of God. 14

We have 'a moral duty', we are 'under obligation' to walk like Jesus. We must fear God even as he feared God. 174

We may have the spirit of love (through the new birth) and the spirit of a sound mind (through the word of God), but be completely lacking the fear of the Lord and therefore have no spirit of power working in us. 60

we see an intertwining of faith and the fear of God that form the foundation for a strong salvation. The fear of God prepares the heart for salvation and faith obtains that salvation. 126

What is this new covenant that God promised? It is the covenant of grace and fear. 114

Without the fear of God we will have no power in prayer, no might to overcome sin, and no depth of spiritual understanding of what is going on in our life. 60

Without the fear of God we will not long wait for God's promise, nor his supply. We will grow tired and soon, like King Saul, we will stretch out our hand to take it into our own hands (1Sam 13:8-10). 162

Without the fear of God, the promise of God is either unattainable or unenjoyable. Even if the promise is received, it cannot be kept or enjoyed without the fear of God. 32

Thanksgiving: The Fruit of Our Labors

To produce anything of enduring substance and quality requires great labor, cost, planning, and time. It will involve more than a little uncertainty, knocking and seeking, trying doors, several failures, and of course much faith and patience in order to inherit the blessing of accomplishing the Lord's vision for something. The writing and publishing of this book has been all that and more. I truly expected this work to be in print 5 years before it was. I, myself, have grown through this process and learned many things 'not to do'.

It is with much thanksgiving to God first that he did not give up on me, but continued to instruct, to inspire, and to provoke to finish this work. There were many, many times I was so discouraged with the process, not of writing, but of getting this work published, that I was ready to quit and forget I had ever started such an endeavor. (The joy was truly in the writing of this work and not in the publishing of it.) If anything reflects his glory and his truth in this book, it is to the Lord GOD Almighty and his marvelous Spirit that all praise, honor, and glory are due. Any fault, error, or short-coming is certainly due to me and the limit of the understanding of God's ways to which I have attained. As I am always urging others to do, I myself am continually trying to press on, as it is written, "But grow in grace, and *in* the knowledge of our Lord and Saviour Jesus Christ. To him *be* glory both now and for ever. Amen." 2Pe 3:18

Much of this work was done in secret, in the wee hours of the night, day after day laboring to produce something for God's glory – perfecting, refining, rethinking, rephrasing. Along the way there are always those who as friends and co-workers come alongside at God's set time to fill in the gaps that one person cannot possibly all do. I would thank most of all my wife with whom none of this could have happened. It was her who lent me to the Lord to have the time to do this and who bore the burdens of a home and of children. She has truly shared this vision with me and has, during it, been willing to give up all to glorify the Lord. I thank her from the bottom of my heart. She has the very talents and gifts, which in many areas I lack. She has been a co-laborer at my side, and her excitement for this book has been at times even greater than my own. Thank you wifey!

I would also like to thank New Covenant Christian Center, International. I would not be where I am in the Lord, living for his glory, without all of you. You are my joints and marrow, the very body of Christ to me, and truly you are for his glory! David prays in Psalm 20 that help would be sent him from the sanctuary and he would be strengthened out of Zion (i.e. the congregation of the saints). Truly this has happened many a time in my life through you all. I love you New Covenant. There has never been a body of faithful disciples like you. Stay strong in truth and in righteousness and in the power of his might.

Thanksgiving: The Fruit of Our Labors

Glorify God in your body and in your spirit, for you are the Lord's – you are the apple of his eye! May you come to know how much he truly loves you.

The gratitude in my heart always overflows for Mr. Kim C. Gossett, a true father in the faith, a man like Paul, who has suffered the loss of all things, and has been an example in "doctrine, manner of life, purpose, faith, longsuffering, charity, patience, persecutions, [and] afflictions" (2Tim 3:10-11). Without you as my friend I would still be lost and wandering in the mire of Christianity. It is because of you and your heart to raise and train men of God, that the kingdom was manifest to me so long ago on my first journey to Kenya, Africa, at your side. Thank you for showing me the world through Jesus' eyes! My journeys to the nations with you have been the fulfillment of my heart. Though not involved directly in the book, the meat of what is here, the teaching of righteousness, the call to holiness, the exposing of the doctrines and traditions of men is because of the endless hours of preaching, counsel, and godly exhortation that you continually give out. May the Lord continue to strengthen you and those at your side as you build the kingdom of God one soul at a time.

Many thanks to those of you my friends who diligently took the time to read the book and review it for me and gave me your insights and criticisms. Many were unwilling or too busy, but those who did have my abundant thanks. I am thankful for your love and honesty and your commitment to help, but most of all that you love Jesus in spirit and in truth. Ros, an especial thanks to you. You took on this project as if it were your own. Your labor helped keep this project alive.

Special thanks go to "For His Glory" and all the hours you spent laying the foundation for the book cover. I owe you a debt of love and thanks, Raymund and Michelle. I can't wait until you are doing full-time what you have been called to do 'for his glory'. Magnus, thank you so much for your attention to detail and the great artwork. It has been a true pleasure working with you. You helped in many ways. Dan, you were one of those whom God brings in at the last minute to save the day. Thank you for doing all the layout adjustments and fine tuning. It never could have been printed without you. Last of all I thank Jason, a man of great humility and servitude, without whose help just at the right time, this work would still just be in a computer and not in print.

Chapter photos from Dreamstime and Photos.com
with explicit rights and permissions

Cover art and graphic design by Magnus Andersson
of Innervision Design Inc.

Cover layout and fine-tuning by Dan Snyder

An Epilogue: Enduring Fear of God

The fear of the LORD will endure beyond all the passing fads, fashions, and thought systems of man. Though many despise it, think evil of it, try to stamp it from existence, or twist it into their own making, yet God has established his fear, like his word, to endure forever (Ps 19:9). When we understand the awesomeness of his word, the appropriate response to it is to tremble in the fear of God. May your life, thoughts and heart be rooted in the transforming ability of the fear of the LORD. It will protect you and guide you all the days of your life, if you do not forsake it. The fear of the LORD is the beginning of wisdom and the source of so many of the blessings that God would bestow in the life of those who are pleasing to him. The following scripture passages are dedicated to the fear of the LORD, being the most focused on it than any other: Psalms 34, 112, and 128. You would do well to meditate on them often.

Why Satan Hates the True Fear of God

"Hast thou considered my servant Job?" Job 1:8

The one man whom God holds up before the face of Satan in the entire Old Testament was Job. God boasts of his servant to the devil by telling of his godly virtues. "And the LORD said unto Satan, Hast thou considered my servant

Job, that *there is* none like him in the earth, a perfect and an upright man, <u>one that feareth God</u>, and escheweth evil?" Job 1:8 We have shown in the course of this book that being "a perfect and an upright man" is the fruit of none other than being a man that fears God. We have also shown that eschewing or departing from evil is the fruit of fearing God. Thus, the root of all that God was able to boast in concerning Job sprang from this single, foundational virtue, that he was a man that feared God.

This virtue and its ensuing fruits are *so important* in fact that God would hold them up, not only for the devil to see, but also for all of us to see. This is why God begins the book of Job with this same display of Job. "There was a man in the land of Uz, whose name *was* Job; and that man was perfect and upright, and <u>one that feared God</u>, and eschewed evil." Job 1:1 It would not be an understatement, then, to say that the whole theme of the book of Job focuses around the fear of God, both its fruits and the fight of faith to maintain it.[263]

God's rebuke of Satan concerning Job was that Job was "one that feareth God". Satan himself heard this rebuke quite clearly and knew that this was the real issue which he was being rebuked for. This is evidenced by Satan's response. "Then Satan answered the LORD, and said, Doth Job <u>fear God</u> for nought?" Job 1:9 Notice Satan does not challenge or attack Job's perfection, nor his uprightness. Neither does the accuser of the brethren challenge or attack Job's eschewing evil. Satan challenges this singular virtue: the fear of God that is in a man's heart. This will be our challenge and the attack we must weather as well. As soon as you choose the fear of the LORD in your life Satan himself will dig into your heart with all fury and bring accusation after accusation. He will say, "Do you really fear God?" This is the one thing that the devil cannot allow to abide in the heart of God's children: the true fear of God. This is why he has all his various counterfeits of the fear of God and all his enemies of it.[264]

It is the true fear of God that will cause us to both depart from evil and to have a perfect and upright heart before him. This is why the fear of God is the beginning of the wisdom of God. These, the god of this world, Satan, cannot endure, for they are a continual rebuke to him. He once walked in the wisdom of God, now he walks in his own wisdom. We think Satan only accuses us, but his real accusations are in fact leveled against God. Thus, God exhorts us as his own sons and the fruit of his labors, "My son, be wise, and make my heart glad, that I may answer him that reproacheth me." Pr 27:11 God desires to use us as

---

[263] I pray this will transform your next reading of the book of Job and make the importance of the fear of the LORD spring up in your heart, especially your understanding of the depth of the struggle we have to maintain it.

[264] For the false fear of God, see the chapter "Cheap Imitations and Artificial Substitutes" and for the enemies of the fear of God, see the chapter "Warning Signs of Losing God's Fear". Both are in the book <u>Losing the Treasure of the Lord</u>.

his answer to the accuser. God's answer to Satan's accusations and reproaches was, "Have you considered my servant Job ... <u>that feareth God</u>?" (Job 1:8)

The Hidden Wisdom of God: The Fear of God

The LORD wants our changed lives to be the justification for his actions to forgive us and to save us. "But wisdom is justified of all her children." Lk 7:35 God *will* have something to answer the devil, who reproaches him, when we walk in God's wisdom, the hidden wisdom, which is the fear of God. This is the wisdom which is hidden from the world (and sadly also from the church at large): the wisdom of God that springs from the fear of God.

Why do I call the fear of God the hidden wisdom of God? First, because the beginning of wisdom *is* the fear of the LORD. Second, because when we seek after wisdom, what do we find? We find the fear of the LORD. Speaking of seeking after wisdom, Solomon writes, "If thou seekest her as silver, and searchest for her **as *for* hid treasures**; Then shalt thou understand the fear of the LORD, and find the knowledge of God." Pr 2:4-5 Notice how in this verse he speaks of seeking and searching for the hidden treasure of wisdom. Thus, the hidden wisdom of God is none other than the fear of the LORD. No one can partake of this hidden wisdom who lacks the fear of God. "But we speak the wisdom of God in a mystery, *even* the <u>hidden *wisdom*</u>, which God ordained before the world unto our glory: Which none of the princes of this world knew: for had they known *it*, they would not have crucified the Lord of glory." 1Co 2:7-8 The princes of this world do not know fear of God. Thus, they do not know even the beginning of wisdom, for it is hidden from them because of their lack of God's fear!

But how may we be wise in spiritual wisdom so that God may bring rebuke to Satan without the fear of God in us? We cannot be wise without the fear of God, for it is the very beginning of wisdom. Without the fear of God we are in truth foolish sons that dishonor our Father. Without the fear of God we cannot make the heavenly Father's heart glad – for he has nothing to answer on our behalf. This is the inestimable treasure of the fear of God in our life. If you would outwit the enemy of your soul, you must have the hidden wisdom, which is the fear of God, working in you. This is the answer God would have for each of us unto our accuser: "Hast thou considered my servant ... one that feareth God, and escheweth evil?"

The fear of God is just as important as the word of God in terms of being in our heart. Without the word of God we do not know *how* to please God. Without the fear of God we do not *want* to please God. We need both today and Satan knows it. We desperately need the willingness to do God's will, and this is what the fear of god is given to us for. Thus, Paul exhorts us, right before speaking of how God works in us to will and to do of his good pleasure (v13), "work out your own salvation <u>with fear and trembling</u>." Php 2:12

What Satan Comes for

Let us look again at what Satan comes for. We know that "Satan cometh immediately, and taketh away the word that was sown in their hearts." Mk 4:15 By this we know that Satan cares nothing about us, it is the Word he is after. Those on the way side (those who have never been born again), Satan would keep them at all costs from the word of God, for the Word is the light that illuminates our darkness and shows us the pathway to the truth that is found only in Jesus, the source of all wisdom and knowledge. The Word contains the power for change and the very source of God's life, so it is called in the Greek the *sperma* of God. The Word is the life-creating force in our heart. We have seen that God would cause his people to fear him by giving them his word. The word is designed by God so that it produces the fear of God which in turn brings about godly change in us (Ps 55:19).

If we consider the parable of the sower of the seed in more detail, we see that Satan only comes for the word among those that are on the wayside (i.e. in the unsaved). Whereas for those who have known the truth and come to believe the word, he has a different scheme. For the rest, he does not come so much for the word, for he knows he cannot take the word out of us, for we are born again <u>by the word of God</u> (1Pe 1:23). The word is literally in our very being. Thus, what he comes to do instead amongst the saved is to make the word of God unfruitful and of none effect. He does this in two ways.

The Extraction of the Fear of God from Christian Leaders: Removing the Power of the Word from the Church through False Doctrine

First and foremost, Satan removes the life-changing power of the word of God from the church by mixing the word of God, diluting and polluting it so that it can no longer change those who hear it. The pure word of God is corrupted and made strengthless through men's traditions and doctrines, even as took place in Jesus' day (Mt 15:6/Mk 7:13). This is why men's traditions and doctrines rule Christianity, rather than the authority of the scriptures. How can Satan accomplish this? Because he works on Christian leaders to remove the fear of God from their hearts first of all. He does this by getting them to fear man and to please man, rather than God alone. The fear of man brings a snare upon a person's life so that Satan, through the power of the soul and temptation, can now manipulate, use, and lead that person where he wants.

Without the fear of God it is impossible to escape the fear of man. We have shown this earlier, that the fear of God will drive out the fear of man, *or* the fear of man will keep us from the fear of God.[265] Once the fear of man is working in

---

[265] This was discussed in the section 'Eradicating the Fear of Man', in the chapter "Replacing Our Many Fears with God's Singular Fear".

a leader's heart, he cannot but envy others. This is the testimony of King Saul's life. The fear of God is envy's cure, but without the fear of God, every leader will become envy's victim. Ministers will measure themselves by themselves and compare themselves among themselves, which the scripture says is not wise (2Co 10:12).

The snare of the fear of man will now cause them to "receive honour one of another, and seek not the honour that *cometh* from God only" (Jn 5:44). This is what was in Jesus' day with the Pharisees and Doctors of the Law, each trying to obtain the highest seat in the house.[266] This is no different than what we have in our day with the well-renowned Pastors, Bishops, and plethora of ministers who are Doctors, all trying to obtain the honor that comes from men, especially of being "the fastest growing ministry" in their local area or in America.

The Extraction of the Fear of God from the Body of Christ:
Removing the Power of the Word from the Church through the Strength of the Flesh

The second way the devil makes the word fruitless is through the flesh. Once man's doctrines replace the purity of the conviction of truth it is easy now to have the flesh rule in the life of the believer. It was the word that proceeded from men who feared only God that brought forth the conviction of sin and the call to repentance. Without the apostolic and prophetic calls to repentance and the two-edged sword to bring conviction, there is little desire, strength, or even vision in men to overcome the world.

How does Satan accomplish this? Through getting us to forsake the Lord through carnal and natural desires and occupations. Effectively, he removes the fear of God from the word of God. The god of this world would have the redeemed put away a good conscience by putting away the fear of God. For the saved, Satan does not so much care that they have the word of God – for <u>even he himself uses the word of God to deceive</u> (Lk 4:9-11), and certainly so do his ministers of righteousness (2Co 11:15)! So we must see, it is not just the Word that Satan comes for among the saved – for there are many who read the Bible today who grow further and further from God by false doctrine. All of us may see the word before our eyes. We may all hear it each week. But we will never be changed by it, if our heart is void of the fear of God. Because men do not fear God, they will not change (Ps 55:19).

Thus, Satan comes immediately to steal the word from them that are lost. But among them that are saved, it is not the word alone that Satan comes to steal. Ultimately, it is the capability to produce the fear of God in us that Satan hates the word for. As long as no fear of God is produced by the word we see or hear, he will allow us to freely have all the word we desire! This is why when

---

[266] Jesus repeatedly had to deal with the self-exaltation of men seeking seats of position: Mt 23:2,6, Mk 12:39, Lk 11:43, 20:46.

one is caught up in the doctrines of men, all things may appear to go smooth. We may be "Ever learning, and never able to come to the knowledge of the truth." 2Tim 3:7 The knowledge of the truth that is spoken here can only be had through the fear of God. "The fear of the LORD *is* the beginning of knowledge: *but* fools despise wisdom and instruction." Pr 1:7 We may have a form of godliness, but the power therefore (i.e. the fear of God) is 'denied, *rejected*, and *contradicted*' (2Tim 3:5).

All things may seem to be going smoothly in the Christian's life until the hour they first hear the preaching of the kingdom of God which brings in God's authority and the fear of God. From that time, great resistance is brought forth by the adversary of their soul. Behold the Pharisees and Sadducees, who feared men but did not fear God. These were men who studied and even diligently searched the scriptures (Jn 5:39-40). They appeared as righteous men, full of peace and blessing. They greeted people in the market places in the name of the Lord.[267] But their encounters with Jesus were of a totally different nature. They came into sharp conflict with Jesus every time because he preached and taught the kingdom of God, God's manifest authority, which had the power to change men and to expose the works of darkness.

Satan has always hated and tried to remove the fear of God from this earth. This is why he so resists the kingdom of God because, it through the apostolic mantle[268] brings in the fear of God. Satan has done a masterful work amongst the church today. Why will so many depart from the faith in the last days? Why will there be a great falling away first, before the return of the Lord? Because men will put away the fear of God and so put away a good conscience. God's promise as to how he would keep us in the covenant of grace is through the fear of God. "And I will make an everlasting covenant with them, that I will not turn away from them, to do them good; but I will put my fear in their hearts, that they <u>shall not depart from me</u>." Jer 32:40

The Fear of God Especially Reserved for the Last Days Remnant

We cannot afford to be without the fear of God in these last days. God has specially reserved it for the remnant that will turn from their ways to seek him with a pure heart. "Afterward shall the children of Israel return, and seek the LORD their God, and David their king; and <u>shall fear the LORD and his good-</u>

---

[267] Greeting in the markets: Mt 23:7, Lk 11:43, 20:46.

[268] This is why every NT writer (except James) wrote about the fear of God: Matthew (Mt 10:28, 27:54, 28:4,8), Mark (Mk 4:41, 5:33, 9:6,32, 10:32, 16:8), Luke (Lk 1:12,50,65, 2:9, 5:26, 7:16, 8:25, 9:34,45, 12:5, 23:40, 24:5, Ac 2:43, 5:5,11, 9:31, 10:2,4,22,35, 13:16, 26, 19:17, 22:9), Paul (Rom 3:18, 11:20, 13:3-4,7, 2Co 5:11, 7:1,11,15, Eph 5:21, 6:5, Php 2:12, Col 3:22, 1Tim 5:20, Heb 4:1, 5:7, 10:27,31, 11:7, 12:21,28), Peter (1Pe 1:17, 2:17-18, 3:2,15, 2Pe 2:10), Jude (Jude 1:12,23), and John (Rev 11:11,18, 14:7, 15:4, 19:5).

ness in the latter days." Hos 3:5 Why does he particularly look forward to the last generation to fear him and to fear his goodness? First, because he knows gross darkness (in the form of wickedness) will cover the earth (Isa 60:2, Jer 13:16). This gross darkness will consume so many who are not watching in vigilance and not giving glory to God through the fear of God, because they lack the fear of God. Second, because the fear of God is the only way the bride of Christ can truly prepare himself for the Lord's coming. She must clothe herself with the glory of the fear of God, His fear.

This is why God so loves the fear of God and longs for us to have it in abundance. It is what keeps us in covenant relationship with him. It will turn us from *our* way and cause us to turn toward him in repentance, and it will prepare us for him. The heavenly Father has created it to endure forever, and he is still looking for those who will choose the fear of the LORD.

The Need for Growing in the Fear of God
"so terrible was the sight, that Moses said, I exceedingly fear and quake" Heb 12:21

We have seen the enemies of the fear of God are many. When we see any of these manifesting in our life or heart we must know that we are departing from the fear of God. Witchcraft and adultery are serious signs we have no fear of God. We have spoken much already concerning the link between the fear of the LORD and humility, and between the fear of the LORD and contentedness (which will put to death covetousness). If we have no regard for the word of correction, then we have little, if any, fear of God. If we do not freely acknowledge the truth when it is spoken, no matter who it is spoken by, or if we justify our own actions and deeds by "extenuating conditions", then we must know we are falling away from the fear of God. When we do not hear the word of God and receive its admonishments, we are departing from God's fear. When we can take advantage of another person we have the first evidence that we are losing our fear of God. Lastly, we looked at how dreams may lead us astray from God's fear, if we do not measure all things by the word of God and keep our desires crucified. These are all warning signs we should now recognize. These are the foghorns to keep us from shipwrecking the fear of God in our life and being without a spiritual compass.

We cannot afford to lose the fear of God in our life. It is a gift from our Father above by his Spirit. It is a gift of inestimable value which will keep us, protect us, and provide for us. Yet, we cannot think merely because we have the fear of God that we have arrived. Oftentimes in terms of spirituals we tend to look only at whether we have something or whether we don't. Are we saved? Are we baptized in the Holy Ghost? Do we fear God? This is clearly the first order of business, but once we have received them we are called in each case to grow up into them. Indeed, the first and most important thing concerning God's gifts is that we have received them. Without salvation we are lost. Without the baptism of the Holy Ghost we are powerless. Without the fear of God we cannot please God, for true faith springs from the fear of God. Yet we are still called to grow up into even these: "grow up into him in all things, which is the head, *even* Christ" (Eph 4:15). And concerning being filled with the Spirit, we are to be continually filled (Eph 5:18), as scripture shows in Acts over and over again. Remember, we are to grow up "unto the measure of the stature of the fulness of Christ" (Eph 4:13).

Let us consider an example. When we are born again and indwelt with the Spirit he fills us with all the fruit of the Spirit. They are *his* fruits and when he takes up residence in us they come with him. But who may say, "I have all patience or all faith"? We may have much, for example, of the fruit of joy in our character from the Holy Spirit's working, but still be weak and seemingly barren in temperance. We can never say, "I have enough of these graces in me." We can never say, "I have enough love, enough patience, enough faith, or enough of the fear of the LORD." We are called to ever be growing in all the graces.[269] Even so we must grow in the grace or gift of the fear of God, which the Spirit brought into us when he came (Isa 11:2).

There are varying degrees of God's graces that are working in us. So we see also with the fear of God. Several times in scripture we see the true fear of God coming upon people greatly. So we see when God magnified his servant Samuel that "all the people greatly feared the LORD" (1Sam 12:18). When God brought judgment against the covetousness, dishonesty, and hypocrisy of heart that dwelt in Ananias and Sapphira and slew them, great fear came on all the church *and* all them that heard (Ac 5:5,11). When God demonstrated his sovereign power to create wild storms and then to cause them to suddenly cease when it fits him, men were moved to fear him exceedingly – both the men aboard the ship with Jonah (Jnh 1:16) *and* the apostles in the lake with Jesus (Mk 4:41).

But we also find men who greatly feared the LORD, not so much because they experienced God's great workings, but because of the depth of their hope in his mercy. Such people had often seen or were experiencing the suffering from the judgments of God because of the disobedience of the nation of Israel, and therefore in the fear of the LORD they hoped in his mercies (Neh 1:11). There were some who, like Nehemiah's brother, Hanani that *"was* a faithful man, and feared God above many." Neh 7:2 Obadiah, the governor of Ahab's house, dwelt around such great wickedness and saw the judgments of the LORD which came as a result of it. So we see he was a man who "feared the LORD greatly" (1K 18:3).

---

[269] Some examples of growing in some of these graces: grow in love (2Th 1:3, 1Th 3:12, 4:9), grow in gentleness (Php 4:5, moderation = gentleness), grow in faith (2Th 1:3), grow in patience (2Th 3:5, 1:4).

Let us look closer at Obadiah, whose name means 'servant or worshipper of Jehovah'. Obadiah had stirred up the fear of God into a flame until he greatly feared the LORD. The word 'greatly' in 1Kings 18:3 comes from the root word which means 'to *rake* together; a *poker* (for *turning* or *gathering* embers)'. How appropriate for stirring up the flames of holiness within our vessel! This is what each of us needs to do within the hearth of our own heart.

> Let the sincerity of our love for Jesus be seen
> by our growth in this grace of the fear of the LORD.

This is very much like what Paul exhorted his son in the faith to do with the gift of God that was in him. "Wherefore I put thee in remembrance that thou <u>stir up</u> the gift of God" (2Tim 1:6). Remember, the fear of God is a gift from him, just like salvation or the baptism of the Holy Ghost. Just like these others gifts we must grow up into the fullness of the fear of God. And though the fear of God does not come by the laying on of hands as the gift that Paul speaks of to Timothy, yet the embers of it may be stirred up into a blazing flame just the same!

> Therefore, as ye abound in every *thing, in* faith, and utterance, and knowledge, and *in* all diligence, and *in* your love to us, *see* that ye abound in this grace also. I speak not by commandment, but by occasion of the forwardness of others, & to prove the sincerity of your love. 2Co 8:6-8

We must learn to *abound* in this grace of fear. As we have begun in it, let us also learn to perfect it. Even though we may have the fear of God, the fear of God may be yet weak within us, just as any grace of God. It may be very present in some areas, yet still lacking in others. The scripture reveals that some fear God less, while others more. Do we fear the LORD hardly or greatly? "He will bless them that fear the LORD, *both* <u>small</u> and <u>great</u>." Ps 115:13 Revelation speaks twice of those who fear God and who fear his name "both <u>small</u> and <u>great</u>" (Rev 19:5, 11:18). Thus, the fear of the LORD may range in us from *not at all* to *small* to *great* and even *exceedingly*.[270]

We may have the micro-fear of the LORD or the mega-fear of the LORD or anywhere in between.[271] It all depends on whether we continue to grow in the fear of the LORD by daily choosing it. When we choose this day to serve the LORD, then we are in fact choosing to fear him, for he seeks those who will worship him, and the highest form of serving God is worshipping him in spirit and in truth. If we only have a small fear of God, let us cultivate a greater fear

---

[270] Feared exceedingly: Jonah 1:16, Mk 4:41, Heb 12:21.

[271] The Greek words used for 'small' and 'great' respectively in Revelation 19:5 and 11:18 are *mikros* (our modern day 'micro') and *megas* (our modern day 'mega').

of God by knowing the mighty God: his judgments, his wonders, and his person. Let us also by our choices grow in the fear of the LORD so that our fear of God is great.

Let the sincerity of our love for Jesus be seen by our growth in this grace of the fear of the LORD. It is spoken of the wise man that he fears and out of that fear he takes action. "A wise *man* feareth, and departeth from evil" (Pr 14:16). Let us accordingly exercise the fear of the LORD in our life to depart from evil and to draw nigh to God in a way that is pleasing and acceptable to him. Let us never depart from it. "Happy *is* the man that feareth **alway**: but he that hardeneth his heart shall fall into mischief." Pr 28:14

Men do all they can to rid themselves of the fear of God, fleeing from it and trying to hide from being naked, open, and honest before the all seeing eyes of God. Men count themselves happy when they have no fear of God, yet scripture records just the opposite. It is in fact a curse from God – a judgment of his displeasure expressed toward us because of the hardness of our hearts – that we do not have the fear of God working within us. "O LORD, why hast thou made us to err from thy ways, *and* hardened our heart from thy fear?" Isa 63:17 Rather, than being on some higher plane with God if we have 'graduated' from the fear of the Almighty, we actually are under his judgment as evidenced by the fact that our heart is hardened or *unfeeling* toward the fear of God! And the result? We will err and go astray from his ways. The fear of God keeps us in the narrow way. The lack of the fear of God causes us to drift and wander away, erring from his ways.

But how may we grow in that which we do not desire? We cannot! We must first know the goodness of the LORD, before we are ever able to overcome our fear of being condemned by him out of hand. Even the reason we come to draw from the breasts of Christ the pure milk of the Word is because we have *tasted* of his graciousness. "As newborn babes, desire the sincere milk of the word, that ye may grow thereby: **If** so be ye have tasted that the Lord *is* gracious." 1Pe 2:2-3 We must cultivate a desire for the fear of God before we will ever seek it and before we will ever choose it.

> *"For a man hardly grows in the increase of any grace*
> *until his heart is united to it,*
> *and until it is made lovely in his eyes."* [272]

---

[272] Bunyan, p. 155. Note that John Bunyan said this, not of the grace of God in general, but specifically concerning growing in the "grace of fear"!

Resources: Table for the Hungry

If you are looking for more sound Biblical teaching centered around the kingdom of God and not from the doctrines of men, please enjoy these teachings and materials. Proceeds from these resources go to New Covenant World Outreach which feeds the poor, clothes the naked, visits those in prisons and hospitals, and preaches the kingdom of God around the world.

Books/Booklets

Where is the Fear of GOD? Finding the Treasure of the Lord
Where is the Fear of GOD? Losing the Treasure of the Lord
The Gospels in Concert: Putting the 4 Gospels in Divine Order
The Epistles in Concert: Putting Acts & the Epistles in Divine Order
Christianity versus the Kingdom of God
The Growing Process [a chart]

Tape Series

Christianity vs. the Kingdom of God
The Pillars of the New Covenant
Discerning Soul from Spirit
The Healing of the Heart
The Fatherhood of God
Learning to Overcome
Hope Set Before Us
A Place of Refuge
Consider Jesus
Heart Care

Contact

Let us know of your desire or need and we will get back to you as soon as we can. To contact us you may email us at info@MoreAbundantLife.com or feel free to visit us at www.MoreAbundantLife.com to learn more. There you can order the tape series. Find the latest news about how our ministry in Kenya is going by visiting our blog: KingomMinistryInKenya.BlogSpot.com. Mail correspondence is via: More Abundant Life, P.O. Box 24526, San Jose, CA 95154.

www.ingramcontent.com/pod-product-compliance
Lightning Source LLC
Chambersburg PA
CBHW060456090426
42735CB00011B/2007